Work, Employment and Unemployment
Perspectives on Work and Society

Edited by Kenneth Thompson
at the Open University

OPEN UNIVERSITY PRESS

Milton Keynes · *Philadelphia*

Open University Press,
12 Cofferidge Close, Stony Stratford,
Milton Keynes MK11 1BY, England
and
242 Cherry Street,
Philadelphia, PA 19106, U.S.A.

First Published 1984

British Library Cataloguing in Publication Data

Work, employment and unemployment.
1. Industrial sociology
I. Thompson, Kenneth,
306'.36   HD6955

ISBN 0-333-10594-7

Library of Congress Cataloging in Publication Data

Main entry under title:

Work, employment, and unemployment.

 Bibliography: P.
 Includes index.
 1. Work—Social aspects. 2. Industrial relations.
3. Industrial sociology. I. Thompson, Kenneth A.
HD4904.W645 1984   306'.36   84-16683

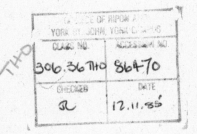

Text design by Clarke Williams

Typeset by
Mathematical Composition Setters Ltd.,
Ivy Street, Salisbury, Wilts.

Printed in Great Britain by
M & A Thomson Litho Limited,
East Kilbride, Scotland

Contents

Editor's Introduction

This volume of contributions to the sociology of work appears at a time when, perhaps more than ever before, problems of work are at the forefront of public consciousness and debate. It is not surprising, therefore, that they are also at the forefront of sociological theorizing and research. Whereas, for a time at least, sociological interest in work issues was fragmented and dispersed across a number of subspecialisms – industrial sociology, sociology of organizations, sociology of the professions, etc. – there is now a much more focused interest in a set of issues and debates that are at the centre of sociological analysis. One reason for this is that the economic crisis has raised questions about all the fundamental structures and processes of our society: What is work and what is it for? Why is it divided up, organized and rewarded in the ways that it is at present? Could it be different? Why do we think about it in the ways that we do? How far are these things determined by forces outside our control? The combined contributions of sociologists from different specialisms, bringing together their various perspectives on these issues, are presented here in the firm conviction that such a combination offers the best hope of finding answers to these questions.

Not everyone is prepared to look to sociology for guidance in understanding problems associated with work. Sociology, for reasons to be discussed, devotes some of its efforts to developing theories about work, and this sort of questioning meets with resistance. Some people think they already have all the answers, and do not take kindly to sociologists raising doubts. Other people hold the firm conviction that academic disciplines have little to contribute to understanding what they regard as 'common-sense' issues or practical matters. We are all familiar with Henry Ford's dismissive comment that 'History is bunk'.

The same kind of superficial reaction is often met by sociology among industrialists and politicians, even though it is a reaction based on little knowledge of the work that sociologists produce. In the absence of such knowledge, industrialists and politicians advance solutions to the problems of work that are founded on crude psychological notions about what motivates individuals to work, or on narrow 'marginalist', economic models that abstract economic processes from their historical and social institutions. When the solutions do not work, even the economists and psychologists are scorned. It does not seem to occur to those who do not take the trouble to investigate what sociology has to say, that psychological and economic processes can only be understood if proper attention is paid to the wider and underlying social context. (Some of the relevant contextual factors with regard to the history and ideology of work are discussed by Kumar in Chapter 1 below, and with respect to fundamental structural processes by Littler and Salaman in Chapter 2.)

A good example of an issue that sociology can illuminate is that of the introduction of new technology, which is often put forward as a solution to problems of low productivity and lack of competitiveness. Politicians sometimes give the impression that a new economic dawn will break on us if only there is more investment in new technology and if engineers are given more power and prestige. Sociologists who undertake the theoretically informed research into the functions and consequences of the introduction of new technology in the production process (or the 'labour process'), show that the crucial issue is how technology is combined with human labour, and why certain work designs are preferred to others. Many of the chapters in the first half of this book deal with this issue: for example, Thompson (Chapter 5) on the labour process and its main tendency under capitalism; Littler (Chapter 6) on similarities and differences in East European factories; and Dunkerley and Casey (Chapter 9) with respect to work cultures and technology, viewed in terms of a historical case-study of a naval dockyard. Armstrong (Chapter 7) shows how work designs and management strategies for controlling labour are affected by competition between different professional groups within management, particularly with regard to engineers.

This sort of questioning of superficial diagnoses of problems of work, which combines critical thinking with empirical research, is characteristic of the 'debunking' aspect of sociology that, it might be thought, should commend it to the Henry Fords of the world. Unfortunately, this is not always the case, especially if it reveals the warts on the face of capitalism, as in Huw Beynon's study, *Working for Ford* (1973), or in other circles when it reveals the less than unblemished face of East European socialism (as in Littler, Chapter 6 below). Nor is sociology popular when its critical thinking discloses the sectional interests served by particular ideologies of work, whether it is the professional ideology of engineers, or other groups which have a vested interest in having their version of events accepted (a theme taken up by Armstrong *et al.* in Chapter 8, when they examine the role of ideology in shop-floor industrial relations).

Of course, sociologists have not been slow to purvey ideologies, but this is countered by the discipline's institutionalization of processes of systematic argument and criticism – processes which sometimes upset students, who wish sociologists would agree among themselves and give straightforward answers! Even the commitment to empirical research, which leads sociologists to search for evidence about what is happening to work as experienced in the factory or office, does not produce straightforward answers which students, industrialists or politicians might prefer. This is partly because sociologists are also opposed to 'mindless empiricism'. The point was well formulated by the man widely acknowledged as the founder of sociology, Auguste Comte (1798–1857), a thinker whose advocacy of a society run by industrialists and bankers (although advised by sociologists!) should commend him to the Henry Fords or like-minded politicians: 'No real observation of any kind of phenomena is possible, except in as far as it is first directed, and finally interpreted, by some theory' (Comte, 1851, discussed in Thompson, 1975, p. 21).

The articles in this book have all been chosen because they make important theoretical contributions to the direction and interpretation of the sociological observation of work. (A companion volume is devoted to more experiential accounts of different aspects of work – C. Littler (ed.), *The Experience of Work*, 1984). The contributions are divided into two main sections. After an introductory section, on 'Issues and Trends', the chapters in the first main section, 'Organization and Control of Work', deal with various aspects of the organization and control of work, mainly within capitalism, but with some reference to non-capitalist systems – the division of labour, labour markets, the labour process and deskilling, work cultures, professions, management ideologies and industrial relations, and agriculture as a section within the global division of labour. The second half of the book, 'Work and Society', examines the changing nature and position of work in our society and the effects on various groups and institutions – women, the family, education, the young unemployed, leisure, and people as consumers.

It can be seen that this represents a very wide coverage of issues concerning work, which correspond to the radical changes that are occurring, especially the economic changes that have brought about widespread unemployment and restructuring of work, the introduction of new technologies, shifts in sectoral distribution of jobs from manufacturing to services, increases in the numbers of women employed and in part-time work, and changes in the global division of labour. Every part of our lives is affected by these changes, from our individual self-images to our experiences in areas outside the sphere of paid employment, such as home and leisure. Many people are puzzled and distressed by the changes and cannot understand why they are happening; those who might be expected to accept some responsibility, in government or industry, sometimes claim either that the causes are beyond their control, or that things will work out for the best provided everyone co-operates, even if co-operation seems to favour some people and to penalize others. Our aim, in this book, is to provide theoretical and analytical guides to the investigation of the causes and effects of those changes. The main focus is on long-term and fundamental processes, which entails probing beneath the surface of events in an attempt to discern underlying structural factors in the social system that might explain these tendencies.

At the beginning of the book (Chapter 1) and towards the end (in Chapter 16), we raise some basic questions about the ideology of work in our society and to what extent it determines people's identities and self-images. There are clearly heavy psychological and social costs entailed in an ideology which creates the impression that a person's identity can be equated with his or her occupation. The costs for the unemployed are evident, but so are those for women (who tend to occupy more part-time and low-wage jobs, and do unpaid work). It raises questions about educational policies which put too much emphasis on early vocational training, thus summoning up the scene in *Brave New World*, mentioned by Kumar, in which embryos destined to be rocket-maintenance men are decanted upside down, so that 'They learn to associate topsyturvydom with well-being'.

Moorhouse criticizes both classic studies in the sociology of work and in Marxism for 'reducing life to labour and being to occupation', and for not taking account of the fact that as production has changed so has consumption, the relative affluence of post-war capitalism having justified an ideology which links the acquisition and use of consumer goods to values which emphasize the importance of the search for personal identity and authenticity. It could be that the ideological idolization of work, which has been common to both capitalism and socialism, is now being challenged by technologies which make it redundant and a consumerism which dethrones it to a purely instrumental-subordinate status. Whether through necessity or choice, society may be forced to re-examine the ideology of work and to question its appropriateness in an age when full-time and lifelong paid employment is no longer a possibility for many people, and for others it does not constitute their main source of personally fulfilling and socially productive activity. (The relation between work, employment and leisure is discussed by Kumar in Chapter 1, and in relation to work in the informal economy by Pahl in Chapter 11; the implications for unemployed young people are the subject of the study reported on by Roberts *et al*. in Chapter 15.

There have been significant developments in the study of work over the last ten years, and these are reflected in this book. It was in 1974 that Harry Braverman published his *Labor and Monopoly Capital: the Degradation of Work in the Twentieth Century*, which took up, after years of neglect, a subject that had been central to Marx's analysis of capitalism – the labour process. By 'labour process' Marx meant the system of production in which labour power, in association with technology, is organized and utilized so as to produce an end product which has a use and which, under capitalism, is a commodity that can be exchanged on the market. Braverman set out to show how and why the labour process had assumed new organizational forms in different periods of capitalist development, although always governed by the fundamental drive towards capital accumulation.

Braverman's central thesis was that the main tendency in the capitalist labour process is towards deskilling – the knowledge and skills of workers are constantly being incorporated into management functions or into machines, so as to reduce labour costs and make labour more controllable, and this is explained as a necessary consequence of the pursuit of surplus value by capitalist enterprises. This thesis has been much criticized and modified. Two prominent criticisms are that Braverman did not take sufficient account of the alternative strategies to that of deskilling which employers adopt to maintain their control, nor did he allow for the effects of workers' resistance. Other critics would regard the thesis as unproven on the grounds that it is not clear whether the undermining of existing skills does not generate new ones to a degree that the net result is an increase in skill. The thesis and some of these criticisms are discussed at length by Thompson (in Chapter 5), and with regard to Soviet-type societies by Littler (in Chapter 6); Armstrong (in Chapter 7) considers how competition between different professional groups within management can give rise to different control strategies.

An important reason for going beyond Braverman in distinguishing different types of management strategy is that it then becomes possible to connect the analysis to the study of dual or segmented labour markets (see Freedman, Chapter 4). For example, it is possible to distinguish two contrasting management strategies for controlling labour. The first is the 'direct control' described by Braverman, where managers attempt to obtain the compliance of the labour force by close supervision and maintaining discipline by minimizing worker responsibility through bureaucratic organization and the techniques of scientific management. The other strategy is that of 'responsible autonomy', where workers are allowed considerable independence in the work situation, provided they conform to the overall aims of management. The second strategy is applied to professionals, some service workers and certain skilled technical workers (such middle-class and skilled manual occupational groups will seek to exclude outsiders and maintain the security of these 'job shelters'). The 'direct-control' strategy is most stringently applied to those in weak positions in the segmented labour markets, who have little chance of breaking into other job markets (this applies particularly to ethnic minorities and women workers, along with unskilled and semi-skilled sections of the working class in general).

It is clear that Braverman's thesis has stimulated a vigorous debate. More importantly, perhaps, it gave a new focus to studies of work. Or rather, he helped to bring back a perspective that was shared by most of the great political economists of the eighteenth and nineteenth centuries, including Marx, before the subdivision into specialized social sciences produced a fragmentation of perspectives. It is a perspective that focuses on the *division of labour* in order to identify the connections between economic processes and social relationships. This revised, classical concept of the division of labour recombines three topics that have frequently been treated separately: (1) sectoral patterns of employment; (2) occupational or skill structure of the labour force; (3) organization of tasks at the workplace (cf. Garnsey, Chapter 3). It also relates these to wider social divisions, particularly the divisions created by the different interests of the major classes, which the early political economists regarded as self-evident. As Garnsey stresses, the division of labour is not determined by a neutral force – technology – but is the outcome of a given distribution of power and serves specific (usually class-based) interests.

Although the revived 'political economy' perspective owes much to the reinvigoration of Marxist theory, as demonstrated by Braverman, it is important to stress the line of continuity with other early political economists, such as Adam Smith and Adam Ferguson. The failure of some theorists to acknowledge these antecedents can give the unfortunate, and usually unjustified, impression of a narrowly biased perspective. The impression can be avoided if it is pointed out that, for example, political economists before Marx posed the question of the choice of new forms of division of labour associated with new forms of technology in terms of promoting labour discipline and reducing wage costs through 'deskilling' (see Garnsey, Chapter 3, for examples).

The contributions to the second half of the book are also concerned with the division of labour, but more in terms of its ramifications and effects outside the workplace, with regard to individuals, groups and institutions. Pahl (Chapter 11) considers the implications of sectoral changes in employment – such as whether an increase in service jobs is likely to make up for the decline in manufacturing jobs, and whether changes are occurring in the balance between the formal economy and the informal economy. The subject of the domestic division of labour is taken up by Oakley (Chapter 12) and Finch (Chapter 13), with particular reference to the implications for women; Finch also looks at the impact of male occupational roles on wives. The problems of preparing young people for work and for coping with the experience of unemployment are discussed in Chapters 14 and 15. The issue of the problems created by current ideologies of work, which is raised with regard to unemployed young people in Chapter 15, is tackled from a different angle by Moorhouse (Chapter 16), who claims that sociologists have overlooked the potent effects of the ideology of consumerism in determining workers' orientations and self-images.

In conclusion, Richard Brown (Chapter 17) combines a discussion of the changing shape of work with an account of changes in sociological approaches to the study of work, so as to show how both must be located in specific historical contexts. The challenge that faces us, as this book seeks to illustrate, is to develop perspectives on work which are relevant to current events and problems, but which are sufficiently theoretically informed so that they can disclose the fundamental structures and processes that shape those events and give rise to the problems.

This book, along with its companion volume (*The Experience of Work* edited by Craig Littler), forms part of the teaching materials for the Open University course, *Work and Society*. In preparing the book I have been greatly helped by the suggestions and assistance of the *Work and Society* course team: Robert Bocock, Rosemary Deem, David Dunkerley, Ruth Finnegan, Elizabeth Garnsey, Peter Hamilton, Margaret Kiloh, Craig Littler, Mary Maynard, Manuela d'Oliveira, Graeme Salaman, Stephen Wood. Professor Richard Brown, of the University of Durham, who has acted as the external Academic Assessor to the course, has provided helpful comments.

I am also particularly grateful to Joan Higgs and Michelle Kent for their secretarial assistance.

Kenneth Thompson
March 1984

References

Beynon, H. (1973) *Working for Ford*, Harmondsworth, Penguin

Braverman, H. (1974) *Labour and Monopoly Capital; the Degradation of Work in the Twentieth Century*, New York, Monthly Review Press.

Littler, C. (ed.) (1984) *The Experience of Work*, London, Heinemann Educational Books.

Thompson, K.A. (1975) *August Comte: the foundation of sociology*, London, Nelson.

Acknowledgments

1. Reprinted from *New Universities Quarterly* 34, 1979 – 80, by permission of *Universities Quarterly*.
2. Reprinted from C. Littler & G. Salaman, *Class at Work*, Batsford, 1984, by permission of B.T. Batsford Ltd.
3. Reprinted from *Theory and Society* 10, 1981, by permission of Elsevier Science Publishers.
4. Reprinted from M. Freedman, *Labor Markets: Segments and Shelters*, Allanhead, Osman & Co., 1976, by permission of Rowman & Allanheld.
5. Reprinted from P. Thompson, *The Nature of Work*, Macmillan, 1983, by permission of Macmillan, London and Basingstoke.
6. Original article by Craig Littler ©The Open University 1984, by permission of the Open University.
7. Original article by Peter Armstrong ©Peter Armstrong 1984, by permission of the author.
8. Reprinted from P.J. Armstrong, J.F.B. Goodman & J.D. Hyman, *Ideology and Shopfloor Industrial Relations*, Croom Helm, 1981, by permission of Croom Helm Ltd.
9. Original article by David Dunkerley and Neil Casey ©David Dunkerley and Neil Casey 1984, by permission of the authors.
10. Original article by Peter Hamilton ©Peter Hamilton 1984, by permission of the author.
11. Reprinted from *International Journal of Urban and Regional Research*, 4, 1980, by permission of Edward Arnold Publishers.
12. Reprinted form A. Oakley, *Subject Women*, Martin Robertson, 1981, by permission of Basil Blackwell Ltd.
13. Reprinted from J. Finch, *Married to the Job*, Allen & Unwin, 1983, by permission of George Allen & Unwin Ltd.
14. Reprinted from *Educational Analysis*, 2 1981, by permission of Falmer Press Ltd.
15. Reprinted from *Leisure Studies*, 1, 2, 1982, by permission of E. & F.N. Spon and Associated Book Publishers (U.K.) Ltd.
16. Reprinted from *Sociological Review*, August 1983, by permission of Routledge & Kegan Paul PLC.
17. Original article by Richard Brown ©The Open University 1984, by permission of the Open University.

SECTION 1

Issues and Trends

This opening section sets out some of the main issues and trends in the sociology of work. Krishan Kumar puts work in perspective for us by his reminder that it is a social institution, and like all social institutions it has a history and an ideology. How it has seemed to people at one time is not how it seems at another, and what seems to be a just reward to one person may seem to another to be the result of exploitation. Social anthropology and comparative sociology reveal wide differences between societies in the ways in which they situate work and give it meaning; for example, non-industrial societies are much less likely to make the distinctions that are made in industrial societies with regard to spheres such as work, leisure, family and religion. An awareness of these background differences is essential to an understanding of the historical and ideological premisses that lurk behind some of the problems of work as they are defined in our society. Kumar maintains that when we are faced with questions about the 'necessity of work', we need to ask: what work, how much, and by whom?

Littler and Salaman focus attention on the historical trends and structural processes of capitalism that give rise to many of the problems of work and lack of work in our society. The same processes that give capitalism its dynamism, such as competition, the drive to increase productivity and lower costs, the search for new markets, innovation and technological development, also give rise to individual and social problems. Although capitalist and socialist systems of work organization share some characteristics and some common problems, they are also different in some important respects, as is made clear in this chapter (and also in Chapter 6).

1 The Social Culture of Work: Work, Employment and Unemployment as Ways of Life

KRISHAN KUMAR

All labour is directed towards producing some effect. For though some exertions are taken merely for their own sake, as when a game is played for amusement, they are not counted as labour. We may define labour as any exertion of mind or body undergone partly or wholly with a view to some good other than the pleasure derived directly from the work.

(Alfred Marshall, *Principles of Economics*, 1890).

As soon as we begin to look at this, we see how curiously limited is the vision of human excellence that has got built into our society, and that we have made do with up to now. It is a vision that is inextricably bound up with the market society. And the sad truth is that it is a vision of inertia. It is almost incredible, until you come to think of it, that a society whose keyword is *enterprise*, which certainly sounds active, in in fact based on the assumption that human beings are so inert, so averse to activity, that is, to expenditure of energy, that every expenditure of energy is considered to be painful, to be, in the economist's term, a disutility. This assumption, which is a travesty of the human condition, is built right into the justifying theory of the market society, and so of the liberal society. The market society, and so the liberal society, is commonly justified on the grounds that it maximises utilities, i.e. that it is the arrangement by which people can get the satisfaction they want with the least effort. The notion that activity itself is pleasurable, is a utility, has sunk almost without trace under this utilitarian vision of life.

(C.B. Macpherson, *The Real World of Democracy*, Oxford, 1966)

Writing recently in the *Guardian* of the plight of three unemployed teenage 'punks', Jill Tweedie commented:

For the first time in history, we have created a society that has given every one of its members aspirations towards individuality and yet is slowly withdrawing the major method whereby such individuality can be expressed – work.

The concern is impeccable: and yet we stir uneasily. The equation between the person's work and his individuality is being made too directly. Certainly it is a conventional one. Who am I? has so often in recent Western society been answered by another question, What do I do? A man's work was his being. But here, too, an equation of another sort is made. 'Work' equals 'job'. Identity and occupation are seen to go together – an association carried to absurd lengths in Huxley's *Brave*

Krishan Kumar, in *New Universities Quarterly*, vol. 34, 1979/80.

New World, where embryos destined to be rocket maintenance men are decanted upside down: 'They learn to associate topsyturvydom with well-being: in fact, they're only truly happy when they're standing on their heads.' The sets of equations – work: job: identity: individuality – begin to take on alarming features.

The confusions are readily understandable. Work is a social institution: and, like all such institutions, it has a history. How it has seemed to people at one time is not how it seems at another. Once a curse – 'in the sweat of thy brow shalt thou eat bread' – it could come to seem a blessing – 'laborare est orare' – and then again an affliction, 'shunned like the plague'. Nor were these judgements necessarily shared by all the people at any given time. Where work was fulfilment to one man or group it could be seen as defilement to another man or group. As far as work is concerned, the saying 'one man's meat is another man's poison' can carry the sense, not of the relativity of tastes and values, but of the brute fact of exploitation. Work has, in other words, not merely a history but an ideology.

The question is, where do we now stand? What has work come to mean? What is the nature of the connection between work and employment? How far should we be trying to find employment for people, rather than seeking to help them to work? What is now implied by the phrase, 'the necessity of work'? What work, how much, and by whom? These are properly questions for a series of essays, not just one. Here I simply want to map out the background to these questions, to suggest the historical and ideological premises that so often lurk unexamined behind them.

I

All societies accept the necessity of work in order to survive. For most societies, for most of the time, work is simply a fact of existence which they must accommodate to. There are always some people who, as rulers, warriors, and priests, escape the more burdensome kinds of work by persuading or forcing others to do it for them. Most societies, too, contain collective fantasies of the Garden of Eden or Land of Cockaigne type, where food and comforts abound without the need to work. And there are even some societies, of the hunting and gathering type, where as Sahlins has shown economic life is so simple and needs so undeveloped that their members have a degree of 'leisure' unheard of until the era of 'the affluent society' of the West.[1]

But it makes little sense in the case of most of these societies – pre-industrial or non-industrial – to ask our typically modern questions about work, leisure, identity, and the like. Such questions presuppose a separation of spheres which does not exist. Their life of work, play, family, religion, and community forms a continuous or over-lapping set of activities, no more to be divided up than the separate cells of a piece of living tissue. This does not mean of course that people work all the time, any more than it means that they play, or pray, all the time. The categories collapse and convert into one another in an almost infinitely flexible way. The Dogons of the Sudan, Keith Thomas tells us, employ the same words to indicate both cultivating the ground and dancing at a religious ceremony, for to them both are equally useful, and equally prayerful, forms of activity. A terracotta from Thebes shows four women rolling dough into loaves to the sound of the flute. Recreational activities flow out of economic needs: horse-racing (according to a twelfth-century account) developed out of the practice of allowing the animals at Smithfield market to show their paces in a sort of primitive selling-plate. Or out of kinship and community relations: in friendly form, as with the convivial wakes and ales, or in ferocious competition, as with the bloodthirsty football matches between rival villages in pre-industrial England.[2]

Just as 'leisure' comes out of work, so work itself is heavily impregnated with needs and obligations of a ritual, religious, and recreational kind. The clearest example of this is the medieval European guild. Thomas writes:

> The model craft guild, maintaining standards and a sense of professional pride, permitting all to work their way up from apprentice to master, allowing masters and journeymen to work side by side, invoking the comforting patronage of a saint, helping the poor and sick among its members, and combining economic functions with religious and convivial ones, must have produced a very different attitude to work from that to be found today in a large factory or steel works.[3]

Work, moreover, is regulated by the task, with its characteristically irregular rhythms in which labour and leisure are intermingled.

> The working-day lengthens or contracts according to the task – and there is no great sense of conflict between labour and passing the time of day.[4]

The irregular pattern imposed by the task is heightened by the irregularity of the working week, and the working year. People work for as long as is needed to meet traditionally-defined needs, and no more. Many an English artisan honoured 'Saint Monday', and showed a pious disposition to give due homage to 'Saint Tuesday' as well. 'The work pattern was one of alternate bouts of intense labour and of idleness, wherever men were in control of their own working lives'.[5] A standard argument against raising the wages of workers in eighteenth-century England was indeed that they would thereby work less. Their needs being satisfied by less work, they would prefer more leisure to more pay. The priorities still occasionally show themselves among more traditional workers today. A time-hallowed set of values supported the chronic absentee mineworker who, pressed as to why he managed only four shifts, replied 'because I can't live on three'.

Given the confusion or conflation of categories, it is neither easy nor particularly profitable to work out how much 'leisure time' is enjoyed by the populations of non-industrial societies. But for at least one reason such an exercise is important. Industrial peoples harbour profound prejudices and illusions about non-industrial peoples, one especially potent one being that they are all bowed down by a lifetime of unremitting toil. What studies there are suggest a quite different picture. Sahlins calculates that the workday of the Australian Aborigines – the time spent in subsistence activities – is about 4 – 5 hours of intermittent and not very demanding labour. An even lower figure is arrived at for the South African Bushmen. 'Hunters', says Sahlins, 'keep banker's hours, notably less than modern industrial workers (unionised), who would surely settle for a 21–35 week'.[6] The ancient Romans, following what one student has called 'man's ineradicable tendency to convert his fast days into feast-days', so piled up festival days that it is estimated that in the middle of the fourth century AD Roman citizens had 175 days a year off.[7] For the European Middle Ages, contemporary evidence suggests that agricultural workers spent nearly a third of the year in leisure, while Paris craftsmen, for instance, worked for only about 194 days in the year – that is, nearly half the year was leisure time.[8]

Such figures are not of course to be taken too literally. But they do at least do something towards putting our present position in the industrial societies in perspective. What they suggest in fact, and what is borne out by all else we know about the nature of work in non-industrial societies, is that the coming of industrialisation marks a clear watershed in the history and ideology of work. One superficial but still quite telling indication of this lies in the fact that the hours of work actually go up, sometimes startlingly, for the populations of the industrial societies, at least in the early stages. Factory workers in nineteenth-century Europe worked a 70 and even 80-hour week. It took a hundred years for them to return to the working hours roughly equivalent to that of the guildsmen who were their medieval forebears. But far more important than these quantitative measurements is the transformation in the very concept and meaning of work brought about by industrialisation.

II

The Greeks, we know, had a low opinion of work in the conventional sense.

> A state with an ideal constitution cannot have its citizens living the life of mechanics or shopkeepers, which is ignoble and inimical to goodness. Nor can it have them engaged in farming: leisure is a necessity, both for growth in goodness and for the pursuit of political activities.
>
> (Aristotle, *Politics*, 1328b)

It is a mistake, however, to think that the contempt for work was a contempt for manual or bodily labour as such. Physical and manual effort was frequently extolled in the case of both athletes and artists. It was not work *per se* that was degrading but, as Aristotle's remarks suggest, the status of being a *worker*. Being a worker meant having to work for one's living, hence being tied, like an animal, to necessity. Greek thought was consistent throughout in the view that the labour of one's body which is necessitated by its needs is slavish. Hence occupations which did not actually consist in labouring, yet were undertaken not for their own sake but in order to provide the necessities of life, were assimilated to the status of labour.[9] By the same token, the free citizen who had the leisure to devote himself to the truly human pursuit of politics or (later) philosophy, was allowed and indeed encouraged to practise manual skills. The important distinction was always that between work performed as a matter of animal need or necessity, and work freely chosen and executed, the only human way of work.

This attitude partly explains the institution of slavery, and the justification of it, at least in Greek eyes. As Hannah Arendt has argued:

> The opinion that labour and work were despised in antiquity because only slaves were engaged in them is a prejudice of modern historians. The ancients reasoned the other way around and felt it necessary to possess slaves because of the slavish nature of all occupations that served the need for the maintenance of life... The institution of slavery in antiquity, though not in later times, was not a device for cheap labour or an instrument of exploitation for profit but rather the attempt to exclude labour from the conditions of man's life. What men shared with all other forms of animal life was not considered to be human.[10]

But of course needs, such as for shelter and subsistence, which man did inescapably share with other animals had to be met; and these needs were supplied by the labour of slaves, free artisans, and foreigners. Hence in practice, if not in principle, a fundamental wedge was driven between the 'leisured classes', those who did not work for a living, and all those who, however wealthy they became, continued to follow an occupation in the world of work. Freedom, defined as an escape from the sphere of necessity (labour), came to be seen as an aristocratic prerogative. This has been a tradition, corrupted into a prejudice, of extraordinary strength and resilience. It survived both the Roman and the medieval eras. It is to be found, alive and vigorous, among the eighteenth-century Whig aristocracy (not least, no doubt, at Wentworth Woodhouse), as well as among the nineteenth-centry planter aristocracy of the southern states of America; and there are many signs of its persistence today.[11] In a peculiarly ironic twist, there was even the invention of the term 'the aristocracy of labour' (in its pre-industrial, not the bastardised nineteenth-century form) to describe those workers who possessed in the world of work a faint echo of the attributes of the 'man of independent means': being their own boss, having their own tools, setting their own pattern and times of work, and so on.

Christianity modified this classical, aristocratic tradition; but in ways which for a long time devalued work even further, making it partake even less of the good life than it had in the eyes of the ancient philosophers. There were, however, contradictory pressures within the Christian attitude to work. In what one might regard as the 'optimistic' strain, there was the view of man's work as a human mimesis of the original act of divine creation. This was a view that gained particular prominence among Renaissance humanists: man as 'the second just creator after Jove', the Prometheus who stole the creative fire from the Gods. As an important subsidiary theme within the 'optimistic' tradition, there was the popular emphasis on the human life of Christ, the humble carpenter who gathered to himself equally human workers and continued an active life in the world, countering the influences of the rich and powerful. In the right circumstances, such a popular tradition could explode with revolutionary force in peasant rebellions and millenarian movements, with their hopes and demands of a communistic, egalitarian society in which the claims and organisation of work were central.

But even within the 'optimistic' tradition there were ambiguities. Christ the carpenter, after all, downed tools in favour of his mission, and drew his disciples away from their crafts. The non-worldly or other worldly strand in Christianity – what John Passmore has seen as the Augustinian as opposed to the this-worldly Pelagian emphasis[12] – repeatedly came out as the dominant ideological force. It appealed not simply to the mystics, but to the orthodox theologians and the Church Establishment, the more so as it seemed to continue the classical, Platonic, tradition. With the decline of the city state and the rise of the 'cosmopolis', Plato's followers increasingly rejected the older idea of politics as the highest activity of free men. Politics was now also relegated, along with work, to the mundane world of the *vita activa*: the ideal life was the *vita contemplativa*, the life of philosophic contemplation of the 'real forms' that lay behind worldly appearances. Such an approach squared well with the temperament and intellectual outlook of some of the best minds in the Christian world. In the theology of Aquinas, strongly influenced by Aristotle, work is indeed rescued from the contempt in which the Greeks held it. But only, as it were, to be damned even more competely as an activity of the incorrigibly lesser realms of the human world, as compared with the divine order. As an end in itself, Aquinas would have regarded it with even greater incomprehension than the Greeks. At best work can be a helpful discipline in preparing the individual for a fit state of religious piety. P.D. Anthony thus sums up the orthodox position:

> The worker might contribute to the mutual exchange of services for the sake of the good life, but the good life was the end and it was not to be measured in ergonomic or economic terms. The church developed a new doctrine of the importance of work but strictly as an instrument of spiritual purpose. The Benedictine rule emphasised the spiritual danger of idleness and ordered regular work at fixed times of the day in order to reduce it. The church also recommended labour as a penance on good scriptural authority emanating from man's fall. Work was a discipline, it

contributed to the Christian virtue of obedience. It was not seen as noble, or rewarding, or satisfying, its very endlessness and tedium were spiritually valuable in that it contributed to Christian resignation.[13]

Protestantism cut across both the 'optimistic' and the 'pessimistic' strands within the Christian attitude to work, and prepared the way for the distinctly modern conception. The legacy of work as a curse put upon Adam and his seed persisted: work was not seen as fulfilment, it was a relentless, joyless activity performed in the spirit of asceticism. But the truly radical innovation was the elevation of the place of work in the life of the individual, and of society. Protestantism broke down the barrier between everyday life and spiritual life, between the monastery and the market place. To work diligently and soberly in one's 'calling' became a central requirement of the Protestant way of life. It was a spiritual duty, an expression of one's faith and piety far surpassing any good works that might be performed in an eleemosynary spirit. With the Calvinist doctrine of a pre-destined elect, work took on even greater urgency. As Max Weber argued, success in worldly life became the sign of election in a world where no action of a conventionally religious kind could be the means of salvation. The psychological need to know whether one was chosen was transformed into an intense, almost neurotic, striving for recognition in the world of men, for such attainment might at least be the outward manifestation of inward grace.

Whether as cause or effect it does not matter here; but at the same time, and in the same places, as Protestantism was giving to work a uniquely spiritualised status, labour was increasingly being discovered as the fundamental factor of production, and a unique source of value. Between the sixteenth and the eighteenth centuries, *homo rationalis*, the model for pretty well all speculation on the human condition up till then, began to give way to *homo laborans*. The speed of this historic shift, as well as its momentousness, still seems insufficiently appreciated. In a complete reversal of the traditional ordering, in which man's rational capacity was seen as the faculty that raised him above the beasts, there developed a naturalistic conception in which man was defined precisely by the capacity that linked him to the rest of nature, the capacity to labour.[14] The industrial revolution was bound to enhance that conception. The fantastic and unprecedented productivity of man linked to machines beggared any other description of him save as producer. Such a description we find pre-eminently in Marx, in whose system labour appears not simply as the source of all productivity but as the expression of the very humanity of man, his 'species-being'.

With industrialism, work is placed at the centre not just of man, but of history. Work is the means by which man makes himself. It is also the means by which he constructs his whole world. Starting with Rosseau's celebration of the craftsman in *Émile*, there develops a tradition of thinking about work in which work is treated with an almost metaphysical pathos and intensity. Work, quite simply, as a philosophy and an activity, becomes a secular religion. No longer, as in the Protestant ethic, does religion sanctify work. Work now sanctifies religion. The claims for work grow in scope and urgency as the nineteenth century progresses, in the writings especially of Schiller, Hegel, Saint-Simon, Fourier, Marx, Tolstoy and Zola. In Ruskin and Morris they reach a culminating point. In the case of Morris in particular one has the feeling that to be deprived of work – fit work – is to be deprived of a soul, to be left in a dark void.[15] It is in this tradition that we get most of our modern humanist definitions of work as 'the first moral category', as Roger Garaudy has stated it. Here, typically, is David Meakin:

Work – and not least manual work – is an integral part of our humanity and our intelligence. It dictates not only our relationship to nature, to our environment, but thereby also the working and scope of our consciousness itself, for consciousness is born of that active confrontation with nature.[16]

Or Tom Kitwood:

> In a fundamental sense, work may be regarded as the exercise of a person's powers in the constructive transformation of the world: an expression of individuality, an enhancement of the sense of being alive, and the most powerful of social bonds beyond the family.[17]

The shift to industrialism produced a further emphasis, and a further equation. Not only was a man's being to be defined by his work, but his work was now also increasingly defined and determined by his *job*, his occupation in the formal money economy. The industrial revolution methodically undermined the older system whereby work, family, and leisure life were all of a piece, performed as an undifferentiated whole. Technical changes, together with other such changes as urbanisation, took work out of the home and into a specialised setting, the factory (and somewhat later, the office). To be 'at work' was henceforward to be 'in work', to be employed as a 'worker' in the formal economy. (Even the 'self-employed' performed their labour in and for the formal economy.) By the same token, all activities outside the formal work setting were devalued as non-work, as 'unproductive'. The woman's work in the home, for instance, formerly on an equal footing with that of the man in the domestic economy, which shaded off insensibly into the wider money economy, now came to be regarded as marginal to economic life. 'Home' and 'work' were specialised and separated out, along with 'leisure' and 'religion'.

While this fragmentation clearly involved a decisive (and debilitating) narrowing of the concept of work, it had the unexpected effect of enhancing the status of work even further. For work-as-job was now linked firmly to the economy; and the industrial revolution, for the first time in history, made the economic realm supreme. It was the sphere of activity which was both the central dynamic of the society and the source of its central values. The industrial economy was 'the unbound Prometheus', and all roles and activities linked to it shared in its glory, just as those which didn't, such as that of the priest, shrank in status and significance. Hence the final equation of work with job, following upon that of work with identity, doubly underscored the importance of work. The question, 'Who am I?', which would formerly have been answered almost everywhere in terms of religion, family or place of origin, could now really be answered only in terms of the occupation a man worked in.

III

But here is the paradox. The celebration, the idolisation almost, of work, proceeds against a background of its imminent redundancy. As Meakin says,

> Looking back from our vantage point, it seems ironic that the industrial revolution leads to a conscious realisation of the ethical value of work in all its fullness – and especially those qualities enshrined in the artisanate – at the very moment when those same values are seriously threatened and perhaps doomed by the advent of machino-facture.[18]

It is important to stress that this is not simply an aspect of our own contemporary predicament. The challenge to the ethic of work was implicit in the very phenomenon, industrialism, which provoked the most passionate advocacy of that ethic. From the very start industrialisation aimed at eliminating the human factor in production altogether. Eric Hobsbawm notes that

> the original cotton factory already strove after the ideal of becoming a gigantic, complex and 'self-acting' (as it was then called) automaton, and each technical innovation brought it a little closer towards this object.[19]

And where machines did not (yet) actually displace labour, the goal of the early industrialists was to make that labour as routine and machine-like as possible. The main difficulty of the early factory system identified by Andrew Ure in his *Philosophy of Manufactures* (1835), was

> in training human beings to renounce their desultory habits of work, and to identify themselves with the unvarying regularity of the complex automaton.

The more skilled the worker, the more intractable to discipline. The solution must be to organise and mechanise work in such a way as to withdraw any process which required 'peculiar dexterity and steadiness of hand...from the cunning workman', and to place it in charge of

> a mechanism so self-regulating, that a child may superintend it. . . . The grand object therefore of the modern manufacturer is, through the union of capital and science, to reduce the task of his work-people to the exercise of vigilance and dexterity – faculties speedily brought to perfection in the young.

Or, as Josiah Wedgwood more pithily put it, the ideal was 'to make such machines of the men as cannot err'.[20]

The dilemma of the philosophers of work is clear. Objectively, the industrial revolution provided the most eloquent testimony to the truth of the conception of man as worker, or producer. At the same time, in practice it threatened to reduce man's work to a nullity. As industrialism progressed, it ruthlessly undermined the need for all skill and creativity on the part of the worker. It reduced him first to a part of the machine, then, having thus simplified his task to a mechanical routine, eliminated him altogether by a further bout of mechanisation. There was thus an inverse relationship between the capacity of the system to provide creative and satisfying work, and the increasingly agonised assertions of the value and the need of such work – or even work as such – as the essential basis of all truly human activity. Various strategies were adopted to fend off reality. There were attempts to set up co-operative and communal ventures, usually on a pre-industrialised scale and with pre-industrial technology. Nearly all failed.[21] The vanishing world of the medieval craftsman was, in suitably idealised terms, resurrected as the standard of all work, and attempts were made to fuse industrial technology with craft practice. There was, it was recognised, not just *homo laborans*, but more importantly *homo faber*. All European languages, it could be shown, had continued to reflect a critical Latin distinction between *laborare* and *facere* (or *fabricari*), between mere 'labour' or 'toil', and true 'work'. For the Germans there was *Arbeit* versus *Werk*, for the French *oeuvre* as against *travail*. In a desperate stand, Ruskin pedantically proposed that we should distinguish between *'opera'* and *'labor'*, between joyful, creative work, and negative work, 'that quantity of our toil which we die in'. All these efforts, in theory and practice, were of little avail against the increasing tendency of industrial society to reserve interesting work for the diminishing few, and tedious toil for the many.

The circle was squared, temporarily, by Utilitarianism. In a watered-down version of Protestantism, it accepted that industrial work was an intrinsically unrewarding, burdensome, necessity. But the alienated character of work was compensated for by high wages, and by increasing periods of 'free time'. In the

Benthamite 'felicific calculus', the individual trades off the pain of work against the pleasure of leisure. He accepts the 'homelessness' of the sphere of work as the necessary and acceptable price of his being more truly 'himself' in his non-work sphere. As Peter Berger expresses it:

> The typical and statistically normal state of affairs in an industrial society is that people do not work where they carry on their private lives. The two spheres are socially and geographically separate. And since it is in the latter that people typically and normally locate their essential activities, one can say even more simply that they do not live where they work. 'Real life' and one's 'authentic self' are supposed to be centred in the private sphere. Life at work tends to take on the character of pseudo-reality and pseudo-identity.[22]

But the Utilitarian contract turns out to be fraudulent, in at least two ways. There is firstly the fact that we cannot, in practice, so neatly maintain the separation of 'work' and 'leisure'. Long hours of passive employment at work seem to breed long hours of passive employment in leisure. Dull, monotonous, and repetitive work – the normal character of most jobs in industrial society – seems to dampen the capacity for active and enjoyable leisure. Alasdair Clayre, who notes these findings, rightly comments that

> if nothing can repay a man in leisure for the capacities of enjoyment that depriving work has destroyed, then monotonous work is paid for in a coinage which work itself debases, and the entire notion of a fair wage-bargain for depriving work becomes suspect.[23]

But even if leisure can in some sense be held separate from work, how far can it be considered genuinely 'free time', that is, time in which the individual re-composes himself, and establishes a significant identity denied him by the standardising routines of work? The fact is that during the nineteenth century the sphere of leisure was as much 'industrialised' as that of work. As a concept, 'leisure' is indeed an invention of nineteenth-century industrial society, a part of that fragmentation and specialisation that was an inherent principle of the industrial way of life. Right from the start, therefore, it carried the hall-mark of industrialism. It was organised, regulated, packaged, and sold like any other commodity on the market. As Briggs comments,

> the old adage, well known to the nineteenth century pioneering retailers, that the luxuries of today become the necessities of tomorrow, had obvious implications in the world of *homo ludens.*[24]

Burns notes that 'the new leisure of the working classes represented a vacuum which was largely filled, even to begin with, by amusement industries'. Drinking, racing, football, and boxing were reconstituted and heavily capitalised, to be transformed into mass entertainment industries. The spare-time reading habits of the new urban classes were equally well taken care of by the new popular press. Leisure might in a subjective sense be seen as 'time off' work. But in a deeper sense it was part and parcel of the same system that also included work, and the determining pressures were to be seen equally in both spheres. Later, you might very well be employed as a worker by the same corporation that provided your daily paper and saw you safely across the Channel on your packaged holiday. Burns well makes the point that

> the swamping of everyday life by industrialism has not been succeeded by a mere ebbing, or forcing back, of the flood [i.e. in the form of leisure time won]. Social life outside the work situation has not re-emerged; it has been created afresh, in forms which are themselves the creatures of industrialism, which derive from it and which contribute to its development, growth and further articulation.[25]

IV

All these dilemmas of nineteenth-century work and leisure are clearly still with us. The currents of industrialism have continued to flow strongly, and to deepen their course. No longer only manual work, but also white collar and professional work have been subjected to the industrial processes of mechanisation and 'rationalisation', in the Weberian and Taylorian sense. Higher educational qualifications are demanded for work that is itself increasingly less demanding, in terms of skill, responsibility, and the exercise of autonomy. As dependent employees of large-scale bureaucracies, more and more hitherto autonomous professionals find themselves well-paid but relatively impotent actors in an economic and political environment that includes powerful unions and even more powerful multinational élites.[26]

The consequences of all this are equally evident. Work is being questioned on a scale unthinkable to an earlier generation. When at the end of the last century Marx's son-in-law Paul Lafargue produced an attack on the ethic of work entitled *The Right to be Lazy*, he offended both his Marxist friends and his bourgeois critics. Neitzsche's 'Do I work in order to live? No, I live in order to work', was by far the more typical and conventional attitude, as was Freud's response 'love and work' to the question of what were the healthiest activities of the normal balanced person. But today, it is not middle-class drop-outs from the counter-culture but two hard-headed trade unionists, Clive Jenkins and Barrie Sherman, who announce 'the collapse of work', and roundly dismiss the whole ethic of work as bourgeois indoctrination.

> We do not believe that work per se is necessary to human survival or self-esteem. The fact that it appears to be so is a function of two centuries of propaganda and an educational system which maintained the 'idea' of work as its main objective, but which singularly failed to teach about leisure and how to use it... People at present accept that they will be bored if out of work, and so become bored; they believe they will drift, and they drift; they believe that by not working they will become useless, and too many become useless. This need for work is, we would argue, an ingrained and inculcated attitude of mind.[27]

It is not simply of course that people now demand, as a belated counter to the obsession with work, an equal attention to leisure, as an activity with its own valid claims on public policy and the public purse. These demands have in any case been voiced regularly since at least the 1930s, when the 'leisure society' was first anxiously discerned and discussed. The concern now springs more seriously from the perception that the mounting dissatisfaction with work itself seems to be reaching a critical point. Work in the future – it if has any at all – appears to hold out an unending prospect of alienated and irresponsible activity, a desert of meaningless and trivial tasks in factory, shop and office. What work there is left after the widespread application of micro-electronic technology would seem to require of most of us no more than the elementary skills of a junior typist.[28] Such a prospect not surprisingly has begun to keep a few people awake at nights.

In one of the most thoughtful reviews of the problem, two Canadian researchers, Gail Stewart and Cathy Starrs, suggest that our dissatisfaction with work currently reveals itself as a basic anxiety and uncertainty about where we should draw the line between work and non-work.

> For the most part the 'line or turbulence' between the old work ethic and an emerging and different work ethic seems to lie within us rather than between us. We may be disturbed or frustrated or alienated or confused as, in one situation after another, it becomes clearer to us that there are different ethical criteria we can apply

with respect to work, and that the answers are not so clear-cut as they used to be. Whether it is a son's career plans or perhaps an absence of them; our own early retirement; the legitimacy of using office time to do community work; the methods we have used to settle competition for positions or for university entrance; the wondering at night at what has really been accomplished during the day, even though mountains of paper may been processed – all of these may create a turbulence within us that is the surest sign of emerging new concepts of work. Much of this turbulence is not yet visible in public forms but it is readily elicited in personal conversation. While it takes many forms the common theme is a questioning of the old work ethic, and the struggle to find a new mode of working which is perceived as both personally and socially productive.[29]

These thoughts take us into the heart of the immediate issue, the relation between 'work' and 'employment'. For the questioning of the ethic of work is not simply negative. It appears that one way out of the dilemma of alienated work and alienated leisure is to re-define, or re-conceptualise, both 'work' and 'leisure', such that any activity which is personally fulfilling and 'socially productive' can be regarded as work – even if, and in current conditions perhaps especially if, it is performed outside the confines of a 'job' in the formal work economy. Given the expected and enforced increase in 'leisure time', leisure (or unemployment) could be converted from a threat into a promise. It could become the sphere of satisfying and useful activity of the kind idealised by the philosophers of work, and now denied precisely 'at work'.

This has many attractions, and has had a good number of advocates. The French sociologist George Friedmann, for instance, foresaw

> in the society of the future, the flowering of a 'new man' of the artisan type, devoted to the patient and creative fashioning of materials with the aid of manual tools, a new *homo faber* resurrected by leisure.[30]

Stewart and Starrs similarly suggest that 'work' can be and is frequently found elsewhere than in the job economy. It's all a matter of what we choose to call work:

> What is a job? What does it mean to be employed, to be working? Fundamentally it is to find, reflected back to you in the eyes of other people, that they think that what you are doing is worthwhile. It probably helps if you are being paid for what you are doing, and it probably helps if what you are doing is something that most people would regard as an unpleasant activity, something they wouldn't want to have to do themselves, and something that you yourself probably wouldn't do voluntarily. And it probably helps if it is a visible exhausting activity with a visible output. But none of these is essential. What constitutes work is decided by social contract, by social agreement. We construct our social agreements – it is we who decide what constitutes work. Work is what we decide it is... Until very recently we bestowed the legitimacy of 'work' on only a very narrow range of our human activities, carried out in particular times and places... 'Do you work or are you just a housewife?[31]

Everyone can see the immediate sense of this. The amount of work to be done is and always will remain infinite: in making, maintaining, and remaking ourselves, our families, our homes, our environment, our world. The statistics of employment and unemployment are quite irrelevant to this. It is well known how even in the conventional world of employment, a job can properly be done only if the worker goes, as it were, beyond the formal description of the job, putting into it his own 'informal' resources of intelligence and creativity. Look what happens when people 'work to rule'. The chaos that results is a measure of the tenuousness of the distinction between work and non-work even in the formal economy.

The anxieties about the position are of a different kind, and are by no means trivial or philistine (there are many of *those*, but not worth the time). Some arise out of a concern for what is lost when the time between work – conceived as free activity – and employment – conceived as a realm of necessity – is broken. There is a particularly interesting religious tradition here that views this disconnexion with grave alarm. The artist Eric Gill constantly inveighed against 'The Leisure State', with its notion

> that matter is essentially evil and therefore work essentially degrading... Culture, if it is to be a real thing and a holy thing, must be the product of what we actually do for a living – not something added, like sugar on a pill.[32]

The supreme exponent of this tradition is probably Simone Weil, who viewed man's entire being as formed through an 'encounter with necessity' through work: a necessity which he can never in the end escape, and which it is dangerous for him ever to lose sight of. Weil was particularly concerned that, if the increased productivity achieved through automation made men feel free of material needs, they would come to inhabit an illusory world of freedom, the prey of arbitrary fantasies. I quote the passage from *Oppression and Liberty* at length because it seems to me particularly fine:

> We have only to bear in mind the weakness of human nature to understand that an existence from which the very notion of work had pretty well disappeared would be delivered over to the play of the passions and perhaps to madness; there is no self-mastery without discipline, and there is no other source of discipline for man than the effort demanded in overcoming external obsticals. A nation of idlers might well amuse itself by giving itself obstacles to overcome, exercise itself in the sciences, in the arts, in games; but the efforts that are the result of pure whim do not form for a man a means of controlling his own whims. It is the obstacles we encounter and that have to be overcome which gives us the opportunity for self-conquest. Even the apparently freest forms of activity, science, art, sport, only possess value in so far as they imitate the accuracy, rigour, scrupulousness which characterise the performance of work, and even exaggerate them. Were it not for the model offered them unconsciously by the ploughman, the blacksmith, the sailor who work *comme il faut* – to use that admirably ambiguous expression – they would sink into the purely arbitrary. The only liberty that can be attributed to the Golden Age is that which little children would enjoy if parents do not impose rules on them; it is in reality only an unconditional surrender to caprice. The human body can in no case cease to depend on the mighty universe in which it is encased; even if man were to cease being subjected to material things and to his fellows by needs and dangers, he would only be more completely delivered into their hands by the emotions which would stir him continually to the depths of his soul, and against which no regular occupation would any longer protect him.[33]

Something of the same force, and even of the same criticism, can be seen in Hannah Arendt's objections to Marx's vision of the future society. Marx, it will be remembered, looked forward to a communist society in which abundance was such that material needs, the 'realm of necessity', were totally satisfied. Men would exist primarily in and for the 'realm of freedom', which

> begins... where that labour which is determined by need and external purposes ceases. It is a realm in which there takes place 'the development of human potentiality for its own sake'.

He goes on:

> The shortening of the working day is its fundamental prerequisite.
>
> (*Capital*, Vol III)

If freedom is to consist in an end to labour, what will men actually do in the future society? Marx makes some notoriously vague remarks about hunting and fishing, but it is in fact fairly clear that what he had in mind was largely what most people would call 'leisure activities'. The trouble is that he nowhere indicates how the labouring mentality of pre-communist man would be transformed in such a way as to make his work in the realm of freedom truly creative and productive. Arendt, noting 'the fundamental contradiction which runs like a red thread through the whole of Marx's thought', comments:

> The fact remains that in all stages of his work he defines man as an *animal laborans* and then leads him into a society in which this greatest and most human power is no longer necessary. We are left with the rather distressing alternative between productive slavery and unproductive freedom.[34]

In practice, Arendt suggests, no qualitatively new activities will emerge, no principle appropriate to 'the public realm' of human action as opposed to 'the private realm' of (animal) labour:

> Neither abundance of goods nor the shortening of the time actually spent in labouring are likely to result in the establishment of a common world, and the expropriated *animal laborans* becomes no less private because he has been deprived of a private place of his own to hide and be protected from the common realm. Marx predicted correctly, though with an unjustified glee, 'the withering away' of the public realm under conditions of unhampered development of the 'productive forces of society', and he was equally right, that is, consistent with his conception of man as an *animal laborans*, when he foresaw that 'socialised men' would spend their freedom from labouring in those strictly private and essentially wordless activities that we now call 'hobbies'.[35]

It is probable that the 'leisure as work' (or 'work as leisure') theorists can deal adequately with these warnings. They are, however, valuable as a caution against a too careless identification of 'leisure activities' with worthwhile and productive work – quite apart from the force of Weil's worrying insistence on the requirement to keep in touch with 'natural necessity' as a condition of human fulfilment and proper understanding. It is notoriously easy to conceive the society of abundance, or even – what is by no means the same thing – the society of no (formal) work, as a sort of Disneyland of leisure time pursuits. Those projections which look forward to a future in which work centres on the 'informal economy' or 'the household economy'[36] are less likely to fall victim to these seductions. But they still need to specify carefully and concretely what kind of work will be performed, how it will be organised, and above all what will be the nature and degree of its dependence on the 'formal economy' of alienated labour and advanced technology.

To come finally to a view which most forcibly stresses the need to maintain the connection between work and employment. The basis of this view is Freud's observation that work is man's strongest tie to reality. It follows from this, for many thinkers, that this function is best performed when work is most highly institutionalised. Unemployment, on this view, is unacceptable even if the unemployed are as financially secure as they would be if employed, and despite all the 'free time' that is released for their varied use.

Marie Jahoda, drawing on her own study of an unemployed community in the 1930s – the Marienthal study[37] – stresses the extreme psychological disintegration brought on by unemployment. She considers a wide range of more recent studies of attitudes to work, and they serve to confirm her view that while there is much dissatisfaction with work, for the vast majority 'having a job is better than being unemployed, even beyond the financial implications'.[38] Kitwood's survey of English adolescents similarly shows that anxiety about employment prospects has become a major feature of the way adolescents view their future, especially when the time for taking action draws near. Conversely, there is virtually no indication that unemployment would be considered a desirable alternative to having a job, even if the remuneration were comparable to a normal wage.[39]

Both Kitwood and Jahoda are at pains to emphasise what Jahoda calls 'the latest consequences of employment as a social institution, which meet human needs of a more enduring kind'. As Kitwood puts it:

> When a boy or girl personally accepts the label 'unemployed', the subjective environment changes, it becomes a state of inactivity and lassitude, where personal powers cannot be adequately used or expressed...At least for indigenous, English adolescents, it seems that there are no social life-worlds specifically adapted to the unemployed condition...Employment, for all its deficiencies, at least provides an arena for social development, and an acceptable general role.

Jahoda offers a more elaborate list of the beneficial 'latent consequences of employment':

> First among them is the fact that employment imposes a time structure on the waking day; secondly, employment implies regularly shared experiences and contacts with people outside the nuclear family; thirdly, employment links an individual to goals and purposes which transcend his own; fourthly, employment defines aspects of personal status and identity; and finally, employment enforces activity. It is these latent 'objective' consequences of work in complex industrialised societies which help me to understand the motivation to work beyond earning a living; to understand why work is psychologically supportive even when conditions are bad and by the same token, why unemployment is psychologically destructive.

She concedes that other social institutions – schools, clubs, and so on – can provide one or more of these psychological supports.

> I know of none, however, in our society [apart from work], which combines them all and, in addition, has as compelling a manifest reason as making one's living. It is equally true that nobody prevents the unemployed from creating their own time structure and social contacts, from sharing goals and purposes with others or from exercising their skills as best they can. But the psychological input required to do so on a regular basis under one's own steam is colossal.[40]

It may well be that we are dealing with a historical time-lag here, as both Kitwood and Jahoda accept. Work and employment have been associated, as a matter of necessity, for so long that the effort that will be needed to separate them without seriously damaging consequences is bound to seem enormous. A helpful step in that direction would be to show where, and in what manner, the disconnection has been made on a reasonable scale and for a sufficient length of time to show that it can be done successfully. At any rate perhaps history is catching up with us. If the widely quoted and increasingly widely accepted (even, if press leaks are to be believed, in many government departments) projection of five million (or 20 per cent of the workforce) unemployed by the 1990s in Britain comes about, we will have no choice but to seek to ensure that 'unemployment' can be as fully satisfying a way of life as employment. We are faced with a future in which unemployment will be a normal, not aberrant experience for the mass of population. Since we are all potentially among the unemployed, this has now become much more than a matter of pleasant speculation about other people's lives.

Notes

1. Marshall Sahlins. 'The Original Affluent Society', in his *Stone Age Economics* (Tavistock Publications, 1974), pp. 1–40.
2. For these examples, see Keith Thomas, 'Work and Leisure in Pre-Industrial Society', in *Past and Present*, no. 29 (Dec 1964), pp. 50–66.
3. Thomas, 'Work and Leisure', p. 55. Thomas acknowledges that this is an idealised picture. For a more sceptical account of work in pre-industrial England, see P. Laslett, *The World We Have Lost* (Methuen, 1965). The conventional sociologist's view of the pre-modern age is well exemplified by Professor Herzberg and his colleagues:

   Life in primitive societies is hard and filled with backbreaking toil. There is relatively little opportunity for individual growth and development because of the necessity for constant emphasis on sheer subsistence. In a society which spends 70 or 80 per cent of its labour on the mere growing of food there is relatively little left over for the fullest development of the individual.

   F. Herzberg, B. Mausner & B. Snyderman, *The Motivation to Work* (Wiley, 1959), p. 121.
4. E. P. Thompson, 'Time, Work Discipline, and Industrial Capitalism', in *Past and Present*, no. 38 (Dec. 1967), p. 60.
5. Thompson, *ibid.*, p. 73.
6. Sahlins, 'The Original Affluent Society', pp. 34–5.
7. H. Wilensky, 'The Uneven Distribution of Leisure: The Impact of Economic Growth on Free Time', in *Social Problems*, vol. 9 (Summer, 1961), p. 33.
8. Thomas, 'Work and Leisure', p. 63.
9. On this see Hannah Arendt. *The Human Condition* (Doubleday Anchor Books, 1959), pp. 72–3.
10. Arendt. *The Human Condition*, p. 74.
11. It is not too fanciful to see in many of the claims and practices of the *jeunesse dorée* of the 1960s a reassertion of just this aristocratic principle.
12. John Passmore, *The Perfectibility of Man* (Duckworth, 1970), chs. 4–6.
13. P.D. Anthony, *The Ideology of Work* (Tavistock Publications, 1977), p. 37.
14. I am not denying of course that older conceptions of the *homo rationalis* persisted for a long time, especially in the period of the Enlightenment. But even then the assumptions were being severely undermined by the psychology of the English and Scottish thinkers – Locke, Hume, Smith.
15. For two useful studies of this tradition, see A. Clayre, *Work and Play: Ideas and Experience of Work and Leisure* (Weidenfeld and Nicolson, 1974); and David Meakin, *Man and Work: Literature and Culture in Industrial Society* (Methuen, 1976).
16. Meakin, *Man and Work*, pp. 1–2.
17. T. Kitwood, *Disclosures to a Stranger: Adolescent Values in Advanced Industrial Society* (Routledge and Kegan Paul, 1980).
18. Meakin, *Man and Work*, p. 4.
19. E.J. Hobsbawm, *Industry and Empire* (Weidenfeld and Nicolson, 1968), p. 146.
20. Quoted Meakin, *Man and Work*, p. 22.
21. For a sympathetic account of some of these ventures, see Dennis Hardy, *Alternative Communities in Nineteenth Century England* (Longman, 1979).
22. Peter Berger (ed.), *The Human Shape of Work* (Macmillan, New York, 1964), p. 217.
23. A. Clayre, 'Improving the Quality of Work', in *New Universities Quarterly*, vol. 30, no. 4 (Autumn, 1976), p. 441. That people, however, still think in terms of the Utilitarian contract is indicated by E. Chinoy's survey of American car workers in the 1950s. As David Riesman wrote in his introduction to Chinoy's book:

   Chinoy's interviews show work to be part-time imprisonment, through which one pays off the fines incurred by one's pursuit of the good – or rather the good time – life at home and on vacation.

   E. Chinoy, *Automobile Workers and the American Dream* (Doubleday, 1955).
24. Asa Briggs, 'The Organisation of Leisure', *The Times*, 11 October 1969.
25. T. Burns, 'Leisure in Industrial Society', in M.A. Smith, S. Parker & C.S. Smith (eds.) *Leisure and Society in Britain* (Allen Lane, 1973), pp. 45–6.

26. For an excellent account of these changes in work, see H. Braverman, *Labor and Monopoly Capital: The Degradation of Work in the Twentieth Century* (New York, Monthly Review Press, 1974); and see also *Work in America*; Report of a Special Task Force to the US Secretary of Health, Education and Welfare (Cambridge, MIT Press, 1973). It seems worth mentioning here that a recent study of workers in Peterborough (by M. Mann and R. M. Blackburn) showed that the most 'skilled' aspect of their work is in *driving* to it. There is less skill required when they enter the factory or office than in manipulating the controls of the car.

27. Clive Jenkins and Barrie Sherman, *The Collapse of Work* (Eyre Methuen, 1979), p. 141. And as further evidence of a shift in trade union thinking, cf. this comment by Sir Len Murray, General Secretary of the Trades Union Council, on the problem of 'surplus labour' in the industrial economy:

> Looking further ahead, it isn't so much that we need a new policy to deal with the situation, I believe we need a whole new philosophy. This is becoming recognised and accepted throughout Western Europe and throughout the whole of the capitalist industrialised countries. When I say philosophy, I mean we've got to get away from what I have on one or two previous occasions called Old Testament economics: 'In the sweat of thy brow shalt thou eat bread', that work is good and non-work is bad, that work is good and leisure is to be deplored...I see this as an opportunity rather than a threat – to increase the amount of active leisure or active non-employment, if you like, in Society.

The Times, 24 August 1977.

28. For the impact of micro-electronics on work and employment, see Colin Hines, *The 'Chips' are Down* (Earth Resources Research Ltd., 1978); Jenkins and Sherman. *The Collapse of Work*; I. Barron and R. Curnow, *The Future with Microelectronics* (Frances Pinter, 1979); and, best of all, the CIS Report, *The New Technology* (Counter Information Services, 1979).

29. Gail Stewart and Cathy Starrs, *Re-working the World: A Report on Changing Concepts of Work* (Public Policy Concern, Ottawa, 1973), pp. 19–20.

30. George Friedmann, *The Anatomy of Work: Labor, Leisure and the Implications of Automation* (Free Press, New York, 1961), p. 108.

31. Stewart and Starrs, *Re-working the World*, pp. 36–7.

32. Eric Gill, quoted Meakin, *Man and Work*, pp. 141, 155.

33. Simone Weil, *Oppression and Liberty* (Routledge and Kegan Paul, 1958), pp. 84–5.

34. Arendt, *The Human Condition*, pp. 90–1.

35. Arendt, *op. cit.*, p. 101.

36. See, e.g. Scott Burns. *The Household Economy* (Beacon Press, Boston 1977); Hazel Henderson, *Creating Alternative Futures; The End of Economics* (Berkeley Publishing Corporation, New York, 1978); James Robertson, *The Same Alternative* (London, 1978); J. I Gershuny, 'Post-Industrial Society: The Growth of the Informal Economy', in *Futures*, Feb. 1979; J.I. Gershuny and R.E. Pahl, 'Britain in the decade of the three economies', in *New Society* (3 Jan, 1980).

37. Now re-issued: M. Jahoda, P.F. Lazarsfeld and H. Zeisel, *Marienthal: The Sociography of an Unemployed Community* (Tavistock Publications, 1972).

38. Marie Jahoda, 'The Impact of Unemployment in the 1930s and the 1970s', in *Bulletin of the British Psychological Society* (forthcoming).

39. T. Kitwood, *Disclosures to a Stranger*. I am grateful to Dr Kitwood for the opportunity to see part of this work.

40. Jahoda, 'The Impact of Unemployment in the 1930s and 1970s'.

2 The Social Organisation of Work

CRAIG LITTLER AND GRAEME SALAMAN

Our basic premise is that the individual experience of work, with all the problems this can bring, is structured and patterned in ways which can be described in terms of class structuring, and that these patterns of experience, deprivation and opportunity are themselves the systematic product of economic and social processes. It is not enough merely to describe the patterning of the highly unequal distribution of work rewards and deprivations, we must also seek to understand and explain these phenomena by reference to underlying social and economic processes. Such is the objective of this chapter.

Evolution of Monopoly Capitalism

We have noted that the basic capitalist dynamic which organises the design of work, the nature and direction of investment, the structuring of large-scale organisations, the search for new products, markets and technologies, is the search for profit. Under capitalism, work is organised to achieve a level of profit sufficient not only to remunerate the owners of capital, and ensure that capital is not transferred elsewhere, or put to other uses, but also to ensure a constant process of re-investment in new technologies, markets, products, and work systems, so that the firm is constantly improving its competitiveness: The process goes like this:

> Competition inexorably pushes firms to seek out new ways to gain an edge, to recapture old markets and conquer new ones. Not only are old technologies and practices stretched to their limits, but capitalists constantly search for new productive methods. In the economist's language, entrepreneurs expand production out along their cost curves, but competition robs them of their expected profits. The entrepreneurs are thus driven to reinvest profits or borrow more funds, hoping that innovation or expansion will lower their entire cost curves and thereby reclaim the lost margins. But soon their competitors will also adopt any innovations and prices will decline to reflect that event. Once again, the stage is set for a new competition, this time with fewer competitors surviving to fight the next battle, a battle to be waged on a much grander scale.[1] (Edwards, 1979, pp. 39–40)

This is the natural order of things – the 'facts of life' – under capitalism. The imperative for firms to accumulate has urgent implications for the nature and distribution of the inequalities of working life. But the requirement for firms to compete to survive, and thus to accumulate capital for further investment, is exacerbated by the chronic instability of capitalism. The development of new

Craig Littler and Greame Salaman, *Class at Work*, London, Batsford, 1984; Chapter 3.

technologies – of fundamental revolutions in technology – leads to a trans-formation of the whole productiive technology of the economy, and thus to increased profitability. But the gradual spread of the new technology must lead, after a sustained phaśe of accelerated accumulation, to a prolonged phase of decelerating accumulation, i.e. renewed under-investment and the reappearance of idle capital. Each of the cyclical movements which characterise the history of capitalism contains the same essential elements: an initial phase distinguished by technological innovation when accumulation, growth and profit rates accelerate; and a secondary and related phase when profits decline, and accumulation decelerates. Once profits begin to decline, investment falls, and managers prefer cost-reducing rationalisation and invention, aiming for the re-achievement of a satisfactory level of profits through attacks on the working class and attempts to reduce the cost of labour.

Since the late sixties the capitalist world has been experiencing a particular, and well-documented, form of crisis. Initially during the sixties the problem was one of over-accumulation in relation to labour supply, with a consequent fall in profitability, as Table 2.1 illustrates.

Table 2.1 Rates of profit for industrial and commercial companies, 1960–75.

| | Percentages before tax | | | | |
	1960	1965	1970	1973	1975
UK	14.2	11.8	8.7	7.2	3.5
USA	9.9	13.7	8.1	8.6	6.9
France	11.9	9.9	11.1	10.2	4.1
Japan	19.7	15.3	22.7	14.7	9.5

Source: Glyn and Harrison (1980), p. 12

The tendency indicated by Table 2.1 was considerably accelerated by the success of organised labour during this period to achieve some increases in real wages. One result of the coincidence of labour shortages, the rise in real wages, and the attempts by firms to continue to accumulate was rising levels of inflation, as firms marked up prices to maintain profits. Government responses to inflation took two forms – attacks on wages through various forms of wage control, social contract, wage freeze, etc. – and measures of economic policy which attempted to control money supply and reduce demand.

By the 1980s the problem of the UK, and to a lesser but still serious degree, of capitalism as a whole, was clear: stagnation. Profits declined drastically, falling by the mid-seventies in the UK, France and Italy, to less than one third of the level of the early sixties (McCracken, 1977). Production was down – by 1979, down by 18% of the level of 1963–73. Unemployment was up – by 1979, by about 10 million in the capitalist world compared to sixties levels. And investment was down – down to three-quarters of the level which would have been reached if pre-1973 levels had been maintained (Glyn and Harrison, 1980, p. 25). An important factor in this stagnation, particularly as it affected the UK economy, was the relative power of the working class (at least up to 1979) to resist the exacerbation of its exploitation:

> Britain became the only imperialist power which proved unable to increase the rate of exploitation of its working class significantly during or after the Second World War.... From a capitalist point of view the result was evident: an erosion of the

rate of profit, and a much slower rate of economic growth and accumulation than in the other imperialist countries. (Mandel, 1978, p. 179)

Mandel's assessment established that under conditions of deep economic crisis, Marx's analysis of the role of labour/capital conflict in establishing the precise level of profitability explains why a major capitalist and governmental response will be various forms of attack on labour power and attempts to cheapen labour. We shall be able to assess the applicability of these likely outcomes as we proceed with our analysis of the nature and extent of work inequalities, for throughout this analysis two major questions should be borne in mind: what are the origins of these variations, these inequalities (or, how do these relate to the basic dynamics of the society and the economy?), and what impact do these highly differential experiences have on the formation and consciousness of group resistance and organisation? We shall return to these questions frequently.

At this stage, the major determining factor should be clear: capitalism depends upon constant pressure on firms to compete, to accumulate, to reinvest. Firms must compete to survive, but competition is, at least in some areas, increasingly fierce; firms must be profitable to compete, but profits are falling. What effects will these basic difficulties have on the development of the characteristic employing organisation in this phase of capitalist development? And what strategies and options are open to, and preferred by, the owners and controllers of such organisations under these difficult conditions? The remainder of this chapter is devoted to a consideration of these questions.

The first point to make concerns the organisation of capitalism in its 'late' or 'monopoly' phase. Capitalism at this stage demonstrates two key inter-related features: firstly, the institutionalisation of processes of capitalist control, ownership and decision-making, such that these processes, once the preserve of individual owners or senior managers, are now specialised and handled by expert departments or agencies according to elaborate, rational criteria. The functions of capital have thus become differentiated (ownership from control; aspects of control from each other, etc.) and removed from the personal competence of individuals. Internally, within the enterprise, functions have been separated and bureaucratised. Externally, the enterprise, now publicly-owned (ownership itself is now differentiated), is locked into an elaborate and constraining series of relationships with financial institutions, expert agencies and government bodies. These large firms are usually highly diversified, with a large range of products, and a multi-divisional structure which has often grown through takeovers. A major trend in advanced industrial capitalism has been towards the concentration of more and more areas of economic activity in the hands of the large multi-divisional corporations (Chandler, 1977; Scott, 1979).

Secondly, the nature of the average enterprise has changed: a process of monopolisation has occurred. Through competition, many firms have found it harder and harder to survive, while even larger firms have managed to gain large shares of the market, and thus monopolistic profits. Helibroner reports that in the USA in 1968, the largest 100 firms controlled as great a proportion of corporate assets as did the top 200 in 1941 (Heilbroner, quoted in Nichols, 1980, p. 29). In Britain the 100 largest firms in 1970 produced about 40% of manufacturing net output, against 16% of output in 1909. Prais makes the further point that the growth of large firms is directly related to the role of financial institutions: 'The vast funds placed at the disposal of…institutional intermediaries, by being invested preferentially in large quoted companies, have contributed to financial pressures which have encouraged the formation of large industrial groups.' (Prais, 1976, p. 135.)

Table 2.2 Enterprise size in manufacturing 1958–78

Enterprise size (number of employees)		2,000 and over	5,000 and over	10,000 and over	20,000 and over	50,000 and over
Number of	1958	469	180	74	32	8
enterprises	1978	428	179	83	37	10
Percentage of employees working for	1958	45.8	34.3	25.0	17.3	7.3
these enterprises	1978	56.2	44.6	34.6	25.0	12.5

Sources: (1958) *Historical Record of the Census of Production 1907–1970*, HMSO, 1978, Table 10. (1978) *Report of the 1978 Census of Production*, PA 1002, HMSO, 1981, Table 12.

With reference to the scale of employment of these large firms, it has been calculated that in both the USA and UK, about 25% to 27% of employees are engaged in manufacturing enterprises with over 20,000 employees. Furthermore, in 1978 half the manufacturing labour force in the UK was employed in enterprises with over 3,000 employees. As Prais concludes, it appears that there is '...an important long-term tendency towards increasing concentration...inherent in our economic system' (Prais, 1976, p. 167) (see Table 2.2).

There is a close relationship between the evolution of large firms, the institutionalisation and differentiation of internal control processes, and the development and role of external financial agencies. As Scott remarks:

> The massive growth of 'institutional' shareholdings is thrusting the insurance companies, pension funds, banks etc. into positions of effective possession of industrial companies. These financial companies are themselves...increasingly subject to impersonal possession. A complex system of intercorporate shareholdings and credit relations is emerging, within which particular corporations are controlled by the specific constellations of interest which have effective possession. (Scott, 1979, p. 174)

The characteristic enterprise within monopoly capitalism is highly differentiated functionally, is located within a complex and indispensable series of external financial arrangements and ties, and is increasingly large, in terms of numbers of employees, output and market share.

But what strategies and options are open to the owners/controllers of these large firms? And what impact may these strategies have on the inequalities of working life?

First, we must dispel any suggestion that the institutionalisation of capitalism, the depersonalisation and differentiation of capitalist functions, and the differentiation and dispersal of the ownership of the corporation, through public, joint-stock ownership, implies any radical alteration in the priority of profit and accumulation. The logic of the market for the modern, large-scale, monopolistic, financial-capital funded corporation is to cut costs in order to increase its share of the market. While the prevalence of monopolistic firms involves a reduction in the extent of competition (for there are now fewer competitors) it also involves an increase in the intensity of competition between the surviving enterprises. Moreover competition becomes increasingly international in form.

It has been suggested, in opposition to this view of the survival, indeed amplification, of the significance and urgency of profitability, that the emergence of the manager-controlled, publicly-owned enterprise signals the transition from the priority of profit, to the priority of more socially conscious objectives. In fact the emergence of institutional ownership and dominance of financial organisations, if it signals any change in this respect, probably marks a move towards a more rational purposive and efficient pursuit of the necessary objective of the capitalist enterprise: profit. All that has changed is the move towards long-term profit maximisation. As Mandel notes, in monopolistic competition,

> Company strategy aims at long-term profit maximisation, in which factors such as domination of the market, share of the market, brand familiarity, future ability to meet demand, safeguarding of opportunities for innovation, i.e. for growth, become more important than the selling price which can be obtained immediately or the profit margin which this represents. (Mandel, 1972, p. 232)

In other words, the time-horizons of companies may change, but even large multinationals cannot bear substantial losses for more than three years running.

What then of the strategies and objectives of these firms under such conditions of declining profitability? As has been stressed, the corporation is still required to pursue long-term profit maximisation. This has direct implications for management/worker relations and for work organisation. The corporation's efforts to increase profitability – some of which are described below – may directly involve interventions in the class relations which exist between employers and employees. The search for profit inevitably occasions attempted alterations in the relative shares of profit and wages, and the wage/effort bargain. The organisation of the firm, and the strategies and objectives of the firm, must pertain to the balance of strength between capital and labour. This is the first, crucial point about corporate strategies: that despite rhetoric about efficiency and productivity and use of such neutral terms such as modernisation and rationalisation, they inevitably and centrally involve attempts to re-order class relations in terms which increase the relative advantage to capital, through manipulating the cost of a unit of labour, the relative size of profit.

Secondly these corporate strategies not only reflect class relations between labour (wages) and capital (profit), they have a direct impact on levels of class consciousness, and thus on concrete class relationships. As Gintis has remarked

> the profitability of production will depend intimately on the consciousness of workers...capital production will be organised not only to produce a marketable commodity but also to reproduce, from period to period, forms of worker consciousness compatible with future profits. (Gintis, 1976, p. 42)

In other words the capitalist, in seeking to achieve profits, must also consider the forms and levels of consciousness of the employees (Littler and Salaman, 1982). To seek profits from alienated labour inevitably raises acute problems of control. The forms of corporate and state strategy described below all reflect the major priority of capital profit and the continued generation of profits. In so doing, however, they also raise a series of major contradictions between mutually opposed tendencies – the need to specify and exploit versus the need to reproduce the conditions for this and further exploitation.

Those 'managerialist' writers who have used the dispersal of ownership as evidence of qualitative changes within the capitalist system ignore the fact that this, in as much as it has occurred, actually makes it easier for big stockholders, and institutions, to exercise a dominant influence on the corporation. The argument also overestimates the significance of individual motives in capitalist life. Capitalism does not depend on individual motivation – on the regular emergence, each generation, of a cohort of rapacious Gradgrinds. Capitalism creates its own systemic imperatives: be profitable, or go under. The emergence of new forms of financial organisation and control, the increasing concentration of production in ever larger units, the centralisation of money capital in ever larger financial units and the increasing depersonalisation and institutionalisation of capitalism itself represent not the transformation of capitalism but a key stage in its development (Scott, 1979).

We shall see that the organised, rationalised, specialised attempts by senior managers of large-scale corporations to ensure the profitability and efficiency of their corporations during a time of increasing competition and declining profitability have serious implications for the design of work and the nature and distribution of work inequalities. We shall consider these various strategies and implications under a number of discrete headings: work design and control within the corporation; the international movement of capital; and the role of the state.

Work Design and Control within the Corporation

Numerous writers have noted that a major characteristic of the modern, large-scale, institutionalised corporation is the professionalisation and rational-isation of planning. Within the large corporation, decisions on products, markets, technologies, etc. have enormous financial implications, and once the early returns from technological innovations have declined drastically, profits are dependent on the ever more detailed and scrupulous planning of corporate decisions, and the elimination of waste and inefficiency. With profits declining, and competition mounting, every aspect of corporate functioning must be rigorously considered and evaluated. The function of such planning, as Galbraith and many others have noted, is to attempt to reduce or at least to foresee, the inherent uncertainty of the market. Mandel sees this as an 'inherent constraint' within late capitalism: '. . . to increase systematic control over all elements of the process of production, circulation and reproduction. . .' (Mandel, 1978, p. 240). As we shall see, this constraint has numerous implications for corporate control over many aspects of corporate life and over the corporation's employees, and indeed for the concentration of state power over social and economic life. But the most significant aspect of the inherent constraint is that it requires tight control over wages and other costs, and also over all aspects of the development of the corporation's products and methods: research and innovation, materials, markets, technologies, investment decisions, forward planning and the basic decisions as to what, where, and how production will take place. Most of all, the 'inherent constraint' requires ever more and more corporate influence over the direction, quantity, quality, and intensity of workers' effort. Declining profitability, increasing competition and the overall requirement of general corporate planning and rationalisation requires greater control over work, not simply in order to increase levels of production, but to maximise the flexibility and efficiency of labour.

Each long wave of economic activity involves an expansion based on technological innovation and product improvement. Often indeed each wave is associated with a distinctive technological/product phase – nineteenth century engineering, early mid-twentieth century motor cars and aeroplanes, late twentieth century electronics – which is associated with a particular geographical location (UK, USA, Japan) and which, initially, gives its host economy an enormous lead. However, as innovations are disseminated, and as technological leads are reduced, profitability comes to depend on detailed improvements in techniques of production, on the smoothing out of the basic unchanged product design. Of particular significance during this phase, of embellishment rather than radical technical/product innovation, is the control and manipulation of labour.

But if the detailed and tightly specified control of labour becomes even more salient during periods of declining profitability (particularly in those economies which are still largely dependent on a now out-moded stage of technological development, with its associated products), it is not unequivocally clear just how the imperative to accumulate under these circumstances is translated into particular forms of labour/capital relations. A major contribution to this debate is that of Harry Braverman (1974), who argues that this imperative results in the increasing predominance of a particular form of work design – one which maximises the control of labour, while cheapening it and making it more transferable: the deskilling of manual and office work, in accordance with the precepts of Taylorism or 'scientific management' – fragmentation of work, the reduction of jobs to minimal elements, the removal of all elements of discretion, etc.

Capitalism under crisis then faces a major dilemma, since it represents a major thrust and a major contradiction within current developments in work design and work organisation. The dilemma is an old one, recognised frequently by commentators and by managers themselves. Basically, it is this: the essential relations between capital and labour, occurring within the context of institutionalised competition, force the employer to seek increased control over the quantity and quality of workers' work efforts. Yet in so doing, relationships between employer and employees can so deteriorate as to lead to a further increase in control, surveillance, and specification, and a further withdrawal of commitment on the part of the work force. This deteriorating spiral of management/worker relations has been described by Fox (1974) and Gouldner (1954). One way of viewing this dilemma is in terms of capital's simultaneous need for two distinct and occasionally opposed forms of control.

However, if a common response to the problems of profitability is to seek even tighter control over labour – increasing the specification of effort, and the quality of effort – such actions soon reveal a basic paradox: that the tighter the control of labour power, the more control is required. No degree of specification can ever remove the essential element of labour power: that it relies ultimately on the worker's willingness to co-operate. Short of removing the worker from the production process completely through automation and the use of robots – both increasingly popular options – the employer sooner or later is forced to seek to recover workers' willingness by harnessing their participation. Numerous management writers have described and extolled the Japanese system of management whereby workers' commitment is apparently achieved (with enviable consequences for productivity and quality) by delegating a degree of responsibility and quality control to the workers themselves (Cole, 1979; White and Trevor, 1983).

Productivity, writes Lester Thurow, can be made to 'bubble up' from the shop floor through changing organisational structure so that worker commitment is re-engaged. Taylorism is reaching a stage where its inherent logic is so plain, and so alienating, that it is becoming counter-productive:

> American firms are being run out of business not slowly, but quickly. General Motors is experimenting with small groups of workers – 'quality control circles' – to control productivity, not because they like them but because they feel they must. If they don't do something new, they will be driven out of business. (Thurow, 1981, p. 4)

Ford of Europe has recently been involved in similar experiments. As we shall see, the imperatives of accumulation, and the pressures of declining profitability, cause employers to place increased emphasis on the control and motivation of workers.

The International Movement of Capital

Increasing interest in the control of labour and its productivity is but one of a number of basic options open to the employer. As Mandel notes:

> Capital today has two ways available to it of reconstructing the industrial army: on the one hand, the intensification of capital exports and the systematic suffocation of investments at home, i.e. sending capital where there is still excess labour-power, instead of bringing labour-power to excess capital; on the other, the intensification of automation, or, in other words the concentration of investment to set free as much living labour as possible... (Mandel, 1978, p. 182).

Our first requirement is to plot the extent of this international movement of investment, then to see its implications for employment practices both in the base economies and those where the investment is placed. It is crucial to appreciate that in the last twenty years of the twentieth century we are dealing not simply with a world-wide structure of national economies, but with a world international economic system. We do not mean to imply by this that the world capitalist economy will be uniform, stable and even in its organisation. On the contrary, a major feature of this system is precisely that it is differentiated into areas of unequal development with central and peripheral areas and economies. Indeed one of the most significant features of the world capitalist economy is the nature of the relationship between centre and periphery, the industrialised West and many undeveloped, dependent economies. The international division of labour requires many societies to participate in the world order in ways which exclude many economies from the benefits enjoyed by the central, metropolitan economies. We follow Wallerstein in stressing the unity of the world economy, its lack of overarching political structure and its dependence on the 'market' as a basis for redistribution of surplus (Wallerstein, 1974, p. 348).

One of the major institutions of the world economy is the multinational company. If we define multinationals as companies with at least 25% of their turnover, investment, production or employment being generated outside their country of origin, then 75 to 85 of the 200 largest American and European companies fall into this category (Mandel, 1978, p. 321). In early 1972 '...the total turnover of all companies which have been described as multinational was estimated to be between 300 and 450 billion dollars...in other words, approximately 15%–20% of the gross social product of the whole capitalist world.' (Mandel, 1978, p. 322.) The development of multinational corporations, and the increasing tendency for these corporations to extend their operations overseas, reflects the fact that the internationalisation of production encourages the internationalisation of capital. An increasing proportion of international trade takes place within the same multinational company, as internal transfers. For example, many of the cars 'imported' into Britain represent the internal transactions of General Motors or Ford.

The multinational corporation becomes the typical characteristic form of economic organisation within late capitalism. Several pressures drive it to international investment; in a number of spheres merely local production is no longer sufficient in quantity to achieve acceptable levels of return on the amount of capital investment necessary; the limitation of sales in home markets drives companies to find markets outside the national boundaries; the increasing search for new products and high profits forces companies to establish international production for international markets; the existence of different tax laws, of different state policies for encouraging investment, of various forms of tariff restrictions and protectionist arrangements, encourages multinationals to locate production within potential market areas in order to avoid tariffs, or to take advantage of concessionary tax arrangements. As Frobel *et al.* demonstrate in their exhaustive survey of investment abroad by West German corporations, between 1961 and 1976 '...the number of foreign subsidiaries belonging . to the companies surveyed...increased fourfold...the number of employees abroad by these companies increased fivefold between 1961 and 1974.' (Frobel *et al.*, 1980, p. 21). In some industries the proportion of investments going abroad is extraordinarily high. The authors calculate that in the first six months of 1976, as much as 70% of investment from the German electrical engineering industry went abroad.

If, as many authors now argue, the changing circumstances of world capitalism, and the search for profits, forces the characteristic modern capitalist enterprise to reorganise production internationally, what are the preconditions, and more importantly, the implications for work organisation and employment practices, of these developments? Can we find any connections between them and the constant struggle between capital and labour, with capital attempting to increase its control over the specification and quantity of worker effort, and over worker willingness, or acquiescence?

The major preconditions for the development of the international division of labour are straightforward: the development, or existence, of a world-wide reservoir of labour (which, as we shall see, represents a major attraction for foreign investment and production), the development of technology and work organisation such that the international fragmentation of production processes is possible, with the consequence that relatively untrained labour can be employed; and the development of technologies which make the actual location of production largely irrelevant to geographical distance – that is, communications and transport technologies.

The major advantages of locating production internationally are equally obvious. The increasing concentration by large-scale corporations within the home economies, on work rationalisation, seeking more productive machinery, and reducing the size and skills of the work force, is less and less adequate; corporate survival is now dependent on the location of production at sites where labour power is cheap, plentiful, well-disciplined and acquiescent. Rationalisation at home and productive relocation abroad are twin strategies with the same objective, and each strategy can support the other, in that location abroad, or the threat of it, can have consequences for the attitudes and commitment of the original work force.

Numerous writers (most notably Braverman) have noted how the principles of Taylorism – deskilling, fragmentation, task specification, etc. – reflect and help to achieve the objectives of capitalism through cheapening labour, making it more productive, more transferable and less central to the decision-making side of the production process. But Frobel *et al.* make a further point: these principles are now increasingly applied by corporate management on an international, no longer a merely national, basis. Calculation about investment, work design, technologies, are now made on a global basis:

> ...the present-day conditions for the world-wide valorisation of capital mean that capital must completely recalculate the allocation of the elements of the manufacturing process to the most advantageous combination of 'factors of

production' as regards the cost of the final product, *on a global basis* – taking into account the enormous reserve army of less skilled workers which has recently come into existence. In many instances, the end result of this calculation...will be the relocation of industrial production (and subassembly) to new sites, chiefly in the developing countries with their practically inexhaustible reservoir of unskilled and extremely cheap labour-power. (Frobel *et al*. 1980, p. 133)

There can be no doubt that in the developing countries, labour is cheap, hardworking and congenial. Listen to an investment brochure from Malaysia:

> Oriental women are famous throughout the world for their dexterity. With their small hands, they work fast and pay great attention to detail. Who could be better qualified by nature and tradition to raise the efficiency of an assembly line?... Wage rates in Malaysia are among the lowest in the region, and women-workers can be employed for about US $1.50 a day.(Quoted by Lipietz, 1982, p. 42).

Workers in many third world societies are 'super-exploited' – that is, they are not even paid enough to sustain them and their families, but are subsidised by the labour of other members of their families (Frank, 1980, pp. 157–87). Super-exploitation of third world workers has a number of implications. They work more hours than their counterparts in the West; Frobel *et al*. calculate that they receive between 10% and 20% of wages in the traditional industrial societies; usually they can be hired and fired at will (Frobel *et al*., 1980, pp. 34–5). Often, the host society can offer 'attractive' anti-union legislation; internal work control can be supported by external policing, unionists can be harassed; 'trouble-makers' persecuted; space and safety provisions are frequently much less than can be expected in the West. A comparison of wage levels, hours of work, safety provisions, fringe benefits, etc. – between work and working conditions in the underdeveloped countries and in the traditional industrial societies – shows that

> Working conditions...compel the labour-force in free production zones and world market factories in the underdeveloped countries...to achieve levels of productivity and intensity of labour which correspond to the most advanced current levels in the world, and to...tolerate wage levels which are not much higher than those which prevailed in Manchester capitalism's heyday. (Frobel *et al*., 1980, p. 36)

Thus a characteristic feature of corporate decision-making and corporate strategy in late capitalism is the 'rationalisation' of labour and work at home and the transfer of industry to areas abroad where labour is cheaper and can be 'super-exploited', with consequences for wage rates, accidents, working conditions, and most significantly, profits. What implications does this transfer of investments have for the quality of work? Are there any relations between capital's efforts to increase control over labour at home, and the transfer of investments overseas? We shall now turn to a consideration of these questions. Three points must be made.

First, the preceding section makes it clear that the modern firm is now international in its organisation, and that corporate decisions about what, how and where to produce and to market, take place on the basis of global calculations of costs, benefits and profits. This development means that it is no longer feasible to conduct a complete analysis, or explanation of a particular organisation, or indeed of employing organisations within any particular economy, without consideration of the location of that corporation and that economy, within a global division of labour. As we shall see, and as Frobel *et. al*., Frank, and Mandel describe, it is not possible to restrict an analysis of a Texas Instruments factory in Taiwan, or a National factory in Malaysia, a textile mill in any free production zone anywhere in Asia, Africa or Latin America, simply to local conditions, markets, and economies. Increasingly it is true that what occurs within and to a particular enterprise, or indeed to a particular economy or industry, can only be understood in terms of the global division of labour within which it is situated.

Secondly, and more specifically, any analysis of working conditions within factories in third world countries must recognise that these conditions – this level of 'super-exploitation' – is not merely an accident of geography, an unfortunate and passing 'stage' in development, or an outcome of some purely local combination of culture, history and national character, nor an outcome of some national moral deficiency – the lack of 'drive' so over-developed elsewhere. The working conditions under which so many third world workers suffer are a systematic outcome of a global division of labour whereby the continuing impoverishment of the third world – or at least of most societies within this category – is often encouraged and reproduced by the investment and production policies of multinational corporations. Frobel *et al*. report, for example, that on the basis of their investigation of the local benefits of world industrialisation and the emergence of numerous free production zones,

> Whereas. . .the economic yields for the countries concerned are in most cases slight and in some cases even negative, corporate profits are massive. As a result of the industrial enclave character of world market orientated industry, corporate profits do not even indirectly increase the local national income, for example through reinvestment, and conversely negative develoments in the local domestic economies have hardly any impact on the rate of corporate profitability. (Frobel *et al*. 1980, p. 378)

For any consideration of the inequalities of working life, this conclusion is very serious indeed. It means that we cannot, under the auspices of such an enquiry, restrict our attention to the (relatively) privileged West.

Furthermore, as numerous writers have recently noted, the 'survival' in various guises, of forms of labour and of labour/capitalist relationships which ostensibly seem characteristic of pre-capitalist economic forms, is a direct and systematic outcome of the global division of labour. The 'super-exploitation' described by Frank, Frobel *et al*., and Mandel involves three key elements: increase in the intensity of work; extension of the working day, and payment of labour below its value (Osorio, quoted in Frank, 1981, p. 161). Frequently super-exploitation is accompanied by oppressive, coercive control of labour itself. As Corrigan has argued, the expansion of capitalism means the expansion of unfree labour: 'Unfree labour is not a feudal relic, but part of the essential relations of capitalism (Corrigan, 1977, p. 438). Such unfree labour takes a variety of shapes: historically, workers having the status of indentured servants; forms of slavery or forced migration; migration as coercive circulation; or the employment of migrant workers or guestworkers. The point about such workers is their exposure and vulnerability to some degree of legalised coercion in their work relationships. Unlike the classic labourer who is 'free' (legally) to terminate his or her employment, the unfree labourer finds such freedom circumscribed by law, indenture, immigration policy, and similar restrictions.

The expansion of capitalism into new areas does not necessarily involve traditional forms of coercive control. For example, the willingness of some companies to finance the setting up of factories in mainland China indicates a corresponding willingness to trade ownership and direct control for other benefits. Processing contracts, whereby the Chinese agree to supply a certain quantity of product for, say, five years in return for capital equipment and working capital, provides a guaranteed source of supply to the foreign firm and offloads all problems of labour control and labour effort onto a socialist state (Lockett and Littler, 1984).

Thirdly, if working conditions in third world countries are seen as part of a global division of labour, then, by the same token, working conditions in the West are related directly to conditions prevailing elsewhere. This relationship has a number of aspects. We have remarked that rationalisation at home and investment abroad are part of the same process: the search for profits under competition. Also, investment abroad affects workers and working conditions at home both directly, in that it may mean the export of jobs, and more indirectly in that the threat to invest overseas can and frequently has been used – for example by Fords – to discipline workers, win concessions and strengthen management's hand during negotiations. Workers in the traditional industrial countries will thus be exposed to labour intensification and to unemployment, and their resistance undermined by the threat of further foreign investment. Frobel *et al*. calculate, for example, that a conservative estimate of foreign employment by German productive industry is 1.5–1.6 million workers in 1975, and report that 'Falling or stagnating employment in Federal Germany, and rising employment abroad have characterised developments in many companies for a number of years, especially the large combines' (Frobel *et al*., 1980, pp 285–6). Unemployment, redundancies, short-time working, declining real incomes at home; abroad, unemployment, underemployment, 'super-exploitation', and deskilled, simplified tasks – the multinational corporation with its international profit calculations can be responsible for all these effects.

Multinationals provide a framework and a calculus for determining comparative labour productivities. For example, the British Chloride company, which started the 1970s with a predominantly home-based organisation, embarked on a major programme of acquisitions abroad between 1972 and 1975. This involved the takeover of about ten companies in Europe, five in North America and others in Australia and South Africa. Within the space of a few years the Chloride group was a multinational with a reorganised management structure. One of the most obvious results of this multinational development was the management's ability to measure the performance of British workers against those in its overseas subsidiaries. In 1977 this led to the introduction of new intensified work practices and effort norms, which in turn drove the normally peaceable workforce into a two-month strike and occupation of the factories (*Financial Times*, 22 July 1977). This availability of international comparisons leads to a world-wide commodification of labour.

The Role of the State

The third major feature of capital's response to increasing competitive pressure, during late capitalism, is an attack on organised labour. We have noted that in a sense the first two strategies, rationalisation and foreign invesment, also carry implications for the control of labour both directly through increased rationalisation and surveillance, and indirectly through the capacity to locate production in areas with 'good' industrial relations records. However, alongside these initiatives, the period of late capitalism also demonstrates an increase in state attacks on labour and on labour unions, both direct and indirect. It is to these state initiatives that we now turn.

In general we find that this period is also, and relatedly, one of greatly increased state intervention. Mandel argues that the shortening of the turnover time of fixed capital, the acceleration of technological innovation, and the increase in the cost of major projects, produces '. . . an inherent trend under late capitalism for the state to incorporate an ever greater number of productive and reproductive sectors into the "general conditions of production" which it finances' (Mandel, 1978, p. 484). State economic interventions have taken a number of forms: collective provision (of such things as welfare, housing, health services), demand management to achieve a 'satisfactory' level of unemployment, demand, inflation, etc., and central planning, to achieve co-ordination, develop investment and reduce market anarchy.

However, such increased state intervention is not necessarily the neutral, merely technical operation it is often presented as. As we have noted, a critical feature of modern capitalism and the economic crises it is experiencing is the struggle between labour and capital, and its potential impact on levels of profitability. Under these conditions, capital attempts to tighten control over the production process and over production costs (including, crucially, labour costs).

The state usually plays a major part in relations between capital and labour, by seeking both to limit the power of labour in struggles and negotiations and to influence the outcomes of these. Such interventions, of whatever nature, are all occasioned by the declining rate of profit, and by the fact that this is recognised to be partly due to the increased strength of organised labour. State interventions therefore are aimed directly at reducing this strength, and at persuading workers to accept less money for more work.

These interventions take a number of forms: ideological attacks; attacks on organised, that is unionised, labour, direct efforts to reduce wages, and attacks on welfare provisions. These elements are frequently closely connected, such as to constitute strands of a recognisable political platform, increasingly adopted by conservative and other parties under the slogans of 'less government'. Ironically, many state efforts to reduce the power of organised labour are justified by reference to the advantages of reduced government intervention in economic life.

Ideologically, the new conservatism argues the neutrality of the economy, and the powerlessness of governments in the face of overwhelming economic forces. Clearly, to argue that direct economic Keynesian interventions are impossible would, in the light of post-1930s government economic policies, be ludicrous. What is argued instead is that such Keynesian interventions actually compound the problem – inflation/unemployment – *in the long run*. The economy is defined in moralistic terms. Its pathologies are occasioned by overindulgence, undeserved extravagance on a societal level. The solution is to strip away the paraphernalia of government intervention and support, the 'artificial' creation of demand, for these only increase the tendency to inflation. The causes are defined in terms highly analogous to those applicable to individual immorality – greed, over-indulgence, extravagance. The problem itself is never in doubt: it is inflation, the consequence of licence.

This view has a number of key elements: that the economy is essentially analogous to an individual's earning and consumption patterns, writ large; that individual extravagance is responsible for large-scale economic problems; that the major problem, the number one issue, is inflation; that this can only be conquered by permitting the re-emergence and ascendancy of basic economic forces too long masked by the interventions of governments seeking to buy short-term solutions; that an untrammelled economy, wherein the forces of supply and demand are allowed unrestricted movement, and where individuals' basic entrepreneurial instincts are permitted free rein, is the only means of ensuring ultimate, long-term, economic 'health'.

These ideas have very definite implications. First, they seek to depoliticise the responsibility of government for economic matters. Such matters – levels of unemployment, recession, bankruptcies, inflation, interest rates, etc. – are defined as (a) the consequence of earlier governments' attempts to buy their way out of trouble by stimulating demand artificially; (b) the consequence of individuals' greed, laziness, etc. They are presented then as not being related to current government philosophies, or action. Such action seeks simply to re-establish a state of affairs wherein these problems will ultimately disappear.

Secondly, they present the problems themselves as unfortunate consequences of individuals', and earlier governments', misguided courses of action. The government is not responsible and is unable, even if willing, to intervene productively without actually exacerbating matters. Thirdly, these ideas define the major problems as being inflation – a symptom of our times, a consequence of our unrealistic expectations, our unwillingness to pay our way in the world, our unwillingness to earn the luxuries we aspire to.

These ideological efforts have a second major strand. This concerns the nature and function of unions, and relations between labour and capital. Unions are defined as having exceeded their proper role, as having grown too strong (and thus being largely responsible for inflation by enabling workers to gain benefits greater than those they 'deserve' by their efforts). Unions are seen in the same light as Keynesian economic policies – as interfering with the necessary re-establishment of the basic economic forces – supply and demand – through the imposition of over-manning, the closed shop, etc. Furthermore, on many occasions, relations between labour and capital, when these become explicitly relations of conflict, are not defined in terms of industrial relations, class conflict, negotiations over levels of pay, but are regarded as threats to law and order, or relatedly, as issues of freedom. As such they often become open to the intervention of the police to ensure the maintenance of law and order, and the courts, to protect individuals' (usually employers') 'rights'. These definitions have importance in reducing the strength of labour's capacity to resist and organise successfully, quite apart from their direct impact on each particular struggle. For such ideas serve to weaken support for unions by holding them responsible for large-scale economic ills; and seek to make illegitimate the issues and resources and strategies typically employed in industrial disputes.

The ideological elements described above are accompanied by more concrete developments in law which seek to reduce such hard-won concessions as have been won by unions, and to make unions more vulnerable to employers' tactics in industrial disputes, and to governmental control. Once again the law is used to buttress employers' strength in industrial conflicts and negotiations and to attack directly any union tactic which might have proved to be of particular use, such as secondary picketing.

Attempts to lower the price of labour takes two classic forms, used as functional alternatives: direct intervention by government in levels of wage increases through formal wage control or varieties of 'social contract'; and indirect, through allowing an increase in unemployment to take place.

The point of wage control, whatever form these efforts may take, is quite clear, and has been frequently reiterated by government spokesmen: it is to push down real wages below the levels of inflation – in short, to reduce the price of labour and to lower real incomes. However, the experience of successive governments throughout the seventies demonstrated the two major weaknesses of all forms of wage freeze or wage control, regardless of how they were presented to workers and voters: firstly, wage control does not work over long periods, but merely delays workers' demands; and secondly, it tends to encourage politicised conflict between employees and unions on the one side and the government of the day on the other. The explicit intervention of governments in relations between labour and capital, no matter how this may be defined by government spokesmen as necessary for the 'national' good, and as an attack on 'extremist' unionists, nevertheless inevitably forces direct confrontation with labour, and government itself may be the loser (as in the 1974 general election, called on the platform – 'Who runs the country?'). The record of the seventies also shows, however, that without some form of wage control the relative strength of labour in relation to capital is increased and unionised labour is consequently able to achieve considerable improvements in wages thus, ultimately, occasioning a reduction in capital's profitability. The solution to this dilemma – that wage control is necessary for capital but too dangerous and ineffective to apply – lies in the functional alternative to wage control: unemployment.

In arguing that unemployment represents a strategy, rather than an unfortunate and unavoidable development outside the control of any government, it is necessary to show that unemployment is at least in part attributable to government policies on wages and government spending, and that increasing levels of 'natural' unemployment play a major part in reducing workers' bargaining strength and, hence, their wage claims. Concerning the origins of mass unemployment, it is important to note, as Glyn and Harrison point out, that this increase is not simply the consequence of technological development, with jobs being automated. Automation only means mass unemployment when market stagnation leads to old plant (and workers) being scrapped to make way for new, which would not occur if markets were expanding. As these authors remark:

> The fundamental cause of the massive rise in unemployment under Labour was a major slowdown in the rate at which markets, and hence production, grew. Government spending and workers' consumption stagnated because of conscious government policies. (Glyn and Harrison, 1980, pp. 127–8)

It is, however, with the policies of the Thatcher government that the use of unemployment and other anti-labour policies achieves its fullest expression.

Thatcherism as a political philosophy contains a number of discrete elements, the most important of which are monetarist economic policy, and reduced public spending and state support for nationalised industry. The justification of these policies is that with credit difficult to find, and more expensive, inefficient firms go out of business; production is concentrated in efficient sectors and efficient firms; management is forced to rationalise organisation and production. At the same time, workers' confidence and aspirations are reduced: 'People are understandably reluctant to take a tough stand on job conditions if bankruptcy seems possible and the chances of finding another job are low.' (Glyn and Harrison, 1980, p.139.) At the same time the strength of unions is undermined, in practical terms, by high unemployment among union members, which irrespective of members' willingness, reduces unions' income and their capacity to finance industrial action.

There can be no doubt that government ministers are and were well aware of the role of unemployment in the struggles between labour and capital, and sought deliberately to use this strategy to 'cool off' expectations and to reduce bargaining strength. Gunder Frank points to 'Essentially the same austerity policy of deliberate recession, masquerading behind a fig leaf of "fighting inflation" (Frank, 1980, p. 113). He goes on to make the central point, revealing the ideological and practical aspects of monetarist policy – that it reduces worker strength, while at the same time disguising its origins and implications:

> Capital's real intention is not to combat inflation, which is created by monopoly capital and helps all capital reduce real wages. The real point is to increase profits by reducing real wages through various means, including inflation and unemployment. However, to the extent that it is still impolitic to admit to wanting to increase unemployment, it sounds better to say that inflation is public enemy number one. (Frank , 1980, p. 124)

As he also remarks, a major element in the ideological side of this offensive is to decrease public concern about unemployment: by re-defining 'natural', therefore unavoidable, rates of unemployment, asserting that it was an international problem, not merely a British one; by asserting its links with (neutral and unavoidable) technological developments – the notorious 'chip' in particular; and by linking unemployment with militant industrial action and with 'irresponsible' wage demands. These ideas could be given considerable edge when allied with attacks on 'scroungers'. In this way the general problem of unemployment, and each individual case, could be defined as the consequences of economic forces unleashed through collective and individual greed and immorality.

Conclusions

This chapter has attempted to describe the basic dynamics of contemporary capitalism as these have impact on corporate strategy, and the development of work forms and modes of organisation. The starting point for the analysis was the centrality of profit for the capitalist enterprise, and the inevitable significance this has for relations between labour and capital. The fact of profit as the mainspring of capitalism places capital and labour in definitionally conflictful relations though there may be no actual conflict taking place between employers and workers. The chapter considered recent trends in levels of overall profitability, and assessed the impact of the recent crisis in profitability on corporate strategy. It was stressed that corporate efforts to increase profitability under crisis conditions take at least two major forms: labour intensification, technological innovation and the rationalisation of work design and procedures; and the international movement of capital. Both occur within the context of increased state interventions in management/ worker relations.

Throughout, it has been stressed that efforts to improve profits are at the same time efforts to improve control, either through increased specification of effort (or through re-locating production in areas where such specification can be more easily achieved) or through influencing worker attitudes and commitment. Any attempt by capital to solve its problems of profitability, and particularly the two forms of solution most frequently adopted by the large, multinational corporations which increasingly dominate the economies of the advanced industrial societies, inevitably involves the basic relation between capital and labour, and represents an attempt by capital to re-order the relative strengths and advantages of this relationship in its favour. Such efforts are considerably assisted by the increasing intervention of the state in this relationship. However, as we have suggested, they raise certain recurring contradictions, the main one being the tension between the two essential but to some degree mutually incompatible dimensions of control.

References

Braverman, H. (1974), *Labour and Monopoly Capital*, New York, Monthly Review Press.
Chandler, A.D. (1977), *The Visible Hand: The Managerial Revolution in American Business*, Harvard University Press.

Cole, R.E. (1979), *Work, Mobility and Participation: A Comparative Study of American and Japanese Industry*, University of California Press.

Corrigas, P. (1977), 'Feudal Relics or Capitalist Monuments?', *Sociology*, vol. II, no. 3, pp. 411–480.

Edwards, Richard (1979), *Contested Terrain: The Transformation of the Workplace in the Twentieth Century*, Heinemann.

Fox, Alan (1974), *Beyond Contract: Work, Power and Trust Relations*, Faber and Faber.

Frank, André Gunder (1980), *Crisis: in the World Economy*, Heinemann.

Frobel, Folker, Heinrichs, Jugen, and Kreye, Otto (1980), *The New International Divisions of Labour*, Cambridge University Press.

Littler, C.R. and Salaman, G. (1982), 'Bravermania and Beyard: Recent Theories of the Labour Process', *Sociology*, vol. 16, no. 2, pp. 251–269.

Glyn, Andrew and Harrison, John (1980), *The British Economic Disaster*, Pluto Press.

Glyn, Andrew and Sutcliffe, Bob (1972), *British Capitalism, Workers and the Profit Squeeze*, Penguin.

Gouldner, A.W. (1954), *Patterns of Industrial Bureaucracy*, New York, Free Press.

Lipietz, A. (1982), 'Towards Global Fordism?', *New Left Review*, vol. 132, March/April, pp. 33–47.

Gintis, H. (1976), 'The Nature of Labour Exchange and the Theory of Capitalist Production', *Review of Radical Political Economics*, Summer, vol. 8, no. 2, pp. 36–54.

Lockett, M. and Littler, C.R. (1984), *Management and Industry in China*, Heinemann.

Mandel, Ernest (1978), *Late Capitalism*, New Left Review Editions, Verso Books, London.

McCracken, Paul (1977), *Towards Full Employment and Price Stability*, Paris, OECD.

Nichols, Theo (1980), *Capital and Labour: A Marxist Primer*, Fontana.

Prais, S.J. (1976), *The Evolution of Giant Firms in Britain*, Cambridge University Press.

Scott, John (1979), *Corporation, Classes and Capitalism*, Hutchinson.

Thurow, Lester C. (1981), 'Death by a Thousand Cuts', *New York Review of Books*, vol. XXVIII, no. 20.

Wallerstein, Immanuel (1974), *The Modern World System*, New York, Academic Press.

White, M. and Trevor, M. (1983), *Under Japanese Management*, Heinemann.

SECTION II

Organization and Control of Work

One of the outstanding positive features of developments in the sociology of work during the last ten years has been a broadening of focus to take account of relations between work, economic processes and social divisions (particularly class divisions). This is not so much a new focus as a welcome return to an older perspective – that of the political economists of the eighteenth and nineteenth centuries, whose concern about the social problems brought on by the Industrial Revolution led them to formulate fundamental questions about the forces that determined the distribution and design of work. As Elizabeth Garnsey shows (Chapter 3), these early political economists, even before Marx, used the concept of the division of labour as the means by which they could identify the connections between economic processes and social relationships. It formed the basis of hierarchies of power and advantage in society, and so questions about how work was divided up, controlled and remunerated were regarded as central to the study of society. The specialization of separate disciplines in the social sciences led them to concentrate narrowly on those variables that they considered to be the province of their particular discipline, and the broader issue of the causes and consequences of the division of labour became neglected. It was the reinvigoration of Marxist theory which largely brought about the emergence of a new political economy approach, and this stimulus has reinvigorated the sociology of work.

The subject of labour markets, and the ways in which they are segmented and operate according to different principles, is a good example of a topic that overlaps the fields of economics and sociology, and tends to be neglected because disciplines see it as marginal to their interests. Freedman (Chapter 4) shows its relevance to helping to explain a number of important phenomena: the differential bargaining power of various groups of workers; the fragmentation of working-class consciousness; its political effects, as in the case of the American labour movement, which is divided into interest groups and single-issue causes; the reasons why women and minorities are often confined to insecure and low-paying jobs, and the dual-income character of many families today, which combine female earnings from low-paid, unprotected jobs, with male earnings from relatively better-paid, sheltered jobs, and so allows families to meet socially-defined standards of consumption.

The significance of the labour-theory approach to the sociology of work, as discussed by Thompson (Chapter 5), is that it attempts to locate work activity within the total productive system and thus within the structures and processes of the wider society (and in capitalist society this means, predominantly, class relations between capital and labour). The crucial issues in the debate about the labour process, stimulated by the work of Braverman, concern deskilling and the resultant degradation of labour, posited as a necessary consequence of the continuous pursuit of surplus value by capitalist enterprises. Braverman's thesis was that the knowledge and skills of workers are constantly being incorporated into management functions or into machines, and the result is that workers are employed in jobs below their capacities, which also renders them more easily controlled by management. The two main criticisms discussed are that Braverman's thesis does not take account of alternative management strategies or of workers' resistance.

A frequent criticism of Braverman is that, in explaining management strategies in terms of the tendencies and imperatives of capitalism, he is guilty of political bias, because similar management strategies and work designs are to be found in socialist societies. Littler (Chapter 6) examines this criticism, and the various explanations offered by Braverman and others for the similarities, and also points out some important differences.

The point about alternative management strategies being neglected by Braverman is taken up by Armstrong (Chapter 7), who shows how management strategies reflect the interests and ideologies of different professional groups within management – engineers, accountants, personnel specialists, etc. The most famous case, that of 'scientific management', or 'Taylorism', which treated management people as a human engineering problem, can be seen to have reflected the ideology and professional interests of engineers. Why the engineers were succesful in promoting that management strategy at a particular time is explained in terms of historical factors. Historical and cross-cultural comparisons reveal the links between management strategies and the fortunes of various professional groups.

Whatever might be the rivalries and tensions between professional groups exercising the functions of management, they are slight compared with those between capital and labour. However, despite the publicity that is given to strikes and the supposed 'bloody-mindedness' of shop-floor militants, the marvel is that workers do obey orders, most of the time, and acknowledge the right of management to give them. If, as most of the early political economists were prepared to admit, there are classes with conflicting interests involved in capitalist production, how does it arise that the representatives of one class give the orders and the others obey? Armstrong *et al.* (Chapter 8) examine the contribution that ideology makes to the functioning of shop-floor industrial relations and the settling of disputes.

Ideology is an important component of culture. To some extent there is a dormant ideology in a society's culture, and this is manifested in the terms used in shop-floor disputes, which Armstrong *et al.* show to usually favour the case of management and to leave workers in a disadvantaged position of having to argue their case in terms which have a built-in bias towards the interests of management. However, there are workplace and occupational cultures which are incorporated in work practices and vary over time and from one workplace to another. An awareness of these cultural differences can assist in understanding workers' resistance to new technologies or work designs, and the reasons for so-called 'demarcation disputes', which are often pictured as purely selfish or irrational attachments to outmoded practices. Dunkerly and Casey (Chapter 9) provide a historical case-study of conflict and change in a naval dockyard, which demonstrates the usefulness of this sociological-historical method for the analysis of the relationships between technology, work cultures and the organization of the labour process.

The advantage to the sociology of work of adopting a political-economy approach, linking the division of labour at the micro-social level of the workplace and enterprise to the macro-level of divisions in society, is illustrated by most of the chapters in the first half of this book. However, the discussion of debates and theories about the incorporation of agriculture within capitalism (by Hamilton, in Chapter 10) enables us to see the intermediate-level connections (the level of different sectors of the economy, in this case agriculture), and the global level beyond the single society. It is an essential corrective to an over-parochial perspective in the sociology of work, which can neglect the obvious importance of multinational enterprises and the global division of labour between developed and less-developed economies.

3   The Rediscovery of the Division of Labor

ELIZABETH GARNSEY

Introduction

The division of labor is a central concept in social and economic thought. It provides the means by which the connections between economic processes and social relationships can be identified. It forms a basis of hierarchies of power and advantage. Yet the division of labor has for long been treated as a secondary phenomenon, at one remove from the main focus of analysis in both economics and sociology. Modern macroeconomic studies have been concerned primarily with its bearing on industrial structure or income distribution, while sociologists, even those according it considerable importance, have not subjected it to systematic analysis in its own right. In this paper I argue that the ingredients for an adequate analysis of the division of labor were provided by the classical political economists, and that a shift of interest away from this theme was the consequence of the demise of classical political economy and the emergence of economics and sociology as distinct academic subjects. The recent revival of interest in the subject has coincided with the emergence of a 'new' political economy. This is largely an outcome of the reinvigoration of Marxist theory. Its exponents, however, do not acknowledge their ultimate antecedents; they do not stress the line of continuity with the themes of the early classical political economists which Marx's writings provide. I argue that the fate of the division of labor in recent social and economic writings throws into question the usefulness of prevailing boundaries between the social sciences.

I use division of labor to refer to the differentiation of work tasks, imposed and remunerated in some specific manner and organized in structured patterns of activity. (Though unpaid labor in the household and community are important aspects of the division of labor, for the present, I will be concerned with paid employment.[1]) When contemporary social scientists have investigated the division of labor, their studies have tended to come under one or other of the following headings: (1) sectoral patterns of employment (in agriculture, manufacture, etc.): (2) the occupational or skill structure of the labor force: (3) the organization of tasks in the workplace. Although the threefold distinction is a viable one, the categories overlap to an extent which is not clearly discernible in many studies. For each category of analysis, the concerns of investigators have been disparate and largely unrelated to issues and problems which arise in connection with the other dimensions of the question. Thus economists interested in patterns of economic growth have examined labor shares in various industries and put forward explanations of sectoral trends in employment.[2] These studies provide a simplified theory of the division of labor in one of its manifestations, but

Elizabeth Garnsey, in *Theory and Society*, vol. 10, 1981, pp. 337–58 few branches of economics have received less systematic attention.[3] Again, studies in organizational theory and industrial sociology have been concerned with aspects of the detailed division of labor primarily insofar as they impinge on labor productivity and the social psychology of workplace relationships. Meanwhile, the aspect of the division of labor which actually provides the central framework for the analysis of income distribution and social stratification, the occupational structure, has not in itself been an object of inquiry.[4]

The classical political economists recognized the three dimensions of the concept of division of labor and saw them as closely interrelated. They also recognized the important distinction between the subdivision of work tasks on the one hand and the allocation of workers to sets of work tasks or work roles (occupational specialization) on the other. While the nature of and demand for the final product and current production methods impose constraints on the way in which work tasks can be divided up, technology does not in itself determine the division of labor among the workers carrying out these work tasks. Here other factors such as bargaining strategies and training arrangements come into play. The notion that technology represents an autonomous, self-generating force which imposes its own constraints on the division of labor is not to be found in the classical writers: it was alien to the humanist premises of enlightenment thought from which early political economy evolved. In contrast there is extensive recourse to technological determinism in contemporary writing on the division of labor. In part this has been the deliberate outcome of the delimitation of fields of study. Narrowing the range of inquiry by the adoption of a 'rule of abstention' may be necessary and fruitful. The advantages have been set out by Gluckman, who advocates the adoption of a 'rule of disciplined refusal to trespass on the fields of others', but recognizes that this rule should be applied with circumspection. He points out that it is 'fruitless to demarcate as a relatively autonomous and independent system a set of regularities which depend essentially on events and relations between events outside that system'.[5] In studies taking occupational structure as their starting point and in others considering micro-aspects of the organization of work, the relative autonomy of the variables under consideration has been assumed. The causes of change in the system of relationships examined have been taken as lying outside the scope of analysis: the division of labor has been treated as exogenously determined, by technological exigencies and macroeconomic processes.

Simplifying assumptions of this kind have diverted attention from the factors encouraging or preventing the introduction of new forms of the division of labor. We have to look to the recent revival of political economy for analyses which focus on the interrelationships between economic, technical, and social factors affecting the labor process. Braverman's *Labor and Monopoly Capital* (1974), an investigation of the organization of work and the structure of occupations in the USA in this century, has been the most influential of these studies. Braverman defended Marx against the charge of technological determinism, arguing that the capital intensive, deskilling, and labor displacing features of modern industrial technology are to be accounted for with reference to the structure of constraints and incentives created by the property relations of capitalism. Braverman found in Marx's footnotes to *Capital* reference to the rationale advanced by Charles Babbage in 1832 for subdividing the work process in order to lower skill levels and cut wage costs. In many ways this provided the starting point for his analysis of the 'degradation of work' in the twentieth century. Other writers have taken up other aspects of the issue. Thus Marglin, adopting a historical approach, argued that it was not the need to improve efficiency but the quest for greater control over workers which provided the major incentive for the reorganization of work through the application of new technology and the introduction of the factory system. Stone has attempted to show that a hierarchical division of labor has been introduced by management as a divisive strategy aimed at controlling the labor force independently of considerations of efficiency.[6]

These studies have a number of weaknesses, notably the failure to analyze the response of labor to attempts to alter the organization of work.[7] Workers have not passively accepted changes imposed by management; as Lazonick has observed, there has been a 'continual process of conflict, compromise and even cooperation between capitalists and workers over the form and content of the components of technical change'.[8] In general, a more critical approach in the application of Marxist categories to features of the labor process has been advocated by those who have most recently taken up the new political economy. But the early attempts at a radical political economy were important in reframing issues of inquiry. It is noteworthy that Braverman was writing from outside any academic setting and was not therefore hampered by existing frameworks in sociology and economics, when he posed the question that had not been faced since the time of Marx: How are the prevailing division of labor and the direction in which it is developing to be explained? To sum up: the new political economy returns in a number of respects to a form of analysis that predates the development of the specialist social sciences. These writers can draw on a range of explanatory factors which lie beyond the scope of either economics or sociology. They analyze the division of labor as the outcome of a given distribution of power, they reject the premise that technology is neutral, and inquire into the ways in which the direction of technological development has served specific interests.[9]

The Intellectual Background: From Classical Political Economy to Marx

Classical political economy was primarily concerned with problems of growth, value and distribution. But in each case the division of labor was seen as an integral aspect of the problem at hand. In part this was a logical outcome of the labor theory of value; labor being the ultimate source of value, the judicious organization of the division of labor could lead to the creation of greater output for a given number of workers. In the *Wealth of Nations* Adam Smith maintained that 'The owner of stock which employs a great number of labourers necessarily endeavours, for his own advantage, to make such a proper division and distribution of employment that they may be enabled to produce the greater quantity of work possible.'[10] In an expanding economy this greater output was seen as conducive to the accumulation of stock that made possible still more refined forms of the division of labor.

> It is the stock which is employed for the sake of profit which puts into motion the greater part of the useful labor of every society. The plans and projects of the employers of stock regulate and direct all the most important operations of labour and profit is the end proposed by those plans and projects.[11]

The 'improvement in the circumstances of society' followed directly. Thus the division of labor, while limited by the size of the market and contingent on the prior accumulation of capital, was seen as playing a central part in the process of transition to a state of 'general opulence'. ('As the accumulation of stock must, in the nature of things, be previous to the division of labour, so labour can be more and more subdivided only as stock is more and more accumulated.'[12]) Changes in the division of labor were accorded a role analogous to that attributed to technological advance in modern theories of growth. The division of labor embraced virtually all forms of technical progress, via 'progress in the arts' which was seen to proceed with it and result from it.[13] The importance of machines which 'facilitate and abridge labour' was recognized, but these were not viewed as disembodied engines of growth nor considered apart from the institutional context in which they were created.

Through the process of accumulation and the system of distribution of rent, profits, and wages, the connections between the division of labor and the constitution of the three great classes of society (landowners, capitalists, and laborers) were seen by the classical political economists to be largely self-evident. A systematic analysis of these interrelationships was beyond the brief they set themselves. Their references to the links between division of labor, changes in productivity, the accumulation of capital, and the distribution of wealth are scattered, but the connections are implicit in their writings. Marx acknowledged his debt to British political economy. Subsequently in non-Marxist economics and sociology the links between the analysis of class and the division of labor were broken and have still be be reformulated. Marx represents the major line of continuity with early political economy: the ideas of the classical economists are to be found in the new political economy, transmitted and transmuted by Marx. It is paradoxical that Marx's writings should provide this link, given his wholesale rejection of the liberal individualist premises underlying this body of thought. But Marx was explicit about his debts to earlier thinkers:

> No credit is due to me for discovering the existence of classes in modern society or the struggle between them. Long before me, bourgeois historians had described the historical development of this class struggle and the bourgeois economists the economic anatomy of classes. What I did that was new was to prove (1) that the existence of classes is only bound up with particular phases in the development of production.[14]

As he himself pointed out, Marx's analysis of the division of labor drew heavily on the work of Ferguson, Smith, Lemontey, and Say. He claimed as his own contribution that he had 'shown for the first time that division of labour as practised by manufacturers is a specific form of the capitalist mode of production.'[15] It was not until he had immersed himself in the study of the eighteenth and nineteenth-century political economists that Marx elaborated his theoretical analysis of the development of the capitalist mode of production and the class relations attendant upon it. Marx argued that the classical economists obfuscated the exploitative nature of the wage system which conceals the transfer of surplus value to those in a position to purchase and control the labor power of others. It was not the identity of their sources of revenue that made of wage laborers, capitalists, and landlords three distinct social classes. Rather, it was the extent of control over the means of production, as embodied in property relations, sanctioned by the legal system and backed by the coercive powers of the state, which determined class formation. Yet in spite of his major objections to the classical economists' interpretations, Marx insisted that 'the anatomy of civil society' could only be ascertained by their methods.[16]

A number of themes with which the classical political economists were concerned have recently come to be considered important areas for theoretical enquiry and empirical research. Among them we can identify the following as centering on the division of labor in various ways.

Productive and Non-Productive Labor

It was held that economic growth was both influenced by and had a direct effect on the distribution of employment among different branches of the economy. Adam Smith devoted considerable effort to countering the arguments of the French physiocrats that agriculture was the sole productive sector. His version of the theory was criticized by Marx, who maintained that 'we need a definition of labour which is derived not from its content or its result but from its social form.'[17] In contemporary economics the problem of productive labor is raised in the 'deindustrialization' debate and in sociology in the analysis of the class situation of workers in the service sector.[18]

Technology and the Control of Labor

The question of *choice of technology* was also posed by the classical economists in a way that now appears highly relevant. The introduction of new forms of the division of labor associated with new forms of machinery was seen to be necessary in order to improve a manufacturer's competitive position in the market, but these constraints were related to wage strategies and to the promotion of labor discipline. The reduction of wage costs (through the levelling of the skills required of labor) and the possibility of maintaining maximum control over the labor force were seen as important effects of the new organization of work tasks. Adam Ferguson pointed out as early as 1776: 'Every undertaker in manufacture finds that the more he can subdivide the tasks of his workmen and the more hands he can employ on separate articles, the more are his expenses diminished and his profits increased.'[19] Here Ferguson made the important distinction between the breakdown of work tasks and the allocation of workers to specific tasks or groups of tasks, to which we referred earlier. If in the production of a given article it is possible to employ large numbers of workers (each on subdivided tasks), it will be possible, assuming 'unskilled' labor is available at low wages, to lower total wage costs. This point was passed over by Adam Smith in his discussion of wages. The argument was taken up again, and its implications spelt out in detail, by Charles Babbage, writing in 1832:

> The master manufacturer, by dividing the work to be executed into different processes, each requiring different degrees of skill or of force, can purchase exactly that precise quantity of both which is necessary for each process: whereas, if the whole work was executed by one workman, that person must possess sufficient skill to perform the most difficult, and sufficient strength to execute the most laborious of the operations into which the article is divided.[20]

Babbage describes here a strategy for the allocation of workers to tasks, taking into account the 'skills' required for the performance of the subdivided work tasks. It is worth noting that in the numerical example he provides the skill level of various workers is a simple attribute of the sex and age of the workers: this suggests that the notion of skill itself is, under these conditions, mainly defined in terms of customary pay. By employing women and children in place of 'skilled male workers', labor costs could be reduced by half *with a given breakdown of work tasks*. Had adult male workers been assigned to the same complex of work tasks, wage costs would have doubled in Babbage's example. Moreover, this wage and skill combination strategy was likely to have a favorable effect, from the employer's viewpoint, on labor discipline. Machinery can, as Babbage pointed out, to some extent afford 'checks against the inattention, the idleness or the dishonesty of human agents', and so, as Marglin has recently argued, ensure maximum application of labor in the course of the production process.[21]

The need to control the workforce was implicit in much of what was written about the organization of the division of labor in new manufacturing concerns. The arguments were set out most crudely (and quoted with relish by Marx) in Andrew Ure's *The Philosophy of Manufactures* (1835). Ure pointed out that the main difficulty in the introduction of Arkwright's spinning fingers lay

> in training human beings to renounce their desultory habits of work and to identify themselves with the unvarying regularity of the complex automation. To devise and administer a successful code of factory discipline, suited to the necessities of factory diligence was the...noble achievement of Arkwright.

And, further,

> By the infirmity of nature it happens that the more skilful the workman the more self-willed and intractable he is apt to become, and of course the less fit component of a mechanical system in which by occasional irregularities he may do great damage to the whole. The grand object, therefore, of the modern manufacturer is *through the union of capital and science* to reduce the task of his work people to the exercise of vigilance and dexterity – faculties, when concentrated to one process, speedily brought to perfection in the young...[22]

If Andrew Ure thought this an admirable process, it had been deplored by earlier writers, for example, by W. Thompson in his *Inquiry into the Principles of the Distribution of Wealth*:

> Knowledge, instead of remaining the handmaid of labour in the hands of the labourer to increase his productive power,... has almost everywhere arrayed itself against labour,... systematically deluding and leading (labourers) astray, in order to render their muscular powers entirely mechanical and obedient.[23]

The introduction of new technology was seen by these earlier writers to be connected with wage strategies which together determined the pattern of work tasks to be imposed on various groups of laborers. Partly for this reason, technological advance was treated by the classical economists as a concomitant of the division of labor, not as an autonomous process. The fragmentation of work tasks which resulted from the use of labor under increasing mechanization had been viewed with some alarm by the early classical political economists. Ferguson, for example, reflected that 'thinking itself, in this age of separations, may become a peculiar craft.'[24] But the fragmentation of work was viewed as an inevitable outcome of the growth of manufacture and increases in productivity by Babbage, Ure and others writing in the 1830s and 1840s. As classical political economy went into decline in the 1830s, writers set about providing a rationale for the prevailing division of labor. Their complacency was hardly challenged by economists or sociologists until the recent revival of political economy.

Wage Strategies

The classical political economists saw that the wage contract reflected the nature of power relations in wage bargaining and made for open or suppressed antagonism between classes in society. In the *Wealth of Nations*, Adam Smith analyzed the basic asymmetry of the bargaining position of laborer and master. It stemmed essentially from property relations: 'this original state of things in which the labourer enjoyed the whole produce of his own labour could not last beyond the first introduction of the appropriation of land and the accumulation of stock.'[25] The concentration of stock, or capital, made for an unequal bargaining position between wage laborers and employers: 'common wages of labour depend upon contract (between the labourer and the owner of stock), two parties whose interests are by no means the same. The workmen desire to get as much, the masters to give as little, as possible. The former are disposed to combine in order to raise, the latter in order to lower, the wages of labour.'[26] Moreover, 'the masters being fewer in number can combine more easily and the law authorizes, or at least does not prohibit, their combinations.' 'Masters are always and everywhere in a sort of tacit but constant and uniform combination not to raise wages of labour above their actual rate.'[27] Smith also discusses the strategies available to laborers to maintain or raise their wages; he recognize that collective action was essential, but difficult to organize, and argued that the best interests of the laborers could be met by the growth of the economy, under which conditions the rising demand for labor would bid up wages.

Smith went so far as to say that 'the labour time of the poor in the civilized countries is sacrificed to maintaining the rich in ease and luxury'.[28] But he was also convinced that the poor in a civilized state were still better off than they would be in a Savage State. The laboring classes benefited directly from the 'growth of opulence, which extends itself to the lowest ranks of the people', and such growth could, Smith maintained, only be ensured by the prevailing system of distribution: 'Something must be given for the profits of the undertaker of the work who hazards his stock' (in enterprises which eventually benefit the community as a whole and which would not be undertaken without the inducement of profit). Class antagonism, as reflected in the wage contract, could, in Smith's view, be transcended for this reason. 'The interest of the second order, that is, those who live by wages, is as strictly connected with the interest of society as is that of the first (the proprietors).[29]

Ricardo's line was more radical. He argued that 'the interest of the landowner is always opposed to that of all other classes of the community'.[30] But Ricardo was unaware of the ideological implications of his own work, and was surprised when he was attacked as the enemy of the landowning classes. His theory of value, in setting profits against wages, also indicated the basis for inevitable conflict between capitalists and workers. But as far as Ricardo was concerned, he was simply drawing up an abstract analytic model from which certain deductions could be made.[31] The kind of society presented as an alternative affected interpretations of the interests of the various classes in the prevailing social order. Claims could be made for common class interest in the existing order when the alternative was presented (as by Smith) as the Savage State, but when the alternative society was conceived as Guild Socialism or, eventually, Communism, the radical implications of Ricardo's statement, 'the cause of profit is that labour produces more than is required for its support', became manifest.

Shifts in the Focus of Economic Analysis

The preface to Ricardo's *Principles of Political Economy* begins as follows:

> The produce of the earth – all that is derived from its surface by the united application of labour, machinery and capital – is divided among three classes of the community, namely the proprietor of the land, the owner of the stock or capital necessary for its cultivation and the labourers by whose industry it is cultivated.

We have seen that, via the division of labor, the question of the relations between these classes forms a central part of the subject matter of classical political economy.[32] But in the late nineteenth century, simultaneously in a number of European countries, the marginalist revolution shifted the focus of economic thought. Jevons, Menger, and Walrus emphasized the methodological advantages of abstracting from historical and institutional considerations in the interest of providing economic models capable of generating predictions from the minimum of assumptions. There is debate over the nature of this shift in interest during the late nineteenth century. The environmentalist explanation (as put forward by Bukharin, for example), was that the economics of marginal utility reflected the individualist outlook of the bourgeoisie, and its emphasis on the psychology of the consumer was characteristic of the newly dominant rentier class. Schumpeter, in contrast, accounts for the advent of marginalism as a purely technical innovation. He argues that 'in analysing economic phenomena, categories other than those suggested by the class structure of society have proved more useful, as well as more satisfying logically'.[33] Whatever the reasons for the shift of emphasis, its effects were to focus attention on the laws of choice in economic situations and on scarcity as the basis of value in exchange. With this shift in emphasis came the notion that wages and profits could be analyzed without reference to the social and political relations between employers, risk takers, and wage earners. The rewards which the market process afforded were held to reflect the aggregate effects of transactions determined by considerations of scarcity and consumer preference. The relations between the classes which supplied land, labor, and capital did not fall within the scope of a strictly economic analysis, as this was now defined.[34]

The marginal revolution, which converted political economy into modern economics, left untended and unreclaimed many of the areas of inquiry partly cleared by the classical economists. It is generally recognized that the study of welfare, income distribution, and economic growth were left aside in the new economic theorizing, but the division of labor was also a victim of the intellectual putsch. With the advent of marginalism the division of labor could be taken as given, as the outcome of 'the prevailing state of technology'. With the demise of political economy there was no further attempt to analyze the division of labor in its relation to technological innovation, except as the residual category.[35] The counter-revolution in economic thought occurred in part for ideological reasons, because the ideas of the early classical economists carried disturbing implications which became increasingly unacceptable in the political climate of the mid-nineteenth century. Marx developed the radical potential of political economy to the full, but so little direct impact did his theories have on British and American academic thought that the reaction against the themes of the early political economists cannot be interpreted simply as a reaction against Marx, but as a genuinely internal development. It occurred despite J. S. Mill's attempts to defuse and make acceptable the arguments and conclusions of the classical political economists. Indeed Mill's attempts were probably doomed by his acceptance of Ricardo's theory of value, in which wages and profits are set in inverse relation to each other, suggesting the basis for endemic class conflict between workers and capitalists.[36]

Weber and Marx

The marginalist revolution took some time to reach Germany, where the historical school resisted the call to abstract from historical and institutional contexts in the analysis of economic life. It was because Weber was writing in this tradition that he provided an analysis of class that was grounded in the study of the economic institutions of different societies. It has been suggested that Weber's conception of capitalism contained a 'critical marginalist element' because he emphasized rational calculation as a fundamental characteristic of the capitalist enterprise. Weber wrote: 'The doctrine of marginal utility treats human behaviour as if it proceeded...under the control of commercial calculation...The mode of treatment of commercial bookkeeping is thus if anything the starting point of its construction.'[37] But Weber's interests diverged markedly from those of the economists propounding marginalism: his emphasis on rational commercial bookkeeping as the characteristic feature of the capitalist enterprise was symptomatic of his search for the institutional forms which promote and maintain certain types of outlook and behavior. In the development of stratification theory Weber's discussion of social honor or prestige has been of special importance. However, his analysis of class phenomena was designed to show how these are rooted in economic relationships, until recently this aspect of Weber's analysis has been underemphasized in stratification theory. Nevertheless, Weber, though he described himself as a political economist, was not predominantly concerned with theories of distribution and productivity. His account of the division of labor is an account of the social relations which it engenders and does not provide the basis for a theory of economic and social development. In this he differs from the classical political economists and Marx.[38]

Marx had been concerned with the complex of processes of production distribution, and exchange. In its fully developed form, his theory of class is at one and the same time a theory of economic development. The interconnections between changes in the economy and developments in the class structure were explored in increasing detail in Marx's work in the years between *The Communist Manifesto* and *Capital*. In *Capital* Marx is concerned with relations between rates of profit and wages, with the ways in which investment funds are obtained, and with processes of concentration and consolidation of productive units; with the effects of economic cycles and with the entire process of capital accumulation and its impact on the working population. *Capital* is a study of 'the capitalist mode of production and the relations of production and exchange appropriate to that method'. He argued that the process of capital accumulation is crucial in distributing the working population among the various sectors of the economy over time and in shaping the occupational or skill structure of the labor force. Thus in Marx's mature analysis the social division of labor follows from the specific forms taken by the process of capital accumulation. But with the increasing specialization of economics and sociology the process of capital formation has come to be regarded as an economic phenomenon, the effects of which on the occupational structure can be taken as given by sociologists. Accordingly, while the influence of Marx on class theory has remained overwhelming in many respects, until very recently sociologists have concentrated on those parts of Marx's analysis which are furthest removed from his analysis of structural economic processes. Interest has centred on the subjective aspects of class, on class images and identification, and the location of class position.[39] Studies of the division of labor have, again until recently, been focused on the effects on the outlook and experience of workers of specific position in the occupational division of labor, and in particular on the psychological dimensions of the concept of alienation.

The occupational structure at the macro-level has been taken as the starting point for the analysis of social stratification, not as a phenomenon requiring explanation in its own right. In many sociological writings the economy is treated as the stage-set within which differentiation and stratification take place. While social and political relations are seen as relations between individuals and groups, economic relationships are reified: changes in the economy are conceived as mechanistic and technologically determined. Thus to some extent the atrophy of the mode of analysis that Marx applied has been the outcome of the transformation of political economy into economics and the relegation by economists of the analysis of the political and social relations between groups engaged in the division of labor to a sociological analysis beyond their brief. But sociologists have not taken on the task of analyzing the causes of change in the occupational division of labor.

Durkheim

It may be easy to accept that Weber had limited interest in the division of labor as such: to make the same assertion about Durkheim is to go against the widely held assumption that he ensured that the division of labor would be enshrined as one of the central concerns of sociology. However, Durkheim did not furnish a viable analysis of the links which the division of labor provides between economic processes and social relationships.[40] His conception was too broad for this purpose, since he was interested in the entire process of structural differentiation; too narrow because his approach led him to view prevailing features of the division of labor as pathological and to focus on their psychological impact. The manifestations of *anomie* were to be found in the attitudes and behavior of individuals lacking social ties and obligations. The weaknesses of Durkheim's approach stem in part from the lack of empirical content to his analysis of the causes of the division of labor. He considered only the relevance of geographic features, population density, growth of towns, etc., in promoting division of labor. His interest in the subject was stimulated by his objections to Spenser's theory that social harmony is ensured through the mutual cooperation which evolves as each individual pursues his own interests in society. Durkheim was convinced that some sort of social regulation was prior to and inherent in the social division of labor. He was also, therefore, opposed to Adam Smith's notion that the division of labor arises through the natural propensity of men to truck and barter. The shortcomings of his explanation are familiar. Because, in his account, the division of labor provides for its own regulation and represents the resolution of the potentially disruptive competition for resources in an expanding society, he had to interpret evidence on irregularities as transitory and abnormal features of society. This is in clear contrast with the type of account Marx was able to put forward to explain alienation, which he could relate to the structural contradictions of the capitalist mode of production. Durkheim's account of the social processes giving rise to the division of labor included the operation of a set of self-correcting mechanisms. These were set into action automatically (*'tout se passe méchaniquement'*) so that manifestations of the failure of these internal mechanisms of society to ensure cohesion and integration through the division of labor must be transitory and abnormal. Thus (as Georges Friedmann pointed out) the normal in the sense of the empirically general forms of the division of labor in industrial society become the abnormal in Durkheim's analysis.[41]

Sociological perspectives have tended to obscure the very different objectives and explanatory schemes pursued by Marx and Durkheim in connection with the division of labor. There is no doubt that Durkheim's preoccupations influenced subsequent social research, but their effect has been to relegate the analysis of the division of labor as such still further to the background. Interest in Durkheim's concept of *anomie* has encouraged emphasis on the 'mental state' implied by Marx's concept of alienation, the opposition between Marx and Durkheim being presented as embodying different conceptions of human nature and human needs.[42] While this is a valid perspective, to concentrate on the contrasting ways of relating certain types of mental condition to certain types of social condition can divert attention from the very different objectives and explanatory schemes pursued by Marx and Durkheim. The sections of *Capital* devoted to the empirical and analytic description of the nature and functions of the division of labor in large-scale manufacture have been largely ignored in the sociological literature.

They had to await analysis by investigators unaffected by sociological approaches to the division of labor.

Recent Sociological Analyses of the Division of Labor

Against my claim that the division of labor has not been a central area of analysis since the decline of classical political economy, it might be said that structural differentiation is an important topic in sociology. Structural differentiation,[43] however, is a much broader notion than division of labor, viewed as simply one of many aspects of the process by which the performance of more specialized functions is carried out by increasingly variegated social units in complex societies. The idea that structural differentiation proceeds spontaneously as a manifestation of the 'logic of industrialism' has diverted sociologists from analyzing in detail the processes of change in the occupational division of labor. The areas in which the detailed division of labor (under other names) has continued to provide a focus of analysis are the sociology of organizations and industrial sociology. There is a mass of case studies on various aspects of work organization, undertaken for the most part in order to ascertain the factors which inhibit or promote increases in productivity. In the bulk of these studies, technological constraints are assumed to be the primary factors determining work organization; the evidence on the extent of management discretion in the establishment of work roles and of the importance of custom and practice is not followed up. Some writers, notably Trist and Bamforth, have developed the notion that technological demands place limits on the range of feasible work organization, but that the work organization has social and psychological dimensions which are independent of technology as such.[44] But the framework of analysis used by them has not been generally adopted and their approach has not been systematically applied to other industries. Many case studies provide no more than a set of *ad hoc* hints to managers on how to promote efficiency and raise productivity.[45]

The managerial bias in industrial sociology becomes evident when one attempts to assemble information on the extent to which organized labor has been able to maintain some control over the detailed division of labor. There is little adequate or systematic discussion of this issue in the literature on industrial sociology; most studies suggest that unions have concentrated on pay demands and have left the determination of changes in the organization of work, the detailed division of labor, to management. But there is much scattered evidence to the contrary, workers have resisted, often successfully, attempts by management to reduce their autonomy in the work process.[46] Craft unions in particular aim at retaining control over the determination of job content and the allocation of workers to jobs. The literature on structured labor markets shows how trade unions have successfully generalized conditions of primary employment established for workers whose productivity depended on firm-acquired skills to other workers in the same firm and industry.[47] Whether a job receives a skilled or semi-skilled grading is often a manifestation of conflict of interest and relative bargaining position between groups of workers and employers and can bear little relation to actual job content.[48] More critical attention has been devoted to the causes and consequences of change in the organization of work in the industrial relations literature, especially that adopting a historical approach, than in mainstream economics and sociology. However, these studies lack a common theoretical framework and the evidence they assemble has not been assimilated in the economic and sociological literature.[49]

A number of writers have deliberately attempted to avoid a management perspective and, as in the case of *The Affluent Worker* study, to build on existing theoretical work and provide a link between the analysis of aspects of their problem at the macro-levels.[50] In no small part, the importance of the *Affluent Worker* study lies in its revelation of the possibility of linking the analysis of workers' position in the detailed division of labor with analysis of broader changes in the occupational structure. Thus Lockwood, Goldthorpe, *et al.*, began with the socio-technical environment (the work situation of the individual) which is related to broader phenomena through the concept of a market situation (the possession of skills which differentiates occupational groups in labor markets). These concepts, first elaborated by Lockwood, provide a basis for connecting the outlook and experience of workers with the labor market forces prevailing in a given occupational environment.[51] But in the course of the research undertaking, the thrust of the argument shifted in reaction to the unexpected discovery of the importance of workers' prior orientations in determining their perceptions and expectations.[52] The importance of these factors is convincingly demonstrated but as a result of the change of emphasis, the relevance of shifts in the occupational division of labor is revealed only indirectly and in passing, mainly through reference to the work experience of immediate kin of the workers themselves. The potential of the approach, as originally outlined, for linking work experience and market position of individual workers to broader changes in the occupational division of labor has not yet been realized.

In contrast with the political economists who emphasized the entrepreneur's need for control over his labor force, many recent writers deliberately avoid analyzing factors connected with authority in explaining the prevailing division of labor. Kemper, for example, states

> For analytic purposes I have considered only the technical workflow in this examination of systems of divided labour....I have omitted...the structure of authority. I do not mean to slight the concept of authority but to treat the pattern of technical workflow as analytically primary.[53]

But the pattern of technical workflow is not self-generating. Even where needs arise spontaneously (as for medical attention) they have to be transformed into work tasks to be met, and to that extent the workflow itself is determined by decisions of authorities, as the classical political economists recognized. A more fruitful sociological approach may be that which sees the division of labor as a process of social interaction. Here again, however, the problem of the material basis of the interaction arises. The significance of work relationships does not derive solely from the cash nexus. The division of labor is undoubtedly a process by which participants 'define, establish, maintain and renew the tasks they perform and the relationships which these presuppose,' as Freidson puts it. He goes on to say:

> The limits to interaction...are sufficiently broad and permissive that a variety of bargains is possible for the participants. It is in that variety that we see the division of labour ultimately as a process of social interaction whereby the participants create their specialized tasks and their work relationships.[54]

But the only way of relating an analysis of this kind to the material base of the division of labor is by investigating the interests at stake, the incentives to bargain in certain ways, the capacity to manipulate the scene of negotiation, the constraints limiting alternative definitions and responses. It is not possible to get very far with an interactionist approach until the range of alternatives, the reality of options available to participants (as opposed to responses which are predetermined) is traced out, and this requires an examination of economic and technical constraints on alternative ways of organizing work tasks and defining occupational roles.

Technology and the Social Relations of Production

We have seen that the early political economists were interested in the relationship between technology, work organization, and the incentives leading entrepreneurs to introduce new forms of the division of labor. These were all notions on which Marx elaborated, but which have only recently come under scrutiny in connection with Marx's writings on the division of labor.

The early political economists saw developments in the division of labor as conducive to efficiency. But it was only when the demands of efficiency came to be *identified* with new techniques that technological progress was, as it were, cut loose from its institutional context and became reified in social and economic thought as a disembodied, exogenous force. The analytic rationale for this development was provided by the assumptions of the new discipline of economics as it emerged in the late nineteenth century, in which market forces were seen to impose on producers least-cost methods of production and to ensure the efficient allocation of labor and capital throughout the economy. Paradoxically, this view took hold at a time when the assumptions of perfect competition which underwrote it were becoming patently inapplicable, as monopolies came increasingly to control features of the product market. Nevertheless, in economic analysis the prevailing division of labor in any industry was seen as the natural outcome of competitive market conditions requiring least-cost production techniques. If this set of propositions was adopted for simplicity's sake in economic analysis, sociological writers took over an even more simplistic version of the same sequence. Clearly the institutional arrangements which structure entrepreneurial and managerial decisions are of a social and political character, but for the most part in sociological writing they are treated as on a par with technological exigencies, that is, as lying outside the scope of analysis. The institutional context in which investment decisions are taken, which in turn affect employment practices, are not viewed as a 'sociological problem'.

For industrial sociologists it is unclear whether incentives to profit maximization, and the complex of inducements and constraints affecting decisions to alter the organization of work tasks and roles, are to be treated as within or beyond the scope of analysis. This type of problem simply did not arise for the early political economists, or for Marx, as we have seen. Whether or not they adhere to Marxist categories, recent studies in political economy share an approach which frees them from the boundary problems besetting analyses using the categories of conventional social science.[55] In contrast, the intrusion of boundary problems relating to the division of labour can be illustrated from almost any contemporary analysis of social stratification. Parkin's stimulating and original article on social closure and class formation furnishes one example:

> Industrial solidism relies increasingly for its effects not simply upon the capacity for social mobilization, but also upon the capacity for social and economic dislocation. Workers in a number of key industries now enjoy a form of social leverage arising from their 'disruptive potential' which is quite distinct from the *social facts* of organizational unity.... It is not merely the potential for collective action that governs the effectiveness or otherwise of solidaristic forms of closure but also *the purely contingent features of production*.[56]

Parkin is distinguishing here between the problems of organizing for strike activity and the impact of a strike, which depends on the nature of the goods or service produced and the role of the striking workers in the production process. But to call the latter set of economic factors 'purely contingent features of production' and oppose them to the *social* factors of organizational unity is to withdraw from analyzing the division of labor and to perpetuate a distinction between the social and economic spheres which hamper analysis of the contemporary class system.

Conclusion: The Division of Labor and the Analysis of Social Class

The division of labor is a topic that overlaps or falls outside current academic demarcations. But it can be argued by extension that the analysis of other issues that do lie within the accepted subject matter of existing disciplines is hampered by boundaries which have outlived their usefulness. Boundary problems are nowhere more apparent than in current writing on social class. Much of this is characterized by doubt over the relevance of variables which are not unequivocally social facts but are also economic, political, or technological facts. Class analysis involves not only mapping persons to given positions in the occupational hierarchy, but also the study of the determination of the occupational structure.[57] However, the occupational division of labor needs to be examined in relation to changes in property ownership, investment patterns and the entire cycle of production, consumption and distribution. For such an investigation, the existing stock-in-trade of sociological analysis is insufficient. Nor can economic analysis in its present state provide an adequate description and explanation of the class system. New perspectives which span conventional academic boundaries are required.[58]

If we are to have a better understanding of the processes of change in the occupational structure at the regional and national level which accompany economic growth, we need more information on the causes of change in the division of labour in the workplace. Studies of change in the organization of work in particular industries under various conditions should identify economic and technical factors which operate not in a social vacuum but in a context in which employers and workers pursue their own interests and goals with varying success according to the distribution of power. If our knowledge about the division of labor is increased by the recent revival of interest in the topic, we should also obtain a better understanding of problems of economic growth and class structure. It was with good reason that these problems first aroused the interest of the classical political economists in the division of labor.

Notes

1. See E. Garnsey, 'Women's Work and Theories of Class Stratification', *Sociology* (1978), pp. 223–43.
2. C. Clark, *The Conditions of Economic Progress*, 3rd edn. (Macmillan, 1957); H. Leibenstein, *Economic Backwardness and Economic Growth* (Wiley, 1957); S. Kuznets, *Economic Growth of Nations. Total Output and Production Structure* (Harvard University Press, 1971), chs. 5 and 6; P.T. Bauer and B.S. Yamey, *The Economics of Underdeveloped Countries* (Cambridge University Press, 1957).
3. G. Routh's study has provided the only work of analysis and reference on occupational change available. See G. Routh, *Occupation and Pay in Great Britain 1906–1979* (Macmillan, 1980). Sociologists writing on 'Post-Industrial Society' have tended to produce a simplified version of the account of the sectoral reallocation of labor put

forward by economists following Colin Clark (e.g., D. Bell, *The Coming of Post-Industrial Society*, (Basic Books, 1973): The theorizing on the basis of which accounts of 'Post-Industrial Society' are drawn up is at best highly simplified; this leads to a misrepresentation of the nature of recent changes in the demand for goods and services. See the critique of Bell by J. Gershuny. *After Industrial Society? The Emerging Self-Service Economy* (Macmillan, 1978).

4. See E. Garnsey, 'Occupational Structure in Industrialized Societies: Some Notes on the Convergence Thesis in the Light of Soviet Experience' *Sociology* (1975), pp. 437–58.

5. E. Devons and M. Gluckman, 'Modes and Consequences of Limiting a Field of Study', in M. Gluckman, (ed.) *Closed Systems and Open Minds* (Aldine Publishing Co., 1964), p. 161. (Professor J. Barnes drew my attention to this book.)

6. H. Braverman, *Labor and Monopoly Capital* (Monthly Review Press, 1974); S.A. Marglin, 'What Do Bosses Do?' in A. Gorz, (ed.), *The Divison of Labour* (Harvester Press, 1976); K. Stone, 'The Origin of Job Structure in the Steel Industry', *Review of Radical Political Economy* (1974), pp. 113–73; cf. A. Friedman, *Industry and Labour: Class Struggle at Work and Industrial Sociology* (Macmillan, 1977).

7. Extensive debate has been aroused by the appearance of the neo-Marxist studies on the division of labor. See e.g. T. Elger 'Valorization and Deskilling; a Critique of Braverman', *Capital and Class* (1979), pp. 58–9. Recently a number of studies which dispense with the more rigid categories of Marxist analysis have appeared, focusing on the division of labor and its implications. See esp. J. Rubery, 'Structured Labour Markets, Worker Organization and Low Pay', *Cambridge Journal of Economics* (1978), pp. 1–19; and papers by W. Lazonick, F. Wilkinson and J. Zeitlin, in 'The Labour Process', Market Structure and Marxist Theory', *Cambridge Journal of Economics* vol. 3, no. 3 (1979).

8. Lazonick, in 'The Labour Process', p. 258.

9. Against my claim that the division of labor has not been a central area of analysis since the decline of nineteenth-century political economy, it might be objected that structural differentiation is a central one.

10. A. Smith, *The Wealth of Nations*, Book I,ch. VIII; also Book II Introduction; R.H. Campbell and A.S. Skinner, (eds.) (Oxford University Press, 1976), pp. 104, 277.

11. *Ibid.*, Book I ch. IX, p. 266.

12. *Ibid.*, Book II, Introd., p. 277.

13. *Ibid.*, Book I, ch. VIII.

14. K. Marx, Letter to Wedermeyer, 1852, in *Marx and Engels Selected Works*, vol. I (Progress Publishers, 1969–70), p. 528.

15. K. Marx, *Capital*, vol. I, ch. XIV, sections 35.

16. K. Marx, *A Contribution of the Critique of Political Economy*, M. Dobb (ed.) (Cambridge University Press, 1971), p. 20. For a detailed account of the evolution of Marx's thought on the division of labor, see Mehboob Ali Ratansi, 'Marx, the Division of Labour and Social Theory', unpublished Ph.D. thesis, Cambridge (1978).

17. K. Marx, *Theories of Surplus Value*, cited by M. Dobb, *Theories of Value and Distribution since Adam Smith* (Cambridge University Press, 1973), p. 61.

18. See e.g. R. Bacon and W. Eltis, *Britain's Economic Problem: Too Few Producers* (Macmillan, 1976) and G. Carchedi, 'On the Economic Identification of the New Middle Class', *Economy and Society* (1975), pp. 1–85.

19. A. Ferguson, *An Essay on the History of Civil Society* (1767) ed. Duncan Forbes (Edinburgh University Press, 1966), p. 181.

20. Ch. Babbage, *On the Economy of Machinery and Manufactures* (Charles Knight, 1832), p. 172. It should be remembered that Babbage advocated 'that a considerable part of the wages received by each person employed should depend on the profits made by the establishment' (p. 250). Among other advantages would be the total removal of all real or imaginary causes for combinations' (p. 254). Babbage's idealism was tempered with realism and he recognized that capitalists would fear to embark on the system he advocated 'imagining that the workmen would receive too large a share of the profits' (*ibid.*).

21. Marglin, 'What Do Bosses Do?'

22. Cited by K. Marx *The Poverty of Philosophy* (Foreign Languages Press, 1978). p. 136 (emphasis added).

23. W. Thompson, *Inquiry into the Principles of the Distribution of Wealth* (London, 1824), p. 274.
24. *Ibid.*, p. 281.
25. A. Smith, Book. I, ch. VIII, p. 82.
26. *Ibid.*, p. 83.
27. *Ibid.*, p. 84.
28. Cited in R. Meek, *Smith, Marx and After* (Chapman and Hall, 1977), p. 11.
29. Smith, Book I, ch. IX, p. 266.
30. Cited by Ph. Deane, *The Evolution of Economic Ideas* (Cambridge University Press, 1978), p. 111.
31. *Ibid.*, pp. 33, 131.
32. Smith discussed the constitution of the 'three great classes' in Book I, ch. XI.
33. J. Schumpeter, *History of Economic Analysis* (Allen and Unwin, 1961), p. 551.
34. R. Meek, 'Marginalism and Marxism', in R. Black, A. Coats, *et al.*, *The Marginalist Revolution in Economics* (Duke University Press, 1973), pp. 233–45.
35. In contrast, as we have seen, Smith chose to incorporate mechanization into his definition of the division of labor. But neither labor nor machinery should be treated as a residual category; both sets of factors interact in determining the organization of work.
36. Deane, *Evolution of Economic Ideas*.
37. Cited in G. Therborn, *Science, Class and Society* (New Left Books, 1976), pp. 313, 314.
38. M. Weber, *The Theory of Social and Economic Organization* (New York, Free Press, 1947), sec. II.
39. Giddens is one of the few sociologists to have examined features of the division of labor as a preliminary to the analysis of social class (or 'class structuration'). See A. Giddens, *The Class Structure of the Advanced Societies* (Hutchinson, 1972).
40. In *De la division du travail social* (Presses Universitaires de France, 1967).
41. Cited in S. Lukes, *Emile Durkheim, His Life and Work* (Allen Lane, 1974), p. 174.
42. S. Lukes, 'Alienation and Anomie', in P. Laslett and W.G. Runciman, (eds.), *Philosophy, Politics and Society*; series 3 (Oxford University Press, 1967).
43. On this concept see N. Smelser, *The Sociology of Economic Life*, 2nd edn. (Prentice-Hall, 1976), pp. 150ff.
44. E.L. Trist and H.M. Bamforth, 'Some Social and Psychological Consequences of the Longwall Method of Coal-getting', *Human Relations* (1951), pp. 3-38.
45. D. Silverman, 'Formal Organizations or Industrial Sociology?' *Sociology* (May 1968), pp. 221–238; *The Theory of Organizations* (Heinemann, 1970).
46. Friedman, *Industry and Labour*.
47. Rubery, 'Structured Labour Markets, Worker Organization and Low Pay'.
48. See J.E. Mortimer, *Trade Unions and Technological Change*, (Oxford University Press, 1971), p. 37 for reference to the unions' case against productivity bargaining, criticized as 'a means of curtailing the autonomous influence of workers over working arrangements, practices and conditions'.
49. Some promising theoretical perspectives are suggested by W. Brown, 'A Consideration of Custom and Practice', in *British Journal of Industrial Relations* (1972), 42–61 and by A. Fox and A. Flanders, 'The Reform of Collective Bargaining from Donovan to Durkheim', *British Journal of Industrial Relations* (1969), pp. 151–80.
50. J.H. Goldthorpe, D. Lockwood, F. Bechofer and I. Platt, *The Affluent Worker*, vols. 1–3 (Cambridge University Press, 1968).
51. D. Lockwood, *The Blackcoated Worker. A Study in Class Consciousness* (Allen and Unwin, 1956).
52. This point was made by Gavin Mackenzie, 'The Affluent Worker Study. An Evaluation and Critique', in F. Parkin (ed.), *The Social Analysis of Class Structure* (Tavistock, 1974).
53. T. Kemper, 'The Division of Labor; A Post-Durkheimian Analytic View', *American Sociological Review* (Dec. 1972), pp. 739–53.
54. E. Freidson, 'The Division of Labor as Social Interaction', in M. Haug and J. Dofny (eds.) *Work and Technology* (Sage Publications, 1977).
55. See nn. 6–7.
56. F. Parkin, 'Strategies of Social Closure in Class Formation' in *The Social Analysis of Class Structure*, emphasis added.

57. For this argument see Garnsey (nn. 1 and 4). I accept the point made by Poulantzas that to focus on forms of consciousness of social actors in the class system and on the question of how individuals achieve class membership through social mobility (the concerns of most stratification studies) is to leave aside the prior question of the structural determination of class positions. See N. Poulantzas, *Classes in Contemporary Capitalism* (New Left Books, 1975). I would go on to argue that this problem requires a systematic analysis of the factors giving rise to the occupational division of labor. This is a central task of class analysis, though class relations are not limited to relations of paid employment. Class is an exhaustive concept, in the sense in which participation in the division of labor is not. By virtue of entering into social relationships, people become members of a class society without necessarily playing a role in the occupational division of labor.

58. Possible approaches are discussed by Anthony Giddens in his Postscript to the second edition of *The Class Structure of the Advanced Societies* (Hutchinson, 1981).

4   The Search for Shelters

MARCIA FREEDMAN

The term 'shelter' suggests several different, but related themes. First is the relationship of job protection mechanisms to the determination of annual earnings, where 'shelter' implies retreat from competition and the sum of arrangements that give workers strong claims to their jobs. Second, 'shelter' signifies a search for protection against adversity and the mitigation of the effects of unemployment, disability, illness and old age.

The most simple, sheltering mechanism arises when work is decasualized, when the daily shape-up is no longer the mode, and when employment is stabilized. This step is consonant with increasing capital intensity and labor specialization. More complex mechanisms evolve as workers begin to bargain about the terms and conditions of continuing employment, the typical vehicle being the trade union or employee association.

Finally, the search for shelter involves worker organizations in attempts to invoke the power of the state for the furtherance of their occupational interests. Such activities result in special applications of licensing laws; the establishment of quasi-public accrediting bodies; legislative lobbying on matters of economic concern; and the exercise of leverage arising from identification as a political constituency.

No mechanism or instrument renders workers impervious to loss. When demand slackens, they are still fired or laid off, although previously agreed upon arrangements for severance pay or unemployment benefits may soften the blow. For those who continue to work, however, shelters constitute a protection against sudden shifts of pay and status. A loose labor market is a deterrent to the strengthening of shelters, but for those who are employed, the existence of shelter gives the group a means of resisting threats to wage scales and working conditions.

Stability

The growth of structure – those rules that make more rigid the terms and conditions of employment – is encouraged when the costs of rapid adjustment outweigh the benefits. The same factors that obviate continual changes in production methods also obviate a daily shape-up for workers. With stable cadres and explicit work rules, large organizations are a fertile ground for the development of formal mechanisms like civil service regulations, collective bargaining agreements, and the creation of internal labor markets that in turn reinforce stability.

While some jobs have undergone considerable structuring in this way, by no means all of them have experienced the progression from informal to formal arrangements; from temporary to permanent, from transient to fixed. Employing

Marcia Freedman, *Labor Markets: Segments and Shelters*, New York, Allanhead, Osman/ Universal Books, 1976; Chapter 7.

organizations exhibit quite contrary needs for *both* stability and flexibility. Commercial farms, for example, need a small permanent workforce and a large flexible manpower pool at harvest time. The rhythm of activity and the long hours of operation in retailing encourage the hiring of part-time workers. Seasonal patterns of production in such industries as apparel and construction results in regular layoffs and intermittent employment. Even in highly concentrated, capital-intensive industries where product markets are favorable, attempts to avoid or slow down increases in fixed costs produce such phenomena as satellite enterprises, contracting out, and franchising – all of which seek to transfer to others the burdens of flexibility.

Enforcing Job Claims

The modal activity that occurs in the labor market is not competition among individuals, but bargaining among groups. The notion of occupational entities is familiar in nineteenth-century economic theory in the guise of 'noncompeting groups'. It has become conventional, following Cairnes, to assume that competition prevails *within* such groups, but it is worth remembering that the four groups Cairnes sketched (unskilled laborers, artisans, producers and dealers, and the learned professions) reflected the class structure of Victorian England,[1] rather than occupational categories consciously operating as groups in their own interest.

Interestingly enough, it was Adam Smith who provided an earlier clue to the processes that segment the labor market. In his attack on the monopolistic practices of journeymen corporations and on the restrictions on movement imposed by the administration of the poor laws, he was protesting existing impediments to the realization of net advantages from a free choice of employments. Workers left to their own devices would find both their proper place and their proper price.[2] In his view, the chief obstacle to achieving a free market was the 'spirit of corporation': the coming together of special interests capable of extracting from the State protections that gave them the character of so many small distinct states within the body politic.[3]

Neither Adam Smith, nor any later economist, ever envisioned labor as perfectly homogeneous, substitutable or mobile. What the classicists counted on was the independence in the market of innumerable individuals. The expectation that each would make his distinctive contribution was, in fact, at the center of classical economic theory. Schumpeter has made the point that 'nobody, either before or after A. Smith, ever thought of putting such a burden on the division of labor. With A. Smith, it is practically the only factor in economic progress.'[4] For the Utilitarians who followed, the spontaneous division of labour gave rise to a natural identity of interests whose harmony

> becomes ceaselessly more perfect through the multiplication of specialities which results from the multiplication of needs and from the progress of the sciences.[5]

But this very proliferation of specialties lies at the heart of systematic market imperfections. Classical economists believed in the atomistic effects of the division of labor, and neoclassicists have simply carried this belief along as part of their theoretical baggage. It turns out, however, that as economic activities become more diverse, more and more occupations emerge, differences among industries contribute additional distinctions, and the 'spirit of corporation' becomes manifest in ever more imaginative guises. In the economic realm, we have witnessed various combinations in restraint of trade; in the political realm, the appropriation of state power for protectionist purposes; and in the social realm, the cultural residues of defining 'inferior' groups. Just as in Adam Smith's day, the purpose is protection in the market.

The language of alleged risk-takers indicates the importance of protection. Individuals seek 'tax shelters', 'hedge' their investments, diversify. More significantly, corporations engage in 'price leadership', enjoy tax 'incentives', and, in the special cases of military and space hardware, become virtual subsidiaries of the public treasury. In all of these activities, the key is to invoke the power of the state in pursuit of private interest.

In the labor market, maximizing group interest and minimizing risk rests on exclusion, which may be justified on the grounds that people are not members of certain associations, that they lack credentials or seniority, or that their age, sex or race is inappropriate. Whatever the particular exclusionary mode, the purpose is to constitute barriers to entry into preferred occupations.

Those aspiring to establishment in the labor market recognize the necessity to acquire their 'cards' – professional certification, state license, civil service status, or union membership; they know, in fact, a good deal about the practical workings of the emulative ethic. Nowhere fully systematized, this operational knowledge of what it takes to 'compete' consists of more than a conviction about the monetary return on investments in education and specific occupational training: it also includes insights into the potential value of organizational attachment and the advantages of long tenure.

The attempt on the part of workers to seek shelter is perfectly understandable: as long as the public system designed for social protection has critical weaknesses and is flawed by inequities, a worker responsible for other family members has to be concerned with sheltering the job and its earnings. Behind the data and the concepts are real people with real anxieties, doing the best they can, and no more inclined to take risks than the next person or the next organization.

The troubles flowing from the labor market system of group-by-group advantages, partial job protections, and political bargaining that developed in the post-World War II era came into sharper focus in the recession of the 1970s. As long as the rate of economic growth, conventionally measured in gross national product, was rising, the system, with some patches here and there, seemed to work along the utilitarian lines laid down for it. The centrepiece of policy, whether acknowledged or not, was the well-being of male heads of households. If there were problems in the transition from school to work, they disappeared from concern as succeeding cohorts matured out of the youth labor market. If women had 'secondary' jobs, it was because the majority preferred them. Furthermore, the lot of minorities was improving, especially among the younger age groups, and it seemed likely that succeeding generations would reap their fair share of both opportunities and outcomes. Most of all, an ever-larger gross national product would insure more real income for everyone without any need for redistribution.

The reduction in the growth rate shattered this optimistic consensus and revealed the fragile logic that informed it: First, it became clear that the system has grown more complex, chaotic and unmanageable. Each increment of privilege makes rational reform more difficult. The inequities created by tying all important social and economic protections to employment[6] became obvious when previously advantaged workers found themselves living on the margins as the poor had done for so long.

Most important of all, the proliferation of groups with fragmented interests has a continuing effect: it makes stalemate the most likely outcome in crisis situations. Struggles occur, not only between, but also among, the 'ins' and the 'outs'.

Small-scale bargains do not add up to political consensus; they do not even produce political conflict over clearly-drawn issues. Rather, they lead to what can only be described as thrashing around in a sea of ambiguity, where it is difficult not only to assess the greatest good, but even to decide on the greatest number.

The institutional arrangements that allocate employment, determine its quality and create sheltering arrangements in the labor market have developed over time and are no more fixed than other features of American social, economic and political life. The study reported here describes two cross-sections in this development, secular trends in institution-building that for good or for ill are bound to influence responses to new situations.

The Segmented Labor Market

The empirical basis for distinguishing levels of protection available to employed Americans is labor market segmentations. There is no claim that the analysis produced a model or a fixed number of segments. It is a preliminary investigation of the forces producing segmentation and an assessment of their relative importance. The basis of the empirical work is an important distinction between occupation and industry. Labor market segments have a variety of sheltering mechanisms, some of which relate to occupations *across* industries and others which relate to occupation *within* industries. Because both have important effects, segmentation depends on locating jobs and including, as independent variables, those factors that identify the interactions between particular occupational and industrial attributes.

It is not enough to investigate blue-collar jobs, or to focus on manufacturing industries, as a number of empirical studies have done. To be sure, the typical opportunities and pay scales of craft, operative and laborer jobs vary by industry. Low-wage sectors, like textile, apparel, furniture and lumber, are characterized by low capital intensity, lack of market power, relatively small firm size and narrow promotion ladders. Stable and well-paid employment, on the other hand, is more likely to occur in large establishments with sufficient market power to treat labor costs as quasi-fixed, and experience on the job as the customary route to advancement. But none of these conditions is necessary. In construction, firms are small and occupations are not linked to one another, yet the local organization of unions means that all firms in contract construction face essentially the same labor costs, passed along in prices charged to owners.

Whatever the distinctions and refinements that may be introduced in the analysis, blue-collar occupations and manufacturing industries are a diminishing proportion of total employment. Yet, little empirical work has been done on white-collar and service jobs and on non-manufacturing industries generally. The results of this study, which includes the entire structure, show that it is in distinguishing these growing occupational groups from each other, that the segmentation, rather than the duality, of the labor market emerges. By now it is clear that all white-collar jobs do not have desirable characteristics, either in income or in working conditions. Furthermore, they derive their protections (or lack of protections) from quite different organizational and bargaining features.

Managers, who are becoming increasingly professionalized, have patterns similar to blue-collar workers in that their earnings and promotional opportunities are a function of the size and market power of their firms. Professionals, on the other hand, owe their position to the nature of their occupations, which tend to be similar across industries. Credentials alone are insufficient to shelter them; what is required is the occupational exclusiveness that comes from control over training, certification and entry. In this study, these elements of sheltering mechanisms were represented by licensing coverage.

Nonprofessional, nonmanagerial white-collar jobs have experienced high growth rates since World War II because of the growth of the industries that employ them in large numbers, but they vary greatly in the scope of their labor market protections. The relative position of technicians and nonoffice clericals is strongly affected by industry. Plant clericals and technicians in manufacturing are similar to blue-collar workers, while, for a distinct subgroup like telephone operators, even the monopoly position of their employer offers few advantages. For the stock clerks and cashiers in retailing, peripheral status is exacerbated by the low wage-scales of the industry, in turn related to the relative weakness of the firms in that market.

Office clericals, like professionals, tend to hold similar positions across industries, but at a much lower level of stability and earnings. In contrast, service workers, who are generally among the lowest-paid of all major groups (always excepting such occupations as policemen and firemen, which were treated as technicians in this study) vary both by occupation and industry.

Underlying the distinctions outlined above is the typical pattern of annual hours of work. During any given year in the sixties, from 54 to 59 percent of those with work experience worked full-time, year-round.[7] Intermittent and part-year work were associated with low wages, adverse working conditions, and the absence of prospects for promotion. Turnover in this part of the market was high, and the instability of these jobs was a major factor in the secular unemployment rate.[8]

Some of the increase in poor-quality employment resulted from the growth of part-time scheduling. 'Voluntary' part-time grew twice as fast as total nonagricultural employment. Altogether, part-time jobs, both voluntary and involuntary, were 17 percent of the total in 1971.[9] Given the advantages to employers who sought flexibility in their labor supply, it was not surprising that a loosening of arrangements on one side of the occupational structure accompanied a tightening on the other.

The influence of 'class-of-worker' as a variable is clearest in the large category of nonprofessional, nonmanagerial white-collar jobs. For a long time, these groups in the public sector benefited to the extent that security was a tradeoff for income. After 1960, however, the movement to bring salaries into line with the private sector and the collective action of worker groups resulted in relatively greater pay increases and higher scales than for comparable jobs outside government service.[10]

The Allocation of Jobs and Family Income

During the sixties, about half of the available jobs provided long-term stability and security. The probability of white men moving into these positions as they matured was far greater than the probability of women or members of minority groups doing so. These groups were more likely to find employment in short-term, insecure positions or in long-term, low-paying jobs.

Conventional explanations for this allocation of the labor force rest on concepts like worker 'quality' and 'productivity', with a flavor of *post hoc* justification that has a way of shifting to suit circumstances. If, for example, incumbents can maintain themselves in sheltered positions, the rationale for excluding the young may include references to unreliability or lack of experience. On the other hand, mature workers with weaker job protections may be moved aside so that employers can allegedly benefit from the more recent training (and the lower wages) of new entrants.

In general, however, better jobs tend to be reserved for men of 25 to 45, in the so-called 'prime working age'. The secular trend for a rising age of full-time entry into the labour market was reinforced at the end of the sixties by a slowdown in the expansion of jobs suitable for establishment. As a group, young entry workers are far better educated in a formal sense than ever before, but the prospects for economic utilization of their education have diminished. When jobs are scarce, the opportunity costs of education are reduced, thus encouraging enrollments and lengthening the queue of ever-aging youths waiting for a chance to secure appropriate employment. Meanwhile, the relatively unschooled minority find it difficult to gain even a foothold.

If men encounter an age-related rationing system in the market, women experience job segregation related to their typical dual roles. Their position at work tends to be defined in terms of family income. Combining the earnings from low-paid, unprotected jobs with the earnings from well-paid, sheltered jobs permits many American families to meet socially defined standards of consumption. As more and more married women have entered the labor market, this type of two-earner family has become increasingly prevalent in the middle range of the income structure.

A family seeking a somewhat different combination, one that avoids career preoccupations and offers a freer life-style, faces difficulties directly related to the inequities of shelters. Suppose, for example, that a married couple concludes that, instead of the husband playing the major role as economic provider, both the husband and the wife should pursue modified careers through part-time jobs. Total family income might be adequate, but neither worker could expect to hold a job with prospects for either advancement or security.

Furthermore, since social welfare benefits are in large measure tied to employment, such a family would forego that part of income received by a full-time worker in the form of fringe benefits. They could, of course, finance these benefits in the private market, but, given that supplemental pay averages about one-fifth of total compensation, it is unlikely that they could insure themselves against certain kinds of risk without considerable real income loss. They would have to purchase their own hospital and health insurance, for example, at considerably higher rates than those afforded by a group. They would be eligible under private pension plans only if they worked somewhat more than half-time. If they persisted in meeting their immediate economic needs with two part-time jobs, their social security benefits at retirement might well be calculated on a smaller base than if one person had earned all the income.

The domestic difficulties involved in both husband and wife pursuing careers (or even just holding down steady jobs) are by now adequately described, but each proposed solution involves another type of cost.[11] Since the costs are often nonpecuniary, there is no coin by which to compare them or even to predict when certain costs may be transformed into benefits. Childlessness is one such fuzzy category. If the marked trends of the early seventies continue with respect to later age of marriage and the sharp decline in the birth rate, the number of women seeking what have hitherto been masculine careers will increase. Buoyed by a new sense of themselves, they will be keen competitors who will demand recognition as the length of their job tenure increases. By and large, however, the combination of employer insistence on flexibility, the type-casting of jobs, and the difficulties facing those who attempt to balance their dual roles, will leave the majority of women in a secondary position in the labor market for some time to come.

The very fact, however, that many jobs continue to be socially (if not legally) labelled 'female', and that women are concentrated in the peripheral segments of the market, creates enormous hardships for women who have to support their families. The number of these families has grown steadily, with the increase proportionately greater among blacks. From 1968 to 1973, the percent rose from 9 to 10 for white families, and from 28 to 35 for black families. With adverse opportunities in the labor market, it is no surprise that, including income from all sources, over one-half of these black families were below the low-income level, compared to about one-quarter of the white families.[12]

For black families as a whole, the slow movement toward parity with whites after World War II reached its peak in1970 when the black – white ratio of median family income was 64 percent.[13] The data may be interpreted as showing the same tendency for polarization as the labor force as a whole: those workers who were able to move into sheltered positions improved their position and those who remained outside were so much the worse off. In 1971, the black–white income ratio began to go down, a leading indicator of the hard times ahead and the cyclical reverse of minority gains.

The weakest families are those with the most tenuous relationship to employment. Their willingness to accept public assistance is a measure of lack of confidence in their ability to succeed at work, a confidence that ironically is undermined in proportion to their aspirations and devotion to the 'work ethic'.[14] Perhaps, as Ernest Hemingway concluded, the only difference between the rich and poor is that the rich have money, but the difference between the poor and everybody else (including the rich) is that the poor have virtually no political power. If they are unable to make a living at work, they can expect only a bare minimum of economic protection from the state.

Mobility

The chief concerns of American workers are well-documented. Even in relatively prosperous times they worry about health and safety hazards on the job; about not being able to pay their bills if illness prevents them from working; about inadequate earnings to meet their usual expenses.[15] At best, their hope has been to experience incremental gains in real earnings, at worst, to be protected from adversity and insecurity. Such concerns would seem to be far more compelling than the striving for status that characterizes our folklore. Biographies of American leaders are replete with drama, and they testify to the fact that many who were poor or near poor in Abilene, Whittier and the Lower East Side went on to fame and glory. These stories encourage the view that occupational success is an individual sequence in a more general morality play in which Everyman triumphs through the possession of merit, the exercise of initiative, and the capacity to defer gratification. Correlatively, failure is the legitimate wage accorded those of lesser worth, punier ambition and more independent habit. The life stories of most people, however, involve small movements in search of modest gains, and their personal histories are to high drama as a school auditorium is to the Broadway stage.

Perhaps because upward mobility involves relatively short 'social distances',[16] it seems to have lost some of its traditional force as myth. In industrialized societies, parents presumably always hoped for better things for their children.

And children in their turn often had to settle for less. What seems different now is the blurring of the success criterion, particularly in the middle ranges of the occupational structure.

The reasons are not hard to find. The race for upward mobility, that 'agreed-upon undebated premise of our politics', may be a great historical metaphor, but it suffers from an internal contradiction. Since it is impossible to enjoy *both* equality of opportunity at the starting line *and* equal opportunity to advance along the way,[17] the contest becomes like the caucus race in *Alice in Wonderland* as organized by the Dodo:

> First it marked out a race-course, in a sort of circle, ('the exact shape doesn't matter,' it said) and then all the party were placed along the course, here and there. There was no 'one, two, three, and away!' but they began running when they liked, and left off when they liked, so that it was not easy to know when the race was over.[18]

Many sensible people, faced with the 'staggered, endlessly multiplied starting lines'[19] of such a race are likely to withdraw, preferably to a position from which the movement of events is more predictable. For everyone who aspires to higher status, there is someone else willing to settle for a different kind of success, for example, as an over-the-road truck driver, a job where high income substitutes for high status. The most menial jobs gain adherents in this manner if one accepts as testimony the long-enduring waiting list for employment in the New York City Sanitation Department where the pay and benefits for garbage collection are exceptionally high.

Those already employed in the stable, middle-range jobs have had opportunities to improve the quality of those jobs. During the sixties, for example, policemen and firemen achieved markedly higher earnings and benefits through a combination of formal and informal bargaining pressures. When room at the top of the occupational structure is limited, workers will seize what opportunities are available to make their jobs more 'important', more secure and, above all, better-paid.

The Role of Interest Groups

Improvement in the quality of jobs requires some form of activity on the part of workers. We speak of collective bargaining in the context of unions and organized labor, but many nonunion groups engage in similar activities for the same purposes. Particularly in the United States, bargaining among interest groups has long been a political norm.

Alexis de Tocqueville, reflecting on equality of opportunity in America and the strivings of men to expand their gratifications, noted that '...the desire of acquiring the comforts of the world haunts the imagination of the poor, and the dread of losing them that of the rich'.[20] The endless associations formed by Americans 'in order to procure the things they covet' seemed admirably suited to a developing United States. The framers of the Constitution, inspired by an anti-monarchical animus, created a system of checks and balances designed to limit the power of the state. Within this loose governance, men were free to pursue their own ends, theoretically as individuals, but practically in a multitude of limited-purpose groups. It is quite in keeping with this tradition that American worker groups should be both fragmented and narrowly focused.

Alliances on which bargaining power depend are limited in scope by the necessity for members to adhere to the same goals and policies.[21] If bargaining among interest groups is the mode, the groups themselves must perforce adopt a narrow definition of their respective missions. The fate of the National Labor Union and the Knights of Labor illustrates this point. For all their weaknesses, these early trade unions viewed the problems of workers in the context of national issues that were best addressed by political means. The American Federation of Labor, on the contrary, developed its activities and programs around much narrower and more immediate aims. In the ideological struggles of the 1890s, the AFL rejected even the moderate socialism of the trade union movement that would lead to the establishment of the British Labour Party in 1906.[22] By the turn of the century, the AFL had not only formulated the distinctively American pattern of negotiating piecemeal gains sector by sector, but had elevated that pattern to a principle.

Samuel Gompers' vision of the future remains a classic statement of the goal as it has come to be defined, not only for union members but for all wage and salary workers:

> ...securing day by day and week by week and month by month and year by year, a little today, a little tomorrow, adding, gaining, moving forward, every step in advance, and never taking one receding step except it be to plant the foot forward firmer than ever before.[23]

Gompers, who accepted the necessity of corporate growth and economic concentration, perceived trade unions as a countervailing force, '... labor's constructive contribution to democratic regulation of large scale production ...'[24]. It was, in fact, a bargaining concept that eschewed broader forms of collective action and that lay well within a developing ideology of pluralism.

The whole point of joining together with others is to provide a 'haven of protection' intermediate between the state and the individual.[25] In a pluralistic society, the necessity for such association often overrides the doubts, the fears, and sometimes even the outright hostility of goup members. The compartmentalization of attitudes emerges from an Opinion Research Center survey in which the majority of members rated their union leadership as 'fair' to 'poor' and blamed unions for inflation and problems of international trade.[26] Yet negative assessments do not typically result in rank-and-file revolt, much less in eschewing the benefits of membership.

The activities of associations go beyond protection in a defensive sense. In seeking better bargains, they also may invoke state power on their own behalf, at times blurring the boundaries between themselves and government. Associations of workers are not alone in this endeavor; they are not even the pace-setters. Business and financial interests seek and obtain welfare legislation in the form of tax provisions, influence on – or control of – public regulatory agencies, tariffs, contracts or direct subsidies. During the recession of the mid-seventies, even free-enterprise ideologues looked to Washington for rescue and treatment for their ailments through the unsystematic application of individual 'bail-outs'. When Americans have been directed to help themselves, their response from the beginning has been to form into groups, and it has been only a brief historical step from cooperative barn-raising to the maintenance of effective Washington lobbies.

Several features of this system have particular relevance to labor market segmentation. In the case of licensing, members of an occupation often have effective control of the governmental regulating apparatus. In other instances, the connection is attenuated, as in labor relations legislation where equity considerations constrain the anti-union practices of employers without obviating them altogether. Other examples are more specialized, like the Davis–Bacon Act which mandates union wage scales for public construction.

If groups are the principal actors, their politics is accommodation of interests on a case-by-case basis, on the assumption that the sum of successive bargains is an automatic self-regulating society. It is a curious elevation of an old homily to a definition of the public interest: 'If you take care of the little things, the big things will take care of themselves.'

The same equality in the marketplace that was formerly ascribed to individuals is in effect now ascribed to groups. But, while less powerful groups may gain concessions from the more powerful, the weak and unorganized have little hope of gaining anything. The inevitable outcome of both conflict *and* cooperation among groups is inequity, and the very workings of the system militate against attempts to redress the balance.

An illustration of this thesis emerges from attempts to enforce equal rights legislation. In its administration of Title VII of the Civil Rights Act of 1964, the US Equal Employment Opportunity Commission (EEOC) has sought voluntary compliance with the law through informal means of conciliation. A study of these efforts (with respect to race) between 1966 and 1971 showed that the net impact of the 'cause finding' and conciliation procedure was small. 'On the average, there was little perceptible difference in minority employment conditions between firms inolved in successful conciliation and similar firms who were not.'[27]

While progress in reducing discrimination has occurred since 1971,[28] the way labor markets operate is not helpful to the women and minority-group members who are the objects of the legislation. As diffuse population groups, they have no claim to occupational exclusiveness. In an expanding economy, classes protected under the law can hope to gain equal representation, but in a period of contraction, their rights come into conflict with the seniority principle. In that situation, only an individual who can demonstrate *individual* suffering from past discrimination at the hands of the employer, can hope to gain his or her 'rightful place'. Meanwhile, the quality of the jobs themselves is in no way affected, and worker hopes remain centered on finding a way, through more equalitarian practices, of moving to a job with better promotional opportunities.

It was Tocqueville, of all optimists, who most eloquently expressed the concern for the 'new species of oppression' that might arise in a world where

> ...each...is a stranger to the fate of all the rest – his children and his private friends constitute to him the whole of mankind; as for the rest of his fellow-citizens, he is close to them, but he feels them not; he exists but in himself and for himself alone; and if his kindred still remains to him, he may be said at any rate to have lost his country.[29]

Fragmentation of interests and unequal distribution of power tend to undermine both national and international purpose because new decisions in one sphere cancel the results of previous decisions in others. Bargaining will not soon wither away on the American scene. But even partial consensus on goals might result in more fruitful and equitable bargains that could obviate a 'new species of oppression'.

Notes

1. J.E. Cairnes, *Some Leading Principles of Political Economy* (London; Macmillan, 1874), pp. 64–74.
2. Adam Smith, *The Wealth of Nations* (New York; Random House (Modern Library Edition), 1937), ch. X.

3. Elie Halevy, *The Growth of Philosophic Radicalism* (Boston; Beacon Press, 1955), p. 118. Although the logic developed by Smith required a thorough policy of nonintervention by the State in economic affairs, juridical systems based on so-called 'artificial identification of interests' quickly made their way back into the concepts of the nineteenth-century Utilitarians. Halevy discusses their rationale for putting the good of security above the good of equality – specifically, for the State to protect the property of the rich against the poor.
4. Joseph A. Schumpeter, *History of Economic Analysis* (New York; Oxford University Press, 1954), p. 187.
5. Halevy, *Growth of Philisophic Radicalism*, p. 488.
6. We are not here considering the advantages enjoyed by holders of wealth nor the connections between wealth and power, but only the effects of the employment system on wage and salaried workers and those engaged in small-scale self-employment.
7. US Department of Labor, *1972 Manpower Report of the President* (Washington; Government Printing Office, 1972), Table B-14, p. 210.
8. See Robert E. Hall, 'Why is the Unemployment Rate so High at Full Employment?' *Brookings Papers on Economic Activity 3: 1970*, (Arthur M. Okun and George L. Perry, eds., Washington; Brookings Institution, 1971), p. 393.
9. *1972 Manpower Report of the President*, Tables A-24, A-25, pp. 188–90.
10. For some examples for local governments, see Stephen H. Perloff, 'Comparing Municipal Salaries with Industry and Federal Pay', *Monthly Labor Review*, vol. 94 (October 1971), pp. 46–50.
11. William Goode, 'Family Life of the Successful Woman', in Eli Ginzberg and Alice Yohalem, (eds.), *Corporate Lib: Women's Challenge to Management*, (Baltimore; John Hopkins University Press, 1973), pp. 97–117.
12. US Bureau of the Census, 'The Social and Economic Status of the Black Population in the United States', *Current Population Reports*, P-23, No. 46, (Washington; Government Printing Office, 1973), Table 52, p. 68, and Table 19, p. 29.
13. US Bureau of the Census, 'Money Income in 1973 of Families and Persons in the United States', *Current Population Reports*, P-60, No. 97, (Washington; Government Printing Office, 1975), Table 10, p. 25.
14. Leonard Goodwin, *Do The Poor Want to Work?* (Washington; Brookings Institution, 1972). For support of the position that 'welfare' is the last defense, see Bradley R. Schiller, 'Empirical Studies of Welfare Dependency; A Survey', *Journal of Human Resources*, vol. 8 (Supplement, 1973), pp. 19–32.
15. Survey Research Center, University of Michigan, *Working Conditions Survey* (Washington; Government Printing Office, 1971), Table 4.1, pp. 106–7. These are not their only worries, but they lead the list of important labor standard problems.
16. Peter M. Blau and Otis Dudley Duncan, *The American Occupational Structure*, (New York; Wiley, 1967), p. 119.
17. Garry Wills, *Nixon Agonistes* (Boston; Houghton Mifflin, 1970), p. 236.
18. Lewis Carroll, 'Alice's Adventures in Wonderland', *Complete Works of Lewis Carroll* (New York; Modern Library), p. 37.
19. Wills, *Nixon Agonistes*, p. 238.
20. Alexis de Tocqueville, *Democracy in America*, Henry Reeve, tr. (New York; Schocken, 1961), vol. II, p. 154.
21. When the merger talks of the National Education Association and the American Federation of Teachers broke down – in spite of the occupational identity of the two memberships and the similarity in their strategies – the ostensible reason was a difference in attitude toward the AFL-CIO.
22. For an account of the ideological struggles of the American trade-union movement in the nineteenth century, see Gerald N. Grob, *Workers and Utopia* (Chicago; Northwestern University Press, 1961).
23. Quoted by Grob, *Workers and Utopia*, p. 192.
24. Samuel Gompers, *Seventy Years of Life and Labor* (New York; Dutton, 1925), vol. II, p. 20.
25. Philip, A. Selznick, *Law, Society, and Industrial Justice* (New York; Russell Sage, 1969), p. 37.
26. Reported in 'Trouble Plagues the House of Labor', *Business Week* (28 October 1972), p. 67.

27. Arvil V. Adams, *Toward Fair Employment and the EEOC: A Study of Compliance Procedures under Title VII of the Civil Rights Act of 1964* (Columbus, Ohio; Center for Human Resources Research, Ohio State University, 1972), p. 127.
28. See, for example, the industry-wide consent decrees in telephone (1973) and steel (1974).
29. Tocqueville, *Democracy in America*, Vol. II, p. 380.

5 The Labour Process and Deskilling

PAUL THOMPSON

New Beginnings: Theory and Practice

A central factor in the return to a workplace focus was the breakdown of the illusion of industrial concensus. Throughout the industrial world, recorded workplace conflict dramatically increased from the period of the middle of the 1960s. Even at this time the unofficial strike rate was so high in Britain as to justify a Royal Commission, which produced the Donovan Report (1968). In other countries a higher peak of industrial and social conflict was reached, as in the mass strike waves in France in 1968 and Italy in 1969. But as the impressive collection of evidence on European class conflict by Crouch and Pizzorno (1978) found, the significance lay in the nature as well as the scale of the action.

Pizzorno notes that they were 'chiefly struck by the new types of qualitative demands' (Crouch and Pizzorno, 1978, vol. 1, p. xi). Activity and demands showed a marked shift towards issues beyond wages. Case studies from various countries, notably France, Belgium and Italy, gave a wide range of examples of struggles over the control of line speeds and piece work, authority relations in the plant, challenges to job hierarchies and classification schemes, over general upgradings, and so on. Although these are prominent examples, it is a long-term trend, as Kumar notes: 'The changing pattern of strikes, especially since 1945, gives further evidence of an increasing restlessness about the quality of working life and the nature of the job itself' (1978; p. 285).

The Degradation of Work: the Braverman Thesis

In one of the first studies of the labour process, Gorz (1976a; p. vii) argued that the capitalist division of labour had been forgotten as a source of alienation until it found itself at the centre of many of the struggles just described. The subsequent awakening of sections of Marxist thought to the process of production led not only to a questioning of the 'tyranny of the factory', but also to the whole historical evolution of the world of work. To take the new beginnings further required a precise and detailed examination of the productive process. Braverman was the first to provide this, and in a manner which deliberately eschews any attempt to accompany it by an explicit theory of class consciousness and social change.

This preference for the 'objective' features of work and class has been the subject of much subsequent criticism. But the clarity of purpose, breadth of research and theoretical originality ensured its prominence, regardless of weaknesses. The latter point concerning originality is important, because

---

Paul Thompson, *The Nature of Work*, London, Macmillan, 1983; chapters 3 and 4 (abridged).

Braverman's centrality arises also from the particular and distinct perspective advanced. One of the many writers using Braverman as a reference point for discussion of their own research sums up the basics of the perspective:

> A certain current in Marxism, seeking to elaborate the concept of the 'labour process' has been influential in representing changes in types and scale of new production technology, as effects of necessary and general 'tendencies' or 'Laws'...proposed as primarily the subordination of the autonomy of manual production workers, through simultaneously decreasing the level of skill in production tasks and increasing managerial control over their execution. (Jones, 1982, p. 179)

In some senses Braverman and others in this 'certain current' have only advocated a return to Marx. Certainly Braverman begins (1974, chs. 1–3) by restating many of the essential features of Marx's theory of the labour process, with the addition of material from modern historians and critical comments on parallel sociological concepts. Indeed, all the major new studies of the labour process – Friedman, Edwards, Burawoy and Gorz – start with similar reminders of aspects of the original approach, although, as we shall see, modifications are proposed in some instances.

There are three aspects that Braverman chooses to emphasise. First, the necessity for capital to realise the potential of purchased labour power by transforming it into labour under its own control, thereby creating the basis for alienation. Second, that the origins of management lay in the struggle to devise the most effective means of imposing employers' will within a new social relations of production different in kind and scope to what had existed before. Third, that a division of labour based on a systematic subdivision of work, rather than simple distribution of crafts, is generalised only within the capitalist mode of production. The separation of work into constituent elements reflects the necessary principle for capital of dividing the craft to cheapen the parts, providing the basis for the subsequent destruction of all-round skills.

Unlike others, Braverman does not seek to alter Marx, and the concepts of deskilling and managerial control are to be found in the original framework. In what sense, then, is Braverman distinctive? Essentially it derives from a successful attempt to *renew* Marx's theory of the labour process and apply it to subsequent historical development, taking a fresh look at skills, technology and work organisation. By doing so, he outlines the greater possibilities for widespread deskilling through the use of new forms of technology and science in the service of capital. In addition there is considerably more scope for tighter managerial control, a process that Braverman argues comes to be located around Taylorism.

Taylorism and control

In retracing the origins of management and hierarchy in work to the combined need for accumulation and control, rather than the imperatives of technology and efficiency, Braverman shares a similar perspective with two other studies often linked to his own (Stone, 1973; Marglin, 1976). For aside from providing more detailed historical evidence on this score, particularly in Marglin, a further emphasis is added: that is, the centrality of the struggle to wrest control of the workplace from skilled craft workers. As we have seen, this degree of control was based on both the existence of craft skills and on methods of work organisation, notably the sub-contracting and 'putting-out' systems.

Whereas Marglin's evidence is largely contemporary to Marx, Stone provides a case study dealing with the steel industry at the turn of the century. She charts how the demands of competition forced employers to try to end the sub-contracting system. Under this arrangement craft workers organised production and even hired their own manual help out of the payments for the amount of tonnage made by employers. To break the 'equal partnership of capital and labour' and introduce labour-saving machinery, it was necessary for employers to make combined use of mechanisation, reorganisation of work that removed planning from the shop floor, and individualistic wage systems. In this battle steel employers increasingly had access to Taylor's emergent theory and practice of scientific management, which was developed within the industry itself.

This is the emphasis taken up and made distinctive by Braverman. He was not the first to note the logical sequence of events that led to Taylorism, as Landes says: 'seen from the hindsight of the mid-twentieth century, scientific management was the natural sequel to the process of mechanisation that constituted the heart of the industrial revolution' (quoted in Kumar, 1978, p. 176). But Braverman showed that as a synthesis of disconnected ideas and experiments concerning the organisation of work, Taylorism was able to 'render conscious and systematic the formerly unconscious tendency of capitalist production' (1974, p. 121) with respect to the control and uses of skill and knowledge.

Hence it is not merely *one* managerial method, nor a *general* science of work, but an essential and defining feature of the capitalist labour process. Taylorism was an explicit recognition that the general managerial setting of tasks, order and discipline was insufficient, even within the factory despotism identified by Marx. Neither was machinery alone a reliable means of control of labour. Braverman argues that as long before this as Babbage's principle of dividing the craft to cheapen the parts, capital had been groping towards a theory and practice of management. By systematically combining together previous insights, Taylorism provided methods of control that could be applied at any given level of technology.

Scientific management was not just a framework of ideas. It was a set of tried and tested practices. As a gang boss in a steel mill, Taylor spent many years perfecting his methods of work organisation in a struggle against what he freely admitted to be perfectly rational means of collective workers' organisation for restriction of output and control of earnings. His battle against 'systematic soldiering' was written up in great detail and reproduced by Braverman, so as to give clear expression to the ideas. Out of his experiences, Taylor developed a series of principles, summed up by Braverman:

> Thus, if the first principle is the gathering together and development of knowledge of the labour process, and the second is the concentration of this knowledge as the exclusive preserve of management – together with its converse, the absence of such knowledge among workers – then the third step is the use of this monopoly of knowledge to control each step of the labour process and its mode of execution. (Braverman, 1974, p. 119)

This summary is not an unwarranted and excessive interpretation. Taylor was quite explicit that because the managers' and foremen's knowledge of the work 'falls far short of the combined knowledge of all the workmen under them' (quoted in Braverman, 1974, p. 101), maximum efficiency and profitability could never be achieved. Therefore management needed to gather together the knowledge possessed by workers and reduce it to their own rules and laws. Furthermore, 'all possible brain work should be removed from the shop and centred in the planning or lay-out department' (quoted in Braverman, 1974, p. 113). Once this had been done management could specify tasks in advance and determine *exactly* how and for how long they should be carried out.

The resultant deskilling could be as effective as through any mechanical means, although it is a by-product, not the purpose of the exercise. This rendering of the labour process independent of craft knowledge was previously noted by the German Marxist, Sohn-Rethel. He argued that Taylorism was a qualitative change in capitalist production, the distinctive feature of which is 'aimed at establishing a novel and clearcut division of mental and manual labour throughout the workshops' (1976, p. 35). But Braverman characterises this more accurately as a separation of *conception* and *execution*, and he goes on to show that further to the separation of mental and manual labour, the tendency is for the former to be sub-divided according to the same rule. Sohn-Rethel also raised the key role of payment structures in Taylor's system, a point recognised by Braverman, but perhaps not given enough weight. As part of work reorganisation, jobs were increasingly tied to individual incentive schemes. Taylor's dream of having a different rate for every worker, so as to eliminate any community of interest, was never a feasible possibility. But aside from emphasising the inseparability of payment systems and labour processes, it did point the way towards attempts to make higher wages compatible with high profits. This idea was taken up by Henry Ford with his 'five dollar day' and by other manufacturers and economists in the aftermath of Keynesianism.

In presenting the above features of Taylorism as necessary components of the capitalist labour process, Braverman is partly accepting Taylor's own definition of his methods as opening up the solution to finding the 'one best way' of organising work. He is thoroughly dismissive of the dominant strands of social science that believe Taylorism to have been superseded by humanistic forms of management. His case does not rest merely on the grounds that these forms are the 'maintenance crew for the human machinery' (p. 87), leaving the Taylorist world of production untouched. The power of the analysis lies in the evidence provided that varied types of scientific management have been *extended* to wider areas of occupational structure.

After proof that Taylorism could be extended from simple to complex production processes (Braverman, 1974, pp. 110-12), the most notable example has been its use in the transformation of clerical labour. The concepts of control flowing from scientific management, allied to complexities of scale, required an expansion of administrative and office tasks. This 'paper replication of production' in the office was first based on the mental labour stripped from manual work through Taylorism. But the monopoly over conception and planning did not survive the pressures to transform office work into an administrative labour process in its own right. Taylor himself had no doubt that the costs of production could be lowered by sub-dividing mental labour and subjecting it to control and measurement (Braverman, 1974, p. 127).

Previously, clerical labour had been a relatively small part of production expenses, largely self-supervising and concerned with 'whole tasks'. But as early as 1917 the application of scientific management began to lead to the 'breakdown of the arrangement under which each clerk did his or her own work according to traditional methods' (Braverman, 1974, p. 307). Under the control of office managers, all clerical work began to be investigated for the most effective means of standardisation and rationalisation. In addition, piece work and incentive schemes began to be introduced.

It must be stressed, however, that these measures were effected *prior* to the extensive *mechanisation* of office work. However, Braverman argues that it signalled that 'manual work spreads to the office and soon becomes characteristic of the tasks of the mass of clerical workers' (1975, p. 316).

Deskilling: science and technology in the service of capital

Despite the extensive, if uneven and varied, spread of scientific management, Braverman recognises that Taylorism alone was not a sufficient basis for the further transformation of the labour process by capital. Both as a system of control, and as a means of deskilling, it was subject to a number of constraints. Braverman points out that 'Taylorism raised a storm of opposition among the trade unions' (1974, p. 136), because of the realisation that it was an effort to relieve workers of their job autonomy and craft knowledge. But, as is consistent with the methodology of the book in omitting reference to organisation and struggles, workers' resistance is only briefly mentioned, and only then as an example of understanding the consequences of scientific management, rather than a substantial limit to its development.

Such constraints are seen more in terms of the inadequate scale of production for meeting the cost of 'rationalisation', and in the limited degree of scientific-technological advancement. It is to the latter that Braverman gives prominence, arguing that Tayorism began to coincide with a new scientific technical revolution. He restates Marx's view of science following labour into becoming an object of capital, thus restoring, along with other studies like Gorz (1976a), a critical analysis of the forces of production. But both these writers go further by giving considerable historical evidence of twentieth-century research and technical innovation aimed at reducing production costs.

New techniques and machinery are able to increase productivity rapidly through greater intensity of work, recalling Marx's own account of the development of new forms of surplus under the impact of large-scale industry (Palloix, 1976). Yet these elaborations of Marx's concepts are an unacknowledged comment on the limits of the original writings. For although Marx showed how science and technology aided mechanisation which strengthened the subordination of labour and deskilling, retrospectively it can be seen to be a clearly incomplete process. In comparison large companies, allied to state intervention, particularly in the post-war period, were able to hasten the planned use of research in technology and product design. These developments went beyond the former, largely spontaneous innovation evoked by the production processes.

The subsequently more intensive and sophisticated mechanisation brought about faster and more efficient machinery, which was incorporated 'within a management effort to dissolve the labour process as a process conducted by the worker and reconstitute as a process conducted by the management' (Braverman, 1974, p. 170). New forms of machinery offer capital the opportunity to extend by mechanical means what had previously been attempted by means of organization and discipline. Even in the sphere of scientific management, Taylor's followers and successors were able to improve methods of control through technical advance. Gilbreth, for example, added the concept of *motion* to time study, the chronocyclograph providing a visual record of body movements. These elementary movements, named *therbligs*, became standardised data that could replace direct observation, thus constituting a more efficient means of measurement and control.

As Gorz has noted, 'Science, then, has helped to turn work into a strait jacket' (1976c, p. 172). But is has also deepened the trend towards deskilling and task fragmentation, which is most commonly associated with the emergence of the assembly line. Indeed, for some writers, notably those influenced by Italian labour process theory, assembly production is *the* characteristic form of mechanisation. Palloix asserts that this development, labelled *Fordism*, innovated and extended Taylorism, the flow line principle allowing for greater mechanical control by management, while high day-wage rates regulated the supply and conditions of labour. The unskilled assembly worker is therefore seen as a central result of accelerated mechanisation.

Braverman recognises the innovative role of Fordism, but concentrates on the more general development and effects of mechanisation. One of his examples concerns machine tools and the introduction of numerical control systems. He shows how metal cutting has become virtually automatic. Numerical tapes control the movement of the tool, relieving the worker of the need to be in close control of the machine. Work tasks can be more easily fragmented between operators, who are required to know less; conceptual knowledge is placed in the hands of programmers. As computerised techniques become more complex, even the machine specifications for programming can be stored on the tapes, thus extending the deskilling process upwards.

Supportive evidence exists in the research of Noble (1979). Visits to twenty-four plants established that 'in nearly every case management had attempted to transfer skill from the shop floor to the programming office, to tighten up lines of authority, and to extend control over all aspects of production' (1979, p. 323). One of the interesting things he shows is that there were other ways of automating machine tools that retained operator skills and control, but he also shows that competitive pressures and deliberate managerial choice of the most effective means of control excluded this possibility. This strengthens Braverman's point that although conventional engineering approaches treat machinery as a technical given, different conceptions of machinery embody alternative designs and uses.

Once again Braverman establishes how mechanisation spreads to the office (1974, pp. 326–48). Computer systems developing from simple card punching, through data processing to the latest microchip technology for handling information, have been the basis for the transformation of white-collar labour. Although initially it had some craft characteristics, data processing was quickly adapted to a new, highly specialised and hierarchical division of labour: 'the concentration of knowledge and control in a very small portion of the hierarchy became the key here, as with automatic machines in the factory, to control over the process' (Braverman, 1974, p. 329). Braverman approvingly refers to managerial sources that suggest that the computer will be to administrative workers, even at lower and middle-management level, what the assembly line was to manual employees. Although Braverman's research was published before some of the more recent office technology was introduced, his preliminary examination of machinery such as word processors indicated a strengthening of existing trends.

Regardless of which aspects of mechanisation are stressed by the different theorists mentioned, the theme of generalised deskilling as a necessary feature of the capitalist labour process is a common feature. Gorz refers to the historical tendency towards the 'dequalification of the direct producers' (1976b, p. 57), while Palloix argues that the tendency towards equalisation of work is part of a double movement of capital (1976, p. 57). The analysis of this strand of labour process theory is therefore directly supportive of Marx's homogenisation thesis, whereby the development of capitalist production erodes the differences between types and categories of work.

Variations of conditions and time-scale within the deskilling process *are* recognised. Each of the theorists referred to is concerned to point to vital contradictory processes involved. At the start of a cycle of technical change and work restructuring there is often a partial inversion of the general tendency. Widespread deskilling is often accompanied by an increased 'qualification' of a smaller layer of workers involved in planning, programming and similar tasks. But the general tendency immediately tends to reassert itself as the enhanced skills are subjected to similar sub-specialisation and the embodiment of skills in more complex machinery. Braverman's evidence of the progressive deskilling of computer programmers is a major example of this type of development.

It is therefore believed that the allied tendencies towards deskilling and increased managerial control will persist *through* changes in technology and work organisation. Braverman argues strongly that the dominant sociological view of automation as qualitatively different from mechanisation is profoundly mistaken. There is a continuum between the two precisely because technological developments are incorporated into the same underlying methods of organising the labour process. He draws extensively on the detailed study of automation by James R. Bright of the Harvard Business School who said: 'I was startled to find that the upgrading effect had not occurred to anywhere near the extent to which it is often assumed. On the contrary, there was evidence that automation had reduced the skill requirements of the operating workforce' (quoted in Braverman, 1974, p. 220).

Even in those industries where operators have been eliminated from the physical process of production – such as chemicals – the supervision of machinery in more congenial surroundings has often been confused with actual increases in the uses of skills and knowledge. These misleading perceptions of early process automation in the work of Blauner (1964), Cotgrove (1972), Goldthorpe *et al.* (1968) and others, has been convincingly refuted by the 'ChemCo' case studies of Nichols and Beynon (1977). The work in control rooms *was* less arduous, but it could also be stressful, lonely and meaningless. In addition to the 'scientific work', there was also 'donkey work': 'For every man who watched dials another maintained the plants, another was a lorry driver and another two humped bags or shovelled muck' (Nichols and Beynon, 1977, p. 12).

Process operators *do* have to be alert, knowledgeable and capable of reacting intelligently to the control machinery, and the group task nature of the work has traditionally made it resistant to scientific management techniques. But the practical utilisation of high skill levels was often a characteristic of the *early* stages of automated process plant. Research shows that the emphasis on problem-solving and teamwork referred to by Blauner has declined as the reliability and sophistication of the plant increased (see Hill, 1981, pp. 97–8). In addition, the latest round of microprocessor technology is enabling management to expand the *self-acting* character of control systems, leading to deskilling of operatives and maintenance staff, although this results in a contradiction between excluding operators from the routine running of the plant and yet having to rely on them to deal with unusual events that go beyond the capability of the computer' (CSE Microelectronics Group, 1980, p. 79).

The Deskilling Debate

The issues of increased deskilling and managerial control have emerged as the two main areas of debate in labour process theory. Emphasis has been placed on the extent and nature of the trends, and their impact on the degradation of work. It is very difficult to separate the two questions. For example, Braverman has argued that the labour process has been affected by technical transformations and the reorganisation of work associated with scientific management. However, deskilling is not only a product of the incorporation of science and technology into capital, it is also interconnected with Taylorism.

As a strategy for managerial control, resting on the separation of conception and execution, skills are inevitably fragmented and routinised. Cooley comments: 'Seventy years of scientific management have seen the fragmentation of work grind through the spectrum of workshop activity engulfing even the most creative and satisfying jobs' (1981, p. 49). Nevertheless, the technical and control dimensions of Taylorism can be partially distinguished. Debates on the latter question have focused on Taylorism as one of the options for a capitalist *strategy* for organising workers and their work. This is distinct from the technical transformations affecting the use of skills and other aspects of the worker's capacity to labour. Retaining this distinction, this chapter will only discuss scientific management where it relates to the latter issue.

The focus of the rest of this chapter will be on the degree to which skills have been transformed and eroded through capitalist development, and the extent to which such changes can be described as a degradation of labour. An important weakness of the existing deskilling debate has been that research has centred on what has happened to craft work. Naturally this reflects the evidence deriving from our greater knowledge of the period from the turn of the century to the impact of mass production industries. Consequently the question of craft skill is examined first. The substantive theoretical issues are discussed primarily in relation to such evidence, despite more recent vital changes in labour and product markets, workers' organisation, and other factors. Our knowledge of how contemporary changes in work and technology are affecting skills and experiences is of course inevitably limited.

It is not only Braverman who argues that deskilling is an inherent tendency of the capitalist labour process. A number of recent studies have reinforced the concept, either at the level of general theory (Brighton Labour Process Group, 1977) or in detailed case studies (Zimbalist, 1979). The Zimbalist collection is directly supportive of Braverman's central thesis that deskilling is a long-run tendency: 'in an absolute sense (they lose craft and traditional abilities) and in a relative one (scientific knowledge progressively accumulates in the production process)' (Zimbalist, 1979, p. xv). It is noted that the tendency is constrained only by the uneven development between and within industries, or what Braverman refers to as 'the nature of the various specific and determinate processes of production' (1974, p. 172).

The Brighton study is more critical, noting the necessity to take into account the specific effects of different phases of accumulation, as well as worker resistance, in that they are mediating factors to changes in the labour process. Nevertheless, deskilling is taken to be one of three 'immanent laws of the capitalist labour process' (Brighton Labour Process Group, 1977, p. 16). Deskilling is said to be inherent in labour functions that are intended to achieve maximum possible speed, cheapness, replaceability, standardisation and calculability for the needs of capital. The authors are also quite clear about what deskilling involves, naming three aspects: the replacement of skilled workers by machines or machine operatives; the division and sub-division of jobs, with any remaining skill allocated to a few specialised workers; and the fragmentation of the remaining semi- or unskilled tasks. The latter is recognised as constituting only a tendency dependent on the particular division of labour and work organisation.

Yet the significance of the deskilling debate does not lie solely in the analysis of trends in the nature of work. Of equal importance are the potential consequences for class consciousness, action and organisation. Labour process theory is strongly connected to Marxism, and Marxism is ultimately a theory of social change, as well as of social structure. Although Marx did not systematically declare the relations between his analysis of changes in the labour process and class struggle, it was clearly implied that the trends towards homogenisation and degradation of labour were important aspects of class formation: objective preconditions for the transformation of society by the proletariat. Such themes have been taken up by contemporary Marxists: for example, Cooley (1981, p. 49) argues that technological proletarianisation will increase the likelihood of an alliance of scientific and technical workers with the working class and with progressive movements.

Taking these factors into account, critics have challenged the assumptions of leading writers such as Braverman both on the extent *and* the consequences of deskilling (see Wood, 1982, for the most comprehensive assessment and reference to other commentaries). However, there are two major problems in embarking on an examination of this debate. First, the connection between changes in the labour process and their consequences for class formation and action are not always spelt out. We have already noted that Braverman deliberately excludes the component of working-class organisation and subjectivity.

The problem is further compounded by a lack of explicit theoretical consideration of concepts like homogenisation, although Braverman makes general reference to 'The giant mass of workers who are relatively homogeneous as to lack of developed skill, low pay, and interchangeability of person and function' (1974, p. 359). Ironically, the only direct comment on issues concerning the consequences of labour-process changes for class struggle is in a short commentary that Braverman made in relation to some of his early critics. Here he recognises that the value of such analysis 'can only lie in precisely how well it helps us to answer questions about class consciousness' (1976, p. 122). Unfortunately, aside from a widely noted assertion of the revolutionary potential of the working class, the point is taken no further.

Second, it is not always clear what changes in skill are being measured against. Systematic definitions of skill are surprisingly hard to come by in the literature on deskilling. We have already seen how the Brighton study gave a detailed definition of the latter phenomenon, but nothing as exact on skill was forthcoming. Despite a chapter entitled 'A Final Note on Skill', Braverman avoids a positive definition. As Putnam (1978) points out, skill tends to be defined negatively and by implication, as part of Braverman's case against the sociological 'upgrading thesis'. This critique centres upon an attack on misleading statistics, training times and a confusion between skill and *dexterity*.

However, the general picture built up in the assessment of changes in the labour process is that skill is largely based on knowledge, the unity of conception and execution, and the exercise of control by the workforce. This ties in with one of the few attempts to define skill closely, as 'knowledgeable practice' within 'elements of control' (Council for Science and Society, 1981, p. 23). But in most cases skill is measured less by a formal definition than by historical context and comparison. The central starting point of many studies has therefore been the nature and transformation of *craft* labour.

Craft: Destruction and Resistance

As Rubery (1980, p. 256) notes, 'The decline in skills in Braverman is essentially viewed from a craft perspective: before the advent of mechanisation and scientific management, craft workers could control the work process, for knowledge of it was stored in the craftsmen themselves.' This is not an idiosyncrasy of that author.

A powerful set of writings has been developed which uses the craft experience to understand major changes in the capitalist labour process.

The perspective

The central theme is that general skills are reduced to job-specific ones, largely as a result of mechanisation. The skills and knowledge of craft workers were crucial to production, but over the first quarter of the twentieth century jobs were broken down, allowing companies frequently to dispense with skilled labour.

Historians such as Montgomery (1976, 1979), Hinton (1973) and Stone (1973) stress the essential role of *control* as the basis for the exercise of craft skill. According to Montgomery, industrial craftsmen such as iron and steel workers and miners were able to use this control to regulate the hours, pace and elements of the price of their labour. Much of this power and control was of course related to the subcontracting arrangements, in sectors like mining and manufacturing (Dix, 1979).

Writers like Montgomery and Hinton go further than Braverman by emphasising the *political* importance of craftsmen's organisation in attempts to extend job control into wider movements for workers' control of production. It was politically important, too, in another sense. The battle over craft skills was part of a general struggle by employers in this period to *rationalise* production throughout the USA and Europe. With the gradual destruction of the old labour system, mechanisation in the context of the emergence of the large factory became the framework for decisive changes in work organisation, technology and payment systems.

The stress on the craft period and the erosion of skills by mechanisation and later by scientific management implicitly identifies it with the transition from formal to real subordination of labour (Coombs, 1978). The trend is extended beyond the period described by Marx, and the transition is theorised *as* deskilling by Braverman, Brighton LPG and others, as Cressey and MacInnes (1980) note in their critique of the concepts. Marx's stress on real subordination resulting in the creation of labour as 'living appendages' of machinery is filled out by reference to technical and organisational changes Marx could not have wholly foreseen.

One such development was the assembly line. Gartman's (1979) study of the introduction of assembly work at Ford indicates that shortage of skilled labour and the indispensability of those skills gave a high degree of control to sections of the workforce. But assembly allowed the progressive dividing of labour, the all-round mechanic giving way to specialised operatives. The elimination of skilled workers was also made possible by the emergence of precisely machined and interchangeable parts. In a clear evocation of the idea of real subordination, Gartman comments that 'Ford's mass production methods rendered workers largely powerless and hence gave capital a free hand to step up exploitation' (1979, p. 200).

The other significant development was the fragmentation of even job-specific skills through work reorganisation on Taylorist lines. For example, in the jewellery industry in more recent times, semi-skilled workers who had traditionally done assembly and soldering tasks were confronted with the 'set-up' for the work based on an externally designed process on pre-cut, heat-resistant boards, stamped with the design impressions of the jewellery style (Shapiro-Perl, 1979, pp. 282–3).

It must be said, however, that many writers have been careful to stress the long and uneven process involved in deskilling. Crafts like carpentry and printing have undergone waves of deskilling in the past century, related largely to technical innovation. In the late nineteenth century, machine wood-working technology slowly developed into a strong challenge to the carpenters' craft position (Reckman, 1979). Not only could 'green labour' be introduced to perform task-specific jobs, but changes in the labour process allowed capital to launch an attack on the weakened craft unions. In many cases they were forced to sign working agreements which gave employers unrestricted use of tools, machinery and labour. Nevertheless, skills survived in modified form. Similarly in the printing industry, significant levels of operator skill were retained through a number of technical changes – including the teletypesetter – which allowed newspapers to receive news stories in the form of already perforated tape.

More recent changes in such industries have often provided a more profound challenge to traditional skills. Zimbalist notes that: 'When the computer made its debut in the newspaper composing room in 1962, the eventual extinction of all craft vestiges became a certainty' (1979, p. 108). In carpentry, factory production of house parts (doors, windows, etc.) has been the main source of the challenge, rather than new tools and machinery used by carpenters themselves. Craft-designated work remains, but largely as a result of 'the evolution of a maze of archaic work rules specifying trade jurisdiction, responsibilities and prerogatives' (Reckman, 1979, p. 93).

The craft perspective does not only utilise industrial examples. As in the case of Braverman, the notion of all-round skill and knowledge is often extended to white-collar work. Reid (1978) notes that older clerks working in local government experienced a 'loss of craft' associated with computer-related fragmentation; and similar observations are made by Crompton and Reid (1982) and Glenn and Feldberg (1979). Nevertheless, even allowing for modifications to the general craft perspective, it is still one that is rejected by other theorists as an inadequate means of understanding changes in skills and working patterns.

The critique

Even critics of the above perspectives agree that there *were* varied modes of deskilling from the later period of the nineteenth century. Littler (1978) shows how the decline of the internal sub-contract system led eventually to the introduction of supervisory labour, whereby 'feed and speed' inspectors, quality control and rate fixers fragmented craft control and the traditional foreman's role. However, Littler, like other commentators, argues that Braverman's analysis is permeated by idealised conceptions of the traditional craft workers.

This constitutes one of the two major strands of the critique of Braverman and the deskilling concept, and it has a number of different components. At its simplest level this involves a challenge to the significance given to skilled work of a craft nature. A large proportion of the industrial population was, and is, in non-factory, manual occupations like transport and mining. Although they had a specific type of skill and control of their own, it could not be compared with factory work concerned with discrete operations on separate machines (More, 1982). Even within the manufacturing sector the craft ideal obscures the fact that it was embodied in only a small minority of the working class (Putnam, 1978). This 'romance' is further challenged by Cutler (1978) on the grounds that it was an idealisation of the range of meaningful mental and manual capabilities exercised in the productive process.

This latter point has been consistently raised in more conventional empirical accounts of the period. More argues that it is possible to overestimate the actual degree of craft or skill, rather than dexterity, of such workers. Such arguments overlap with sociological accounts of the social construction of skills as occupational strategies to control recruitment and rewards. The designation of craft work is seen as little more than a restrictive device (Flanders, 1964; Turner, 1962). Hence job control can be confused with genuine exercise of control over the labour process. This distinction allows Monds (1976) to make a very negative assessment of the craft tradition, arguing that, even before Taylorism, craft control had been destroyed by new technologies and anti-union offensives.

These views simply do not square with the substantial amount of evidence already examined indicating the genuine levels of skill, knowledge and control exercised by craft workers. Yet the criticisms do raise a very important point.By elevating craft workers to such importance, there is a danger that an analysis is constructed which unduly *separates* them from *non-craft* workers, many of whom were subject to similar pressures from capital concerning their skills, rewards and working conditions. For example, economic pressures built up in the late 1920s and early 1930s impelling employers to take a greater interest in neo-Taylorite and other rationalisation schemes. But by the time they were implemented, many of the industries had either already shifted to non-craft work, such as in metalworking, or, in the case of sectors like food, drink and tobacco, had been *set up* on the basis of semi- and unskilled labour (Littler, 1982, p. 141).

Furthermore, outside the manufacturing sector work could not involve the same degree of specialisation, and 'involved a considerable degree of control over the process' (More, 1978, p. 4). Work traditionally defined as semi-skilled, such as dockwork, could embody high work satisfaction related to the variety of tasks and problems requiring use of experience and knowledge (Mills, 1979). Factories themselves still often depended on a variety of machines and operations, limiting the degree of specialisation for semi-skilled workers. The gradual development of new forms of work organisation and technology increasingly put non-craft workers under the threat of fragmentation and deskilling. Yet these trends are relatively unrecognised within a craft perspective. This threat did not always become actuality. Paradoxically, in idealising craft work, it is possible to overestimate its destruction.

There were a number of mechanisms that counteracted deskilling, and these mechanisms have acted as the focus for the second strand of criticism of the perspectives associated with Braverman. The main theme of these criticisms is the effect of *worker resistance* on the deskilling process. It is not just a question of Braverman and the others omitting reference to industrial struggles. It is wrong to study craft skills without examining the role of craft *organisation* in mediating the relations between technological development and skill in the labour process.

These are not just general points of criticism. Studies indicate a considerable amount of craft resistance to mechanisation in industries such as building, engineering and textiles (Friedman, 1977; Penn, 1978; Lee, 1980). Such resistance could be quite successful in retaining levels of skill and rewards, with the key role being played by mechanisms of *social exclusion*. Penn shows how spinning and engineering workers were able to maintain structural support for their skills by retaining social control over the utilisation of machinery, and by a double means of exclusion: first, of management from complete control of the work process; and second of other non-craft workers who offered a threat to their position (Penn, 1978, pp. 4–5).

Worker resistance can also have wider consequences. For example, attempts by skilled workers to control the supply of labour at the level of the firm and of society (and thus resist dilution by semi-skilled workers, women entering the labour force, etc.) can create *segmentation* in the *labour market*. This segmentation may help workers to retain skills, as it reduces employers' freedom to interchange the workforce. Furthermore, the question of the effects of the labour market is an independently important aspect of the study of skills and the labour process. The labour market often mediates the pace and extent of changes in work organisation and skill, and its fluctuating requirements can aid workers' tactics of exclusion. The result is the survival of a higher number of craft jobs than the deskilling thesis would appear to indicate. Such markets are themselves reflections of wider local and national economic contexts. A notable example was the situation in Coventry and the Midlands during and after the Second World War. Rearmament programmes and general economic expansion sustained a tight labour market in an area with one of the highest densities of skilled engineering workers in the world. This situation enabled workers to impose the Coventry Toolroom Agreement on the engineering employers, which was to guarantee high earnings and the protection of skilled status until the beginning of the 1970s.

A craft perspective is *not* incompatible with a recognition of worker resistance. Montgomery (1979) shows how workers used both technical knowledge and a code of moral collectivity often embodied in the work rules of unions to enable the continuation of resistance even through difficult periods of mechanisation. Yet the point remains that emphasis on skilled workers too often identifies them as the focal point of changes in the labour process. This takes us back to the theme of worker resistance, for such struggles were not the sole province of those workers. As Friedman (1978, p. 11) argues, it is an error to suggest that the material basis for worker resistance disappears following the spread of modern industry and its consequent partial erosion of skills. In fact the new situation can create the material conditions for successful and organised resistance by the semi- and even unskilled. As the increasing number of semi-skilled workers became proficient in the use of machinery, employers found it more difficult to replace them, and suffered heavy losess if equipment stood idle (Hinton, 1971). Moreover, as both Friedman (1977) and Nichols and Beynon (1977) show, the distinguishing characteristic of class struggle in the twentieth century has been the use of the collective strength of non-craft workers to oppose capital. While this has been largely unconnected with 'skills', it has involved a more extensive use of tactics connected with machine utilisation.

The labour market could also be used advantageously by non-skilled workers. When there was still relatively full employment in the early 1970s, workers in the motor and other industries used their own mobility from job to job as a means of pushing general wage rates up. Labour turnover at plants like Ford's Dagenham was extremely high, although this situation has obviously changed in the new economic context.

What are some of the points of theoretical significance raised by the critique of craft deskilling? For some critics the inadequate understanding of the role of worker resistance in the labour process can be located in the nature or use of the underlying concept of real subordination of labour. Friedman (1978) argues that the successful retention of aspects of skills and control by workers throws into doubt the significance attached to the distinction between formal and real subordination. Cressey and MacInnes (1980), too, would rather discard this usage, and seek to avoid analysing the struggle between capital and labour within what they refer to as an ahistorical formalism that cannot deal with the complex relations of control and skill.

For others, the variation of trends within the workplace bring into question the concept of homogenisation of labour. *Before* the major deskilling offensives, skilled workers were not a homogeneous group, and their position afterwards with reference to the preservation of skills was often a function of relative strengths *prior* to the development of mechanised factory production (Penn, 1978, p. 27). But the argument that it is necessary to look at more *specific* situations doesn't satisfactorily resolve these and other major issues raised in the debate. That requires further examination of a number of key points in more general terms.

The Theoretical Issues

There were a number of apparently contradictory emphases in the previous discussion concerning the relationships between labour markets, workplace organisation and the construction and retention of skills. The aim of this section is to discuss whether it is possible to incorporate critical insights within a labour process perspective.

Labour markets and capitalist development
Labour market theories have developed as means of explaining the persistence of segmented and hierarchical structures of allocation and pricing of jobs in the economy as a whole and within particular firms. Some writers emphasise the impact of technological and industrial change in creating a *dual labour market* (Doeringer and Piore, 1971). The key element of this is the emergence of firm-specific skills that encourage employers to develop wage, employment and promotion policies that will develop a stable labour force. An *internal* labour market will thus be dominant over external market pressures. More radical versions emphasise the advantage to employers of the use of segmented labour markets as a means of dividing and controlling a labour force increasingly homogeneous in composition (Gordon, 1972). There is common ground in the assertion that segmentation creates a number of distinct sectors, usually distinguished by some variety of the terms primary and secondary. The former is the dynamic and technologically changing sector, where skills, crafts and professional work are concentrated. The latter is said to be largely stagnant technologically, flexible to demands outside the framework of the major markets, and requiring and using labour that is undifferentiated, low-skilled and irregular in commitment and access to work, for example immigrant and female labour (see Rubery, 1980, for a full discussion).

Such research therefore has direct relevance to the sphere of skills and work: as Lee puts it, 'the production process is overlain by the market process' (1980, p. 60). In practice, he argues, the labour market operates as a series of social filters between skill and the wider economy and class structure. An examination of the workings of labour markets can provide an important source of modifications of labour process theory. The most important point raised by both Lee and Rubery is the absence of a theory of wage and price determination in studies like Braverman's. The assumption of an immanent tendency towards deskilling relies heavily on the views held by Babbage and Marx that dividing the craft cheapens the parts. But this assumes too readily that 'the effect of price competition in employers will always be the same' (Lee, 1980, p. 74). In practice, market factors can alter the pace of technical innovation and affect the bargaining position of workers, and therefore their ability to retain skills.

However, there is a difference between establishing the importance of these factors and mapping out the exact relationships between the labour market and the labour process. There are problems here that can be illustrated by looking at the analysis of Lee, who has made one of the most detailed attempts to explain the interrelationships. Priority is given to examining *systematic* (external) shifts in the size and nature of labour markets. There are said to be two forms of external shift, *industrial*, which pertains to factors like new products and processes, and *cyclical*, which refers to the overall fluctuations in economic activity. A third shift is internal to the workplace and is described as *occupational*. These correspond to the kinds of changes dealt with by Braverman. What is significant about Lee's argument is that external shifts are explicitly given more weight and counterposed to direct deskilling in the labour process itself.

Using official employment statistics and reference to a number of industrial studies, Lee asserts that the percentage of skilled operatives in traditional areas of craft work (engineering, shipbuilding, construction, printing) remains high. This is put down to the operation of industrial and cyclical shifts. While both processes have produced a certain amount of deskilling, this is said to have seldom been the product of change within an industry, but rather the result of new products in new industries that are based on an expanded use of semi-skilled labour. However, this trend is counterbalanced by the creation of new areas of skilled work, often using workers displaced from previous craft jobs, and by the survival of 'marginal' sectors using traditional methods.

While the distinction between deskilled *jobs* and deskilled *workers* is a useful one. Lee does not explain the *relationships* between the labour market and labour process, but merely asserts the domination of one over the other. There is no attempt to examine changes in the nature of work in the occupations discussed, and the study is almost wholly reliant on quantitative and official statistics. The 'skills' represented in such sources inevitably tend to reflect existing *bargaining* frameworks rather than accurate assessments of the level of skill. The growth of new industries, technologies and products does of course create new skills. But Lee does not ask whether the examples he gives – for instance electricians – are subject to the same long-term process of deskilling that have affected the older crafts. Evidence we shall examine later indicates that 'crafts' allied to the new electronic technologies *have* been deskilled, in the case of some electricians by the incorporation of diagnostic skills within the means of testing and repairing machinery.

A serious attempt to link the labour and market processes must give greater emphasis to changes at the point of production. There is evidence that the structures of the labour market may be a partial reflection of what is happening to the nature of work. The erosion of skills has gradually weakened the bargaining position of many skilled workers. Thus workers will act to maintain their position against threats of substitution and competition, and in this battle 'their most effective tactic is to differentiate themselves from potential competitors' (Rubery, 1980, p. 260). This necessitates attempts to control aspects of both the external and internal labour markets, including control of apprenticeships, promotions by seniority, restrictive practices and demarcation, with redundancy agreements working on the basis of 'last in, first out'. These practices are very likely to be harmful to the interests of sections with less of a stable foothold in the labour market, such as women workers.

Far from 'occupational shifts' having little relevance to deskilling, workers' attempts to control and shape labour markets are aimed to *compensate* for loss of skills and bargaining power, and this indicates 'workers' success in regaining some of the control lost through the destruction of the craft system' (Rubery, 1980, p. 259). This suggests that particular attention should be paid to *internal* markets. Such a focus does not leave the deskilling thesis unscathed, as it brings into question once more the concept of homogenisation.

Deskilling does not necessarily lead to undifferentiated work, as the labour process can be reconstituted as a new organisation of production dominated by internal labour markets. As Burawoy perceptively points out, *despite* the separation of conception and execution, the expropriation of skill and the narrowing of discretion, studies like Braverman's have 'missed the equally important parallel tendency toward the expansion of choices within narrower limits' (1979, p. 94). The growth of internal labour markets can therefore act as a counterweight to skill degradation, and this opens up the whole area of the subjective components of deskilling. This is an issue to which we shall return later.

The other area that the study of labour markets rather inadequately directs our attention to is the economic and class relations within which changes in the labour process need to be situated. Too much emphasis in labour process theory has been placed on a generic impulse to deskill, without connecting it to specific economic circumstances. It is true that Braverman does refer to the crucial emergence of 'monopoly capitalism'. But this was a decidedly sketchy framework that was better at analysing the changes in the *structure* of monopoly forms and their labour processes than dealing with the problems and contradictions that capital faces in seeking to 'constantly revolutionise' the system of production. As Elger notes, 'Braverman tends to assume a general congruence between strategies of valorisation and accumulation and deskilling, in which the former is directly lodged within the latter' (1979, p. 83). Yet this may not be the case. For example, mechanisation has to be financed, and this has to be situated within cycles of fixed capital renewal (Coombs, 1978).

But like other critics, Elger and Coombs do little more than indicate the *need* for an analysis of the labour process that would locate transformations in relation to phases of valorisation and accumulation and their contradictions. A more concrete analysis would have to explain the variety of national and international factors influencing workplace changes. We can return to the example used earlier of skilled engineering workers in the Coventry area. In 1971 the Coventry Employers' Association informed the unions that it was attempting unilaterally to abolish the district 'toolroom' rate, signalling a serious attack on pay, shopfloor practices and skilled status.

This was not just a matter of normal worker–employer conflicts; it reflected rapid changes in the ownership and control of the machine-tool industry in the mid-1960s. Several conglomerates moved in and bought up small and medium-sized companies, and the existing larger machine-tool firms attempted expansion and vertical integration with firms producing components and raw materials (see Coventry Machine Tool Workers' Committee, 1979). The state played a significant role through the Department of Trade and Industry and the Industrial Reorganisation Corporation in encouraging rationalisation in order to strengthen the competitive position of British manufacturers in the face of sharp international pressures. In the 1970s international competition further tightened the screw and gave companies a choice: automate or decline further. Subsequent restructuring inevitably had important effects on skills and the labour process in the industry.

This example highlights the role played by *product markets*. In this context, Kelly (1982) shows how the massive growth of the consumer goods sector in the post-war period inevitably put a strain on their assembly-line methods geared to long runs on single products. Firms responded in a variety of ways, through built-in obsolescence, factory or section specialisation, and, most significantly for our purposes, attempts to reorganise the labour process itself: hence the experiments undertaken in job enrichment and enlargement such as at Volvo in an effort to create production flexibility.

Pressure from product and labour markets, plus exhaustion of the possibilities contained in the 'Fordist' model of work intensification, therefore *lead* in a number of directions. Aside from the programmes of work humanisation, other important trends include the moves to decentralise production to smaller units and even to outwork in Italy, and the 'export' of Fordism and other methods of advanced capitalist production to parts of the Second and Third Worlds. This search for cheap and docile labour zones has taken place in Eastern Europe, as well as in countries such as Brazil, South Korea and Turkey (Lipietz, 1982). International developments of this kind have acted to strengthen previous trends towards *runaway shops*, where multinationals transfer production to 'underdeveloped' regions. We therefore have to recognise that labour processes are shaped by the contradictory, rather than unilinear, development of capitalist production.

Worker resistance, skill and job control
There is no doubt that there are *cycles* of deskilling and resistance, and that Lee is right in saying that 'the skilled trades have been declared dead at the hands of mechanisation and deskilling many times, but the defence of craft identity and difference lives on' (1978, p. 3). One manifestation is the consistent practice of 'clawing back' concessions to management on questions of skill and control. Craft control can be re-established at plant level, as engineers did in the early part of this century, using tactics like demarcation disputes (Penn, 1978, p. 12). Recognition of these processes does cast doubt on the viability of Braverman's objectivist methods. The result is that Braverman is surprisingly deterministic concerning the shaping of work by technological change (Mackenzie, 1977), and overreliant on managerially derived evidence concerning skills and control (Elger, 1979, p. 64). This creates the paradoxical situation that while the book clearly recognises the role of class struggle in creating workplace antagonism connected to the degradation of labour (Zimbalist, 1979, p. xii), it ignores its role in the consequent evolution of the labour process.

It is interesting to note that defenders of Braverman, e.g. Zimbalist, rather than make an extensive defence of his methods, tend to argue the long-term ineffectiveness of worker resistance as it has existed. Zimbalist uses his own case study of the printing industry and the inability of craft unionism to reshape or even halt technological development as proof of this point (1979, p. 125). It is important to make a distinction between resistance that is often informal and unorganised, and a conscious and collective struggle. However, either dimension can modify the course of development of the labour process. But the more important question is, does worker resistance actually retain skills? We have already seen the considerable evidence concerning the social construction of skills for bargaining purposes. Lee dismisses this argument. Union power to enforce skills would not work unless it was based on what he calls 'real technical use-values' of skills. Mechanisms of exclusion and construction so as to control entry and regulate the supply of craft labour are independent phenomena in themselves, rather than a means of compensating for deskilling. Unfortunately, talk of 'real skills' was once again largely unsupported by qualitative evidence on the occupations concerned.

The essential confusion is between the ability of workers to retain skills and *job control*. There is considerable evidence that workers can exercise the power to determine elements of working conditions and rewards, *after* deskilling has taken place (Elger, 1979, pp. 74–7; Rubery, 1980, pp. 262, 264). In his case study of electrical workers, Brecher shows how, in the wake of mechanisation and subdivision, the establishment of industrial unionism in the 1930s involved the creation of a substantial amount of direct control over the work process through the grievance procedure, steward system and regulation of production (1979, p. 213). In fact deskilling can sometimes *confer* bargaining power in circumstances where mechanisation replaces craft labour with semi-skilled workers who have been previously unskilled. This enabled such workers to exercise some control over output and in general to extend workplace organisation (Rubery, 1980, pp. 256–63). Once established, it is possible for machine operatives to use that strength, leading Nichols and Beynon to note correctly that: 'Skill is not essential to control' (1977, pp. 108).

What *are* often retained are specific dexterities, which still involve levels of training, if for no other reason than they are the 'tricks of the trade'. Forms of expertise may be narrower than traditional skills, but they can still 'constitute effective obstacles to capitalist initiative' (Elger, 1979, p. 76). Once again, therefore, the struggle in the labour process persists through craft deskilling, and it is unnecessary to deny the importance of the erosion to acknowledge that worker resistance reconstitutes the struggle at a different level. Where does this leave the concept of real subordination of labour?

The lesson is that no amount of deskilling or mechanisation can lead to the *complete* domination of capital over labour. There is always a danger of conceiving of real subordination as a finished and self-contained process. This is particularly the case when allied to major changes in the organisation of production such as the assembly line. Real subordination is best thought of as a *tendency*, and as a *precondition* for a more direct control of labour given by the use of developments in the productive forces (Friedman, 1978, p. 13).

References

Amsden, A. (ed.) (1980) *The Economics of Women and Work*, Harmondsworth, Penguin.

Blauner, R. (1964) *Alienation and Freedom*, Chicago University Press.

Braverman, H. (1974) *Labor and Monopoly Capital: the Degradation of Work in the Twentieth Century*, London, Monthly Review Press.

(1976) 'Two Comments', *Monthly Review*, vol. 28, no. 3.

Brecher, J. (1979) 'The Roots of Power: Employers and Workers in the Electrical Products Industry', in Zimbalist, A. (ed.).

Brighton Labour Process Group (1977) 'The Capitalist Labour Process', *Capital and Class*, no. 1.

Burawoy, M. (1979) *Manufacturing Concent: Changes in the Labour Process under Monopoly Capitalism*, University of Chicago Press.

Conference of Socialist Economists (eds) (1976) *The Labour Process and Class Strategies*, London, Stage One.

Cooley, M. (1981) 'The Taylorisation of Intellectual Work', in Levidow, L. and Young, B. (eds),

Coombs, R. (1978) 'Labour and Monopoly Capital', *New Left Review*, no. 107.

Cotgrove, S. (1972) 'Alienation and Automation', *British Journal of Sociology*, December 1972.

Council for Science and Society (1981) *New Technology: Society, Employment and Skill*, pamphlet, London CSS.

Coventry Machine Tool Workers' Committee (1979) *Crisis in Engineering: Machine Tool Workers Fight for Jobs*, pamphlet jointly with Institute for Workers' Control.

Cressey, P. and MacInnes, J. (1980) 'Industrial Democracy and the Control of Labour', *Capital and Class*, no. 11.

Crompton, R. and Reid, S. (1982) 'The De-Skilling of Clerical Work', in Wood, S. (ed.).

Crouch, C. and Pizzorno, A. (eds) (1978) *The Resurgence of Class Conflicts in Western Europe*, two vols. London, Macmillan.

CSE Microelectronics Group (1980) *Microelectronics: Capitalist Technology and the Working Class*, London, CSE Books.

Cutler, A. (1978) 'The Romance of Labour', *Economy and Society*, vol. 7, no. 1.

Dix, K. (1979) 'Work Relations in the Coal Industry: The Handloading Era, 1880–1930', in Zimbalist, A. (ed.).

Doerringer, P.B. and Piore, M. J. (1971) *Internal Labour Markets and Manpower Analysis*, Lexington, Mass., D.C. Heath.
Donovan Report (1968) *Royal Commission on Trade Unions and Employers' Associations*, 1965–8, London, HMSO.
Elger, T. (1979), 'Valorisation and De-skilling: a Critique of Braverman', *Capital and Class*, no. 7.
Flanders, A. (1964). *The Fawley Productivity Agreements*, London, Faber.
Friedman, A. (1977) *Industry and Labour: Class Struggle at Work and Monopoly Capitalism*, London, Macmillan.
  (1978) 'Worker Resistance and Marxian Analysis of the Labour Process', Nuffield paper.
Gartman, D. (1979) 'Origins of the Assembly Line and Capitalist Control of Work at Ford', in Zimbalist, A. (ed.).
Glenn, E. K. and Feldberg, R.L. (1979) 'Proletarianising Office Work', in Zimablist, A. (ed.).
Goldthorpe, J.H., et al (1968), '*The Affluent Worker: Industrial Attitudes and Behaviour*, Cambridge University Press.
Gordon, D.M. (1972) *Theories of Poverty and Underdevelopment*, Lexington, Mass., D.C. Heath.
Gorz, A. (ed.) (1976a) *The Division of Labour: the Labour Process and Class Struggle in Modern Capitalism*, Brighton, Harvester Press.
  (1976b) 'The Tyranny of the Factory', in Gorz, A. (ed.).
  (1976c) 'The Technology, Technicians and Class Struggle', in Gorz, A. (ed.).
Hill, S. (1981) *Competition and Control at Work*, London, Heinemann.
Hinton, J. (1971) 'The Clyde Workers' Committee and the Dilution Struggles', in Briggs, A. and Saville, J. (eds), *Essays in Labour History*, London, Macmillan.
  (1973) *The First Shop Stewards Movement*, London, Allen and Unwin.
Jones, B. (1982) 'Destruction or Redistribution of Engineering Skills: The Case of Numerical Control', in Wood, S. (ed.).
Kelly, J. (1982) 'Useless Work and Useless Toil', *Marxism Today*, voll. 26, no. 8.
Kumar, K. (1978) *Prophecy and Progress:the Sociology of Industrial and Post-Industrial Societies*, Harmondsworth, Penguin.
Lee, D. (1978) 'De-skilling, the Labour Market, and Recruitment to Skilled Trades in Britain', Nuffield paper.
  (1980) 'Skill, Craft and Class: a Theoretical Critique and a Critical Case', *Sociology*, vol. 15, no. 1.
Levidow, L. and Young, B. (eds.) (1981), *Science, Technology and the Labour Process*, London, C.S.E. Books.
Lipietz, A. (1982) 'Towards Global Fordism', *New Left Review*, no. 132.
Littler, C.J. (1978) 'De-skilling and Changing Structures of Control', Nuffield paper.
  (1982) 'De-skilling and Structures of Control', in Wood, S. (ed.).
Mackenzie, G. (1977), '*The Political Economy of the American Working Class*', British Journal of Sociology, June.
Marglin, S. (1976) 'What Do Bosses Do? The Origins and Functions of Hierarchy in Capitalist Production', in Gorz, A. (ed.).
Mills, H. (1979) 'The San Francisco Waterfront: the Social Consequences of Industrial Modernisation', in Zimbalist, A. (ed.).
Monds, J. (1976) 'Workers' Control and the Historians: a New Economism', *New Left Review*, no. 97.
Montgomery, D. (1976) 'Workers' Control of Machine Production in the Nineteenth Century', *Labor History*, no. 17.
  (1979) 'The Past and Future of Workers Control', *Radical America*, vol. 13, no. 6.
More, C. (1978) 'De-skilling in Historical Perspective', Nuffield paper.
  (1982) 'Skill and the Survival of Apprenticeship', in Wood, S. (ed.).
Nichols, T. and Beynon, H. (1977) *Living With Capitalism: Class Relations in the Modern Factory*, London, Routledge and Kegan Paul.
Noble, D.F. (1979) 'Social Choice in Machine Design: the Case of Automatically Controlled Machine Tools', in Zimbalist, A. (ed.).
Palloix, C. (1976) 'The Labour Process from Fordism to Neo-Fordism', in Conference of Socialist Economists (eds).
Penn, R. (1978) 'Skilled Manual Workers in the Labour Process', Nuffield paper.

Putnam, T. (1978) 'Skill and Technical Education: Getting Beyond Braverman', Nuffield paper.

Reckman, B. (1979) 'Carpentry: the Craft and Trade', in Zimbalist, A. (ed.).

Reid, S. (1978) 'Computers and De-skilling: Some Preliminary Observations from a Case-Study in Local Government', Nuffield paper.

Rubery, J. (1980) 'Structured Labour Markets, Worker Organisation and Low Pay', in Amden, A. (ed.).

Shapiro-Perl, N. (1979) 'The Piece Rate: Class Struggle on the Shop Floor: Evidence From the Costume Jewelry Industry in Providence', in Zimbalist, A. (ed.).

Sohn-Rethel, A. (1976) 'The Dual Economics of Transition', in Conference of Socialist Economics (eds).

Stone, K. (1973) 'The Origins of Job Structures in the Steel Industry', *Radical America*, vol. 7, no. 6.

Turner, H.A. (1962) *Trade Union Growth, Structure and Policy*, London, Allen and Unwin.

Wood, S. (ed.) (1982) *The Degradation of Work? Skill, De-skilling and the Labour Process*, London, Hutchinson.

Zimbalist, A. (ed.) (1979) *Case Studies on the Labor Process*, London, Monthly Review Press.

6 Soviet-type Societies and the Labour Process

CRAIG LITTLER

The Soviet Union was a society whose leadership took power with a dual goal – to modernize Russia and to create a socialist alternative to the capitalist societies of Europe and North America. Thus, the Soviet Union was the first society to pose the issue of whether modernization could be separated from European capitalist civilization. Instead of a nationalistic capitalism, the path taken by Japan in the early decades of the twentieth century, the Soviet leaders offered a vision of a non-bureaucratic state where the workers controlled the means of production and where accelerating economic progress would lead forward into a classless society.

However, neither Marx nor Engels had provided much of a blueprint for the construction and administration of a non-capitalist economy.[1] In the absence of concrete guidelines, the pressures of the immediate post-revolutionary period (foreign invasion, civil war, and the threatened collapse of industry) pushed the new Russian leaders away from high-risk, experimental policies. Thus, Lenin adopted a fairly conservative development strategy, consisting of copying the newly emergent giant enterprises of the capitalist world, concentrating on heavy industry in the urban centres, and extracting as much surplus from the backward peasantry as was politically feasible, at least until the task of heavy industrialization was well underway.

Similarly, Lenin embraced the latest managerial methods of capitalism, namely the ideas of Frederick Taylor and the practices of Henry Ford:

> The Soviet Republic must appropriate for itself, at whatever cost, the most valuable conquests of science and of technology in this field. We shall be able to bring about socialism precisely in the measure that we have succeeded in combining Soviet power and the Soviet system of administration with the most recent advances of capitalism. We must organise in Russia the study and teaching of the Taylorite system, its systematic experimentation and adaption. (Lenin, 1969, vol. 42, pp. 72–3)

However, Lenin's endorsement of Taylorism did not determine the nature of Taylorism in the USSR. A fierce controversy over Taylorism took place between 1918 and 1924 and it was this debate and struggle for influence which shaped the nature of Taylorism in the Soviet Union. The major figure was Alexi Gastev – who, before 1917, was known as a worker-poet expounding a romantic vision of industrialism in which men and machines merged: machines were seen as extensions of the human body, while people took on the speed and efficiency of their creations, acquiring 'nerves of steel' and 'muscles like iron rails'. In 1920, Gastev founded the Central Labour Institute which had the responsibility of co-ordinating all Soviet research efforts on labour rationalization, and for training industrial instructors throughout Russia.

The Open University, 1984 (Specially written for this volume)

Gastev was in many ways like his mentor, Frederick Taylor; he had a naïve, technicist vision which gave a major significance to the inexorability of technological progress:

> The metallurgy of this new world, the motor car and aeroplane factories of America, and finally the arms industry of the whole world – here are the new, gigantic laboratories where the psychology of the proletariat is being created, where the culture of the proletariat is being manufactured. And whether we live in the age of super-imperialism or of world socialism, the structure of the new industry will, in essence, be one and the same. (Gastev, quoted in Bailes, 1977, p. 377)

In this vein, Gastev advocated nothing less than 'Soviet Americanism', wanting to see the USSR transformed into a 'new, flowering America'.

According to Gastev, the forces of technical change would inevitably affect the levels of skill in industry. He divided all industrial workers into five types, according to the varying degree of skill and creativity required in their jobs. So far as the future of metal-working industries was concerned, he saw the elimination of both the creative craft workers at the top of this skill hierarchy and the workers who did heavy, physical work at the bottom. The processes of mechanization and standardization would expand the third category, namely those whose work was completely standardized and devoid of any subjective element; the individual worker simply follows a set routine. Thus Gastev believed that rationality at the present stage of industrialism demanded a further division of labour in the economy, with increased specialization, job fragmentation and consequent inequalities (Bailes, 1977, p. 381).

A further consequence of the advocacy of an enhanced division of labour was the creation of a technological élite, depriving the masses of workers of initiative and any responsibility for innovation. Instead, Gastev and the Central Labour Institute worked from the top down and sought to create a 'priesthood' of scientific management.

This narrow, élitist, technocrat interpretation of Taylorism was subject to fierce attack within Russia. Gastev was criticized for depriving the workers of all creativity and seeking the militarization of labour, leading to some terrible form of barrack-like existence. Critics such as Bogdanov believed that specialization and associated work inequalities could be largely overcome by a rapid raising of the cultural level of the masses. Similarly, Gastev was attacked for his emphasis on labour intensification and ignoring the psychological and physiological sides of labour – aspects which were being studied in Western Europe as these societies assimilated and modified classical Taylorism (Bailes, 1977, pp. 381, 386–7; Littler, 1982, p. 113).

The Russian controversy over Taylorism was crucial; what was at stake was the question of what should be the proper Soviet attitude to work and the direction that scientific management should take within Soviet society. The controversy was largely resolved at a conference in 1924 (Second All-Union Conference on Scientific Management) at which Gastev emerged with the support of the Party leadership. The conference passed a resolution which affirmed 'the possibility of increasing intensification of labour in those areas of industry where the current level of labour intensification lags behind the corresponding level in capitalist countries'. Furthermore, the fundamental assumptions of Gastev's Labour Institute were recognized as the standards for the entire Soviety economy (Bailes, 1977, p. 392).

Similarly, Henry Ford had a wide influence in the Soviet Union. Ford tended to be viewed not as a capitalist, but as a revolutionary economic innovator. Translations of his autobiography, *My Life and Work*, were widely read in Russia and used as texts in universities and colleges. Apart from the ideological influence, Ford's mass production methods were widely copied in the Soviet Union and Russian engineers visited Ford plants in Detroit in the 1920s in order to learn Fordist methods (Flink, 1975, pp. 71–2).

The ready acceptance of Western mass-production methods continues today. For example, Dido, the Secretary of CGIL (the Italian communist labour federation) visited the Soviet car plant in Togliattigrad which has been built by the Italian car firm of Fiat and commented that:

> The entire project has been carried out on the basis of plans prepared and supervised by Fiat technicians...not only the technical equipment but also the organization of work is of the Fiat type...it is impossible to distinguish the administrative organization... At Togliattigrad...they have adopted not only Western machines but also Western systems of organization. To have a minimum of equilibrium, however, such a system presupposes at the very least the existence of a strong trade union force. But at the present moment such a force does not exist, either in the Soviet Union or in the other countries of Eastern Europe. (Quoted in Holubenko, 1975, p. 23).

Overall, it can be argued that Taylorism and Fordism became not transient phases of Soviet development, simple expedients of the moment, but that they laid the foundations for the division of labour in the USSR from the 1920s through to today.

However, on these foundations have been raised some structures with significant differences from the West. Even when technology has been transplanted directly from the West, it tends to be more heavily manned and to function with labour-intensive auxiliary processes. The large number of 'indirect' workers in the Soviet Union is exacerbated by the managerial practice of labour hoarding – maintaining a labour reserve in order to meet the exigencies of production targets (Garnsey, 1982, pp. 23–4; Ruble, 1981, p. 56). A typical Soviet factory director is faced with uncertain supply links to other organizations and is loath to part with any resources, however marginal. This is particularly so because the Soviet economy often works by 'storming' – a mad rush at the end of a plan period to fulfil targets – which requires a factory-based labour reserve. This plan 'rationality' creates a different economic context to that faced by capitalist managers.[2]

Though Gastev continued to believe in a cultural revolution of work based on Taylorism, by 1928 the cultural influence of scientific management in the USSR was waning. During the Stalin era, Taylorism continued its influence at the level of the division of labour and in defining the functions of workers, technicians and managers, but in relation to the structure of control, socialist emulation (or Stakhanovism) became more important.

The consolidation of a command economy after 1929 entailed the centralization of control over industry by the state and the politicization of all spheres of economic activity. The unions became fairly powerless and lost virtually all influence over hiring and firing, wages and labour protection. Strikes became a criminal activity. However, there were still problems of industrial control: the rapid expansion of industry led to a massive influx of peasants into the factories with huge problems of labour discipline, labour turnover and absenteeism.[3] In 1931, the state introduced prison sentences for violation of labour discipline and labour books to record the work performance of every worker. But authoritarian measures were not enough, and in the 1930s there was a mass movement of 'socialist emulation'.

According to Lenin,

> Socialism not only does not eliminate rivalry but on the contrary creates for the first time the possibility of applying it truly on a large scale, on a massive scale, to

effectively lead the majority of workers into an arena where they are enabled to work positively, develop their capacities.... Our task, now that a socialist government is in power, consists in organising competition. (Lenin, 1962–9, vol. 26, p. 367)

Given this philosophical acceptance of competition, from the end of the 1920s it was socialist emulation – and not Taylorism – which progressively became the central idea in official speeches in relation to the efficiency of work. The development of socialist competition was not conceived in order to undermine the practices of Taylorism: neither the division of work in industry, nor the dynamics of job specialization are affected by socialist emulation. However, there are tensions and conflicts between Taylorism and the emulation campaigns, as we shall see below.

The most famous Russian campaign of labour emulation was the Stakhanovite campaign launched in 1935. Stakhanov was a coal-miner who was selected by the Party and government because he had evolved a new method of organizing the extraction of coal which increased the amount of coal cut per shift by an astonishing amount (from 6 or 7 tons to 102 tons per shift).[4] Stakhanov was quickly given massive publicity by the Party, declared a 'labour hero', rewarded and decorated. 'Stakhanovism', as it came to be called, was assiduously fostered in other sectors of the economy and many workers – 'emulators' – were encouraged to imitate him and achieve enormous increases in output. The Stakhanovites, or shock workers, received various advantages and privileges, such as better housing, medical treatment, and holidays, apart from much larger bonuses. In class terms, the overall effect is to create a labour aristocracy – an effect which continues today. Most factories and mines have their model brigades made up of shock workers, who are chosen for their loyalty to management and who receive the best equipment, first access to materials and the best conditions. This inevitably creates a highly paid, privileged group of up to 25 per cent of the workforce, who, in exchange for their privileges, will tend to support management if any tensions or conflicts occur.[5]

With a Stakhanovite labour system, planned output targets are not set on the basis of working averages or scientifically detected norms, but on the performance of the model brigades. Clearly this can create labour tensions (and there are several accounts of over-zealous Stakhanovites being murdered), but it also runs counter to Taylorism, as one Soviet minister made clear:

The essence of the Stakhanovite movement lies in this: that the Stakhanovist pulverises with his own hands, in practice and not merely in theory, all the so-called technical norms of work. ... Norms based on scientific technique were nothing but a ghost destined to frighten us, a brake to retard us. (Closing speech of the 1st Inter-Trade Union Conference of Stakhanovites, October 1935; quoted in Schwarz, 1952, p. 510).

Stakhanovites, then, are expected to over-fulfil output norms, rather than to conform to 'scientifically established' effort norms as under Taylorism.

But there is a deeper problem than the origin and legitimation of effort norms in understanding the role of Taylorism in Soviet and East European work organizations. The Soviet-type enterprise is an entity characterized by an articulation of specific means of socio-political control, which is difficult to combine with classic Taylorist principles (Lowit, 1983). For example, the selection of all managers and even of lower-level personnel is, often, politically based. The right of the Party to nominate or to exercise veto power at various stages of the selection process is called the *nomenklatura* system. A jaundiced view of this system is best provided by interviews with Solidarity supporters in Poland:

With us, the *nomenklatura* of the Party begins with even manual labour. It is accepted that a workman cannot become a team leader, that is to say someone who directs a group of 5–20 people, if his candidature has not been submitted to the Party committee of the enterprise and approved by it. This concerned all workers whether or not they were members of the Party. With greater reason, it was a practice, an unwritten rule, that everyone above the level of team leader owed to himself to belong to the Party.

Later, this Polish factory worker underlines the effects of this system:

Let us finish with this story of *nomenklatura* and what follows from it: the professional competence of the person entrusted with the post...was a criterion only in a secondary or third position. The most important factor was political loyalty. Such a person could not refuse any order given. And that leads to several consequences. It is normal that in a factory the prime concern is production. However, if those who decide on the quality and quantity of work are themselves mediocre in this field, then the economic results, from the basic team to the level of the national economy, are those you have before your eyes. (Interviews conducted with Polish workers and Solidarity supporters in 1981 by Thomas Lowit and Nicole Fratellini).

Clearly the notion and practice of Party control over management leadership – a dual-control system – is alien to anything written by Frederick Taylor. This was underlined by Bendix, who argued that the structure of authority in Soviet-type organizations represents a different form of bureaucracy, involving a principle of dual government with two interlocking hierarchies of authority. Thus there is a Party representative at the side of every work unit in order to establish guidelines and exert influence (Bendix, 1974, pp. 446–8).

This dual-control principle cuts across the oft-cited notion of one-man management within Soviet organizations. Since 1921, the principle of one-man management theoretically underlies managerial thinking and practice in the USSR. Such a principle is a principle of responsibility, of accountability, for decision-making: it entails a strict hierarchy whereby the control of an organization is assumed by its director and orders emanating from him are obligatory for all personnel. Workers may protest about illegal instructions only once the task is done. However, the principle of one-man rule is limited to hour-to-hour and day-to-day decision-making of a fairly routine nature. Though the role of Party officials is supposed to be confined to policy issues, there is no clear distinction between issues of policy and those of administration. Thus, there is a clear tension between one-man management and the equally sacred principle of the Communist Party's 'right of control' (Ruble, 1981, pp. 54–5).

So far, we have considered the division of labour and structure of control aspects of Soviet-type work organizations and concluded that though there are some differences compared to capitalist organizations (e.g. labour hoarding associated with the extensive use of auxiliary labour; and the dual-control system), nevertheless there are no significant differences in the aspects of work which have so concerned labour process theorists. Soviet-type organizations are hierarchical and Taylorite in their orientation to the division of labour.

However, a full analysis of work organization in the Soviet Union and East Europe does require some consideration of the employment relationship – this is the fundamental relationship between the worker and the employing institution which is constituted not just at the level of the enterprise, but at the level of the labour market, property relations and the state. It can be argued that the full employment and job security of Soviet-type societies does entail a package of benefits and welfare rights that replace the commodification of labour involved in the traditional wage/labour relationship in the West. In most Soviet-type societies there is a labour market: workers can, within varying limits, choose and change jobs. And given the labour shortages in Soviet-type economies, many workers do change jobs in an effort to maximize their advantages: many Soviet enterprises report annual rates of labour turnover of between 70 and 90 percent (Dyker, 1981, p. 55). Despite such rates of turnover, once they are in a job workers have job security, which is maintained both by the trade unions and informal worker processes. Soviet-type trade unions do not generally engage in collective bargaining and are fairly powerless organizations, but they can and do oppose redundancies or press for alternative work at equivalent pay rates. Thus the anxieties of job insecurity and the threat of unemployment is removed from the heads of most workers and the labour market often operates to their advantage. Moreover, despite such devices as the Stakhanovites, there is considerable recent evidence that the relative position of labour feeds through to the shop floor in terms of less burdensome and demanding effort standards and work intensities (Garnsey, 1982, p. 24; MacDonald, 1983. p. 7).

Given the previous discussion, it is possible to outline a model of Soviet-type work organization (see Table 6.1).

Table 6.1 Model of Soviet-type work organisation

Job design	Taylorite, with occupational specialization and job fragmentation. Formalized job boundaries.
Structure of control	Dual-control system, with a day-to-day emphasis on one-man management. Socialist emulation (Stakhanovism), and ideological control. Emphasis on piece-rates.
Employment relationship	Job security. Tendency towards the development of internal labour markets. (See Sziraczki, 1983 for the dynamics of the process in the Hungarian context).

This model is an ideal type, a crude summation of a complex set of realities. Clearly, there are differences between the USSR and East Europe, and between different East European societies. In addition there is still a dearth of information on the day-to-day shop-floor situation in Soviet-type societies. However, assuming that the model does provide a crude picture, then one thing stands out – the model is *not* based on one underlying logic or rationale. On the contrary, there is a series of tensions between Taylorism and certain aspects of the structure of control; between the dual-control system and one-man management as an operational principle; and between the continued existence of a labour market with guaranteed job security.

The model in Table 6.1 also provides us with some analytic leverage in comparing Soviet-type and capitalist work organization. This comparison suggests that the changes in ownership of the means of production arising from the Bolshevik Revolution do not necessarily result in a radical restructuring of the labour process or a significant shift towards workers' self-management. Given that this is so, the key question is why? Are the dynamics of capitalist work organization perhaps the dynamics of *industrial* work organization and industrial society generally? Is the capitalist labour process distinctive to capitalism?

In seeking an answer to these questions, the first point to underline arises out of the earlier discussion of Gastev: namely, that the Soviet leadership made little or no effort to develop new forms of work organization. Garnsey makes this point clearly:

> After about 1927, systematic research and experiment in factory organization were discouraged in the Soviet Union.... Soviet forms of scientific management, even those contrasted with Taylorism, have not avoided the fragmentation of tasks and centralization of authority at work. A serious challenge to the hierarchical division of labour and polarized skill distribution characteristic of Western industry calls for a strong political commitment to the organization of work on the basis of shared knowledge and control of the productive process and sustained experiments with alternative methods of work organization. No such commitment has been shown under conditions of Soviet industrial development. (Garnsey, 1982, p. 22)

A similar conclusion was reached by Braverman:

> Whatever view one takes of Soviet industrialization one cannot conscientiously interpret its history, even in its earliest and most revolutionary period, as an attempt to organize labour processes in a way fundamentally different from those of capitalism. (Braverman, 1974, p. 22)

The reasons why there was no commitment to change and why the problem of deskilling of manual jobs through technological change has not been directly faced in the Soviet Union are still the subject of intense debate. One explanation is that the Soviet-type economies remain in some sense 'capitalist'. This explanation seems to this author to be an intellectual evasion. The relations of production in the Soviet Union are clearly not capitalist. As Garnsey points out, the processes of capital accumulation in Soviet-style economies are essentially different in that the unit carrying out the accumulation process is not the firm, but the national planning agency, such that the choice of techniques is made by planners, not by managers. Secondly, profit is not the objective and shareholders' interests are not at stake, so that enterprise managers do not experience the same pressures felt by capitalist managers to reduce the size of their labour force in response to economic downturns or in order to 'rationalize' production. Thirdly, the processes are not stimulated or reinforced by market competition (Garnsey, 1982, p. 29). In general, Soviet-type economies are governed by a plan rationality and not a market rationality.[6]

A second explanation is a developmental one. The usual reasons advanced by spokesmen in both the Soviet Union and Eastern Europe are that they have been economies in the early stages of industrialization and that only by pressing ahead as fast as possible (which, in practice, means using Western technology and management methods) can standards of living be improved. Generally, there may only be a limited amount of historical space within which a big push/high accumulation strategy can be achieved without unacceptably high economic costs, social tensions or political conflicts (White, 1983, p. 13). More particularly, the Soviet leaders were faced with potential economic collapse and civil war between 1918–21 which threatened to engulf the emergent new society, such that they had to place the greatest priority on restoring 'order' in industry. Secondly, Soviet spokesmen argue that though there may be an imperative need to relieve people from heavy physical labour, boring and trivial work is not a problem. On the contrary, it is well paid and preferable to agricultural work, which it supplants, and there is no lack of willingness to do this work (see Rosenbrock, 1983).

A third possible explanation arises from a world-system view of the modernization of societies. Wallerstein, most notably, argues that definite limits to social divergence are imposed by a capitalist-dominated world economic system: 'Establishing a system of state ownership within a capitalist world economy does not mean establishing a socialist economy. ... It is merely a variant of classical mercantilism' (Wallerstein, 1974, p. 23). Wallerstein's critique of much of comparative theory and research represents an extreme view, but cannot be dismissed. Some Chinese analysts, such as Edward Friedman, have also argued that 'true' socialism is impossible because the pressures of the world market compel socialist leaders to act in a capitalist manner, and to organize their society for competition in world exchange (Friedman, 1979, p. 806). Indeed, it is not just economic competition that acts as a pressure on modernizing societies, but *military* competition. A crucial factor fuelling the take-up of Taylorism and Fordism was the awareness of a link between mass production and a war economy: as Sabel points out, 'a state that did not foster mass production industry invited defeat on the battlefield as well as in the market' (Sabel, 1982, p. 44). In other words, the ability to mass produce cars is the ability to mass produce tanks.

Whatever the explanation of the path taken by the Soviets in relation to the labour process, it had an important effect on Western discussions of the range of potentialities of organizing work. The crucial impact was to foreclose debate and to see technology as the key determining factor which spelt the 'end of ideology' (Kerr *et al.*, 1960; Andors, 1977, p. 19–20). As Chinese developments filtered through to the West in the 1960s and 1970s, they appeared to open up the terrain of debate once again. If the Soviet economy was not a good test case, then the Chinese experience seemed to offer the potentiality to see whether alternative forms of work organization could prevail in a non-capitalist framework, because there did appear to be serious efforts to break away from the Western and Soviet methods of organizing work. In particular, the Cultural Revolution (1966–76) was seen as a process of transforming the age-old pattern of the division of labour, the mental/manual divide, so as to reshape the nature of industrial work (see Bettelheim, 1974). Even more widely, the Maoism of the Cultural Revolution period was seen as a struggle against bureacracy and bureaucratism. The Maoist model of organization, according to King, involved five characteristics:

1. *Anti-hierarchicalism*: This involves a simplification of the organizational structure, on the basis that a minute hierarchical control system stifles the energy and initiative of the masses.
2. *Anti-functional specialization*: It is accepted that some division of labour is necessary, but this should be kept to a minimum, as should departmental specialization.
3. *Anti-expertness*: This is the issue of 'redness versus expertness'. Essentially expertness, or 'expert mysticism', is viewed as antithetical to mass participation.
4. *Anti-administrative professionalism*: All administrative leaders should take part directly in the productive process, so that nobody 'moves his mouth and not his hands'.
5. *Anti-administrative routinization*: It is encouraged to break through unnecessary rules and regulations and to 'reshuffle' organizations. (King, 1977, pp. 367–8).

Given this Maoist ideology, then it did seem as though the Chinese situation provided the commitment to a radical restructuring of the labour process, which could both carry Western theoretical debates forward out of the stasis of convergence theory and provide some guidelines to action for those who regarded more participatory and less bureaucratic organizations as desirable. It is here that we can locate the importance of the Chinese case, beyond the appeal of the exotic and esoteric, to bear on crucial issues which touch the work lives of us all.

However, just as Western academics were catching up with the Chinese experience, it changed before their eyes. Since the overthrow of the Gang of Four in 1976, the reported stress on transforming the division of labour has been much reduced in official policy statements and in reports given to Western visitors. It is now seen as a 'technical' problem rather than a political one and, moreover, as a long-term problem. In contrast, there is an emphasis on 'scientific management' and a widespread interest in Taylorism!

The full implications of these developments have yet to be explored by Western theorists, either in relation to the capitalist labour process or in relation to the development of work organization in the Soviet Union. Perhaps the overriding fact is that the Soviet-type countries have been backward economies, desperate to catch up, and this explains why it is that instead of executing the legacy of Marx, of constructing an egalitarian, non-market society with a radically different labour process, they have created societies which are neither fish nor fowl.

Notes

1. See for example McLellan, (1971, pp. 212–24).
2. Ryapolov (1966), an ex-Soviet manager, says that

    As a rule, enterprises do not work on a regular schedule. . . . In the first 10 days of the average month, most of our workers would do nothing or continue to work illegally on the last month's plan. The second 10 days would be used to produce 10–15 percent of the current month's plan. In the last 10 days of the month, 70–80 percent of the production plan would be fulfilled. Part of our piecework force at that time would work more than 12 hours a day without overtime pay, since it had not earned anything in the preceding 20 days. The last ten days at the plant would resemble a mad rush, (pp. 120–1)

3. Lieberstein (1975, p. 53) says that of the 12,600,000 workers drawn into industry during the First Five-Year Plan (1928–32), 8,600,000 were former peasants.
4. It is doubtful if Stakhanov was the actual initiator of the new work arrangements.
5. Haraszti (1977), describing modern factory conditions in Hungary, paints a rather different picture. He asserts that 'competition has come to dominate our conditions of life' (p. 69), but locates its origin in the pervasiveness of the piece work system. The brigade system does exist, overlaying the rivalries of piece work, but is treated as a formalistic joke: 'The competition between the brigades doesn't stir much water', and Haraszti had no idea about the identity of the other members of his 'First of May' brigade. (p. 67).
6. From a rather different perspective (that of an analysis of the Japanese economy), Chalmers Johnson argues that the Soviet economy is not plan rational, but *plan ideological*, in that state ownership of the means of production, state planning, and bureaucratic goal-setting have become fundamental values in themselves, not to be challenged by evidence of either inefficiency or ineffectiveness (Johnson, 1982, p. 18). There is some truth in this, but it ignores the development of the economic reform movements in the USSR and Eastern Europe.

References

Andors, S. (1977) *China's Industrial Revolution*, Oxford, Martin Robertson.
Bailes, K. (1977) 'Alexei Gastev and the Soviet Controversy over Taylorism', *Soviet Studies*, vol. 29, no. 3, pp. 373–94.
Bendix, R. (1974) *Work and Authority in Industry*, Berkeley, University of California Press.
Bettelheim, C. (1974) *Cultural Revolution and Industrial Organization in China*, New York, Monthly Review Press.
Braverman, H. (1974) *Labor and Monopoly Capital*, New York, Monthly Review Press.
Dyker, D.A. (1981) 'Planning and the Worker', in L. Schapiro and J. Godson (eds), *The Soviet Worker: Illusions and Realisites*, London, Macmillan, pp. 39–75.

Flink, J.J. (1975) *The Car Culture*, Cambridge, Mass., MIT Press.

Friedman, E. (1979) 'On Maoist Conceptualization of the Capitalist World System', *China Quarterly*, vol. 80, December.

Garnsey, E. (1982) 'Capital Accumulation and the Division of Labour in the Soviet Union', *Cambridge Journal of Economics*, vol. 6, no. 1, pp. 15–31.

Haraszti, M. (1977) *A Worker in a Worker's State*, Harmondsworth, Penguin.

Holubenko, M. (1975). 'The Soviet Working Class: Discontent and Opposition', *Critique*, vol. 4, pp. 5–25.

Johnson, C. (1982) *MITI and the Japanese Miracle: the growth of industrial policy, 1925–75*, Stanford, Cal., Stanford University Press.

Kerr, C., Dunlop, J.T., Harrison, F. and Myers, C.A (1960) *Industrialism and Industrial Man*, Harmondsworth, Penguin.

King, A.Y. (1977) 'A voluntarist Model of Organization: the Maoist model and its critique', *British Journal of Sociology*, vol. 28, no. 3, September, pp. 363–74.

Lenin, V.I. (1962–9) *Collected Works*, Moscow.

Lieberstein, S. (1975) 'Technology, Work and Sociology in the USSR: the NOT Movement', *Technology and Culture*, vol. 16, no. 1, January, pp. 48–66.

Littler, C.R. (1982) *The Development of the Labour Process in Capitalist Societies: A comparative study of the transformation of work organization in Britain, Japan and the USA*, London, Heinemann Educational Books.

Lowit, T. (1983) 'Taylorisme et controle social en europe de l'est', mimeo.

MacDonald, O. (1983) 'The Polish Cortex', *New Left Review*, vol. 139, May/June, pp. 5–48.

McLellan, D. (1971) *The Thought of Karl.Marx*, London, Macmillan.

Rosenbrock, H.H. (1983) 'Report of a Visit to Budapest', mimeo.

Ruble, B. (1981) *Soviet Trade Unions: their development in the 1970s*, Cambridge, Cambridge University Press.

Ryapolov, G. (1966) 'I was a Soviet Manager', *Harvard Business Review*, January/February, pp. 117–25.

Sabel, C.F. (1982) *Work and Politics*, Cambridge, Cambridge University Press.

Schwarz, S.M. (1952) *Labour in the Soviet Union*, New York, Praeger.

Sziraczki, G. (1983) 'The Development and Functioning of an Enterprise Labour Market in Hungary', *Economies et Sociétés*, no. 3–4, pp. 517–47.

Wallerstein, I. (1974), *The Modern World System*, New York, Academic Press.

White, G. (1983) 'Revolutionary Socialist Development in the Third World: an overview', in G. White, R. Murray, and C. White, (eds), *Revolutionary Socialist Development in the Third World*, Brighton, Wheatsheaf Books.

7 Competition between the Organizational Professions and the Evolution of Management Control Strategies

PETER ARMSTRONG

Introduction: Two Ways of Looking at Scientific Management

For Braverman, scientific management was nothing less than the 'explicit verbalisation of the capitalistic mode of production' (1974, p. 85). Earlier forms of work organization which relied on traditional craft controls or systems of internal contract were merely transitional forms in which the formal subordination of labour to capital had not yet been fully transformed into the real subordination characteristic of the full development of capitalism (ibid., p. 63; Marx, 1976, p. 1054).

A great deal of valuable work has arisen out of criticism of this apparently simple thesis, notably on the grounds that it confines within the factory the analysis of the means used by capital to control labour, that it romanticizes the craft skills supposed to antedate scientific management, and that it neglects the role of workers' resistance in shaping the strategies adopted by capital (Elger, 1982, pp. 24–7). From the present point of view, however, the most relevant criticism is that of Littler and Salaman (1982): that Braverman, by positing a single control problem and deskilling as a global means of solving it, prematurely foreclosed analysis of the real means used by capital to control labour.

However, opening up the debate in this manner raises afresh the question of the origins of scientific management, a question which for Braverman was resolved virtually as a matter of definition: no scientific management, no fully developed capitalism. It is the contention of this paper that there are lacunae in what might be called the 'labour process tradition' in dealing with questions of this type. In order to show what these are, I will first briefly outline the 'modal' account of the advent of scientific managment and allied techniques which is offered by a sample of prominent post-Braverman writers (Friedman, 1977; Edwards, 1979; Clawson, 1980; Gordon, Edwards and Reich, 1982; and Littler, 1982). Stripped of historical detail and allowing for differences of terminology, their argument runs that employers' reliance on craft traditions (Friedman, Grodon et al.) or systems of internal contract (Clawson, Littler) proved inadequate as means of work intensification under the increased stress of competition brought about by slump conditions. There followed a period of experimentation with piece-rates (Friedman, Edwards, Clawson, Littler), a technique of control which began to fail,

---

in its turn, as workers learned to regulate their efforts as a defence against rate-cutting. It was therefore the employers' need to combat effort regulation which first exposed the necessity for direct physical intervention in the process of production, and it was noticeable that Taylor explicitly directed his methods against 'systematic soldiering'. In post-Braverman writings, then, scientific management and similar techiques appear at the moment when earlier attempts at work intensification were failing for want of precisely the kind of control of production methods which the new strategies promised. If this account is read not simply as a narrative, but as an *explanation* of the evolution of employers' control strategies, it is, as Salaman (1982, p. 51) has pointed out, a functionalist one: the techniques of scientific management seem to appear *because* of the problems which they solved. Moreover they are made to appear as the *only* solution, a position which is quite obviously untenable since Littler's own study of the very different development of the Japanese labour process (1982, p. 46).

A related difficulty occurs in the attempts of some of the accounts to periodize changes in control strategies by relating them to economic crises. The problem here is that there are *always* crises somewhere in capitalist economies, nor is it established that the search for a competitive edge is absent when and where there is no crisis. At the empirical level, the work of Littler (1982) again underlines this difficulty: whereas the experiments with scientific management occurred in the USA in boom conditions, the derivative techniques of the Bedaux system were implemented in this country during a slump.

The treatment of the techniques of scientific management within the 'labour process tradition', then, is arguably deficient in its account of the reasons for their advent, in explaining the precise nature of the techniques and in locating them historically. In these respects, the work of Layton (1969, 1971) offers an important supplementary perspective.

For Layton, scientific management, in its criticisms of traditional supervision and in its claim that the administration of labour should be monopolized by the 'planning department', was a product of the 'ideology of engineering'. This, in turn, was an expression of the resentment of the American mechanical engineers of the day, hitherto accustomed to the ownership or substantial control of small jobbing machine shops (Calvert, 1967, ch. 1), at their subordination in growing bureaucratic organizations as industrial concentration proceeded.

There was nothing even mildly reformist about this ideology: far from expressing hostility to big business, it constituted a claim that engineers were those best fitted to dominate it. Thus, as the same time as scientific management offered techniques for, and an ideological justification of, the control of labour by capital, it derived those techniques from a particular analysis of the management task – an engineering analysis – and made the claim that an application of those techniques called for the installation of a particular group – engineers – as the apex of the developing differentiation within the 'global function of capital'. (This term was used by Carchedi (1977) to denote that assemblage of roles which, in modern capitalism, performs the functions once carried out by the individual capitalist).

What this perspective offers is first of all a convincing periodization of the advent of scientific management: it arose as an expression of the 'ideology of engineering' at the moment when American mechanical engineers, as a group, experienced an abrupt transition from independence to subordination within the developing industrial hierarchies. More importantly, it offers an explanation of the nature of the solution which scientific management offered to the problem of controlling labour. The approach to the physical process of production grew out of the engineers' previous experience of machine design. Workers' movements were analysed and redesigned so as to achieve the most economical sequence, an approach which inherently presupposes the subordination of manual to mental labour and close directive supervision. Moreover there is an analogy between the reduction of skilled to simple labour and the earlier development by mechanical engineers of interchangeable parts as a solution to the problem of co-ordinating production (Clawson, 1980, pp. 76–9). Of course these considerations do not, by themselves, explain why businessmen adopted the techniques of scientific management (when they did): for that we need to return to the considerations emphasized by the labour process writers. What is being claimed is that the two perspectives are complementary and that Salaman (1982, p. 59) is correct in calling for a consideration of the influence of intra-organizational relationships on the development of control strategies and also of the influence of previous systems of ideas on the form they take.

Although it anticipates some later arguments, it is as well at this point to anticipate a major possible objection: that if scientific management was advocated by engineers in an attempt to install themselves at the apex of the global function of capital and if its techniques are now, as Braverman claims, the bedrock of all modern management (1974, p. 87), how it is that engineers themselves do not now dominate the managements of all major corporations? The answer appears to lie in Larson's (1977, ch. 4) analysis of the conditions under which a professional body of knowledge can form the basis of a 'collective mobility project'. Whilst the knowledge base needs to be sufficiently codifiable to be transmitted as a professional culture, it also needs to contain sufficient indeterminacy to debar outsiders from professional practice. In other words, however important their function, professionals can only use it as a basis for social mobility (in this case within the global function of capital), if professional knowledge (in this case a technique for controlling labour) is sufficiently indeterminate to prevent the detachment of the function from the professionals themselves. Unfortunately for the engineers, the techniques of scientific management proved too lucid and could too easily be detached from the ambitions of the engineers, despite Taylor's protestations that scientific management could only be installed as a total system. Thus Bedaux, though a technocrat by personal inclination, was acute enough to market the techniques of scientific management to the family-dominated firms of England in a form shorn of Taylor's Messianic pretensions (Littler, 1982, pp. 105–8).

The Role of Inter-professional Competition in the Generation of Control Strategies

Although the development of the techniques of scientific management occurred early in the differentiation of management hierarchies, it has features which point towards a more general model of the development of management control strategies. For brevity, in what follows I will loosely refer to specialisms within the global function of capital as 'professions'. Such a usage calls for some explanation, since professionalism has traditionally been thought of as in some degree antipathetic to the values of business organizations.

This supposition was derived largely from the assumption that professions could be defined by the possession of certain traits, notably independent ethical or technical standards of performance and collegiate control of these. Besides tending to accept at face value the professionals' own account of the reasons behind their exclusionary practices and demands for autonomy (Roth, 1974), this assumption ignores the possibility that some of the techniques which certain professions attempt to monopolize can form components of the global function of capital and that, in the context of business organization, demands for autonomy may express not so much a desire for independence, but an ambition to be numbered amongst the controllers rather than the controlled. Thus Child *et al.* (1983) see professionalism amongst the staff positions in British industry not simply as a demand to be allowed to work according to the professions' own conception of proper standards, but also as an imposition of these standards on managers in the production function.

It should also be pointed out that, in using the term 'professionals' to denote competing specialisms within the global function of capital, I am not endorsing the notion that all mental labour lies within the capital function (cf. Poulantzas, 1975). It is simply that I am not directly concerned in this discussion with those elements of professional work which constitute productive labour. And whereas certain segments of a profession may lie within what Abercrombie and Urry (1983) call the 'service class' (i.e. that class which discharges the functions of capital), other sections of the same profession may not – although they may nevertheless aspire to do so.

Into this last category fell a section of the American engineering profession at the time of the development of scientific management. The related trajectories of the profession and the techniques which it originated suggest a more general model of the development of management control strategies.

At the time of the development of scientific management, American mechanical engineers had produced a relatively clear occupational ideology, one element of which was a belief that their position within the global function of capital had become unjustifiably subordinate. This suggests that, beyond a certain stage of differentiation, the global function of capital can be seen as a collection of relatively self-conscious specialisms which compete at a group level for access to the key positions of command. At stake is both access to the relative dominance of the profession as a whole and the promotion prospects of individuals whose careers originate within it. There is every incentive for such a competition if Wright (1979) is correct in arguing that there exists an economic return to the function of control, and (for example) the 45 per cent salary advantage enjoyed by British engineers who move into 'general' management (Berthoud and Smith, 1980, p. 38) strongly suggests that he is.

As an expression of the ideology of engineering, scientific management sought to remedy the subordination of the engineer by offering an engineering solution to one of the key problems within the global function of capital – that of controlling labour. Though the problem was, of course, real, the urgency of solving it was also ideologically emphasized by Taylor's criticisms of the inadequacies of traditional management. Generalizing, this indicates that collective mobility for a profession within the global function of capital depends on identifying a key problem confronting capital (which need not necessarily be that of controlling labour), ideologically stressing the inadequacy of existing methods of coping with it (which may be associated with competing professions) and developing a solution based on the techniques of the profession.

As has already been pointed out, scientific management was based on an extrapolation of the principles of mechanical engineering design, in that most of its key characteristics derived from an assumption that human labour could and, for optimum efficiency, should, be designed in the same way as machine movements. Thus the solutions offered by professions to crises within the global function of capital are likely to be generated from their existing bodies of professional knowledge and their specialized techniques. Pre-professional examples of this process were the systems of internal contract and the piece-work payment methods which succeeded them. Both can be regarded as attempts to generalize the petty capitalist motives of the small entrepreneur into methods of controlling labour in relatively large organizations (Littler, 1982, pp. 81–2).

Professions which achieve a pre-eminence within the global function of capital on the basis of solving a problem other than that of the control of labour (for example, that of the realization of surplus), may still influence the control strategy simply on account of their general dominance. Seeing the problem in terms of their professional expertise (or their origin in the case of senior managers who can no longer practise one), they may favour systems of control which they best understand.

One reason for the evolution of control (and other) strategies from pre-existing specialist knowledge is that, for a strategy to function as a means of collective mobility for a profession, the profession needs to retain a monopoly of it. As already pointed out, scientific management let the engineers down badly in this respect: it was too lucid. Its techniques could be divorced from the overall dominance of the engineering profession, despite Taylor's warnings of the perils of doing so. As Braverman put it, though not with quite the same meaning, the techniques of scientific management are no longer the property of a faction (1974, p. 87). Speaking more generally, the continued possession of a control (or other) strategy depends on the profession maintaining a certain mystique and indeterminacy about it so that the strategy can be operated only by themselves.

A feature of internal competition within the global function of capital which is not illustrated by the case of scientific management is the development of clear-cut differentiations of power, privilege and status (horizontal fissures) within competing professions, of the kind analysed in the case of accountancy by Johnson (1977a, 1977b, 1980). However, whereas Johnson argues that horizontal fission tends to occur at the boundary between capital and worker functions, I would maintain that his analysis of accountancy demonstrates that it can also serve to isolate different levels of access to decision-making power and economic privilege *within* the global function of capital. There are at least three reasons for expecting this to occur:

1. By consigning the routine and codifiable elements of its professional knowledge to subordinates, the élite secures for itself the elements of indeterminacy and thus reinforces its grip on the strategy on which its collective mobility project is based.
2. By reducing the size of the élite for whom key positions are claimed, competition for these at the individual level is reduced.
3. An internal hierarchy within the profession creates a managerial element in senior positions within it which reinforces the claim of the élite that their professional practice inherently involves managerial responsibility.

Having sketched out a model of the role of competition within the global function of capital in the development of control strategies, I will now attempt to apply it to the cases of accountancy, engineering and personnel management, since these are the three professions picked out by Gospel (1983, p. 11) as having influenced managerial strategies from the time of the inter-war years. After a brief discussion of the place of each profession within the managerial and directoral élite, the discussion of each will follow the model as laid out above.

Accountants and Other Financial Specialists

As far as can be ascertained, British company directors with backgrounds in banking or accountancy substantially outnumber those with technical training (BIM, 1972), membership of the Institute of Chartered Accountants being the single most common academic or professional qualification in British boardrooms (Institute of Directors Survey, 1965, quoted in Tricker, 1967, p. 20). Further, although the most common first degrees amongst the members of the British Institute of Management (BIM) are in science or engineering (Melrose-Woodman, 1978, p. 16; Mansfield, *et al.*, 1981, p. 8), the pattern of postgraduate study is such that qualifications in business, economics or accountancy predominate amongst the minority (roughly one-third) of members who are qualified to degree level. Moreover the trend over time is strongly in favour of qualification in the business and financial subjects (Melrose-Woodman, 1978, p. 14). Small wonder, then, that between 15 and 20 per cent of final-year accounting students expect to become managers (Solomons, 1974).

Thus understanding accountancy not as a specific professional training, but as that broader range of subjects which include its technologies as core elements, there can be little doubt of its heavy and increasing representation at the key decision-making levels within the global function of capital. Although we are here concerned with the fortunes and consequences of accountancy in this broad sense, much of what follows perforce draws on a literature which has been concerned with the profession specifically. Nevertheless this will still serve to illustrate the processes which have led to the comparative dominance of accountancy as a means of management and its consequences for the control of labour.

In this country, the accounting methods used by early manufacturers originated in the book-keeping techniques used by estate managers, mercantile capitalists and putting-out manufacturers. Although these were quite unreliable, even as a basis for pricing, let alone internal control, these deficiencies were masked for a long time by the characteristic wide profit margins of the era. In the firms of the Industrial Revolution, the clerks who performed this accounting work remained few in number and comparatively poorly paid, whilst their employers were more preoccupied with shortages of engineers and metalworkers (Pollard, 1965, pp 144, 223).

Accountants owed a more substantial early position in the structures of capitalism to the audit requirements imposed by capitalists on each other, some of which were incorporated into law, both here and in the USA (Portwood and Fielding, 1981, p. 755; Boland, 1982, p. 116), just as later specialists in taxation were able to prosper by employing their 'impartiality and dispassionateness' (Stacey, 1954, p. 178) to minimize the tax liabilities of the firms which employed them (Thompson, 1978, p. 397; Boland, 1982, p. 122).

However, at least until the mid-1920s, it was not understood by investors and entrepreneurs that 'In helping to boost company profits, the accountant has been and remains to this day, perhaps the most important management tool of private enterprise' and members of the profession 'rarely ascended to leading positions in trade, industry or commerce' (Stacey, 1954, pp. 168, 176–8, 200–2). In other words, the adaptation of auditing techniques to the problem of internal control within capitals, as opposed to that of regularizing relations between them or between capitals and the state, had not yet begun. Nor had the correlative advance of accountants and former accountants to positions of command within the global function of capital.

What changed matters was the depression of the mid-1930s. If the wide profit margins of early manufacturing industry had forgiven the primitive accounting techniques of the Industrial Revolution, economic crisis, by a reversal of the same logic, helped to advance the cause of accountancy by stimulating a drive to locate and contain costs. It was the evolution of management accountancy in response to this pressure which completed the consolidation of accountancy as a major profession. However, despite proddings from the government during and immediately after the Second World War, the new techniques were not adopted without the vigorous advocacy of the profession itself against the resistance of 'entrepreneurs', suspicious of any 'new fangled administrative overhead' (Stacey, 1954).

Although Stacey is not very clear about the sources of resistance and not very sophisticated in his analysis of its motivation, these developments fit well with the model of an organizational profession developing its original specialism into a comprehensive technique of managerial control in response to a crisis within the global function of capital and using the possession of this technique as a means of collective mobility in competition with other potential or actual incumbents of positions of command.

Studies of the evolution of giant corporations in the USA, carried out by Chandler and his co-workers, cast further light on the rise of accountancy, although, as Littler (1982, p. 50) points out, it is necessary to be careful when applying American experience to this country. In viewing giant corporations essentially as alternatives to competitive markets or cartel arrangements for carrying out the economic functions of co-ordination, monitoring and allocation, Chandler could be said to be using concepts and a frame of reference which virtually define the development of accounting controls as fundamental to the development of giant corporations (Chandler and Daems, 1979, pp. 3–4). However, his historical accounts show that the rise of the accountants was accomplished not as a matter of definition, but by a purposeful restructuring of large corporations in response to the economic crisis of 1920–2. Until that time, the organizational structures of large American corporations were modelled on the line/staff structure first developed on the railways, in which accountants and other financial specialists were amongst the staff advisory to line managers. When applied to multiproduct enterprises, the fundamental weakness of this structure was that it provided no rational way of allocating resources. Because line managers reported only to senior managers, who themselves had functional responsibilities, allocation remained a matter for bargaining and infighting between interested parties. The consequent inability to adjust inventories to demand led to a severe crisis for American corporations in the recession of the early 1920s.

In the pioneering and prototypical restructuring of General Motors, this problem of allocation was solved by creating a multidivisional structure, co-ordinated and controlled by a general office of financial and advisory staff who developed, from the original techniques for controlling inventories, new statistical techniques for more generally controlling, co-ordinating and evaluating the performance of operating divisions (and consequently of their managers). Senior managers were thus divorced from day-to-day operations and, what is more significant from the present point of view, they became financial rather than operational or technical decision-makers. Thus although it was an engineer – Alfred P. Sloan Jr. – who played a prominent part in the restructuring of General Motors, the reorganization was possible because the accounting and financial staffs, formerly in advisory positions, possessed the techniques of auditing and cost accounting (the latter, ironically, first developed by the early industrial engineers) from which could be developed more general methods of control which offered a solution to the crisis faced by the corporation. To put the matter very crudely, accountants displaced engineers and other operational managers from key positions within the global function of capital because decisions of allocation between dissimilar operations could only be made on a common abstract – and therefore financial – basis. However, in applying such an analysis to the United Kingdom, it is necessary to bear in mind a number of contextual differences: first, and most important, that family capitalism persisted far longer in this country than in the USA, and also that here the coincidence of mass markets and mass-production techniques, which stimulated the development of giant multi-divisional American corporations, was less common and occurred later (Chandler, 1977, 1980; Chandler and Daems, 1979). Whereas in the United States of America, the multidivisional form became predominant amongst large corporations in the period 1945–50, in the United Kingdom, the transition was still in progress during the years 1965–70 (Steer and Cable, 1978).

It is important to note that the growth of giant corporations itself is not sufficient to explain the relative ascendency of the accounting profession. For this it was critical that accountants were already represented in the management hierarchies of British and American companies at the time of their growing pains, so that they could profit by offering their characteristic remedies. As has been already pointed out, this early presence was partly a consequence of the audit requirements imposed by the securities market. In Germany and Japan, where the major sources of industrial finance were respectively the banking system (Habakkuk, 1967, p. 167) and government (Littler, 1982, p. 146), it is also the case that accountants are both less numerous and less senior in the management hierarchies of large companies (Hutton, Lawrence and Smith, 1977, pp. 69–87; Lawrence, 1980, pp. 67–74; Coke, 1983). German management, in particular, is dominated by engineers, and the techniques of financial control, instead of forming the stock-in-trade of a specialist accounting profession as in Great Britain and the United States of America, are taught to these engineering managers at undergraduate and postgraduate levels. Although German accounting controls may, in consequence, appear primitive to American eyes, this appears to be compensated by the greater emphasis on manufacture (Lawrence, 1980, pp. 89–95). Interestingly, in a German company studied by Millar (1971), the engineer–managers had devised a decentralized system of production and a 'special' stock-control system, both of which eliminated the need for certain accounting procedures common in the United Kingdom.

The involvement of accountancy in key decision-making positions within the global function of capital has, in Johnson's view (1977a, 1977b, 1980), created a horizontal fission within the profession whereby the activities of the élite which creates, installs and supervises control systems have the effect of routinizing, fragmenting and deskilling the work of their nominal professional colleagues. For the élite, on the other hand, the delegation of routine tasks to subordinates has the effect of sustaining the 'indetermination' of its own activities, thus serving to reinforce its monopoly of them. This monopoly persists, suggests Johnson, not so much as a result of the esoteric nature of the knowledge base, but only so long as it operates in the interests of capital. Testifying to the qualitative differences in different levels of accounting work are the problems of adjustment faced by accountants if and when they are promoted (McKenna, 1978).

Besides these tensions internal to the profession, claims are being made for the territorial extension of the accounting domain, particularly into production management (Burchell *et al.*, 1980) and, in reaction, resistance by operational managers to the control exercised by accountants is a continuing feature of modern corporations. Amongst accountants themselves, at least the Institute of Cost Management Accountants is keenly aware that its members are in competition with other professions and with the members of other accounting institutions for positions of corporate power. At the time of writing, this institute is preparing a report identifying the sources of competition and strategies to deal with it. In particular, it is seen as necessary in the interests of the profession that it should succeed in annexing those parts of information technology which look likely to impinge on its practice, rather than suffer the consequences of the monopolization of these by other specialists (Banyard, 1983). On another front, the more recently evolved subspecialisms of operational research and managerial economics appear to be competing for part of the traditional control function of management accountancy (Tricker, 1967, pp. 371–5) to the accompaniment of mutually denigratory occupational ideologies (cf. Esland, 1980, p. 240).

As a system of control, management accountancy does not, in its pure form, involve physical intervention in the labour of production. However, in the larger sense, it serves to control the labour process in at least three interrelated ways. In one of its aspects, it is is a solution to the problem posed by the demise of the internal contract system: that of how to ensure the loyalty and motivation of salaried managers and so avoid the 'negligence and profusion' which Adam Smith believed would be the inevitable result of their relative economic security (Pollard, 1965, p. 12; Edwards, 1979, p. 31). Budget allocations are used to discipline and control department managers (Tricker, 1967, pp. 73–5), and the development of measures of departmental performance has been linked with practices for the evaluation and reward of their managers (Burchell *et al.*, 1980, p. 16). In this aspect, management accountancy supplements the engineering transformation of the physical process of production by linking managers' careers to their success in increasing the rate of exploitation in their particular departments. Secondly, by rationalizing decisions of allocation (see, for example, McKenna, 1978, p. 13) it enables the concentration of capital and labour on those operations which yield the greatest surplus, so indirectly acting as a disciplinary pressure on those whose livelihoods are linked with those operations which yield the least. Finally, the language and presuppositions of accounting systems (Burchell, *et al.*, 1980) function as vocabularies of motive which set the terms of and limit any challenge by workers and subordinate managers to senior management decisions (Batstone, 1979).

Engineers

According to Gerstl and Hutton (1966, pp. 87–9), about one-third of all mechanical engineers are in managerial positions of some kind, a proportion which rises to over half in the over-55 age-group. However, such figures give quite a misleading impression of the place of engineers in the corporate power structure, since most of these 'managerial' positions appear to involve only the supervision of other engineers or technologists. Only a small proportion of engineers have line supervisors reporting to them (Vanning, 1975, pp. 62–3). To look at the matter another way, even in the engineering industry only one-quarter of the managers have training or experience in engineering (ibid., p. 106). In industry generally, qualifications in business economics or accountancy substantially outnumber those in science or engineering amongst members of the British Institute of Management. At board level, British companies are far more likely to appoint directors with purely financial backgrounds, or even persons possessing only a general aura of eminence than those with any form of technical training (BIM, 1972). More specifically in the engineering industry, in 1952 only one-fifth of all directors had any form of technical qualification, whereas, fully one-third of the companies had no technically qualified director at all (Monck, 1954).

In Victorian England, the rapid mechanization of textile production created the first large-scale market for the embryo mechanical engineering industry. At the time, the manner in which this market was supplied ensured that the engineers themselves participated fully in the global function of capital: they set up and ran their own machine shops in the centres of textile manufacture (Rolt, 1970, pp. 131–8). In other industries too, salaried managers were often engineers by the standards of the day, if only because the lack of differentiation of function made it difficult to separate management from technical expertise (Pollard, 1965, p. 126). The path from this heavy involvement in the global function of capital to the comparative contemporary subordination of the engineer in Great Britain is comparatively uncharted. For example, there are instances in which the persistence of family capitalism in this country (Hannah, 1980, p. 53) ensured the dominance of the engineering interest until as late as the 1950s, but how widespread this pattern was, where it was located and what ended it are matters for future research. With due caution, we shall have to turn to the United States for clues.

Until the end of the nineteenth century, many American mechanical engineers either owned their own small machine shops or, where they were employed by larger firms, had wide-ranging managerial powers (including, for example, responsibility for industrial relations) (Calvert, 1967, ch. 1 and pp. 141–2). Similarly, the early civil engineers had considerable autonomy in overseeing the work of subcontractors on behalf of their employers, although the efforts of some of them to achieve contractor status for themselves were firmly resisted (Calhoun, 1960, pp. 68 and 91–103). This broad and, by today's standards, 'managerial' interpretation of their role by the American engineers of the day is further evidenced by the fact that it was the early industrial engineers who pioneered the techniques of cost accountancy in America (Chandler, 1977, p. 464), not to mention the technocratic vision of scientific management. For Noble (1977), it was the industrial engineers 'who shaped and rationalized the modern corporation, creating a technology of social production in the image of science, and in the process, generated modern management'. Yet, only a decade or so later, large amounts of college-trained engineers were having to be content with routine and increasingly specialized work within the developing industrial bureaucracies, often in positions subordinate to men without technical training (Calvert, 1967, pp. 145–52). Instructively, the cost-accounting techniques pioneered by engineers found their way on to college syllabuses and, by 1926, they were annexed by the specialist National Association of Cost Accountants (Chandler, 1977, pp. 464–5).

This strongly suggests that the loss of position by engineers within the global function of capital during the transformation of the American corporation, described earlier, is partly due to a process of horizontal fission on the model of that described in the case of accountancy by Johnson (1977a, 1977b, 1980). The more narrowly technical work performed by the later (and larger) generation of college-trained engineers, though arguably based on a body of knowledge more esoteric than that of their forebears schooled in the 'shop culture', was fatally (from their point of view) shorn of its role in the appropriation of surplus value. The new engineers were not simply the updated counterparts of the old. Those parts of the professional body of knowledge most intimately concerned with the functions of capital were appropriated by an élite which, although it continued to recruit from the ranks, also had heirs who might be called organization and methods managers or even management accountants, rather than engineers, whilst the more purely technical work and the name of engineering passed to men who were subordinate both in the corporations and in the professional associations.

However, horizontal fission within the engineering profession itself is probably not the whole reason for the relative contemporary subordination of the mass of engineers in Great Britain. A few years after the American engineer, Alfred P. Sloan Junior, reorganized General Motors so as to place operational managers under the financial control of the general office, the British accountant, D'Arcy Cooper created a central technical investigating committee as part of his reorganization of Unilever. This committee – chaired as a matter of deliberate policy by a non-technical manager – was to investigate every technical department in the company and report directly to the board (Wilson, 1970, p. 299). In other words, it appeared to a non-technical senior manager that the solution to a lack of co-ordination of technical operations was to subordinate technical to non-technical decision-making.

The typicality of this case is, at the current state of research, very much an open question. However, the current situation is that the mass of the engineering profession in this country is considerably obsessed with its 'low status', despite the fact that engineers' earnings are said to compare well with those of other professions (Berthoud and Smith, 1980, pp. 45, 34; Finniston, 1980, pp. 185, 60–5). Engineers themselves are clear about who are their more successful competitors within the hierarchies of management – 'The status of Engineering depends on the outlook of higher management. All too frequently, these consist of salesmen and accountants...' (Feilden, 1963, p. 18). Whilst preoccupied with the possibility of a 'collective mobility project' (cf. Larson, 1977, p. 66) for engineering within the global function of capital, engineers also accept individual moves into semi- or non-technical management (the former preferred) as a legitimate professional goal (for American evidence on this, see Perrucci and Gerstl, 1969, p. 102; Rothstein, 1969, p. 85). Attempts to provide for engineers' ambitions by means of 'dual career ladders', so that they can attain high salaries and status while performing purely technical work, have been interpreted as a strategy (presumably thought up by non-engineering senior managers) aimed at deflecting engineers from the positions of real corporate power which are seen as the proper objects of professional ambition (Goldner and Ritti, 1967).

In this country, discussion amongst engineers of the 'problem' of low status has created a well-formed ideology which stresses the dire effects on the nation of allowing the profession's grievances to fester, an ideology which has found forceful expression in a sequence of government inquiries that were run, as it happens, by engineers themselves. This ideology stresses the importance of manufacturing industry to the British economy, the crucial role of engineers in ensuring that designs and production methods in that industry are competitive and that this cannot be achieved so long as engineers are subordinate to non-engineers, with the happy corollary that action should urgently be taken to ensure that engineers quickly move into the command positions of British manufacturing industry (Feilden, 1963, Dainton, 1968; Finniston, 1980). Thus key positions within the global function of capital are now being claimed not on the grounds of offering a superior means of appropriating surplus value, as was the case with scientific management, but on the basis of a distinctive and vital contribution to the productive work itself. The outcome of these attempts will prove a severe test of Johnson's (1977b, p. 106) assertion that the persistence of indeterminacy, on which depends the monopolization of a body of knowledge by an organizational profession, depends not so much on the inherent mystery of the professional knowledge itself, but on whether the monopoly coincides with the interests of capital. In this connection, it is worth remarking that, ominously for engineers, computer technologies are being developed in the direction of routinizing, fragmenting and deskilling the work of engineering designers (Cooley, 1977, p. 39; Cooley, 1981; Rosenbrock, 1977, p. 392).

Even if this analysis proves fallacious, engineers face other difficulties in claiming positions of corporate power on the basis of their technological contributions. As Larson (1977, pp. 25–31) and Collins (1979, p. 174) have argued, professionals are in the strongest position in relation to their clients when they can monopolize the competence not only to practice, but to judge the results of that practice. Engineering activity, however, though esoteric and inaccessible to lay judgement in itself, must end in a physical product or process which *can* be judged by outsiders (unlike, say, the work of accountants which ends as a balance-sheet drawn up by themselves). In the face of this, the profession's ideology must somehow sustain the position that the subordination of engineers to non-engineers is still undesirable. This it nobly attempts, arguing that technological innovation in British industry suffers due to the caution of senior managers ignorant of the 'engineering dimension' (Finniston, 1980, pp. 30–5) and that the quality of design work suffers when supervised by non-engineers (Feilden, 1963; ch. 5). Nevertheless the 'problem' of the openness of engineering to lay judgement remains.

The other difficulty is that of formulating a policy, a problem exacerbated by the horizontal fissures within the profession. Both Feilden and Finniston proposed reforms to engineering education on the one hand and a campaign aimed at convincing senior managements of the importance of engineering on the other. The first course of action premised that it was engineers' lack of business sense and their inability to communicate with non-engineers which kept them from senior positions. In the debates within the profession, this analysis is supported by comparisons with the situation in West Germany, where engineering education includes substantial 'business' elements and where senior managements of manufacturing companies are indeed dominated by engineers (Hutton, Lawrence and Smith, 1977, pp. 69–87; Lawrence, 1980, pp. 67–74). However, it is questionable whether the former is the cause of the latter. As mentioned in the earlier discussion of the accountancy profession, the incorporation of business elements into German engineering education may be a *consequence* of the relative dominance of engineering and subordination of accountancy in German management. This, in turn, is probably related historically to the major role played by the German banking system, rather than the securities market in providing long-term industrial finance (Habakkuk, 1967, p. 174; Millar, 1979, p. 63).

It needs to be borne in mind that the diagnosis of the deficiencies of British engineers is one gathered by the élite of the profession (which overlaps the corporate élite), from employers who (by definition of 'the problem') are mostly non-engineers or, if engineers, are those occupying senior managerial or directional positions in a system of predominantly financial control. As an analysis, it amounts to an acceptance that business sense outweighs technical competence as a claim for senior management positions, and that the problem is not the inability of the non-engineering managers to understand technical issues (cf. Beuret, 1983), but the inability of engineers to explain them simply enough. As a policy, despite substantial changes in engineering education, it has achieved little, as is demonstrated by the similarity of the diagnoses of the Feilden and Finniston reports, separated by almost 20 years. The other side of the policy – that of persuading senior managers of the importance of engineering – amounts, in very simple terms, to a polite request to financial specialists that they should at least share their positions of corporate power with engineers. There is, however, a third possible course of action; the introduction of a system of licensing such as exists, however ineffectively, in the USA (Rothstein, 1969, p. 85), requiring government contractors to employ chartered engineers in appropriate positions. The reactions of the élite within the engineering profession to the restrictions on capital implied by such an approach, one favoured incidentally by an appreciable body of opinion amongst chartered engineers, can be gauged by the fact that Sir Monty Finniston himself ruled out the suggestion on the rather specious grounds that it was *ultra vires* in terms of the charters of the engineering institutions (Finniston, 1980, p. 186).

As the debate continues on how best to further the cause of engineering, structural changes within the profession are also making it clear that the collective mobility project – if it occurs at all – will not be for everyone. The Finniston proposals (Finniston, 1980, pp. 165–6) are only a formalization of pre-existing trends towards a three-tier profession, separated by increasingly rigid credential barriers, in which those elements of business education aimed at suiting engineers for management responsibilities will be taught only to a minority. Indeed, the developing hierarchy within the profession is explicitly one of control, rather than simply one of prestige. It is proposed by the elders of the profession to write into the very definition of the technician engineer and engineering technician grades that they will normally be subordinate to chartered engineers (Engineering Council, 1983). Given that many practising engineering managers have qualifications appropriate only to these lower grades of the profession (e.g. Sorge and Warner, 1980), this could be seen as an attempt to annexe management positions *within* engineering on behalf of the chartered grade, a move which could then serve as justification for claims of suitability for management status outside it.

Speaking generally, the approach brought by engineers to the control of the labour process is the systematic redesign and specification of the physical process of production itself, either through techniques such as scientific management (of which engineers no longer possess a monopoly, as discussed earlier) or via the designs of plant or machinery, a process which Edwards (1979) calls the 'technical control' of labour. Both approaches inherently imply a separation of mental from manual labour, a fact which has led some Marxists, arguing at high levels of abstraction, to conclude that the work of engineers and technicians necessarily functions to exploit labour (Poulantzas, 1975, Gorz, 1976a), as if the mental labour of *all* engineers was concerned solely with controlling labour so as to extract (rather than create) a surplus from the productive process. Such a view of the relationship between technical and manual labour quite arbitrarily defines out of existence the possibility of a division of mental and manual labour within the productive process itself, and it has been challenged by the more concrete and historical analysis of Smith (1982). As a further example, Rolt (1970, p. 137) has pointed out that the motive which led Victorian mechanical engineers to develop self-acting machine tools was not the desire of employers to displace skill, but the desire of technical men to overcome its limitations.

More specifically on the question of technical control, although it is true that engineers have looked for and achieved technological innovations in areas where the control of labour was proving a problem (Habakkuk, 1967, p. 152; Bruland, 1982), that their choices in machine-tool automation have been such as to maximize control rather than efficiency (Noble, 1979), and that some chemical engineers have been conscious of devising labour processes along with their plant designs (Hales,

1980, pp. 55–8), there are insufficient grounds for that leap into technological determinism which argues that all current production technology is 'capitalist', in the sense that it can only be operated within capitalist social relations of production (Gorz, 1976a, 1976b). For example, continuous-flow process technologies were surely introduced primarily in order to corner the super-profits from a temporary technological monopoly, not as a crafty way of inviting labour to discipline itself in the manner described by Blauner (1964). In fact capitalists' priorities may be such that they do not even bother to take advantage of the subtle control potentialities of flow process technologies, as is shown by the persistence of traditional authoritarian management practices in French oil refineries (Gallie, 1978). In my view, therefore, it is a distortion to represent technological control as the kind of solution to a control crisis (cf. Edwards, 1979), by means of which at least that section of the engineering profession which is directly involved might have advanced within the global function of capital. Though technical control certainly exists as a phenomenon, it does so, for the most part, as a by-product of what both engineers and their employers think of as productive labour, and this no more constitutes an entry permit to the directors' canteen for intellectual workers than for their manual counterparts.

The Personnel Specialists

Despite the assertion of Cherns (quoted in Watson, 1977, p. 168) that 'organizational leadership' in post-war Britain had successively passed from engineers, accountants and marketing specialists to personnel departments, Brookes (1979, p. 53) found that only seven of the 173 companies he surveyed had directors responsible solely for personnel and industrial relations. Despite the recommendations of the 1968 Royal Commission on Trades Unions and Employers' Associations (Donovan, 1968, paras 95, 102) that boards of directors should take responsibility for industrial relations, over half of the companies had no director whose responsibilities included these matters (Brookes, 1979) and the characteristic directoral approach to industrial relations appears to be one of studied ignorance (Winkler, 1974). On the other hand, success is relative: the profession itself traces its origins to the 60 or so female welfare workers in British factories on the eve of the First World War (Niven, 1967, p. 42), whereas by 1980 membership of the Institute of Personnel Managers stood at over 20,000 (ACAS, 1980, p. 55).

According to the literature, there is a curious difference between the origins of British and American personnel management. Whereas in the USA, personnel departments were apparently created in order to administer a battery of techniques aimed at dividing and weakening the workforce (Gordon, Edwards and Reich, 1982, p. 138) and the devices of paternalistic despotism such as Henry Ford's 'Sociology Department' (Beynon, 1973, pp. 21–3), the profession in this country, as has been mentioned, claims its origins in factory welfare work. Perhaps the discrepancy arises because, in the more fragmented conditions of British industry, the less benign approaches to the control of labour were performed by employers' associations rather than by managers as such (Clegg, 1979, p. 125). However, these aspects of its origin are not emphasized in the accepted histories of the profession, though Anthony and Crichton (1969, p. 160) do mention the bargaining activities of employers' associations as antecedents.

History is written by the victors, and that of the personnel profession is represented as a struggle whereby 'professionalism' emerged through, and was finally emancipated from the 'welfare image' (Anthony and Crichton, 1969, p. 149). For example, in the inter-war years, welfare workers based outside the factory were excluded from membership of the Central Association of Welfare Workers, care was taken to define welfare work as an aspect of management and even the name of the association was changed so as to emphasize its industrial concerns (Niven, 1967; pp. 51, 52, 61). In Anthony and Crichton's account (1969, p. 164), the former welfare workers 'struggled to find other jobs to do for management which would entitle them to a place on the management team, in order that they could be brought in on discussions of importance such as the determination of wage rates or the deployment of staff'. In other words, it is claimed that corporate power was sought, not in the self-interest of the profession, but as a means of more effectively performing welfare work (see also Watson, 1977, pp. 52–5). Niven's account of the progress of the profession during the recession of 1925–39 is more robust: 'in the recession, welfare workers had to justify their immediate usefulness or founder...welfare supervisors had the courage and adaptability to turn course from welfare to labour and staff management in order to meet new and pressing needs' (Niven, 1967, p. 71). Given that the welfare needs of workers can scarcely have declined during the hungry 1930s it is likely that these 'new and pressing needs' had more to do with maintaining the welfare workers' position in industry than with anything else. Niven's passage suggests that they did so by adapting the existing means of their trade (interviewing, record-keeping and so on) so as to create a new means of labour administration. As late as the early 1970s, this aspect of the origin of the techniques of personnel management was, according to Timperley and Osbaldeston (1975, p. 619), still reflected in the clerical/administrative backgrounds of many practising personnel managers.

Having developed its techniques of control before the Second World War, the profession was well placed to offer them on a post-war seller's market, when full employment made the control of labour a more pressing problem. By the 1970s, the adaptation of professional values to the opportunities of the market had proceeded to the point where a concern for welfare appeared to be entirely submerged beneath a concentration on 'efficiency' (Watson, 1977, p. 198), and this tradition of relatively self-consciously adjusting the service provided so as to advance the profession within the global function of capital has continued (Thomason, 1980, pp. 32, 37).

However useful the personnel specialists may or may not have been, they could only have advanced their profession on the basis of that usefulness by establishing a monopoly of competence. Thus Niven (1967, p. 59) saw a key task of the association as that of combating the employers' tendency to assume that anyone could do the job and persuading them to employ only trained welfare workers. For Thomason (1980, p. 32), the essential difficulty in this is that the human relations and social skills which are part of the profession's stock-in-trade are too indeterminate to form a sufficiently exclusive and distinct basis on which to claim a monopoly (in a way, the opposite difficulty to that faced by the engineers). Like Niven, and with a disarming frankness, he proposes a somewhat artificial credentialism as a solution (Thomason, 1980, pp. 32, 33), without burdening his readers with the usual claims that this is really in the clients' own interests.

Perhaps because they have not yet succeeded in gaining the autonomy which they believe possible and necessary (Thomason, 1980, p. 35), personnel specialists are highly conscious that they face competition for positions of corporate power from engineers, financial and sales specialists. The kind of interpersonal tactics used by individual personnel managers in such situations are most illuminatingly described by Watson (1977, pp. 178–89), in an account which also stresses the active role played by them in defining the problems for which they purport to offer solutions.

Personnel specialists have tried to expand their sphere of influence into production planning and have competed with foremen and costing departments for the function of rate-fixing, on the grounds that they possess specialist knowledge of the effects of incentives. After the Second World War, they increasingly appropriated the training of first-line supervisors and middle managers, on the grounds that the hire-and-fire methods of control, traditional amongst these groups, were no longer appropriate in an era of full employment (Anthony and Crichton, 1969, pp. 166–70). In the industrial context, they have become the prophets of a particular kind of behavioural science, much of which, as Rose (1975, p. 213) points out of the Tavistock researches, can be interpreted as an attack on the trained incapacities of production engineers. Moreover, in the industrial relations field, the general message of the kind of industrial relations policies advocated, for example, by Hawkins (1979) is that short-term expediency in solving industrial relations problems (characteristic of production managers) should be subordinated to a broader, more consistent policy (administered by personnel specialists, and, naturally, from the boardroom).

All this is a particular case of a phenomenon remarked by Child *et al.* (1983), and earlier by Fores and Glover (1978), as particularly prevalent in Britain: that the professionalization of staff positions outside production involves a claim for decision-making autonomy which results in the imposition of the practices of the professions concerned on, and thus the subordination of, the production function. In other words, personnel specialists have ascended within the global function of capital partly by exposing the inadequacies of, and at the expense of, engineers in line management.

The major crisis within the function of capital that has enabled them to do this concerned the control of labour, and it resulted from the persistence of relatively full employment from the end of the Second World War until the early 1970s, although a part may also have been played by the development of capital-intensive technologies, which made it necessary for employers to bargain for their workers to take a responsible attitude towards capital plant in this 'primary' sector of the labour market (Edwards, 1975). Full employment created the conditions for the growth of shop-steward organization, to which the response – first of academics, then later of the Royal Commission – was that the techniques of industrial relations pluralism were a more realistic strategy than the bluff anti-unionism of an earlier generation of engineer/managers (Fox, 1966; Donovan, 1968, p. 264; Flanders, 1975).

The appropriation by the profession of industrial relations pluralism, with its assumption of permanent underlying conflicts of interest, provides the perfect rationale for the curious dual relationship of personnel specialists to the control of labour. On the one hand, this obviously presents problems which must be solved at the level of day-to-day operations, and on the other, their own organizational power and influence depends on the long-term persistence of the problem (Watson, 1977, pp. 183–9). In Turner, Roberts and Roberts' (1977, pp. 35–9) finding that labour problems are most prevalent where personnel specialists are most heavily represented, there is even the suggestion that they may play a part in sustaining the very problems which provide the rationale for their presence. A survey by the Industrial Relations Research Unit, reported by Batstone (1980), points towards a mechanism by which this may occur. By centralizing and formalizing company-level procedures in line with the recommendations of the

Donovan Report (1968), personnel managers have stimulated the development of shop-steward organization and the expectation that something was to be gained by participating in the new bargaining procedures. However, because they lacked influence on top management financial policies, personnel specialists have been unable to satisfy these new expectations. The result has been an increased incidence of conflict with a better-organized workforce.

Another development during the years of full employment worked in favour of the personnel specialists. As part of a high-level strategy for securing the co-operation of labour, governments have introduced, from the 1960s onwards, a mass of legislation offering 'individual rights' to workers on the one hand, and regularizing the position of their trade unions and officials on the other. Although some of these 'rights' proved more apparent than real when put to the test (Lewis, 1981), the complication of the legislation provided personnel specialists with a major opportunity to supplement their somewhat indeterminate human relations skills with a genuinely codifiable and esoteric body of professional knowledge. As Thomason (1980, p. 33) puts it, 'The spate of employee legislation and codes of practice have enabled both the IPM and individual practioners to acquire status enhancing power', and again: 'the state response changed the balance of power as between personnel practitioners and line managers which allowed the former to enhance their discretion'. Put more crudely, personnel managers have used the threat of industrial tribunals to impose their own methods of discipline on lower-line managers and to remove from them altogether the right to sack.

If the personnel profession has traditionally sought its advances within the corporate hierarchy by exposing the shortcomings of production and other line managers, with a view to taking over certain of their former roles within the global function of capital, there are signs that a different strategy is being adopted in relation to financial specialists. Recognizing the corporate ascendancy of these, personnel thinkers are now seeking to present their specialist contribution to the control of labour in forms which they take to be acceptable in terms of the 'dominant utilitarian values and bureaucratic relationships' of the organizations which employ them. Thus quantitative and computerized techniques of manpower planning have been developed in answer to the criticism that personnel departments have not, in the past, provided 'hard' data (Legge, 1978, pp. 79 ff.). There have also appeared the significantly labelled techniques of 'Human resource, *accounting*', and the 'Industrial relations *audit*', but it is not clear whether these attempts to present personnel work as a species of accountancy are meeting with much success.

As with accountancy and engineering, the stress of competition for corporate power appears to be producing a hierarchy within the profession. There are five grades of membership in the Institute of Personnel Management; the 'Member' grade, which numbers about one-fifth of the total, dominates the policy of the Institute and sets increasingly rigorous requirements for entry to its own ranks (Timperley and Osbaldeston, 1975). However, the reported infrequency of formal qualifications amongst personnel managers in industry (Daniel and Millward, 1983, p. 122) indicates that the creation of this hierarchy has not enabled the élite of the profession to monopolize the available top corporate positions. Although there probably *are* hierarchies within personnel practice in industry (in a case observed by the writer, such matters as interviews, issuing warnings and even the more straightforward sackings were all handled by female subordinates), these seem to have developed in an *ad-hoc* manner, unrelated to the formal hierarchy of the profession.

Though subject to negotiation and attempts at territorial expansion, the role of personnel specialists in the control of labour has historically been that of delivering a suitable supply of it to operational departments and helping to movtivate or at least prevent its insurrection once it is there. Such a specialism can prosper in the corporate hierarchy only when these tasks are, or can be made to appear, sufficiently grave a problem not to be handled incidentally by other managers. Whereas the ultimate logic of the engineers' claim to design the physical process of production leads to attempts to destroy workers' resistance to this claim, that of the personnel specialists' position demands that the control of labour, both at the individual and collective levels, should continue to pose a problem, albeit one containable by the specialist techniques possessed by them. Perhaps this contradiction is one reason for the rapidly changing hit-parade of psycho-sociological gimmickry deployed by the profession (the other reason being product differentiation under the stress of competition amongst the associated consultants and semi-academics). These have ranged from comparatively straightforward attempts to explain to workers what they are doing and why, to insultingly childish campaigns such as 'QED' ([save a] quid each day), to highly enjoyable weekend trips on which (according to accounts given to the writer) managers and workers reach out for mutual understanding, but find only a common drunkenness. In a profession with such a strong tradition of offering whatever service promises to advance or secure its own position, more will surely follow – provided, that is, it can find a way of surviving the comparative quiescence of labour imposed by the current recession.

Brief Remarks on Other Competing Groups

Financial, engineering and personnel specialists by no means exhaust the catalogue of identifiable groups engaged in the competing collective mobility projects within the global functions of capital. Here, more briefly than hitherto, I will look at the situation of unspecialized general managers, of sales and marketing specialists, and of systems analysts, both from the point of view of the resources they bring to the intra-corporate competition and of their actual or potential contributions to the control of labour.

General managers
About two-thirds of the membership of the British Institute of Management and four-fifths of company directors in this country are not qualified to degree level (Brookes, 1979, p. 3; Mansfield *et al.*, 1981, p. 8). Indeed, slightly under half of all British managers have no higher education at all (Fidler, 1981, pp. 85-6). Although a proportion of these undoubtedly possess quite specific knowledge acquired on the job, these figures point to a substantial category of British managers, represented at the highest level within the global function of capital, whose stock-in-trade is an ill-defined, though effective ability to get what they want, to motivate or push people, rather than anything which could be called a professional specialism. If these men and women, like the 'traditional' foremen described by Nichols and Beynon (1977, ch. 4) are historically on the way out, they are putting up a good fight of it. Though almost by definition unorganized at the formal level, they possess a well-defined occupational ideology in which the macho virtues of their own 'practicality', 'hard-headendness' and 'realism' are constrasted with the effete theoretical footling associated with any profession requiring higher education and stigmatized at its very worst as 'academic'. *En masse*, managers of this kind are capable of administering a severe culture shock to trainee and even

newly qualified professionals and may be responsible for many decisions to devote future careers to research or teaching. It is likely, then, that people of this kind play a substantial role in the competition for key positions in the global functions of capital, and they do so on the basis of a claimed semi-instinctive understanding of and ability to control their fellow human beings and, through them, the labour process.

Sales and marketing specialists

One of the mechanisms behind the creation of giant corporations in the USA was the integration of mass production with a mass marketing network (Chandler, 1980, pp. 23–5). This implies a penetration of the sales effort into the production function (Baran and Sweezy, 1966), and therefore a tendency for sales departments to be the most powerful in such organizations (Perrow, 1970 quoted in Watson, 1977, p. 168). Clearly, the relative ascendancy of sales and marketing specialists in the global function of capital would initially be on the basis of performing the function of realizing surplus value, rather than appropriating it. However, the motivations and modes of awareness characteristic of the marketing/sales functions *do* appear to be influencing some recent approaches to the control of labour, which have in common that they rely on exposing work groups directly to their customers. Examples of this have taken place in Italy (Pignon and Querzola, 1976) and in a British company studied by the writer, in which groups of workers were made responsible to 'their' customers and required, at intervals, to meet them socially.

Computer specialists and systems analysts

In the kind of competition for corporate power and status described by Pettigrew (1975), the specialisms based on computer technology have already undergone, in America at least, a horizontal fission into a lower routinized branch (programming) and the more indeterminate, less codifiable and therefore less monopolizable skills of the systems analyst (Kraft, 1979). In one of its aspects computer technology makes it possible to deskill, routinize or even replace productive work, either physical or intellectual (Cooley, 1981; Wilkinson, 1983). However, by designing systems which obtain data direct from the point of production, store and analyse it, systems analysts are in a position to compete with existing line managers by offering senior managements an independent means of monitoring productive workers with consequent effects on the autonomy, and even the livelihoods of these line managers. Thus the effect of a system of centralized control installed in a steelworks was to reduce the job of the former production manager to a clerical task which could be performed by an untrained person, while at the same time the power of the computer specialists themselves was increased (Miller and Armstrong, 1966). Whisler (1966, p. 308) has listed a number of effects of installing computer information systems. Those relevant to the process of competition within the global function of capital are (1) that the organizational level of decision-making moves upwards; (2) that the system clearly pinpoints the responsibility for decisions and exposes them to scrutiny; (3) that the ability to handle large amounts of data enables decisions to be linked, thus allowing departmental structures to be destroyed (along with the careers of some of their managers). Finally, Haug (1977) has argued that, by making professional knowledge accessible to outsiders, computer technology creates the possibility of undermining professionalism altogether, a threat of which the profession of management accountancy has recently shown itself to be keenly aware (Banyard, 1983). Although Haug's argument is, to some extent, based on a misunderstanding of the nature of professional knowledge, it is nevertheless a good indication of the nature of the systems analysts' mission.

Fundamentally, then, the success of the collective mobility project of systems analysist within the global function of capital depends, first, on their continued role in the deskilling or replacement of productive physical and intellectual work; second, on their ability to continue cannibalizing their competitors; and third, on their ability to sustain a monopoly of their techniques. None of these conditions is assured. On the second point, for example, the adoption of computer technologies is very much a question of who is likely to be affected by them. Furthermore, as computer technology develops rapidly in the direction of greater 'user-friendliness' (perhaps under the pressure of a demand from non-specialist managers) and systems analysis, as a specialism, responds by divesting itself of this increasingly accessible knowledge base in favour of the more indeterminate skills of 'analysis', there arises the possibility that, like scientific management three-quarters of a century ago, it will cease to exist as a distinct school and become a component of all management. Even if this occurs, however, it seems likely that the workforces in the affected areas will experience the characteristic technology of surveillance associated with the specialism.

Conclusions

With Salaman (1982), it has been argued that, in treating capital as a unitary concept and concentrating on relationships between capital and labour, writers on the labour process have tended towards functionalism in their accounts of variations in the control strategies adopted by capital. Thus successive crises within the function of capital are made to account both for the advent of new control strategies and their nature. In contrast to this perspective, it has been argued that control strategies are based on generalizations of the techniques and knowledge possessed by 'professional' groups in competition for the key positions within the global function of capital. The response of capital to its crises (which need not be specifically of control) is mediated by these professions, which are poised to engage on collective mobility projects within the global function of capital in virtue of their possession of techniques which offer responses to these crises. However, if the knowledge basis of a response strategy is too accessible to outsiders, it can be implemented while failing as a means of group mobility, since the 'profession' may then be dispossessed of its strategy. For this reason, the élites within a profession may attempt to monopolize for themselves the esoteric indeterminate aspects of professional practice, while delegating the routine elements to subordinates, thus producing what Johnson (1977a, 1977b, 1980) called a 'horizontal fission' within the profession.

Relationships between the control strategies produced by the engineering, financial, personnel and other professions have been reviewed and appear to be consistent with such a perspective, although there are considerable gaps in the evidence. For instance, there appears to be little known of the historical evolution of the place of engineers in the control processes and management structures of British companies, and further research is clearly needed in this and other areas.

References

Abercrombie, N. and Urry, J. (1983) *Capital, Labour and the Middle Classes*, London, Allen and Unwin.

ACAS (Advisory, Conciliation and Arbitration Services) (1980) *Industrial Relations Handbook*, London, HMSO.

Anthony, P. and Crichton, A. (1969) *Industrial Relations and the Personnel Specialists*, London, Batsford.

Banyard, C. (1983) 'Future Prospects for Management Accountants', *Management Accounting*, vol. 61, p. 6.

Baran, P. A. and Sweezy, P. M. (1966) *Monopoly Capital: an essay on the American economic and social order*, New York, Monthly Review Press.

Batstone, E. (1979) 'Systems of Domination, Accommodation and Industrial Democracy', in T. Burns (ed.), *Work and Power*, Beverly Hills, Sage, ch. 7.

(1980) 'What have Personnel Managers done for Industrial Relations?' *Personnel Management*, June, pp. 36–41.

Berthoud, R. and Smith, D.J. (1980) *The Education, Training and Careers of Professional Engineers*, Department of Industry, London, HMSO.

Beuret, G. (1983) *Engineers – Servants or Saviours?* CNAA Development Services Publication No. 2.

Beynon, H. (1973). *Working for Ford*, London and Harmondsworth, Allen Lane, Penguin.

Blauner, R. (1964) *Alienation and Freedom*, Chicago, University of Chicago Press.

Boland, R. Jr (1982) 'Myth and Technology in the American Accounting Profession', *Journal of Management Studies*, vol. 19, no. 1, pp. 109–26.

Braverman, H. (1974) *Labor and Monopoly Capital*, New York, Monthly Review Press.

British Institute of Management (1972) *The Board of Directors: a survey of its structure, composition and role*, Management Survey Report No. 10.

Brookes, C. (1979) *Boards of Directors in British Industry*, Social Science Branch Research and Planning Division, Department of Employment Research Paper No. 9.

Bruland, T. (1982) 'Industrial Conflict as a Source of Technical Innovation: three cases', *Economy and Society*, vol. 11, no. 2, pp. 91–121.

Burchell, S., Clubb, C., Hopwood, A., Hughes, J. and Nahapiet, J. (1980) 'The Roles of Accounting in Organisations and Society', *Accounting, Organisations and Society*, vol. 5, no. 1, pp. 5–27.

Calhoun, D.H. (1960) *The American Civil Engineer, Origins and Conflict*, Cambridge, Mass., Technology Press, MIT.

Calvert, M.A. (1967) *The Mechanical Engineer in America 1830–1910: Professional Cultures in Conflict*, Baltimore, Md, John Hopkins Press.

Carchedi, G. (1977) *On the Economic Identification of Social Classes*, London, Routledge and Kegan Paul.

Chandler, A.D. Jr. (1977) *The Visible Hand; The Managerial Revolution in American Business*, Cambridge, Mass., Harvard University Press.

(1980) 'The United States: Seedbed of Managerial Capitalism', in A.D. Chandler, Jr and H. Daems (eds), *Managerial Hierarchies: Comparative Perspectives on the Rise of Modern Industrial Enterprise*, Cambridge, Mass., Harvard University Press, ch. 1.

Chandler, A.D. Jr and Daems, H. (1979) 'Administrative Co-ordination, Allocation and Monitoring: a comparative analysis of the emergence of accounting and organisation in the USA and Europe', *Accounting Organisations and Society*, vol. 4, no. 1/2, pp 3–20.

Child, J., Fores, M., Glover, I. and Lawrence, P. (1983) 'A Price to Pay? Professionalism and Work Organization in Britain and West Germany; *Sociology*, vol. 17, pp. 63–78.

Clawson, D. (1980) *Bureaucracy and the Labor Process: the Transformation of US Industry 1850–1920*, New York, Monthly Review Press.

Clegg, H.A. (1979) *The Changing System of Industrial Relations in Great Britain*, Oxford, Basil Blackwell.

Coke, S. (1983) 'Putting Professionalism in its Place', *Personnel Management*, vol. 15, no. 2, pp. 44–5.

Collins, R. (1979) *The Credential Society: an historical sociology of education and stratification*, London, Academic Press.

Cooley, M.(1977) 'The Contradictions of Science and Technology in the Productive Process', in G. Boyle, D. Elliot and R. Roy (eds), *The Politics of Technology*, London, Longman, pp. 36–45.

(1981) 'The Taylorisation of Intellectual Work', in L. Levidow and R. Young (eds), *Science, Technology and the Labour Process: Marxist Studies*, vol. 1, London, CSE Books, pp. 46–65.

Dainton, F.S. (Chairman) (1968) *Enquiry into the flow of candidates in Science and Technology into Higher Education*, Council for Scientific Policy, London, HMSO.

Daniel, W.W. and Millward, N. (1983) *Workplace Industrial Relations in Britain: The DE/PS1/SSRC Survey*, London, Heinemann Educational Books.

Donovan, Lord (Chairman) (1968) *Report of the Royal Commission on Trades Unions and Employers' Associations*, London, HMSO, Cmnd 3623.

Edwards R.C. (1975) 'Social Relations of Production and Labour Market Structure', in R.C. Edwards, M. Reich and D.M. Gordon (eds), *Labour Market Segmentation*, London, DC Heath, ch. 1.

  (1979) *Contested Terrain: the Transformation of the Workplace in the Twentieth Century*, London, Basic Books (page references to Heinemann edition).

Elger, A. (1982) 'Braverman, Capital Accumulation and De-skilling', in S. Wood (ed.), *The Degradation of Work?: Skill, de-skilling and the labour process*, London, Hutchinson, ch. 2.

Engineering Council (1983) *Consultative Document on Standards and Routes to Registration, 1985 Onwards*, The Professional Institutions Directorate of the Engineering Council.

Esland, G. (1980) 'Professions and Professionalism', in G. Esland and G. Salaman, (eds), *The Politics of Work and Occupations*, Milton Keynes, Open University Press, ch. 7.

Feilden, G.B.R. (Chairman) (1963) *Engineering Design*, Department of Scientific and Industrial Research, London, HMSO.

Fidler, J. (1981) *The British Business Elite: its attitudes to class, status and power*, London, Routledge and Kegan Paul.

Finniston, Sir M. FRS (Chairman) (1980) *Engineering Our Future: Report of the Committee of Inquiry into the Engineering Profession*, London, HMSO, Cmnd 7794.

Flanders, A. (1975) 'Collective Bargaining: Prescription for Change', in *Management and Unions: the theory and reform of industrial relations*, London, Faber (second edition), pp. 155–211.

Fores, M. and Glover, I. (1978) 'The British Disease: Professionalism', *Times Higher Educational Supplement*, 24 February 1978.

Fox, A. (1966) *Industrial Sociology and Industrial Relations*, Donovan Commission Research Paper No. 3, London, HMSO.

Friedman, A.L. (1977) *Industry and Labour: class struggle at work and monopoly capitalism*, London, Macmillan.

Gallie, D. (1978) *In Search of the New Working Class*, Cambridge, Cambridge University Press.

Gerstl, J.E. and Hutton, S.P. (1966). *Engineers: the anatomy of a profession*, London, Tavistock.

Goldner, F. H. and Ritti, R.R. (1967) 'Professionalisation as Career Immobility', *American Journal of Sociology*, vol. 72, pp. 489–502.

Gordon, D.M., Edwards, R. and Reich, M. (1982) *Segmented Work: Divided Workers: the historical transformation of labor in the United States*, Cambridge, Cambridge University Press.

Gorz, A. (1976a) 'Technology, Technicians and Class Struggle', in A. Gorz (ed.), *The Division of Labour*, Brighton, Harvester Press, pp. 159–89.

  (1976b) 'On the Class Character of Science and Scientists', in H. Rose and S. Rose (eds), *The Political Economy of Science*, London, Macmillan, ch. 4.

Gospel, H.F. (1983) 'Managerial Structures and Strategies', in H.F. Gospel and C. Littler (eds), *Managerial Strategies and Industrial Relations*, London, Heinemann Educational Books, ch. 1.

Habakkuk, H.J. (1967) *American and British Technology in the Nineteenth Century: the search for labour-saving inventions*, Cambridge, Cambridge University Press.

Hales, M. (1980) *Living Thinkwork: where do labour processes come from?* London, CSE Books.

Hannah, L. (1980) 'Visible and Invisible Hands in Britain', in A.D. Chandler Jr and H. Daems (eds) *Managerial Hierarchies Comparative Perspectives on the Rise of the Modern Industrial Enterprise*, Cambridge, Mass., Harvard University Press, ch. 2.

Haug, M. (1977) 'Computer Technology and the Obsolescence of the Concept of Profession', in R.M. Haugh and J. Dofny (eds), *Work and Technology*, Beverly Hills, Sage, ch. 14.

Hawkins, K. (1979) *A Handbook of Industrial Relations Practice*, London, Kogan Page.

Hutton, S.P. Lawrence, P.A. and Smith, J.H. (1977) *The Recruitment, Deployment and Status of the Mechanical Engineer in the German Federal Republic*, University of Southampton, Department of Mechanical Engineering.

Johnson, Terry (1977a) 'What is to be known?' *Economy and Society*, vol. 6, no. 2, pp. 194–233.

(1977b) 'The Professions in the Class Structure', in R. Scase, (ed.), *Industrial Society: Class, Cleavage and Control*, London, Allen and Unwin, ch. 5.

(1980) 'Work and Power', in G. Esland and G. Salaman, (eds), *The Politics of Work and Occupations*, Milton Keynes, Open University Press, ch. 11.

Kraft, P. (1979) 'The Industrialisation of Computer Programming: from Programming to "Software production", in A. Zimbalist, (ed.), *Case Studies in the Labor Process*, New York, Monthly Review Press, pp. 1–17.

Larson, M.S. (1977) *The Rise of Professionalism: A sociological Analysis*, Berkeley, University of California Press.

Lawrence, P. (1980) *Managers and Management in West Germany*, London, Croom Helm.

Layton, E.T. Jr. (1969) 'Science, Business and the American Engineer', in R. Perrucci and J.E. Gerstl (eds), *The Engineers and the Social System*, New York, John Wiley, ch. 2.

(1971) *The Revolt of the Engineer: Social Responsibility and the American Engineering Profession*, Cleveland and London, Press of Case Western Reserve University.

Legge, K. (1978) *Power, Innovation and Problem-solving in Personnel Management*, New York and London, McGraw-Hill.

Lewis, P. (1981) 'An analysis of why legislation has failed to provide employment protection for unfairly dismissed employees', *British Journal of Industrial Relations*, vol. 19, pp. 316–26.

Littler, C.R. (1982) *The Development of the Labour Process in Capitalist Societies*, London, Heinemann Educational Books.

Littler, C.R. and Salaman, G. (1982) 'Bravermania and Beyond: Recent Theories of the Labour Process', *Sociology*, vol. 16, no. 2, pp. 251–69.

Mansfield, R., Poole, M., Blyton, P. and Frost, P. (1981) *The British Manager in Profile*, British Institute of Management Foundation Survey Report No. 51.

Marx, K. (1976) *Capital*, vol. 1, Harmondsworth, Pelican.

McKenna, E.F. (1978) *The Management Style of the Chief Accountant*, Farnborough, Hants, Saxon House.

Melrose-Woodman (1978) *Profile of the British Manager*, British Institute of Management Foundation Survey Report No. 38.

Millar, J. (1979) *British Management versus German Management: a comparison of organisational effectiveness in West German aud UK Factories*, Farnborough, Hants, Gower Press Edition, 1981.

Miller, E.J. and Armstrong, D. (1966) 'The Influence of Advanced Technology on the Structure of Management Organisation', in J. Steiber (ed.), *Employment Problems of Automation and Advanced Technology*, London, Macmillan, ch. 17.

Monck, B. (1954) 'The Eclipse of the Engineer in Management', *Egnineering*, vol. 178, pp. 329–34.

Nichols, T. and Beynon, H. (1977) *Living with Capitalism: Class Relations in the Modern Factory*, London, Routledge and Kegan Paul.

Niven, M.M. (1967) *Personnel Management 1913–63*, Institute of Personnel Management.

Noble, D.F. (1977) *America by Design*, Oxford, Oxford University Press.

(1979) 'Social Choice in Machine Design: the case of automatically controlled machine tools', in A. Zimbalist, (ed.), *Case Studies in the Labor Process*, New York, Monthly Review Press, pp. 18–50.

Perrucci, R. and Gerstl, J.E. (1969) *Profession Without Community: Engineers in American Society*, New York, Random House.

Pettigrew, A. (1975) 'Occupational Specialisation as an Emergent Process', in G. Esland, G. Salaman and M. Speakman (eds), *People and Work*, Edinburgh, Holmes McDougall for the Open University Press, ch. 19.

Pignon, D. and Querzola, J. (1976) 'Dictatorship and Democracy in Production', in A. Gorz (ed.), *The Division of Labour*, Brighton, Harvester Press, pp. 62–99.

Pollard, S. (1965) *The Genesis of Modern Management: a study in the Industrial Revolution in Great Britain*, London, Edward Arnold.

Portwood, D. and Fielding, A. (1981) 'Privilege and the Professions', *Sociological Review*, vol. 29, no. 4, pp. 749–73.

Poutlantzas, N. (1975) *Classes in Contemporary Capitalism*, London, Verso Books.

Rolt, L.T.C. (1970) *Victorian Engineering*, London, Allen Lane.

Rose, M. (1975) *Industrial Behaviour: Theoretical Developments since Taylor*, London and Harmondsworth, Allen Lane, Penguin.

Rosenbrock, H. (1977) 'The Future of Control', *Automatica*, vol. 13, pp. 389–92.

Roth, J. (1974) 'Professionalism; the Sociologist's Decoy', *Sociology of Work and Occupations*, vol. 1, p. 1.

Rothstein, W.G. (1969) 'Engineers and the Functionalist Model of Professions', in R. Perrucci and J.E. Gerstl, (eds), *Engineers and the Social System*, New York, John Wiley, ch. 3.

Salaman, G. (1982) 'Managing the Frontier of Control', A. Giddens and G. Mackenzie (eds), *Social Class and the Division of Labour*, Cambridge, Cambridge University Press, pp. 46–62.

Smith, C. (1982) 'Technical Workers: Class, Work and Trade Unionism', PhD thesis, University of Bristol.

Solomons, D. (with T.M. Berridge) (1974) *Prospectus for a Profession: the report of the long range enquiry into the education and training for the Accountancy profession*, Advisory Board for Accounting Education.

Sorge, A. and Warner, M. (1980) 'Manpower Training and Manufacturing Organisation and Workplace Relations in Great Britain and West Germany', *British Journal of Industrial Relations*, vol. 18, no. 3, pp. 313–33.

Stacey, N.A.H. (1954) *English Accountancy: a study in social and economic history 1800–1954*, London, Gee.

Steer, P. and Cable, J. (1978) 'International Organization and Profit: an Empirical Investigation of Large UK Companies', *Journal of Industrial Economics*, vol. 27, pp. 13–30.

Thomason, G. (1980) Corporate Control and the Professional Association, in M. Poole, and R. Mansfield (eds), *Managerial Roles in Industrial Relations*, Farnborough, Hants, Gower, ch. 4.

Thompson, G. (1978) 'Capitalist Profit Calculation and Inflation Accounting', *Economy and Society*, vol. 7, no. 4, pp. 395–429.

Timperley, S.R. and Osbaldeston, M.D. (1975) 'The Professionalisation Process: an aspiring occupational organisation', *Sociological Review*, vol. 23, no. 3, pp 607–77.

Tricker, R. (1967) *The Accountant in Management*, London, Batsford.

Turner, H.A., Roberts, G. and Roberts, D. (1977) *Management Characteristics and Labour Conflict*, Cambridge, Cambridge University Press.

Vanning, M. (1975) *Professional Engineers, Scientists and Technologists in the Engineering Industry*, Engineering Industry Training Board.

Watson, T.J. (1977) *The Personnel Managers*, London, Routledge and Kegan Paul.

Whisler, T.J. (1966) 'The Impact of Advanced Technology on Managerial Decison-Making', in J. Steiber, (ed.), *Employment Problems of Automation and Advanced Technology*, London, Macmillan, ch. 16.

Wilkinson, B. (1983) *The Shopfloor Politics of New Technology*, London, Heinemann Educational Books.

Wilson, C. (1970) *The History of Unilever: a study in economic growth and social change*, London, Cassell Edition.

Winkler, J.T. (1974), 'The Ghost at the Bargaining Table: Directors and Industrial Relations', *British Journal of Industrial Relations*, 12, pp. 191–212.

Wright, E.O. (1979) *Class Structure and Income Determination*, London, Academic Press.

8 Ideology and Shop-Floor Industrial Relations: Theoretical Considerations

P.J. ARMSTRONG, J.F.B. GOODMAN
AND J.D. HYMAN

Basic Concepts

The study of industrial relations has often centred around rules and the processes of rule making. Thus Flanders stated that a 'system of industrial relations is a system of rules' and subsequently defined the subject as the 'study of the institutions of job regulation'.[1] Many writers (e.g. Goldthorpe and Margerison[2]) have taken exception to the formalistic orientation implied by Flanders's concentration on 'institutions', particularly to the implied neglect of the informal processes which have been increasingly characteristic of British industrial relations in recent years. Thus Bain and Clegg, whilst retaining the emphasis on 'the making and administering of rules', broadened their definition of industrial relations to include 'all aspects' of job regulation.[3]

Even this wider emphasis on job regulation has not escaped criticism. Hyman,[4] for example, accepts the importance of rule making in industrial relations but argues that its elevation to the central area of study involves a number of inadequacies. In particular, he considered that the approach results in a definite conservative bias:

> To define industrial relations in terms of rules is to emphasise the relatively defined, stable and regular aspects of employer–worker and management–union relationships: by the same token it is to play down the significance of conflicts of control in the labour market and over the labour process as manifestations of a fundamental and continuous antagonism of interest.[5]

Accepting Hyman's point – that rule making is only a partial form and consequence of the struggle for control – the approach adopted in this study, by focusing on some of the conflictual processes of rule making, can hopefully meet the main thrust of his argument. Provided due attention is paid to these processes there seems no reason why a focus on rules should involve any particular bias.

What, then, is meant by employment rules? At the institutional level there are a number of major sources of rule output: management, trade unions, the institutions of collective bargaining and the relevant agencies of government. The most obvious and tangible rule output of these institutions is in the form of written regulations and traditionally the aggregate of these written regulations has often, following Weber's study of bureaucracy,[6] been considered to comprise the

P.J. Armstrong, J.F.B. Goodman and J.D. Hyman, *Ideology and Shop-Floor Industrial Relations*, London, Croom Helm, 1981; Chapter 2 'formal' rules of an organisation (e.g. Blau.)[7] However, there was from the outset some ambiguity in the usage of the term 'formal rule': there were writers who clearly considered 'formal' rules to include all rules of management origin, whether written or not (e.g. Roethlisberger and Dickson[8]) and such an approach might be considered to open the way to a consideration of unwritten rules from other sources. In industrial relations the recognition of the 'two systems of industrial relations', and especially the formulation by the Donovan Commission,[9] confirmed that it was unrealistic to consider the written output of official union-management negotiations as constituting the whole rule output of joint origin. The post-war rise of shop stewards meant that any realistic picture of workplace rules would clearly have to include the frequently unwritten output of 'unofficial' negotiation. At a lower level still, recognition that in some sectors of British industry there existed a substantial measure of workers' job regulation – or at least workers' restriction of management job regulation – inspired Brown's studies of 'custom and practice'[10] which again made it clear that there were many operational rules which were neither written nor originated with any of the recognised rule-making institutions. When it is finally added that a traditional theme of organisational studies has been the manner in which 'informal' rules supplant written regulations or standing management instructions, it is clear that, unless rules are to be studied in the abstract, the starting-point must be the actual regularities of behaviour involved in the employment relationship. This implies rather a wide definition of the term 'rule'; thus, rates of pay, customary differentials and so on are included as well as the patterns of behaviour which those involved conventionally refer to as rules. With the one proviso that the behaviour must be known to the immediately interested parties (otherwise the regularity might be abruptly ended by discovery), this will form our working definition of a rule. Of course, these regularities of behaviour may coincide with 'formal' rules, with management instructions or negotiated agreements, but equally they may not. As will be amplified later, 'formal' regulations constitute only one of the resources which go into the making of operational rules and there may be other considerations which, from time to time, override such 'official' prescriptions.

For some years one of the dominant theoretical approaches to rule making has derived from the work of Dunlop[11] in which employment rules are regarded as the output of an industrial relations system. It remains debatable whether systems theory can usefully be developed beyond an orderly listing of relevant variables (Gill[12]) and it is open to criticism where extra-institutional processes are concerned (Fatchett and Whittingham).[13] Despite the incorporation of an 'informal system' into the model, there are still difficulties of accommodating custom and practice rule making into the system. In fact, Brown's[14] account of the process of management 'error' and workers' consolidation by which C & P rules become established owes nothing at all to the systems model. One possible line of progress has been suggested by Goodman and his colleagues[15] who differentiated between 'industrial relations' and 'production' systems and described a process of norms originating in the latter and being reinstitutionalised in the former. However, taking these approaches together still does not provide a comprehensive theory as to how rules may come into being outside of the industrial relations system unless, that is, it can be assumed that all rules generated outside of the system are the result of C & P.

If, as has been suggested earlier by Armstrong and Goodman,[16] the term C & P is broadened to include managerial rule making and rules imposed by the use of power rather than appeals to legitimacy, there may be a certain amount of justification in this assumption. If, however, C & P is understood in the conventional sense, as a set of rules maintained by workers and legitimised on the grounds of custom, it will be recognised on reflection that the identification of extra-system rules with C & P is far too restrictive. For one thing it is perfectly possible for rules of this character to originate with management, more especially with the lower ranks. Although management as a whole is, from the systems point of view, considered as a legitimate rule-making institution, it nevertheless happens that operational rules, particularly those originating at lower levels, are sometimes not in accord with directives from senior management nor, indeed, with other rules of institutional origin. In this manner, rules which modify the output of the system may easily originate with management themselves. Nor are extra-system rules invariably legitimised by appeals to custom as is the case with C & P as this is conventionally understood. New rules, indeed, could not possibly be justified in such a manner. Both managers and workers employ a wide variety of arguments to justify 'informal' rule changes. Appeals are made, for example, on the grounds of fairness, of productivity, of the right of managers to manage and on the grounds that workers possess certain property rights in their jobs.

Once this variety of argument is acknowledged, it becomes a matter of observation that it is by no means confined to the justification of 'extra-system' rules. Day-to-day encounters in which managers explain rules they may have made, discussions involving shop stewards and more formal negotiations with outside union officials are all permeated by what are essentially legitimising arguments, many of which actually recur in all three settings. Arguments used to justify informal practices may recur in formal negotiations and senior managers may explain their instructions in the same terms as their supervisors account for their deviation from them. There is in this respect a continuity between extra-system and in-system rule-making processes which has possibly been obscured by the system concept itself. In practice, as Clegg has pointed out, there is no clear dividing line between informal negotiation and the day-to-day conduct of affairs on the shop floor.[17] Nor should this cause much surprise: the arguments deployed in negotiations have often been well rehearsed beforehand in the course of everyday encounters.

We are not, of course, suggesting that the role of legitimising argument has gone unnoticed in the literature. To Fox the 'ideologies of management and collectivities' constitute a resource in the struggle for power.[18] Walton and McKersie refer to 'attitudinal structuring' as a stage of the bargaining process.[19] In the same vein Batstone *et al*, point out that shop stewards, in order to be successful, must couch issues in a form which ensures the 'mobilisation of bias'[20] and, for Partridge, one of the key tasks confronting a shop steward is to define a grievance so as to engage the values of his constituents.[21] In all this there is a clear convergence: it is recognised that the parties to the rule-making process – particularly workers' representatives – must engage effective legitimising arguments in support of their policies. However, the emphasis has usually been placed on the process of doing so, almost as if the selection of the issue has preceded the search for an effective means of legitimisation; as if the discovery of appropriate legitimising arguments were merely a question of technique. It is here, following McCarthy,[22] that we would wish to shift the emphasis more towards the content of such arguments, for it is surely common that the impulse to campaign for rule changes springs from a spontaneous sense of injustice rather than a calculation of advantage which is later cold-bloodedly dressed up in some legitimising argument. Furthermore, one can think of a very wide range of rule changes which would benefit either management or workers but which never become issues, possibly because the balance of power is unpropitious but also (and not unrelatedly) because there is no effective way of legitimising such rule changes. In other words, it is suggested that legitimisation is not merely a technique or tactic but an important constraint on which rule changes are raised as issues. Phelps Brown was not only prepared to recognise such constraints but also to suggest their enlistment in the cause of wage restraint. He wrote that:

> It is fortunate that even in the pursuit of self-interest, we all feel the need for legitimisation. Particular groups in advancing their own claims for certain relative rates of pay have to show that they are fair, and this not only for the purpose of bargaining, but also as a matter of self respect.[23]

In pursuing this theme, Gerth and Mills's[24] concept of a 'vocabulary of motives' is useful. This notion suggests that in any cultural setting there are certain acceptable motives for action (what we will call 'legitimising principles') which are, in turn, embedded in the characteristic world view (ideology) of that culture. Thus, in his 'mobilisation of bias' a shop steward must link his policies to acceptable motives already existing in the culture of his constituents. He cannot invent motives at will and expect them to have the desired effect. The same considerations apply when he presents an argument to management. He must, if he is to be effective, engage with the vocabulary of motives already existing in management culture. These two considerations, we would argue, not only place technical demands on his ability to link cases to principles; they also place limits on the cases he can take up with any expectation of success.

However, the matter goes somewhat deeper. We have spoken as if the shop steward were an uncommitted outsider, as if he were concerned only in a manipulative way with other people's vocabularies of motive. Ordinarily, however, being of the culture of the workforce, it is very likely that his own personal vocabulary of motives largely coincides with theirs, thus enabling him to act in spontaneous rapport with his constituents. Otherwise, and as experienced managers seem able to sense very quickly, he will be easy meat: a representative deserted by his constituents or the feeble advocate of a case he does not believe in. Very often, then, the legitimising arguments advanced in the rule-making process will be advanced in all sincerity, their effectiveness depending not on a calculative appeal but on a pre-existing cultural rapport. It is this which makes it possible for a sense of what is legitimate actually to set the rule-making process in motion. What a junior manager sees as a legitimate rule change, for instance, is also very likely to seem legitimate to his seniors, and so receive their backing, even though he may not actually possess the delegated 'formal' responsibility to make the change.

There are thus a number of aspects to the concept of legitimisation, as we wish to employ it. First of all, corresponding to the concept of a vocabulary of motives, there exist certain legitimising principles in the culture of managers and workers, and these exert some constraint on what can be justified to these groups. Generally speaking, legitimising principles are embedded in the ideological world views of those concerned and are therefore relatively stable. Although, as Fox[25] points out, there are ideological exchanges between managers and workers, the reciprocal influence of their ideologies is largely played out at the society-wide level. At the workshop level, 'vocabularies of motive' consist of fairly limited repertoires of legitimising principles which are largely stable in the short term.

Secondly, there is a mobilisation dimension to legitimisation (shop steward convinces his constituents) as well as a tactical dimension (shop steward attempts to convince his manager). Whilst the mobilisation dimension is virtually a pre-condition of a rule-making initiative (in that it appears to those involved as their actual motive), the importance of the tactical dimension depends very much on the balance of power. However, although it may be possible for one party – particularly management – to ride roughshod over the other's sense of outrage, the price in subsequent resentment and guerilla warfare may be too high. Thus, even where sufficient power exists to impose a rule unilaterally, long-term considerations may counsel some compromise with the opposition's concept of what is legitimate.

Thirdly, there is a public, as well as a private, dimension to legitimisation which is most important when, as is very often the case in industrial relations, questions of legitimisation are actually contested. Suppose, for example, that a worker objects to a new management rule but can find no publicly acceptable legitimising principle to justify his objection. However personally aggrieved he may feel, there is then no way of mobilising his colleagues' support on the issue. It is even possible for such feelings to be shared, for a group of workers to feel individually ill-used, but unless there is some means of transforming their private grievances into a public issue, they will not be able to mobilise effectively. Although the impulse to mobilise may originate in a private sense of legitimisation, the effectiveness of mobilisation depends on linking the issue to what is publicly acknowledged as legitimate. The same distinction applies to the outcome of the rule-making process. A new rule may come into existence because management publicly concede the legitimacy of a case put by the workers. Individual managers, however, may still object to the new rule, albeit on grounds which do not have public currency. Conceding the legitimacy of a rule at the public level, then, may coexist with private discontent. Where this is the case, those concerned may regard the rule as a temporary imposition, to be changed when the balance of power allows.

Fourthly, the practical legitimisation of an operational rule is generally a question of degree. For, if the arguments on one side of an issue prevail (either because of their merit or because they are backed by sufficient power), it does not follow that the opposing arguments suddenly lose their validity. Rules come into being and are sustained against a background not only of the arguments used to introduce them but also of opposing arguments which unsuccessfully challenged them. During the initial states, at least, of a rule's life, this structure of argument continues to be associated with it.

What is emerging is essentially a conflict theory of rule making in industrial relations in which the rival parties use legitimising arguments both to mobilise their own resources and to undermine the unity and resolve of their opponents. It may seem strange that a conflict theory should use legitimisation as its central concept rather than power or interests. Basically, the reason is that we are concerned primarily with rule making at and below the level of the individual firm. The processes involved are on quite a small scale and concern only marginal adjustments to the *status quo*, issues on which there is something approaching a balance of power. In any case, although power is clearly important in determining the outcome of any attempt to change workplace rules, it does not, by itself, determine which rule changes are in question. Power is a generalised resource and the fact that it is exercised does not determine the issues on which it is exercised. It is at this level that questions of legitimisation become important. By suggesting issues on which one's own side can be mobilised and one's opponents ideologically outmanoeuvred, so to speak, the available legitimising principles serve to channel the application of power. Again, if power were sufficient to explain rule changes, these should only occur as a consequence of a shift in the balance of power. Clearly this does occur, for example as a consequence of market or technological changes. Equally, however, rule changes frequently take place with no discernible change in the relative power of the parties. In such cases, and especially where the process of rule change is fairly rapid, power can be considered as a background 'given'. And even when a shift of the balance of power can be observed, questions of legitimisation may still channel the newly available resource in ways which seem worth while and economical.

Much the same remarks apply to the question of interests. So many rule changes would be in the interests of either side that the problem is to account for the selection of those which become live issues. The possibility of legitimisation provides an appropriate principle of selection since it is those interests which can be justified, both to one's own side and to the other side, which can most effectively be pursued. Where workers' interests are concerned there is another way of putting this which may be more familiar: we are saying that false consciousness limits the extent to which workers' ideology reflects their own interests. Interests are thus tacitly present in the proposed model of rule change. At the level under discussion, they are articulated with varying degrees of distortion, through the parties' ideologies and the legitimising principles embodied in them. In fact, the intervening stage between interests and action lends additional dynamism to the model in that rule changes may originate through innovative usages of ideological raw material. A pure interest theory, on the other hand, would require some shift in the parties' interest priorities to set the process of rule change in motion. Of course this may well happen, for example as a result of technological change. Yet even there legitimisation plays its part in that there tends to be pressure towards those rule changes which can be effectively legitimised by reference to the changed circumstances.

Legitimisation for Managers and Workers

In order to see rule making and rule change in context it is as well to remember that they are often part of the management process rather than the subject-matter of industrial relations as conventionally understood. For instance, Storey's[26] survey confirms that, in many workplaces, a wide range of conditions affecting workers is decided by management alone. Evidence suggests that, although successes are achieved by work groups in shifting back the 'frontier of control', such successes are frequently temporary (Cliff[27]) and limited in extent (Fox[28]). Herding's comparative study of American and German industrial relations indicates that there has, if anything, been a decrease in workers' job control in the USA in recent years.[29] Besides this direct control there is a second sense in which workplace rules may be a management product: they may largely follow from technical or marketing decisions which are almost invariably made unilaterally by management. Following the implementation of such decisions, there may be negotiation over the consequences, but the decisions themselves remain firmly in management hands. Furthermore, the generally unchallenged ability of management to make strategic decisions of this kind ensures that any ensuing negotiations take place within parameters which have already been unilaterally determined. Thus, fewer than one in ten of the workplaces surveyed by Storey negotiated over the introduction of new products, whilst roughly half negotiated over redundancies.[30] Yet, in a situation where redundancies are a consequence of a decision to switch resources to the production of new products, any negotiation could concern only the allocation of redundancies, or at most, minor variations in their extent.

Therefore, although management prerogatives may have been spectacularly eroded here and there, and although there may have been some diminution overall, it cannot, as Goldthorp[31] pointed out, be concluded that there has been a serious loss of management authority. What *has* declined, in Goldthorpe's view, is the ability of managers to overstep the bounds of their authority (as accepted by workers) and exercise arbitrary economic power – but note that power here is defined in the very general Weberian sense as 'the probability that an actor will be able to realise his own objectives even against opposition from others with whom he is in a social relationship' (Giddens[32]). Where subordinates accept the exercise of power as legitimate it is usual to speak of authority, in which case authority appears as a sub-class of power. It should be pointed out, however, that this definition does not coincide with Fox's usage, in which power and authority are conceived of as alternatives, nor with that of Batstone and his colleagues, in which power and authority are not distinguished at all (see Fox,[33] Batstone *et al*.[34]). In the sense used here, then, workers largely continue to accept management authority over marketing or technical matters and over much else besides.

The unproblematic exercise of management power is founded in an ideology which confirms its legitimacy. Based, amongst other things, on conceptions of the employers' property rights, on claims to special competence on the part of management (cf. Hyman and Brough[35]), managerial ideology serves to legitimise not only management power but also the ends to which it is characteristically directed which, for brevity, we will subsume under the blanket term 'profitability'.

Actually managers, whether in state or privately owned organisations, may think in terms of efficiency, corporate growth or community benefits rather than profit *per se*. However, these apparently diverse aims all depend upon increasing the economic return from the employment of labour and in that sense are equivalent to the profit motive as far as the effect on the work-force is concerned. Again, managers may express their aims in terms of 'productivity' rather than profit. When coupled with attractive notions of 'enlarging the cake' (e.g. see Stettner[36]) to the ultimate benefit of all the stake-holders in an enterprise, appeals to 'productivity' serve to avoid contentious distributive arguments associated with the term 'profit'. For brevity and the avoidance of confusion in exposition, therefore, we shall speak of profit and profitability as providing the motivating force behind management objectives.[37]

Not only is managerial ideology the characteristic world view of managers themselves; it is also, since managers and their employers are a dominant group in society, a key component of the 'dominant ideology' itself. Furthermore, in Parkin's[38] view, most workers broadly accept the main tenets of the dominant ideology. Whatever specific reservations may exist in the culture of workers there is, therefore, little systematic, across-the-board rejection of managerial ideology (Goldthorpe,[39] Hyman and Brough[40]). To the extent that this is the case, it is proper to speak of management authority rather than power.

In the context of rule making, an unconditional acceptance of managerial ideology constitutes an open cheque. In its pure form it potentially legitimises any rule change which originates with management: in so far as it insists upon an unqualified 'right to manage', it imposes no criteria which rule changes must meet in order to qualify as legitimate. This is also true to a lesser extent of legitimisation based on the object of management policy – profit. Any rule change which increases or is aimed at increasing profit can be legitimised in this way; the only restriction is that the rule change must not be a 'mistake'. At first glance, then, the legitimising principles derived from managerial ideology, in contradiction to what we have said earlier, appear to exert no restriction at all on the management part in rule making. In practice, however, this is not necessarily, the case, principally because managerial ideology has, over the years, accumulated a secondary structure of supportive argument some of which can imply limits on management action (Bendix[41]). For example, if the pursuit of profit is legitimised not as a fundamental right of ownership but by insisting that it is in the long-run interest of the whole community, it becomes that much more difficult for managers to sanction the poisoning of rivers and their workers. If managers justify their power not by appealing to an inalienable 'right to manage' but by representing themselves as the judicial arbitrators of competing interests (e.g. Simon, Flanders, Thomason[42]), it becomes so much more difficult for them to pursue policies which manifestly ignore some of these interests. Paradoxically, then, the secondary accretions of managerial ideology, whilst fundamentally supportive of management power, may also imply limits on its exercise. In practice, these limits of legitimisation may either be self-imposed by managers or may form a resource with which workers, whilst broadly accepting managerial ideology, may challenge the legitimacy of particular management rule-making initiatives.

It is also pertinent to point out that, whilst managerial ideology may be central to the characteristic world view of managers, this may also contain elements of the dominant ideology which are not obviously expressive of the interests either of themselves or of capital. The widespread notion that it is legitimate to expect someone to behave consistently is one such example and, given the right circumstances, such a legitimising principle may imply considerable constraint on management decisions. Indeed, in Brown's[43] discussion of custom and practice, it is evident that the principle of consistency (allied to that of managerial prerogative) is one of the major resources used by workers in establishing the legitimacy of their practices.

However, the use of managerial ideology 'against itself' and the appeal to principles of society-wide application do not exhaust the resources available to workers. Few of them nowadays would accept managerial power or the pursuit of profit without qualification – although it is important to stress that qualification is not the same thing as rejection. Indeed, it is the burden of Storey's[44] paper that what might appear in some quarters to be challenges to management power are in fact moves to set limits to its exercise – in other words, to activate the limits outside which workers do not accept management authority. The implication is that the managerial origin of rules and their relationship to the pursuit of profit still serves to legitimise them unless they impact upon these limits.

It is fruitful to consider this in relation to the body of research on workers' images of society. Such writers as Westergaard and Resler[45] argue that these tend to be fragmentary, inchoate and incomplete rather than coherent and internally consistent. Certainly, full-blown and consistent class consciousness (which implies a systematic rejection of the dominant ideology) is rare. Much more frequently there are elements of class consciousness uneasily coexisting with a background acceptance of the dominant ideology (sometimes in a 'negotiated' version, as Parkin points out[46]). On the whole, then, the bases for legitimising management-originated rules exist in most workers' views of the world, but here and there they coexist with, or are replaced by, isolated 'counter-principles' of legitimisation, elements of a view of the world opposed to the dominant ideology. Workers' resistance to the process of management rule making, or initiatives launched on their own account, may therefore proceed from counter-principles of this kind and, in so far as these counter-principles are expressive of workers' interests, there is some similarity to the deployment of managerial ideology by managers.

However, there is an important asymmetry. Whereas managerial ideology comprises a relatively coherent body of thought, comprehensively expressive of management interests, this is far from the case with the fragmentary counter-ideology available to workers. Whereas managers can justify their actions, at least to themselves and often to workers as well, by citing the principles of managerial prerogative and profitability, either of which will justify virtually any rule change, workers must ordinarily make use of legitimising principles which are relatively specific. One can see this asymmetry most clearly where an extension of the frontier of control is at issue. Managers could (admittedly with varying degrees of effectiveness) represent any extension of their own control as an application of managerial prerogative. Whilst workers might resist on the general grounds of C & P (always supposing that this principle implies a generality of application in their particular culture), they would not normally be able to legitimise extensions of their own control in general terms. At present there is not, in the culture of most workers, anything corresponding to the principle of managerial prerogative which could justify any demand for increased control.

Failing the strategic deployment of managerial ideology or of generally applicable principles (both of which imply some restriction on what can be justified), this means that workers' resistance to management rule changes or demands for changes of their own must be capable of articulation in terms of the counter-principles of legitimisation current in their culture. Since these are of a fairly specific nature, it follows that the need to legitimise workers' demands importantly conditions the demands themselves. For instance, if the principle of parity is used to justify a wage claim, this clearly determines the amount of the claim and who should get it. The interests of the workers would not, by themselves, determine this, since almost any wage increase (and a very large number of other possible rule changes) would also be in the workers' interests.

In summary, the legitimising principles available to managers can be used to justify their rule making in very general terms, only secondarily limited by the supportive arguments of managerial ideology and principles of society-wide application. The principles available to workers, on the other hand, consist of isolated and specific areas of rejection of managerial ideology and have greater limitation on what can be legitimised. Whilst not immutable, this set of available principles is fairly rigid, at least in the short term and as far as individuals are concerned. Legitimising principles in their nature depend on social acceptance and this ordinarily takes time to establish. One cannot, therefore, invent them at will, although ingenious casuistry and strategic choices of argument are certainly possible.

This comparative rigidity means that a large number of the possible rule changes which may be in the workers' interests are impossible to justify themselves with any degree of effectiveness. To put the matter another way, when comparing the rules as they exist with the rules as the available legitimising principles suggest they should be, there is probably very little question in workers' minds as to which are the changes that should be campaigned for, or which aspects of management proposals should be resisted.

Contested Legitimisation

Whereas managerial ideology constitutes a general warrant for rule making, the entry of workers into the rule-making process depends on the engagement of specific principles of legitimisation or any 'universal' principles of conduct which may be applicable or on the possibility of using managerial ideology 'against itself'. On issues where none of these is possible, workers and their representatives are likely to fail in the 'mobilisation of bias' and any desires they may have will then remain individual, fragmented and ineffective. This is the regime in which the legitimacy of management rule making at the public level remains unchallenged even though individual workers may have private reservations. In practice, the process of rule change in this area may seem so natural and its legitimacy so much a matter of common sense that it may not be thought of as rule change at all. Both managers and workers may see it simply as the former 'doing their job'.

Ordinarily, however, industrial relations is concerned with issues on which there are arguments on both sides of the question – where, in our terms, legitimisation is contested. In such cases managers mobilise basically around the principles of managerial prerogative and/or profitability and are confronted by workers mobilised around whichever of their legitimising resources can be linked to the case in hand. This we have referred to as the 'mobilisation dimension' of legitimisation. However, unless the parties are on course for an uncompromising trial of strength, there is also the tactical dimension to consider. Even if naked power is deployed at some stage of the proceedings, it still makes sense for both parties to attempt to convince the other of the legitimacy of their demands. Thus workers' representatives develop arguments linking their position to legitimising principles thought to be acceptable to management and vice versa. Rule changes, or modification to management rule changes, may be justified by workers as beneficial to, or at least not incompatible with, profitability. They may seek to show that their demands actually derive from past management decisions (principle of managerial prerogative) or, at least, do not represent incursions into the present zone of managerial control. The intention is to 'sugar the pill', to undermine the legitimacy of management opposition.

Exactly the same process will ordinarily be taking place on the management side. They will be attempting to demonstrate that the rule changes they desire are compatible with legitimising principles accepted by the workers; that (amongst other possibilities) the new rules involve no more work, that they respect existing property rights in jobs, or that they are aimed at restoring equitable treatment of comparable groups of workers. As an example, one management justified the declaration of redundancies amongst short-term employees (and the subsequent movement of long-service employees into their jobs) by an appeal to the 'trade union principle' of last-in-first-out, and this effectively pre-empted any opposition. However, it is noticeable that these attempts to engage workers' legitimising principles are sometimes accompanied by continued assertions of managerial prerogative and appeals to the profitability principle. Aside from the fact that the latter may contain an element of threat, it might be thought that the insufficiency of such arguments would be demonstrated by the fact of workers' opposition. However, it needs to be appreciated that the world views of individual workers vary somewhat and that there may well be contradictions within the thought processes of individuals. Thus, some workers may doubt whether the issue is really one on which there are legitimate grounds for opposing management. For others there may be a region in which their own principles of legitimisation alternate with an acceptance of managerial prerogative according to the context of discourse. Continued claims based on managerial ideology, therefore, may successfully play on ideological differences within the workforce and on inconsistencies within the thought processes of individuals.

Potentially, at least, both the mobilisation and tactical aspects of legitimisation can exert some influence on the rules which eventually emerge. Workers' representatives must propose rules or formulate objections to management rules in terms which their constituents are likely to regard as legitimate. However ingenious their arguments may be, this will often limit the form of the rules or the objection. Moreover, unless the workers possess an overwhelming short-run power advantage and are willing to use it, the need to engage management legitimising principles, even if only partially, will involve further limitations. In practice, of course, these limits may not be the subject of conscious calculation; still less should the two sources of limitation be understood as successive stages in a process of accommodation. Rather, a steward will formulate his position – as he sees it, 'realistically' – in the light of his knowledge of his constituency and of the management.

On the management side, because of the inclusive nature of managerial ideology, the restrictions on the form of proposed rules proceeds mainly from the requirement to compromise with workers' legitimising principles. Again, the process may be less reflective than this formulation makes it appear: most managers are not looking for trouble and will have a very good idea of what their workers will stand for. Moreover, it is perhaps important to stress that, for some managers, compromise with workers' principles of legitimisation may be part and parcel of what they take to be decent behaviour. If managerial ideology has accumulated supportive arguments based on 'fairness' and the like, the possibility is open for some managers to take these not as unconditional supports for their own position but as serious requirements to be met in practice. Again, it needs to be recalled that some managers, particularly the lower levels of line supervision, have their cultural origins within the workforce and, indeed, in trade unionism. Although managerial ideology may be the characteristic world view of managers, it does not follow that other elements (specifically workers' conceptions of what is legitimate) are absent from the thought processes of individual managers.

Rule changes tend to be accompanied by considerable ideological 'work'. Both stewards and managers rehearse amongst themselves the arguments linking their positions on the latest proposed rule changes to the available stock of legitimising principles. Similar rehearsals take place in encounters between stewards and managers, even though these are frequently irrelevant to the ostensible business in hand (a process described as 'attitudinal structuring' by Walton and McKersie[47]). These serve to discover the grounds of legitimisation claimed by the other side and to develop one's own arguments and perhaps modify one's demands accordingly. Finally, the arguments in developed forms are again played out in actual negotiation (assuming the issue has not been settled before this point is reached) which sometimes seems to serve merely as a ratification of what has already been agreed. In this respect there is an essential continuity in the processes at work in the negotiation and in day-to-day encounters.

It is noticeable that negotiation and conversational encounters also include exchanges of a general ideological character. Managers will refer to the necessity for profit; workers and their representatives will complain of rising living costs and so on. Often these occur as asides, not linked in any obvious way to the main trend of the discussion and sometimes divorced from concrete issues altogether. Whilst this is undoubtedly propaganda of a sort, it would be naive to believe that either party is expecting sudden conversions. When re-stated for one's own side, such rehearsals of ideological basics seem to serve as ritual re-affirmations of group values (cf. Berger and Luckmann[48]) which might be considered as an aspect of the mobilisation of bias. For example, managers of a traditional persuasion may, in private, reaffirm the indispensability of fear as a basis for discipline.

Where exchanges with the other sides are concerned, the intention seems to be to pre-empt the terms of the discussion to ensure that what might be called the 'negotiating climate' favours one's own case. As stated earlier, few workers would reject the claims of profitability even where its requirements conflict with those of certain counter-principles of their own. By reiterating the profit requirement, managers may be attempting to establish that it is this aspect of the contradiction in workers' ideologies which is relevant to the matter in hand. The same seems to be true to a lesser extent of general assertions made by workers' representatives. Provided the conflict with the profit requirement is not acute, few managers would dismiss out of hand arguments based on rising living costs. By reiterating the fact that the cost of living *is* rising workers' representatives are attempting to keep the discussion in a frame of reference favourable to themselves. However, the effectiveness of this particular tactic may often be limited, as managerial ideology also contains the idea that living standards in general can only rise if profitability rises too.

Interwoven with legitimising arguments – and sometimes difficult to disentangle from them – are threats and actual displays of power. Ultimately – 'at the end of the day', as tired negotiators are wont to say – the outcome of the rule-making process must be decided by the balance of power. But meanwhile the new rules (if any) will have been moulded by the necessity of justifying them by reference to principles accepted by whoever possesses significant power. Thus managers, in formulating their policies, will, where necessary or politic, 'economise' on the use of power by formulating them so as to accommodate so far as is possible the principles of legitimisation accepted by the workforce. For workers, on the other hand, their resources of power largely depend on their ability to mobilise, which implies that typically they can effectively pursue only those of their interests which can be legitimised 'for themselves'. In the ordinary way, too, it will pay workers to compromise with management's sense of what is legitimate if they wish to avoid confrontation altogether or to leave management an honourable line of retreat in the event of an actual dispute. It is in this manner that legitimisation enters the rule-making process. Considerations of legitimisation shape the issues on which power is deployed and the tactical deployment of legitimising arguments may also serve as a partial substitute for the exercise of power itself.

It needs to be added that much of the above goes by the board when one of the parties possesses, and is patently prepared to use, an overwhelming power advantage. There may then be little inclination to bother with what the other party considers to be legitimised. However, this is only to say that the theoretical framework is restricted to the conventionally defined subject area of industrial relations. The zone of claim and counter-claim for legitimacy coincides with what Brown termed 'bargaining awareness'[49] and the subjects' central concern with negotiation and bargaining processes (both formal and informal) reflects an assumption that there is, on the whole, something approaching a balance of power over those marginal adjustments which are typically live issues between workers or management.

So far we have discussed the nature of the legitimising argument surrounding single proposed rule changes. Sometimes, indeed, issues *are* dealt with singly. Rules which one side or another regards as deeply unjust are a case in point. For example, a management attempt to clamp down on a developing lateness 'rule' may take place in isolation from other issues.

Frequently, however, the discussion of proposed rule changes takes the form of an exchange. In fact, managers sometimes explicitly propose rule changes in this form. On other occasions, the exchange may be less obvious. In many factories both stewards and managers speak of 'winning some, losing some', almost as if it were a question of taking turns. In this there appears to be an implicit consciousness of the state of debt or credit in the relationship which underlies the arguments on each issue. The state of credit or debt is related not just to numbers of wins and losses but also to whether issues are 'big ones' or 'small ones'.

Yet the process is not one of 'pure' exchange – legitimising arguments are deployed here just as when a single rule change is in question. The reason appears to be that the bargaining process has to establish the 'worth' of the concession offered and sought by either party. Moreover, the valuation of rule changes has a lot to do with their legitimacy. For example, workers cannot expect much in return for a management-proposed rule change which they, themselves, concede is legitimate in itself. Conversely, a rule change which they see as making definite inroads into their rights will command a high price. By proposing rule changes of a type which can be largely legitimised in terms accepted by the other party, one minimises the 'price', so to speak. In this manner, the prospect of legitimising rule changes influences what is proposed and offered during bargaining. The process differs only in complexity from that discussed earlier. Put simply, the parties concede rule changes which they regard as of roughly equivalent illegitimacy and expend much of their argument on establishing what *is* equivalent.

Varieties of the Rule Change Process

Essentially, we have portrayed the set of rules governing employment relationships at factory level as a 'negotiated order' (in the sense used by Strauss *et al.*[50]), as the outcome of processes in which the participants deploy such power and legitimising resources as they possess in their attempts to change the rules in their own favour. However, if the available stock of legitimising principles is, as we have argued, comparatively limited and largely unchanging, it might be thought that the resultant structure of rules would be relatively static also. For a number of reasons that is not necessarily so, the most obvious being that any change in the balance of power is likely to set the process of rule change in motion. For instance, externally negotiated agreements and laws bring with them the possibility of help from outside. Market and technological changes alter the extent to which managers depend on co-operation from the workers, and the labour market obviously influences the workers' power position. Bearing in mind that an existing structure of rules is a compromise, in the sense that both parties will generally have what they consider to be legitimate reasons for attempting to change it, one would expect new issues to be created and old ones to be reopened as a result of any perceived change in the balance of power. Nevertheless, despite the obvious dependence of any resulting rule changes on material factors, one would still expect the deployment of newly available power to be conditioned by the available modes of legitimisation.

Besides affecting the balance of power, external changes may affect both the priorities amongst the parties' interests and the legitimising resources available to them. As an example of the former, technological advance may sharpen the issue of job security for the workforce and that of manning flexibilities for the management. Although the revised set of priorities would still be expected to be articulated through the parties' sense of what is legitimate, one would nevertheless expect the points of pressure on the existing structure of rules to change.

New laws and externally negotiated agreements provide the most obvious example of external changes which alter the available resources of legitimisation.

However, evidence from our fieldwork suggests that laws and external agreements should be regarded, not as absolute constraints on workplace rules, but merely as an addition to the stock of legitimising material. Laws and negotiated agreements 'take time to apply', 'are not reasonable' or are, in some instances, simply ignored. In other words, their practical effect depends on their being invoked and even then they are not immune from counter-argument.

Technological or market changes can alter the implication of the existing stock of legitimising principles since some of these contain blanks (as it were) to be filled in by reference to an existing situation. For instance, the principle of survival (profitability) changes in its implications when a firm is subjected to price-cutting competition. Technological changes might be used to legitimise wage claims invoking the principles of skill or responsibility. On the other hand, they may also legitimise management demands for reduced manning levels or for flexible working, citing the principle of survival. Clearly, there are many possibilities and the outcome depends heavily on the ingenuity and skill of the parties involved. In general, there are a variety of channels through which a structure of employment rules can respond to external changes.

However, there are also internal sources of change. Some legitimising principles, more especially those linked to managerial ideology, constitute a warrant, not so much for pressing towards an ideal state, but for continued pressure in a certain direction. The principles both of managerial prerogative and of profitability legitimise an active interest in changing rules, no matter what may be the current state of play between the parties. In their unqualified form, both are insatiable. By contrast, the principles culturally available to workers seem, broadly speaking, to be defensive in character and therefore somewhat static in their implications, although the trade union leader who succinctly described his goals as 'more' would presumably disagree. It might be added that there is greater open-endedness in the pursuit of management initiatives in a time sense, whilst workers' 'bargaining opportunities' may be periodic. For example, for time-paid workers pay bargaining may be restricted to the annual negotiation, whereas management prerogative and the pursuit of profit allow a continuous search for change and improvement.

Besides the ideological warrant for continued rule-making activity by managers, the process of internally originated rule change may be set in motion by the 'invention' not of a new principle but of a new application of an existing principle. This might occur, for instance, by the realisation that an existing principle might be applied outside its previous, tacitly and somewhat vaguely understood zone of application. In one factory, for example, senior operators were in the process of discovering that they were 'really' supervisors and that the principle of hierarchy (to coin a phrase) therefore entitled them to greater differentials with respect to the workforce than they actually received.

Internally originated rule change may also accompany changes in personnel, especially of senior management, with the newcomers normally being charged, or charging themselves, with the duty of improving labour utilisation, reducing labour costs and so forth. These new managers may take the initiative in implementing, on the basis of their own personal repertoire of legitimising argument, rule changes which have not been conditioned by the existing culture in the factory.

Speaking more generally, it should be pointed out that the availability of stock of legitimising principles does not determine the use to which they are put in practical situations. There is constraint – some demands cannot be convincingly justified – but not determinacy.

It also happens that one rule change, when viewed in the light of existing legitimising principles, may precipitate demands for further changes. Most obviously, a concession given to a particular group of workers may, via the principle of equity, give rise to a demand that all receive the same concession. If, and when, such generalisations of a concession are established, the rationale behind them might ultimately approach the status of principles-in-themselves in that particular factory – though one would not wish to insist on an over-precise distinction between the application of principles and the principles themselves. It is important to add that any feedback from new rules to the characteristic application of legitimising principles is a matter of the *interpretation* of the rules as well as of their actual nature. Thus, 'washing-up time' might be interpreted simply as a certain time allowance and incorporated into a system of legitimisation on that basis. This might then lead to demands for its extension to workers in 'clean' jobs or an insistence on retaining the time allowance when the original job is cleaned up or actual washing time is reduced due to improved facilities. In the longer term, then, there is a further source of dynamism in the interplay between the operative working rules and the characteristic manner in which principles are used to justify or oppose them.

In practice, there is considerable variation in the manner in which rule changes are actually initiated. Managers or workers might, for instance, become conscious of a gap between rules as they exist and what their legitimising principles suggest they should be. This might be followed by one of the parties explicitly proposing the appropriate change in rules. Conversely, managers or workers might be driven to seek justification for a developing practice which the other side suddenly calls into question. In this they would be limited by the relative inflexibility of the available stock of principles. In fact there are many instances in which developing practices fail to engage with legitimising principles (e.g. 'creeping lateness') and the speed and ease with which these are eradicated further demonstrates the importance of legitimisation in rule change. Often a mixture of processes might be involved. There might be a series of probes, experiments and rehearsals of justificatory arguments during which the nature of the proposed rule change and its accompanying modes of justification is developed. The 'proposal' of rule changes is not always a tidy process and this means that it may be a methodological error to seek a 'moment of initiation'. Rather, the process is likely to be one of a developing mutual affinity and interplay between proposed rule changes and their associated legitimising principles. Again, the proposition of rule changes and the deployment of the associated conflicting principles of legitimisation should not be thought of as successive stages. At the same time as workers and managers develop their own positions, both tend to argue them through with the other side on an experimental basis. Then again, the proposed rule changes may be temporarily operated as a *fait accompli* in order to test the likely nature of the opposition. Clearly, such experiments serve to assist in developing an effective mode of legitimisation 'for the other side'. It is a kind of 'low-cost' strategy, a way of testing the water without being committed to swim.

Forms of Legitimising Principle

Besides this variety of process, there is also considerable variation in the form in which legitimising arguments appear. Some principles, for instance, are just that – explicitly announced as principles of greater or lesser generality of application. For instance, during one negotiation, the representatives of a group of craftsmen defended their differentials as customary, as an incentive necessary to ensure a supply of apprentices and as a reward for a craftsman's long training. All three principles were actually spelled out during negotiation. However, when the same representatives had to defend their differential against the argument that other groups of workers were 'really' skilled as well, they did so by insisting on a distinction between skill and experience. Terminological exchanges of this type are extremely important since many words in the industrial relations context carry a heavy ideological load. If, for instance, a man is asked to sweep up, the reply 'but I'm a skilled man' can only be understood once it is realised that the term 'skilled man' carries implicit claims for special treatment and status. A further example is the term 'custom and practice'. In the factories studied by Brown it is evident that a shop steward's declaration that a certain rule is C & P is less a description than a rallying cry summoning workers to its defence.[51]

As might be expected, many verbal usages in the dominant culture reflect and support the assumptions of managerial ideology. The term 'managerial prerogative' itself is a shorthand expression of claims to unilateral management control (as opposed to a description of what managers do, in fact, control). A tendency to describe profitability as 'efficiency' is another case in point, serving to represent opposition to the most profitable course of action as the advocacy of inefficiency, an attitude which some managers in moments of stress are prone to stigmatise further as 'Luddite'. The dominant culture provides a number of categories of workers' behaviour which are assertive of managerial interest. Terms such as 'demarcation' and 'restrictive practice', with their pejorative overtones, serve more to assert the illegitimacy of the modes of behaviour than to describe them. Concepts of this type do more than describe the social reality: they serve also (in Berger and Luckmann's terms[52]) to construct reality as it appears when certain interests are taken for granted.

Legitimising principles can be even more unobtrusive. Quite frequently practices are accounted for by an appeal to 'self-evident common sense'. 'Of course' the supervisor should be paid more than those he supervises. 'Of course' the workers are found other work when the machines stop. Here the investigation of legitimising concepts takes an ethnomethodological turn as one is looking at the ideas which people use to construct their taken-for-granted reality. Obviously, rule changes which can be identified with a shared version of common sense can be very effectively pressed. Opposition to them appears, almost by definition, as nonsensical. In practice, the extent to which 'common-sense' principles of justification are investigated probably depends on the extent to which the researcher and his presumptive audience find the factory practices 'anthropologically strange'.

Apart from these three varieties of legitimising principle, one of the most prevalent legitimising tactics is an appeal to 'formal' (usually written) rules and agreements. Accordingly, these need special mention. On a naively formalistic view, what is in accord with formal rules and agreements would thereby appear to be absolutely legitimised. In practice, this view is a drastic over-simplification. Indeed, an earlier generation of organisation theorists frequently took their basic problem to be the deviation of *de facto* organisational rules from the 'formal' system. However, couching the problem in terms of an opposition of formal and informal rules is somewhat suspect. More recent theorists (e.g. Zimmerman; Bittner[53]) have pointed out that there are methodological problems involved in deciding what a 'formal' system of rules actually is. They have insisted that the real meaning of a formal rule can be discovered only by observing the practical use made of it by 'competent' users of the rule. Such a position is close to asserting that the system of rules as it exists *is* the meaning of the 'formal' system: the apparent distinction between 'formal' and 'informal' rules is seen as resting on an inadequate interpretation of the meaning of 'formal' rules on the part of the observer.

There would appear to be problems with this point of view. For one thing, the possibility of normatively sanctioned rule breaking by 'competent' users is virtually defined out of existence. Secondly, there is the problem of deciding who are the 'competent' users of rules. Nevertheless, the perspective serves to stress that it is the use made of formal rules which matters and not the rules themselves. In this respect the approach is in harmony with the definition of 'rule' adopted at the beginning of this chapter: if the real rules are the actual regularities of behaviour, 'formal' rules are seen as just one of a number of legitimising resources which are deployed in the formation of real rules. The result may be that the real rule coincides with the 'formal' rule (where the meaning of this is unambiguous) but, equally, it may not. Even where there is no question over interpretation, the invocation of formal rules may be insufficient to settle the issue of legitimacy. If, for example, a formal rule has not been consistently applied, its use might be resisted on the unwritten grounds of equity or of C & P. Again, it is perfectly possible for a shared principle of legitimisation to take preference over a formal rule or agreement which contradicts it. Sometimes, too, appeals to formal rules are made by both sides, both claiming competence as interpreters of their meaning (cf. Albrow[54]), and in this manner the same rule may serve as a legitimising resource on both sides of an issue.

When one inquires into the legitimising principles behind the deployment of formal rules, there is some diversity according to their origin. Aside from the fact that written rules are sometimes produced as evidence that the principle of consistency has been observed, it is broadly the case that formal rules of management origin rest on the principle of managerial prerogative and that negotiated agreements (and possibly laws) derive their legitimacy from the fact that workers and managers were, at least notionally, represented in their formulation. But this does not exhaust the legitimacy of formal rules since the legitimising arguments which went into them will still, presumably, lie behind them in their application. For example, a manager may point out that safety requirements not only have the force of law but also were formulated for the worker's own protection.

Notes

1. A. Flanders, 'Industrial Relations: What is Wrong with the System?' (1965), in A. Flanders, *Management and Unions* (Faber and Faber, London, 1975), p. 81.
2. J.H. Goldthorpe, 'Industrial Relations in Great Britain: A Critique of Reformism' (1974), in T. Clarke and L. Clements (eds), *Trade Unions under Capitalism* (Fontana, London, 1977), pp. 184–224: C.J. Margerison, 'What do we mean by Industrial Relations? A Behavioural Science Approach', *British Journal of Industrial Relations*, vol. VII no. 2 (July 1969), pp. 273–86.
3. G.S. Bain and H.A. Clegg, 'A Strategy for Industrial Relations Research in Great Britain', *British Journal of Industrial Relations*, Vol. XII, no. 1 (March 1974), pp. 91–113.
4. R. Hyman, 'Pluralism, Procedural Consensus and Collective Bargaining?', *British Journal of Industrial Relations*, vol. XVI, no. 1 (March 1978), pp. 16–40; R. Hyman, *Industrial Relations – A Marxist Introduction* (Macmillan, London, 1975), ch. 1 and particularly ch. 7.
5. Hyman, 'Pluralism, Procedural Consensus', p. 34. Dissatisfaction with the 'rules'

approach is forthcoming not only from Marxist writers; see, for example, Margerison, 'What do we mean by Industrial Relations?', p. 273.

6. M. Weber, *The Theory of Social and Economic Organisation* (Free Press, New York, 1964).
7. P.M. Blau, *On the Nature of Organisations* (Wiley, New York, 1974), pp. 30–1.
8. F.J. Roethlisberger and W.J. Dickson, *Management and the Worker* (Harvard University Press, Cambridge, Mass, 1939).
9. Lord Donovan, *Report of the Royal Commission on Trade Unions and Employers' Associations, 1965–68* (HMSO, London, 1968).
10. W.A. Brown, 'A Consideration of Custom and Practice', *British Journal of Industrial Relations*, vol. X, no. 1 (March 1972), pp. 42–61; W.A. Brown, *Piecework Bargaining* (Heinemann, London, 1973), especially ch. 4.
11. J.T. Dunlop, *Industrial Relations Systems* (Holt, New York, 1958).
12. J. Gill, 'One Approach to the Teaching of Industrial Relations', *British Journal of Industrial Relations*, vol. VII no. 2 (July 1969), pp. 265–72.
13. D. Fatchett and W.M. Whittingham, 'Trends and Developments on Industrial Relations Theory', *Industrial Relations Journal*, vol. 7. (1976–7), pp. 50–60.
14. Brown, 'A Consideration of Custom and Practice', pp. 42–61.
15. J.F.B. Goodman, E.G.A. Armstrong, A. Wagner, J.E. Davis and S.J. Woods, 'Rules on Industrial Relations Theory. A Discussion', *Industrial Relations Journal*, vol. 6 (Spring 1975), pp. 14–30.
16. P.J. Armstrong and J.F.B. Goodman, 'Managerial and Supervisory Custom and Practice', *Industrial Relations Journal*, vol. 10 (Autumn 1979), pp. 12–24.
17. H.A. Clegg, *The System of Industrial Relations in Great Britain*, 3rd edn (Blackwell, Oxford, 1976), pp. 249–50.
18. A. Fox, *A Sociology of Work in Industry* (Collier Macmillan, London, 1971), pp. 124 *et seq.*
19. R.E. Walton and R.B. McKersie, *A Behavioural Theory of Labor Negotiations* (McGraw Hill, New York, 1965), pp. 184 *et seq.*
20. E. Batstone, I. Boraston and S. Frenkel, *Shop Stewards in Action* (Blackwell, Oxford, 1977), ch. 6.
21. B.E. Partridge, 'Towards an Action Theory of Workplace Industrial Relations', University of Aston Management Centre, Working Papers Series, no. 50 (1976).
22. W.E.J. McCarthy, *The Role of Shop Stewards in British Industrial Relations*, Research Paper no. 1, Royal Commission on Trade Unions and Employers' Associations (HMSO, London, 1966), pp. 16–18.
23. E.H. Phelps Brown, 'New Wine in Old Bottles: Reflections on the Changed Working of Collective Bargaining in Great Britain', *British Journal of Industrial Relations*, vol. XI, no. 3 (November 1973), pp. 329–37.
24. H. Gerth and C.W. Mills, *Character and Social Structure* (Routledge and Kegan Paul, London, 1954).
25. Fox, *A Sociology of Work in Industry*, pp. 124–32.
26. J. Storey, 'Workplace Collective Bargaining and Managerial Prerogatives', *Industrial Relations Journal*, vol. 7 (Winter 1976–7), pp. 40–55.
27. T. Cliff, *The Employers' Offensive* (Pluto Press, London, 1970), pp. 48 *et seq.*
28. A. Fox, 'Industrial Relations: A Social Critique of Pluralist Ideology', in J. Child (ed.), *Man and Organisation* (Allen and Unwin, London, 1973), pp. 207–15.
29. R. Herding, *Job Control and Union Structure* (Rotterdam University Press, Rotterdam, 1972), pp. 178–212.
30. Storey, 'Workplace Collective Bargaining', p. 49.
31. Goldthorpe, 'Industrial Relations in Great Britain', pp. 192–3.
32. A. Giddens, *Capitalism and Modern Social Theory* (Cambridge University Press, Cambridge, 1971), p. 156.
33. Fox, *A Sociology of Work in Industry*, pp. 34–9.
34. Batstone *et al.*, *Shop Stewards in Action*, p. 8.
35. R. Hyman and I. Brough, *Social Values and Industrial Relations* (Blackwell, Oxford, 1975), pp. 199–207.
36. N. Stettner, *Productivity Bargaining and Industrial Change* (Pergamon Press, London, 1969), p. 4.
37. For the ideological content of appeals to 'productivity', see Cliff, *The Employers' Offensive*, pp. 143–62. For evidence that managers actually find it difficult to disentangle

the profit motive from other supposedly independent policy goals, see T. Nichols, *Ownership, Control and Ideology* (Allen and Unwin, London, 1969), pp. 208–45.

38. F. Parkin, *Class Inequality and Political Order* (MacGibbon and Kee, London, 1971).
39. Goldthorpe, 'Industrial Relations in Great Britain', p. 193.
40. Hyman and Brough, *Social Values and Industrial Relations*, pp. 199–207.
41. R. Bendix, *Work and Authority in Industry* (Wiley, New York, 1956).
42. H.A. Simon, *The New Science of Management Decision* (Harper and Row, New York, 1960-); A. Flanders, 'The Internal Social Responsibilities of Industry', (1966), in Flanders, *Management and Unions*, pp. 129-32; G.F. Thomason, *A Textbook of Personnel Management* (IPM, London, 1978), ch. 2.
43. Brown, 'A Consideration of Custom and Practice', pp. 42–61.
44. Storey, 'Workplace Collective Bargaining', pp. 40–55.
45. J. Westergaard and H. Resler, *Class in a Capitalist Society: A Study of Contemporary Britain* (Heinemann, London, 1976).
46. Parkin, *Class Inequality and Political Order*, pp. 88–96.
47. Walton and McKersie, *Behavioural Theory of Labor Negotiations*, pp. 223–77.
48. P.L. Berger and T. Luckmann, *The Social Construction of Reality* Penguin, Harmondsworth, 1967), pp. 110–46.
49. Brown, *Piecework Bargaining*, p. 143.
50. A. Strauss, L. Schatzmann, D. Ehrlich, R. Bucher and M. Sabshin, 'The Hospital and its Negotiated Order' (1963), in F.G. Castles *et al.*, *Decisions, Organisations and Society* (Penguin, Harmondsworth, 1971), pp. 103–23.
51. Brown, *Piecework Bargaining*, pp. 103–5.
52. Berger and Luckmann, *The Social Construction of Reality*.
53. D. Zimmerman, 'The Practicalities of Rule Use' (1971), in G. Salaman and K. Thompson (eds), *People and Organisations* (Longmans, London, 1973), pp. 250–63; E. Bittner, 'The Concept of Organisation' (1965), in Salaman and Thompson (eds), *People and Organisations*, pp. 264–80.
54. M. Albrow, 'The Study of Organisations: Objectivity or Bias' (1968), in J. Gould (ed.), *Penguin Survey of the Social Sciences* (Penguin, Harmondsworth, 1968), pp. 146–67.

9 Technological Work Cultures: Conflict and Assimilation within a Mid-nineteenth-century Naval Dockyard

NEIL CASEY AND DAVID DUNKERLEY

Introduction

The analysis of organization cultures has a long and respectable history and is arguably best characterized by the many empirical investigations in the 1950s and 1960s that employed the case-study method in industrial sociology. In a similar vein, the present study uses the case approach in order to understand and interpret events in a particular type of organization that involved the attempted integration of two technologically distinct groups with their own very distinctive work cultures.

In the first instance, the paper examines the general issue of organization culture and then places this within the context of earlier studies such as those referred to above. From this review a number of specific issues and questions arise that are then addressed through the medium of the case-study.

Although many attempts have been made to arrive at a model of organizations that allows for high predictability of the particular configuration of aspects of structure (e.g. the Aston studies), such attempts have been largely unsuccessful except at the most general of levels. Perhaps the chief reason for this lack of success has been a failure to recognize a rather obvious fact – that each organization is unique and thus has its own individual history and pattern of structure and activity. While there may be similarities between organizations in terms, say, of the degree of centralization and formalization, the differences far outweigh these. Thus, it may be possible to compare a university with a prison in terms of their formal aspects of structure, but the comparison is largely spurious since it does not enable comparison of 'life-forms'; it says next to nothing about what is actually happening in the organizations (their means), nor what they are seeking to achieve (their ends). A sterile, formalized snap-shot is obtained of one moment in an organization's life, viewed from one particular position.

Criticisms of an approach centred upon formal structural characteristics are not uncommon (Burrell and Morgan, 1979; Clegg and Dunkerley, 1980), and many alternative approaches to organization analysis now exist that represent systematic attempts to present an approach that is both realistic and impartial. Interestingly, it is the uniqueness of organizations that not only forms a part of the basic criticism of structural approaches, but this phenomenon also figures centrally in alternative

Neil Casey and David Dunkerley, 1984 (Specially written for this volume)

strategies. It is also worth noting that such recognition was a part of the literature of industrial and organizational sociology long before the dominant trend of the late 1960s, inviting a formalized approach, as shown below.

Organization Culture

To speak of every organization as a unique configuration is, of course, not sufficient to allow further analysis. In what sense is each organization unique; why is there this uniqueness? Such questions can be answered by reference to the fact that uniqueness arises at least partially because of the different culture that each organization possesses. Although all organizations possess a culture, within one organization this phenomenon of culture 'refers to the unique configuration of norms, values, beliefs, ways of behaving, and so on that characterise the manner in which groups and individuals combine to get things done' (Eldridge and Crombie, 1974, p. 89). In the same way that sociologists apply the term culture to a society as a whole, to those factors contributing to the uniqueness of society X compared to society Y, similarly culture can be applied to complex organizations and, as shown below, to parts of organizations. Just as it is possible to refer to the norms and mores, the history and ideology of society, so it is for an organization and its parts. And just as it is the individuals, past and present, who have contributed to the culture of a society, so with organizations. Individuals both inherit culture and perhaps change it during their association with it in both formal and informal ways.

For present purposes, this last issue is important, since if individuals are capable of changing their organizational culture, whether as individuals or through group pressures, other questions are raised. It might, for example, be perfectly reasonable to ask why some individuals wish to change the culture they have inherited and of which they are a part. Equally, it is pertinent to enquire as to how they attempt to do this. Further, how enduring are such changes? Such questions are relevant to organization analysts, since underlying them is the common feature that choice exists. To say this is obviously too broad, since it does not give any clues as to how much choice different people at, say, different levels in the organization have; it says nothing about how, when a choice has been made, it might be implemented, nor with how much probability of success. Nevertheless, and recognizing the reification, 'organizations' do have choice and, indeed, do choose between alternative strategies that may have profound and lasting consequences for an established organizational culture.

The objectives of an organization are clearly the result of choice, as are the means to achieve these objectives. In both cases – for means and ends – it might be assumed *a priori* that the 'choosing' is largely done by those in powerful organizational positions, the managers and/or owners. Rank-and-file members of an organization tend not to be involved in fact in the making of such choices, in spite of the rhetoric of many organizations concerning participation, consultations and shop-floor democracy. Decisions and choices made about working practices tend to be imposed; the introduction of new techniques may be made with only a nominal reference to the attitudes of a workforce; the target markets or the sources of raw materials of a production organization are decided a long way up the organizational hierarchy.

Yet, it is these kinds of choices that, in practice, lead to changes in the culture of an organization, because material changes are culturally negotiated by organizational participants. A decision by a local authority to automate its offices through the introduction of word-processors will have a deep effect upon the culture of that organization. The choice by a university to run down its social science faculty will equally affect the culture. The culture of British prisons has undoubtedly changed as a result of an ideological and political shift towards the award of longer custodial sentences. In essence, then, it can be argued that major cultural shifts can occur through a change in strategy and policy by those in positions of power in organizations, shifts that will affect the social and work lives of the majority, even though they may have had only a nominal influence over the original decision.

In the same way that when discussing the culture of a society it is generally recognized to be something that changes slowly, that is produced over many generations, the same is largely true for organizations. It is common to refer to a 'cultural lag' within society as a whole to describe a situation where the norms and values of that society have not kept apace with other changes of perhaps a technological variety, or those brought about by political change. It is only in very recent years, for example, that a greater public acceptance has come about for homosexuals in British society, even though the practice of homosexuality for consenting adult males has been legal in England for some years. Organizations, too, experience this cultural lag. Changes in technology, for example, have never been welcomed from the days of the Luddites through to the robotization programme at British Leyland. Many reasons can be given for this reluctance to accept imposed change, or any change for that matter, but the unwillingness of individuals to change their values and attitudes rapidly often points to the deep-felt nature of a culture and the desire to retain a pattern of norms to which long socialization has been addressed.

Previous Case-Studies

As suggested above, industrial sociologists and organization analysts have long been interested in and have studied the cultures of organizations either directly or indirectly. Work in the 1950s and 1960s tended to concentrate upon the dimension of technology and the effect this had upon social relations at work ('the 'socio-technical' theorists), whereas later work has addressed more explicitly the question of why change that disturbs an existing static pattern of culture is introduced. In a sense these two approaches operate at different levels – the one emphasizing technology, the other the organization of work processes, notwithstanding the fact that the two may be interdependent.

Those researchers emphasizing the role of technology in defining and redefining an organization's culture can trace their intellectual pedigree back to the human relations movement of the 1930s and 1940s, and more recently to systems theory. From human relations comes the emphasis upon workshop relations to be found in the work of Walker and Guest (1952), Sayles (1958) and Blauner (1964). Sayles's work is the first in a line of studies that is emphatically 'technologically determinist', that is, suggesting that technology has a direct bearing on behaviour. His study enabled him to produce a scheme showing how different levels of skill and interaction characterize different types of work group. He distinguishes four types of group:

1. 'Apathetic': unskilled people working alone with little notion of group solidarity and experiencing low job satisfaction.
2. 'Erratic': unskilled, but with some interaction with others; they

occasionally, but often inappropriately, exhibit solidarity with their fellows.

3. 'Strategic': skilled workers with high levels of interaction, calculative in their dealings with management.
4. 'Conservative': highly skilled, with a strong solidaric identity with their work group; a concern with stability, especially of differentials.

Of course, these four types are highly generalized and, although Sayles's scheme may not directly contribute a great deal to an explanation of reactions of changing culture, the technological influence is obvious.

Assembly-line production has often been the setting for studies undertaken by industrial sociologists and for those expressing an interest in technological effects. Such a production system was an ideal focus in the 1950s and 1960s, since it represented one of the most technologically sophisticated systems in existence. The seminal work of Walker and Guest (1952) highlighted the physical features of assembly-line work and described how the nature of the employed technology prevented social interaction (noise and physical location), how work was essentially an individual operation, how job satisfaction was minimized, and how individuals responded through behavioural reactions such as high absenteeism. Yet, as with the later studies by Goldthorpe *et al.* (1969), an element of calculative instrumental choice seemed evident in the workforce, although this was not discussed by Walker and Guest. The interesting point to emerge and one that, in a tangential sense, will have particular relevance to our case-study, is that different groups may react in different ways to the same technological situation. Overall, both the samples of Walker and Guest and Goldthorpe *et al.* show that there was a voluntary choice made whether to work on an assembly-line for the majority. Although the work may be inherently dissatisfying, the instrumental attitudes of the workforce suggest a level of satisfaction (with income), in spite of the low level of satisfaction (with the work itself).

Again, through an analysis of work situations with varying degrees of technological complexity, Blauner (1964) sees a direct relationship between type of technology and individual reaction to it. His famous inverted U-curve of alienation suggests that the lowest level of alienation (as measured by powerlessness, meaninglessness, isolation and self-estrangement) is to be found in craft production; this increases for machine-minding, reaches a peak in mass production, and drops slightly in process production. Although criticisms of Blauner's conclusions are not difficult to make (especially his operating definition of alienation and his unwillingness to study subjective aspects of alienation), the significant point here is the deterministic nature of the analysis, that an individual's involvement or lack of involvement (alienation) results directly from the nature of social organization, which, in turn, arises directly from the type of technology employed.

As stated above, the human relations movement and systems theory were powerful influences on those researchers emphasizing the role of technology. The technological determinists outlined above were clearly influenced by systems theory, but the tradition now known as the socio-technical approach has far more affinity with it. Silverman gives a succinct description of this approach when he writes that it

> stresses the inter-relationships of technology, environment, the sentiments of the participants and organizational form. Since the nature of these relationships will determine the stability and even the survival of any economic organization, all the variables must be taken into account in empirical analysis and in prescribing change. (Silverman, 1970, p. 109)

Although a number of empirical studies can be labelled as being within the socio-technical tradition (for example, Burns and Stalker, 1961; Woodward, Miller and Rice, 1965; 1967), it is one of the earliest that is both the most celebrated and most typical of the traditions – the study of the Durham coalfield undertaken by Trist and Bamforth (1951). It is worth recalling the study in some depth, because of the interpretations that may be placed upon the results from the point of view of technology and organizational culture.

Traditionally, coal-mining in Britain had employed a relatively simple technology and a stable social organization. The 'stall-and-pillar' method of coal-getting with its small teams of men had facilitated the relatively autonomous, multi-skilled and self-selected work group. In turn, this meant high job satisfaction and consensus between work groups. The immediate post-war period not only was one in which nationalization of the coal industry was experienced, but also the 'hand-got' method of extraction was replaced by the longwall method. The conventional longwall method involved the use of mechanical 'rippers' and specialization by shift. Thus in a three-shift cycle, the total operation was undertaken with one shift cutting the coal mechanically, the next loading the cut coal onto the conveyors, and the third propping the roof, moving the conveyor and cutter and generally preparing for the next shift. In this way, 'a total coal-getting cycle may be completed once in each twenty-four hours of the working week' (Trist and Bamforth, 1951, p. 11).

Technically, the conventional longwall method was highly efficient, but the social consequences were less so, for a variety of reasons. The level of autonomy of work groups was minimized; work groups were no longer self-selected; old loyalties were destroyed (yet these were considered essential in order to face the shared dangers of underground working); supervision, once the preserve of the work group, became more direct and coercive; greater co-ordination by surface management was required. In short, the conventional longwall method was socially a disaster and had a number of predictable consequences – high absenteeism, industrial disputes and lower output.

As a palliative to the conventional system, the 'composite' longwall method was introduced, which attempted to include aspects of the former hand-got method with the technology of the longwall method. In essence, the rigid three-shift total cycle system was relaxed, work groups were more multi-skilled, self-selection for the work groups was re-introduced, supervision was made less direct, and a common paynote payment system by work group was brought back. There is evidence (cited by Marglin, 1974, p. 42) that the composite method produced 20 per cent more coal than the conventional longwall method.

The studies of the composite system are fully described in Trist *et al.* (1963), and it is here that the notion of a socio-technical system is used to explain the dramatic effect the system had. Rather than suggesting that technology *determines* form of organization, Trist and his colleagues refer to technology *placing limits* on organization. The position is, then, that technology and social-psychological factors act as constraints.

It will be recalled that the proposition was forwarded above that an element of choice exists in the matter of organizational culture. The work of Trist *et al.* provides some empirical underpinning for this proposition, since:

> it has been important in demonstrating that the technical systems used by enterprises invariably offer *some* choice in the structure of work relationships, and that the resulting social systems are just as 'objective' and as important in determining effectiveness as the structure of the technical system itself. (Eldridge and Crombie, 1974, p. 109)

Rose (1975, p. 217) is more sceptical, pointing out 'that the notion that choice of organization is possible, given a specific technology and the need to show a profit, is in my view somewhat deceptive'. This debate will be returned to later, when a further aspect – the reasons for change – is discussed.

Leaving aside the question of how appropriate it was for many researchers in the 1950s explicitly to set about empirically testing Weber's ideal-type model of bureaucracy (note the logical inconsistency of even attempting such a test), it is nevertheless the case that writers such as Gouldner (1954), Blau (1955) and Merton (1957) provided some interesting and valuable insights into the workings of modern organizations, centring on the issue of organizational effectiveness and bureaucratic distinctions. Although chronologically illogical, it is worth examining Gouldner's study *Patterns of Industrial Bureaucracy* (1954) so that again, and from a different perspective, the issue of organizational culture can be examined.

Although very much an antecedent to Silverman's (1970) work on an action frame of reference applied to organizational analysis, Gouldner's work examining the pattern of events (in his 1954 volume) and the subsequent description in *Wildcat Strike* (1965) contains an implicit rejection of a systems perspective and an acceptance of what Rose (1975) calls actionalism. Actionalism or a social action perspective can be constructed as an ideal-typical model with the following sequence:

1. What is the historical development of the role-system in the organization?
2. What type of attachment do the members of the role-system have?
3. What strategies of action follow from actors' attachments and definitions?
4. What are the consequences, in terms of patterns of interaction, for the organizational 'rules of the game' in which action and meaning have been constrained? (Clegg and Dunkerley, 1980, p. 279)

Gouldner's empirical analysis suggests that a historical analysis of an organization's role-system needs to be considered from the point of view of the wider environment. The environment acts as a source of meanings for the participants, rather than (as seen above) a determinant of structure and behaviour. The analysis of a gypsum mine and processing plant shows how, historically, a stable period had once existed. Being in a relatively isolated rural community, the actual role-organization had come to depend on traditional community values and structures. The role of rational organization was thus minimal. Instead of the application of formal characteristics associated with bureaucracy, there existed an 'indulgency pattern' of informal relations not simply between workers, but also between them and management. The indulgency pattern was not the result of a technological determinism nor environmental determination. Rather, 'it was dependent upon a common definition of the situation which had developed historically and had never been radically re-negotiated or challenged' (Clegg and Dunkerley, 1980, p. 280).

In brief, the pattern of events described by Gouldner was that when the manager of the local plant died, the head office (with its orientation towards rational organization and profit-seeking) brought in an outside manager. His perception of the indulgency pattern as non-rational and his possession of the orientation of the head office led to him introducing a number of modernizing changes such as the introduction of modern machinery and the imposition of a harsher and more rigidly imposed role-system.

Predictably, worker dissatisfaction increased dramatically as the established value-system was dismantled and as definitions of the situation were radically altered. Where certainties had previously existed, the new situation was characterized by uncertainty. It was clearly inappropriate to appeal for a return to the old values and, in fact, the dissatisfaction was articulated by a demand for higher wages. Although this issue was resolved, the situation of uncertainty remained, with minor skirmishes between management and men. These incidents eventually culminated in a wildcat strike, which, in turn, led to an increased use of power by management – a classic vicious circle.

Gouldner's analysis, then, provides many helpful insights into the analysis of organizational culture. From a position where power appeared to be absent, because organization was based far more on traditions of consent than on coercion, the situation had developed to one where, lacking the traditional ideological supports, organization had to be more explicitly buttressed by power. Furthermore, the analysis has a number of strengths: it is historically based; changes in organization structure are not perceived as being technologically or environmentally determined; different meaning systems can be understood; power and status differentials are highlighted; the social relations of production can be seen to be altered from those in which informal control prevailed to a situation where a highly formalized structure of organization prevails. In short, the complex interrelationship between organization culture, technology and the organization of the work process is more clearly understood. It is also interesting to note that an *ex-post-facto* analysis of events is perfectly feasible.

It has been established so far that the culture of an organization and of its parts may be determined by a multiplicity of factors, both within and outside the organization. The spillover of community values into an organization is clearly important, and within an organization the actual structure, the technology and the organization of the labour process have been shown to be significant. The idea that the latter is largely determined by the type of technology has been shown to be an overstatement and that, rather than technology directly determining the organization of work, it would seem to be more appropriate to refer to it setting limits. Indeed, more recent work than that of Woodward or Blauner has shown that the relationship is not casual, but correlational (Argyris, 1972; Child, 1973). The review above has tended to confirm the suggestion made by Davis, Dawson and Francis (1973) that the issue has polarized into the technological writers and determinists, on the one hand, and the action frame of reference writers, on the other.

A more recent approach, and one with wide currency in contemporary literature, examines the reasons for organisational change of the kind that results in technological change that, in turn, affects the organization of work. As already argued, such changes profoundly affect the organizational culture. One goal, then, is to answer the question of for what reasons technological and organizational change might be imposed (given that choice is available).

Certainly empirical studies do suggest that the search for efficiency is not the sole determinant of the imposition of technology (Beynon, 1974; Nichols and Beynon, 1977), but the historically-based evidence is even more convincing. Fox (1974, p. 179), for example, comments that 'the emergence of the factory owed as much to the drive for closer coordination, discipline and control of the labour force as the pressures of technology'. Equally, Marglin's (1974) historical analysis comes to the same conclusion, that factory production in the nineteenth century was introduced as much an attempt to control the activities of workers as to use the improved technology as it developed. Further evidence is provided by Braverman (1974), Clawson (1980) and Littler (1982).

In concluding this section, a number of issues are raised that are relevant to the analysis of organizational and work culture. An appropriate method of analysis would seem to involve using a historical approach. Given that cultures in any context are generally slow to change of their own volition, a longitudinal analysis would appear essential. Even when external forces to an established culture intervene to change that culture, a long study period is appropriate in order to trace the effects of imposition. The much-debated relationship between changing technology and changing structure clearly needs to be central for there to be an understanding of culture. Reasons for, and effects of, technological change, and indeed cultural change, are empirical questions, as is the exact role and motivation of management in such a situation. Equally, the ability of a particular work group to preserve its long-established traditions and patterns of culture is bound to a particular set of circumstances. Bearing in mind such issues, an actual case-study is now examined in order to explore further the relationship between technology, work culture and the organization of the labour process.

Technology and Culture in a Government Dockyard

The case-study focuses on an instance of cultural contrast arising out of the coming together of two distinctive technological groups with distinctive work cultures. It recounts the institution in 1853 of the steam factory in Devonport Royal Dockyard, after the Admiralty's somewhat belated realization that steam-powered warships could be more effective than those driven by sail, and the basic antagonism between those who worked in wood and those who worked in metal. Over the course of the dockyard's long history, the predominantly craft workforce centred around the shipwrights (dominant both numerically and in terms of status) had developed a strong cultural identity and heritage stemming, at least partially, from the social organization of their work. However, the traditions of this dockyard labour force were widely threatened by the opening of the factories, which brought with them not only an alien organization of work, but managers and workers thoroughly imbued with that work's culture.

This historical setting enabled us to investigate two key issues related to work culture. First, it facilitated exploring the relationship between technology and culture at a specific level. Second, it allowed examination of the incidence and character of cultural conflict, with its implications for working-class cohesion. Clearly this was not a standard case of cultural hostility emanating from the material threat of one group's work domain by a new group because, for the most part, the shipwrights on the one hand and the engine fitters and boilermakers on the other performed different tasks. If it was not a question of technological demarcation, then, where did the antagonism arise from and was it related to technology?

It should be stressed immediately that the positing of a relationship between technology and culture should not give rein to assumptions of technological determinism. Two factors avoid this elementary mistake, the first of which is that the relationship between technology and culture is viewed as reciprocal. For example, although the hand-tool technology of the shipwrights may have encouraged a culture which emphasized personal achievement, respectability and independence, that culture then came to affect the application of new technology with regard to such factors as mechanization and specialization. The second factor is that technology is assessed in the socio-economic context of its imposition. Variables such as the economic basis of the organization, its goals, who precisely imposes the technology, the broad structure of the work process and so on all operate to mould work cultures. Thus, with respect to the contrast between the traditional organization of the state-owned dockyards and the customary arrangement of private industry, after which the steam factories were fashioned, an officer (the dockyard term for managerial staff) noted:

> that the officers of a public establishment are not stimulated by motives of private gain to enforce the full amount of work which the men may be capable of performing. This is a defect inseparable from public establishments but, on the other hand, where work of excellent quality is required, the incentive of private gain is often found to impair the honest performance of the work. (Quoted in Field, 1979, p. 71)

Clearly, then, such varying contexts emphasize that an organizational aspect such as work culture is not determined by technology alone – indeed, technology itself is shaped by its context. This might beg the question of how, if technology is but a component of a larger socio-economic structure, can one talk of cultural differences in terms of technological differences – that is, a woodworkers' culture and an engineers' culture? The answer resides in the distinction between the 'causes' of culture and perceptions of culture. It will be argued that the shipwrights' and engineers' cultures were *'caused'* or sculpted by a multitude of social influences (amongst which was technology), but that it is valid to discuss cultures in technological terms because that is how cultural identities were manifested, perceived and discussed. That cultural distinctions were multi-faceted, then, did not prevent their being labelled technologically.

With these analytical points in mind, we will proceed by examining the work processes of the shipwrights and the engineers in their respective socio-economic contexts, as well as their recognizable cultural identities, the modes of cultural conflict and the relationship between technology and culture.

An adequate understanding of shipwrights' work culture therefore must be rooted in a knowledge of the work processes' context, and in particular the historical peculiarity of the dockyard's role as a state-owned industrial organization fulfilling a military function (Casey, 1983). This latter constraint, in terms of the need to be perpetually prepared for the short-term unpredictability of war, required that the Admiralty maintained a given productive capacity and, importantly, a core of permanent skilled workers (they were known as the 'established' men, preponderant amongst whom were the shipwrights), supplemented by 'hired' men whenever necessary. In addition, the imperative of producing efficient, reliable warships resulted in an unusual stress on quality which, at the level of production, was translated into the encouragement of craft skills and a relaxed pace of work.

The guaranteed provision of state capital to an organization central to the state's protection allowed the Admiralty to pursue these 'uneconomic' policies. Apart from periods of emergency, a rapid return on capital was not necessary, so that speed and economy were not intrinsic to the organization of the work process. Thus, there was a systematic explanation for what nineteenth-century Liberals saw as a 'lax' pattern of supervision and discipline, although the representatives of those Liberals in Parliament did circumvent some of the financial latitude provided by the economic basis (Barry 1863a and 1863b). They ensured that the Admiralty at least paid lip-service to 'economy', a fact realized in wages, which in 'normal times' remained consistently below the market rate.

The twin demands of low wages and a permanent workforce, however, formed a paradox, the solution to which resided in the Admiralty's provision of various alternative benefits – such as a pension, sick pay and holidays for ship's launchings

– with a number of precocious inducements, three of which, for our purposes, should be singled out. The first was the dockyard educational system, which in the absence of mass schooling in the mid-nineteenth century provided a general education for apprentices and some older men. Their 'learning' would appear to have contributed to a belief in their cultural superiority, manifested by their attendance at Mechanics' Institutes long after they were on the wane elsewhere (Bowers, 1971), and their dominant role in local associations such as Friendly Societies (Buck, 1981, pp. 70–71).

The dockyard school was an aspect of a second inducement, that of the labyrinthine promotion system, the dimensions of which could stretch from apprentice to Master Shipwright and from errand boy to skilled labourer. The genuine prospect of promotion (Evidence to the 1859 Report of the Admiralty Committee on Dockyard Economy – hereafter RDE – contains various individual biographies to illustrate this) helped mould work culture in a number of ways.

It inculcated the individual with a competitive ethos (Waters, 1977) and the notion that hard work could gain a commensurate reward (Crossick, 1978, pp. 71–2). More importantly, it resulted in an unusual pattern of management. Shipwrights were not overseen by traditional capitalist managers and supervisors, but either by naval officers (whose knowledge of industrial organization could kindly be described as sketchy) or crucially by craft-trained artisans risen from the ranks of the dockyard network. Not only did their training render them less capable of imposing the kind of vigorous discipline typical of private enterprises (indeed with more to lose, 'misconduct' was less common amongst established shipwrights), but it also engendered a degree of empathy between workman and officers which would seem to have attained a more material plane (RDE, 1859, para. 207 and Chatfield's dissent). The emergence of a defined craft industry, rather than a class identity, amongst the shipwrights can partially be explained by this possibly tenuous, but none the less existent, respect and co-ordination.

The promotion system, with the institution of establishment and the provision of the pension, also served to create overwhelmingly long-term objectives in shipwrights' work lives. They became enmeshed in the structural and ideological dockyard milieu as evidenced by their negotiations of their position in terms of a 'duty to Public Service' (Field, 1979, p. 389). Permanence encouraged the development of locally-rooted family clans of shipwrights (Waters, 1979, pp. 32–3; Buck, 1981, pp. 41–4; RDE, 1859, para. 100) with their implication for various aspects of non-work life such as residential patterns and cultural pursuits.

A third inducement to complicity was the primitive industrial relations machinery offered by the Admiralty in the form of the workmen being able to petition for various claims. This too had cultural consequences, on this occasion for political culture (an issue to which we will return below), because the availability of a formal channel to the employer diminished the need for alignment to national trade unions. Even industrial conflict, then, was a peculiarly dockyard affair. Thus, prior to any detailed consideration of shipwright technology or the specific organization of the work process, we have located various aspects of the socio-economic context which will help characterize the shipwrights' work role in terms of competitiveness, diligence, permanence, loyalty, localization, relative relaxation with regard to the pace of work, and other qualities so common to the British labour aristocracy in the mid-Victorian period. Such traits can be applied to a recognizable technological group, but they were *not* technologically determined; this emphasizes how technological cultures must refer to the wider context. Such an analysis is incomplete, however, because it does not treat culture as process.

Culture is not simply created from above; it is a product of negotiation by the group – the shipwright labour force – itself. This will become apparent now as we examine technology and the actual work process.

The shipwrights of the 1850s possessed a notable degree of control over a predominantly craft technology, the control being in part ceded by the employer and in part gained by dint of the workers' traditional influence. The shipwrights' function in Devonport would appear to have corresponded with that in other dockyards (Waters, 1977 and 1979; Field, 1979). Essentially, it was to construct the hull of the ship from the initial mould through to the rudder, as well as build some small yard craft and undertake repairs.

Their work amassed the shipwrights' status both from within the workforce itself and from many of the officers; thus Chatfield, Deptford's Master Shipwright, described his men as 'a most effective staff, skilful, well-disciplined and of good moral tone' (RDE, 1859, p. 95). The status accrued in part from the dangerous and physical nature of the work, but chiefly it came from the skill and flexibility with which it was executed – that is, its craft value. Mechanization, at least until 1860, was virtually non-existent, leaving shipwrights with their traditional hand-tools, with which they were encouraged to perform not just single skilled tasks, such as rudder-making or the building of masts, but the entire range of work on the hull, so that men could be consecutively employed on a number of quite different jobs. This amounted to a concern with the entire process, giving an apparent satisfaction unknown in more specialized work (Waters, 1979, p. 178) and illustrated in the continuing identification artisans made, and continue to make, with their finished product. In particular, ship's launching were days of great celebration; admittedly everybody received an afternoon off, when of course the hostelries ringing the dockyard walls were always open, but still the bulk of the men were keen to attend the actual ceremony (Field, 1978). Mr Fincham, the Master Shipwright at Chatham, suggested this sense of satisfaction extended into managerial ranks, with the existence amongst the shipwright officers of an 'esprits de corps, which is such a stimulant to exertion' (Observations on the Report of the Committee on Dockyard Economy – hereafter ODE – 1860, p. 60).

The central cultural ramifications of the shipwrights' allotted function, then, were a sense of superiority within an informal dockyard hierarchy, and what might also be described as pride in their process and the product. Such traits were encouraged by the individual skilled craftsman's position within the wider organization of the collective work process. Generally one can point to the employer's carefully structured organization of the work process within which they allowed, and perhaps even nurtured, the adoption of the artisans' own principles of self-control and administration. Obviously the construction of the work day as regards hours, mealtimes, registration (known as 'mustering' in the dockyard), work detail, and so on were organized and upheld by the management (although it should be noted that factors such as the shipwrights' working of daylight hours and their relatively long meal breaks, which allowed many men to go home for lunch, contrasted with other trades). But within this structural configuration, the shipwrights' own work culture was pervasive.

The liberty to exert their cultural influence was owed to some degree to the nature of the technology. Mechanization, specialization and centralization could not or would not be imposed, and this allowed the men a physical and mental freedom. But, as implied here, their fortune was not solely technological. The fact that the craft officers were not trained as supervisors, the Admiralty's fear that excessive interference might mar quality, and the shipwrights' own undoubted acquiescence, given their long-term goals, were all conducive to an environment in which shipwrights, to the disgust of Liberals, had been able to develop and impress their own organization of the work process.

Central to this organization were an informal scheme of gradation based on estimations of ability and experience, internal to the men themselves (Admiralty attempts to impose their own stratification system, known as classification, caused 'an unceasing source of annoyance where the men performed the same work' – ODE, 1860, p. 25 – and met with co-ordinated resistance), a concern with the welfare of colleagues' particularly those less fortunate, and a democratic sense of what was 'fair' and 'unfair'.

The internal scheme of gradation was particularly important. It was most apparent in the annual 'shoal' whereby the work gangs for the year were picked by the leading men (chargehands), taking it in turns to choose (Waters, 1977). It was symbolic for two reasons. First, in as far as the best man was picked first and so on, it was an overt recognition of grading based on ability and experience, and, as such, was a process riddled with tensions. The grading was not, however, confined to one day a year, but was acknowledged by the employer (the number in which one was picked was printed on the muster ticket used in registration and getting paid) and by the men, who used it roughly in deciding who would work where on the hull (the best men were placed on the front and the back where the work required the most skill) (Waters, 1979, p. 178, 20). Apparently, this informal social order was broadly accepted by all – a Devonport officer noted that 'the inferior men know their inferiority and readily take their places' (RDE, 1859, Q 1141). Second, the shoal epitomized the concern with fairness and welfare, because it made sure that men of differing abilities, ages, and characters were shared out so that older and less able men were evenly distributed (Waters, 1979, p. 178).

Within each work gang, options were available (furthermore, individuals could choose to avoid working within particular gangs, if they so desired). Fragmented work groups known as 'squads' could choose their own composition and leader and, crucially, individuals could choose their own 'mate' with whom they would have to co-operate closely and rely on for support and advice. The emphasis here on co-operation and the previous observation regarding the importance of individual competition should not be taken as contradictory, however. As Waters notes for Chatham dockyard:

> The ex-apprentice shipwright was being trained to perceive himself as the organiser of this collective effort through his superior knowledge, and to accept the rationality of controlled competition as a means of selecting the best men for the top of the pyramid but, because of his practical training, he knew that such control must ultimately be based upon cooperation. (Waters, 1979, p. 184)

So, technology and the overall organization of the work process contributed to the shipwrights' recognizable work culture. That this culture, in return, influenced the imposition of technology is best instanced by the fact that, until the change to iron ships, the Admiralty allowed the shipwrights to continue performing their own labouring, thus preventing encroachment on traditional work boundaries.

Nor was their culture a purely workplace phenomenon. Co-operation within the work gangs was paralleled by participation in co-operative consumer ventures. Devonport had possessed a co-operatively-run mill since 1816 (Cole, 1944), the shipwrights, as with other associations, being closely identified with its operation. Similarly, the democracy of the work gangs was followed closely by the shipwrights' political structures and culture. Each group elected representatives onto a committee whose purpose was principally, though not solely, to formulate the annual petition to the Admiralty (Wells, 1977). The shipwright committee had links with other trades (though there is no evidence for relations with steam factory trades) and shipwrights in other dockyards, but – and this confirms the existence of a craft, rather than class identity – connections with national trade unions were non-existent (Casey and Dunkerley, 1982). Also, their independence at work was reproduced outside the Dockyard. It would seem (although further research is needed to confirm these suspicions) that Devonport shipwrights dressed specifically (they wore bowler hats), drank in different pubs, were prominent in certain associations and pursuits, and tended to live in older areas. The orientation to long-term objectives surfaced in a 'moral sobriety'. Shipwrights would appear to have been patriotic, mirroring their role as the means to an aggressive, imperialist end. In short, work in all the facets discussed here had a profound effect in shaping the culture of large sections of a community.

In the dockyard, then, the imposition of a technology and a work process in accordance with given socio-economic constraints, and that process's cultural negotiation and rearrangement by the workforce, resulted in a work group with a recognizable cultural identity – not technologically caused, but technologically perceived. Before moving on to look at the occupants of the steam factory, it should be noted that the shipwrights' cultural superiority was, to some extent, a representation of a privileged economic position. Their value to the Admiralty gave them benefits and incentives which, in turn, made them the most influential group within the yard, possessing an acknowledged, but often resented, status. In other words, the shipwrights had something to protect from any emergent group, of which the engineers of the steam factory were the first since the dockyard network's constitution.

Probably by virtue of their lack of tradition, less is known about the work of engineers in the steam factories (Crossick, 1978; Field, 1979; Waters, 1979). However, it is clear that their particular socio-economic context set them apart from the moment they began to enter the yard in 1844. Initially, we can isolate three key factors. The first is that in our case, the engineers were geographically and administratively distant, because the steam factory was erected on an adjacent site at Keyham. Contact did occur, because some shipwrights had occasion to perform minor repairs in the factory, and engineers were often required to work on board ship, but on the whole the distance did little to encourage cultural cohesion.

Secondly, the engineers were rarely Plymouthmen or indeed from Devon and Cornwall; in the main they hailed from the industrial centres of London, the north of England and Scotland. They had different dialects, eating and drinking habits, leisure pursuits, possibly religious affiliations, etc. and they tended to be younger (Buck, 1981, pp. 23-4). They were culturally distinct before they walked through the dockyard gates.

The third factor, and the one most pertinent as regards work culture, is that the steam factory, because of pressure from *laissez-faire* Liberals and because of its staff, was organized along the lines of private industry. The cost of production and its speed, then, were paramount principles. Employment levels were based on demand as far as possible; labour was attracted by paying a market wage which tended to be noticeably higher than that paid to shipwrights (RDE, 1859, pp. 187–8). Wages, then, replaced the array of benefits and inducements available to the shipwrights. There was no formal promotion scheme, and even trade qualifications were not adhered to in many instances (Waters, 1979, pp. 27–8). This, of course, had the advantage for the employer of avoiding the strong cultural links between officer and artisan as existed in the Master Shipwrights' department in the steam factory, the division between workman and manager was clearly defined.

There were no indentured apprenticeships and no access to the dockyard educational facilities in the factory, and consequently no ideological inculcation of dockyard traditions (Casey, 1983). There was no establishment and no pension, with the result that regardless of conditions at the workplace, engineers did not have the same propensity to stay in the yard for a long time. Also, the Admiralty did not bestow the welfare rights pertaining elsewhere in the yard; John Trickett, the Chief Engineer at Keyham, outlined the quandary:

> as the men get older we shall have great difficulty in dealing with them, as they become incapable of doing their full day's work, we shall have either to discharge him, or the man should be provided for. (RCM, 1861, Q 4343)

He solved his moral dilemma by ruling against a pension, in the belief that men should save for their old age (RCM, 1861, Q 1232).

The engineers thus worked in a less philanthropic environment. Initially, it meant they had little material or emotional investment in the dockyard service, and of course they were not local men, but uprooted 'foreigners'. In their relationship with the employer, exploitation was far more apparent and, unsurprisingly, the response of engineers gave them the label of being more 'troublesome'. Their dissatisfaction, however, was not channelled into an employer's formal conduit; in the absence of any industrial relations machinery, the engineers invited into the yard, despite the Admiralty's refusal to recognize them, national trade unions (Crossick, 1978, p. 79; Waters, 1979, p. 188).

Once again, what we are seeing here is the distinction between technologically *determined* culture and technologically *represented* culture. The engineers' more instrumental and less committed character was, as we have just seen, a product of the economic basis on which they worked, not of the actual work they did, but the large influx of new workers between 1845 and 1855 was again perceived in technological and occupational terms. The work process itself, however, reinforced the perception of differences.

The contrast between the two technologies was stark; the engineers had long since left behind a craft technology for a machine technology, with the perilous trio of mechanization, specialization and centralization. The flexibility of the ship-wrights was replaced in the mechanized factories by a strict adherence to the dictates of the machines to which they were tied. The structure of the work day (engineers worked a 10-hour day all the year round) and breaks (mealtimes were shorter than those of the shipwrights) were shaped by the demands of the technology, because fires had to be kept alight (RDE, 1859, paras 610–11), and differed from the flexible arrangements in the Master Shipwright's department. The pace of work was also strictly controlled, and even though there was still a stress on quality in the factory, it denied the engineers the same scope for indulging their skills. Neither was there the possibility of the development of the close interaction and sense of co-operation which existed on the ship's hull. The thought of the workmen employing their own principles of self-administration was not really relevant.

There was more specialization in the factory, which of course made the engineer more expendable, and probably contributed to his sense of resentment. As a consequence, craft qualifications were not so keenly observed; at Sheerness, labourers were quickly trained as boilermakers and riveters (Waters, 1979, p. 28). Status and pride in work could only be diminished in this environment. Mechanization also allowed centralization in the factory itself and in the individual shops, the consequences of which was a reliance on supervision and discipline to maintain employee compliance. Men specifically trained to supervise and manage, rather than craft-trained officers, oversaw foundries constructed to reveal 'idleness or absence' (RDE, 1859, paras 898–920; ODE, 1860, pp. 33–4). As mentioned before, engineers were less inclined to acquiescence, and certainly the organization of their work process would have exacerbated this, as would management's reliance on a strict code of discipline. John Yale, Keyham's Foreman of Boilermakers, argued against security and for discipline: 'if there is any discontent among the factory people, we pick out the most disorderly, and discharge them' (RDE, 1859, Q 1428).The rigour of factory discipline would not have encouraged an organizational commitment to the dockyard service.

An understanding of the engineers' work culture is perhaps harder to glean, because they were more confined and controlled. In fact, it seems probable that we can learn more from a consideration of traits conspicuous by their absence; we find no reference to 'loyalty' or 'patriotism', to the status of engineers (although clearly lower than that of shipwrights), to family clanships, to sobriety, nor indeed to the 'satisfaction' of work. This would reinforce the picture of a group of workers with a more instrumental attitude to work, little commitment in the dockyard and a consciousness, to some extent, of the exploitation inherent in their position.

That there was cultural conflict between the shipwrights and the engineers is undeniable, but the question is why was there conflict? Except in isolated cases, the engineers did not threaten the shipwrights' work domain, but they did threaten the shipwrights' prestige, influence and material advantages. Strangely, though not illogically, the genuine challenge to the shipwrights had its spearhead at the pinnacles of the two departmental hierarchies, where the historical superiority of the Master Shipwright was being attacked by the Chief Engineer. One of the central recommendations of the 1859 Report on Dockyard Economy was the transfer of far greater responsibilities to the Chief Engineer as a reflection of then-current technological change (RDE, 1859, paras 557, 559, 577–9, etc.). Inevitably, it provoked a counter-attack from the defensive shipwright officers – one was of the opinion 'that Keyham yard should be made independent, as far as possible, of Devonport Yard' (RDE, 1859, Q 1456) – and a snobbery toward 'begrimed engineer officers' (Field, 1979, p. 35).

The artisans must have been aware of the implications of the challenge to their officers. As we have argued, the two departments were organized on two totally different bases. Attempts to wrestle control from the Shipwright department were not simply struggles for power, but for the entire organization of the dockyard service. Victory for the Chief Engineer could have meant an end to establishment, pensions, education and comparatively abundant promotion into the dockyard supervisional and managerial hierarchy. Shipwrights, therefore, were on the defensive. The different values intrinsic to their respective technologies – for instance, skill on the one hand and speed on the other (RC, 1861, Q 2870) – were championed and the snobbery of shipwrights' 'superiors' was repeated at their level.

The attack on the shipwrights' edifice should not, however, suggest that resentment was one-sided. The engineers, despite their higher wages, objected to the shipwrights' receipt of privilege and benefits. As Waters points out, there was 'much rivalry between the engine fitters and shipwrights and much heartburning on the part of the former because the shipwrights always seemed to get the preferences and the upper hand' (Waters, 1979, p. 29). By the early 1860s, we see a reorientation of the attitude of engineers towards a concern for long-term benefits (RDE, 1859, p. 119); indeed a deputation of patternmakers and fitters walked into the 1859 Committee when it was collecting evidence at Devonport, requesting that they be eligible for establishment, superannuation and widows' pensions (RDE,

1859, p. 128). Clearly, then, the inequality of privilege was a source of division.

Conflict was fuelled by the lack of interaction between the groups. The very physical distance which often prevailed was widened by the structure of the two groups' respective days whereby they came and went, and ate and drank at different times. This of course was repeated outside the dockyard gates, in the ways outlined above. Conflict could even become overt and violent (Waters, 1979, pp. 65–6). This would appear to fit into a wider theme; that of the Admiralty's continued policy of 'divide and rule' (Casey, 1983). The Admiralty exploited the yard's heterogeneity by pitting groups against one another to dilute the possibility of a class-based consciousness. The engineers and the shipwrights provide an excellent example of this strategy. Their grievances were different, as were their means of dealing with them, but despite a common enemy (the Admiralty kept shipwright's wages low and the Admiralty denied the engineers a pension) animosity was directed against each other.

The fragmentary and disruptive entry of the engineers was not, however, to have a long-felt legacy. By the 1860s, relations between the two trades were far more amicable and evidence of a cultural distinction is far harder to find. In part, this can be explained with reference to a gradual assimilation, facilitated first by the realization that neither group threatened the other's material position, and second by the breakdown of barriers occurring in the wider community amongst wives, in schools and general working-class popular cultural institutions. This does not, though, tell the complete story. What brought the technological cultures together involved a gradual change in the socio-economic context of the engineers' work and the entry of a third technological group, who threatened both the engineers' and shipwrights' cultural and, more importantly, material position.

In the third quarter of the nineteenth century it is possible to trace the Admiralty's efforts to encompass the engineers and cloak them in the kind of organizational ethos common to the Master Shipwrights' department. The engineers had been virtually the only group to display a – for the Admiralty – problematic militancy, not least as a response to their persistent exclusion from the shipwrights' benefits and inducements. The Admiralty, despite political opposition, sought to solve the problem by including them. In 1859, Mr Stewart, an officer in the steam factory, had come to realize the potential benefits of establishment to both the men and the service.

> You could control these men much better, especially when trade was good, and they would be less likely to stand out in combination when trade was brisk. The men would have more steady employment and they would be more deeply interested in the service. (RDE, 1859, Q 1390)

This attitude heralded the Admiralty's efforts at incorporation over the next twenty years. The gradual rationalization of a promotion system, opportunities for education and a pension were followed in 1876 by engineers being taken on to the establishment (Waters, 1979, p. 265). The employer and the workforce had converged with a single aim; the men to improve their material position (and in so doing, of course, they were profoundly to alter their cultural persona) and the Admiralty to increase their institutional control. The jealousy of the engineers was thus at least partially assuaged.

Perhaps more important in bringing the groups together was the entry of a third group, representing the massive technological change from wood to iron shipbuilding. In private industry, iron construction had been taken over by boiler-makers with the help of new trades such as platers and riveters. When it was decided to introduce the new technology into the dockyards, it constituted a threat to both the shipwrights and the engineers. Following what became known as the Achilles Incident at Chatham in 1862, the unionized boilermakers were kept out of the dockyards and all construction work was given to shipwrights and newly trained labourers; the shipwrights' training was undertaken by none other than the engineers, as the trades were now favourably disposed to each other. (Waters, 1979).

Thus, the Admiralty, following Crimean defects, needed to introduce new technology, but it was opposed to the culture, particularly the political culture, of the groups who worked the new technology. It preferred the work cultures of the shipwrights and increasingly that of the engineers, because they were considered the most propitious for the Admiralty's specific method of reproducing the social relations of production. So the employer compromised. The new technology was introduced, but it was to be handled by men of the traditional culture, moulded in the dockyard's own peculiar context. Technological change would subsequently affect work culture, but at that point the organization of work life *in its totality*, remained basically the same.

Conclusions

What, in essence, this chapter has sought to achieve is some understanding of how culture is produced within an industrial organization. In thus doing, it has aimed at the unravelling of such related variables as technology, work process, work culture and indeed organization. By looking at a particular instance of cultural development, various points were suggested or reiterated.

Our study of work culture confirmed that organizational analyses must be both specific – the shipwrights' culture, for instance, would not fit a general pattern of work culture in capitalist organizations – and historical; again, taking the ship-wrights as an example, their pattern of work would make little sense without knowledge of the peculiar historical development of the royal dockyards. Further-more, the research on Devonport, emphasized the inadequacy of fundamentally structuralist approaches to organizations by illuminating the importance of culture – its creation, production and reproduction – in comprehending how organizations work. Workers are not simply the silent, suffering recipients of a structural subjection courtesy of their situation within the relations of production, but in fact imbue their material position with meaning. They socially negotiate their work role and give it their own expressive form.

As this implies, work culture is produced by workers, but importantly it is bounded. As was noted earlier, some writers have argued that all organisational aspects, including culture, are limited either by technology alone or by the slightly wider realm of the 'work process'. We have shown that the boundaries within which work culture is formed are somewhat wider – they encompass both technology and the work process, but extend to the socio-economic context of technological imposition and work design. In fact, work culture is a realized product of the sum of social groups' social and material work experience and indeed will also be constrained by – a theme deliberately excluded here – extra-organization factors. Thus, to assess work culture in purely technological terms erects artificial barriers within social reality.

However, as we have seen, even though culture is not, in definitive terms, technologically produced, it may be labelled as technological by organizational participants. It may also be labelled in a variety of other ways, such as 'depart-mental' (differences between sociologists and engineers in a university) or 'sexual' ('the girls from the typing pool'), etc. – 'technological' being the method of labelling in our example.

The notion of culture being bounded stresses how it is produced within organizations which reflect and carry wider social divisions. Organizations are class-based institutions and work-group culture, even if it differs between work groups, is *working-class* culture constrained by the limitations of ruling-class controllers. This leads to the conclusion that culture, like technology in the Gouldner case, is a tool which is available for use by the employer. It would seem that the Admiralty encouraged many aspects of shipwright work culture and even moved to protect it when it was threatened in the 1860s. The controller hence used a work culture because it was, not surprisingly given the Admiralty's role in constraining organizational form, complementary to its overall goals, though it needs to be said that culture is not a totally flexible weapon in the hands of an omnipotent ruler; rather, its production is reflexive and interactional. As has been seen, the culture of work groups can influence the choice of dominant groups in structuring organizations. But what is clear is that culture, within organizations as well as without, cannot be divorced from class.

So, analyses of work or organizational culture must mirror the necessary analytical context of 'culture' generally. Culture is not the product of a simple, causal relationship in a static, ahistorical, atomised organization; rather, it develops in a dynamic, historical, whole milieu, as a result of the interplay between imposition and negotiation. As others have observed for society as a whole.

> Culture is the way the social relations of a group are structured and shaped but it is also the way those shapes are experienced, understood and interpreted. (Clarke *et al.*, 1981, p. 53)

References

Argyris, C. (1972) *The Applicability of Organizational Sociology*, Cambridge, Cambridge University Press.

Barry, P. (1863a) *Dockyard Economy and Naval Power*, London, Sampson and Low.
   (1863b) *The Dockyards and the Private Shipyards of the UK*, London, T. Danks.

Beynon, H. (1974) *Working for Ford*, Harmondsworth, Penguin

Blau, P.M. (1955) *The Dynamics of Bureaucracy*, Chicago, Chicago University Press.

Blauner, R. (1964) *Alienation and Freedom*, Chicago, Chicago University Press.

Bowers, C.L. (1971) 'The Development of Mechanics' Institutes in the South West of England during the First Half of the 19th Century', unpublished MA thesis, University of London.

Braverman, H. (1974) *Labor and Monopoly Capital*, New York, Monthly Review Press.

Buck, N. (1981) *An Admiralty Dockyard in the Mid-nineteenth Century: Aspects of the Social and Economic History of Sheerness*, University of Kent, Urban and Regional Studies Unit.

Burns, T. and Stalker, G.M. (1961) *The Management of Innovation*, London, Tavistock.

Burrell, G.A. and Morgan, G. (1979) *Sociological Paradigms and Organisational Analysis*, London, Heinemann Educational Books.

Casey, N. (1983) 'Class Relations in Devonport Naval Dockyard: Methods of Organizational Control', paper presented at BSA Annual Conference, University College Cardiff.

Casey, N. and Dunkerley, D. (1982) 'Naval Dockyard Growth since 1850: an analysis of factors promoting and retarding union growth in a state sector', 3rd EGOS AWG on Labour Unions, Florence.

Child, J. (1973) 'Strategies of Control and Organizational Behaviour', *Administrative Science Quarterly*, vol. 18, pp. 1–17.

Clarke, J., Hall, S., Jefferson, T. and Roberts, B. (1981) 'Sub-cultures, Cultures and Class', in T. Bennett et al., *Culture Ideology and Social Process*, Oxford, Oxford University Press.

Clawson, D. (1980) *Bureacuracy and the Labor Process*, New York, Monthly Review Press.

Clegg, S. and Dunkerley, D. (1980) *Organization, Class and Control*, London, Routledge and Kegan Paul.

Cole, G.D.H. (1944) *A Century of Co-operation*, London, Allen and Unwin.

Crossick, G. (1978) *An Artisan Elite in Victorian Society*, London, Croom Helm.

Davies, C., Dawson, S. and Francis, A. (1973) 'Technology and Other Variables: some current approaches in organization theory', in M. Warner (ed.), *The Sociology of the Work-Place*, London, Allen and Unwin.

Eldridge, J. and Crombie, A. (1974) *A Sociology of Organizations*, London, Allen and Unwin.

Field, J. (1978) 'The Diary of a Portsmouth Dockyard Worker', in *Portsmouth Archives Review*, vol. 3, pp. 40–67.

  (1979) 'Bourgeois Portsmouth: Social Relations in a Victorian Dockyard Town, 1815–75, PhD thesis, University of Warwick.

Fox, A. (1974) *Beyond Contract: work, power and trust relations*, London, Faber and Faber.

Goldthorpe, J., Lockwood, D., Bechhofer, F. and Platt, J. (1969) *The Affluent Worker in the Class Structure*, Cambridge, Cambridge University Press.

Gouldner, A. (1954) *Patterns of Industrial Bureaucracy*, New York, Free Press.

  (1965) *Wildcat Strike*, New York, Free Press.

Littler, C. (1982) *The Development of the Labour Process in Capitalist Societies*, London, Heinemann Educational Books.

Marglin, S. (1974) 'What Do Bosses Do? – the origins and functions of hierarchy in capitalist production? *Review of Radical Political Economics*, vol. 6, pp. 60–112.

Merton, R.K. (1957) *Social Theory and Social Structure*, New York, Free Press.

Miller, E. and Rice, A. (1967) *Systems of Organizations*, London, Tavistock.

Nichols, T. and Beynon, H. (1977) *Living with Capitalism*, London, Routledge and Kegan Paul.

ODE (1860) 'Observations of the Superintendents and Officers of the Dockyards on the Report of the Committee on Dockyard Economy', *British Parliamentary Papers*, vol. XLII.

RCM (1861) 'Report of the Commissioners on the Control and Management of the Naval Yards', *British Parliamentary Papers*, vol. XXVI.

RDE (1859) 'Report of the Admiralty Committee on Dockyard Economy', *British Parliamentary Papers*, vol. XVIII

Rose, M. (1975) *Industrial Behaviour*, Harmondsworth, Penguin.

Sayles, L. (1958) *Behaviour of Industrial Work Groups*, New York, Wiley.

Silverman, D. (1970) *The Theory of Organizations*, London, Heinemann Educational Books.

Trist, E. and Bamforth, K. (1951) 'Some Social and Psychological Consequences of the Longwall Method of Coal-Getting', *Human Relations*, vol. 4, pp. 3–38.

Trist, E., Higgin, G., Murray, H. and Pollock, A. (1963) *Organizational Choice*, London, Tavistock.

Walker, C. and Guest, R. (1952) *The Man on the Assembly Line*, Cambridge, Mass., University Press.

Waters, M. (1977) 'Craft Consciousness in a Government Enterprise, Medway Dockyardmen, 1860–1906', in *Oral History*, vol. 5, Pt 1, Spring 1977.

  (1979) 'A Social History of Dockyard Workers at Chatham, Kent 1860–1914', PhD thesis, University of Essex.

Wells, R. (1977) 'The Revolt of the South-West 1800–1801: a study in English Popular Protest', *Social History*, vol. 6, October 1977, pp. 713–44.

Woodward, J. (1965) *Industrial Organization: theory and practice*, Oxford, Oxford University Press.

10 The Incorporation of Agriculture within Capitalism[1]

PETER HAMILTON

Introduction

Agricultural work is by far the most common productive activity of the world's population, and it is only in the somewhat atypical societies of Western Europe, North America and the Southern Pacific, as well as Japan, that agriculture is not the principal employment sector. Britain, in which less than 2.5 per cent of the workforce is directly engaged in agricultural work, appears to be rather anomalous when compared with her European partners, where the farming population still remains relatively large. Even the USA and Canada, for example, have proportionally larger agricultural workforces that does Britain (USA 3 per cent; Canada 6 per cent). Although it is clear that the experience of agricultural work in Britain is shared by relatively few people, it is also true that special historical factors have produced this situation which are not likely to occur in many other societies.

Agricultural work is a curiously invisible category for both ordinary people and sociologists in Britain, at least partly because of the small size of the agricultural workforce, but also because the current ideological images of farmers and farm workers are not ones which put them at the centre of the stage. Politically, the farming community is not clearly identified, although issues about the Common Agricultural Policy and, more recently conservation have begun to surface. Paradoxically, even the CAP tends to be seen by many people (and especially the 'popular' press) as some hideous consipiracy to handicap the wonderfully efficient British farmers from competing with their 'peasant' colleagues on the continent of Europe, which conceals the fact that the CAP generates large profits for large and relatively 'efficient' farms such as are found in Britain. This is not to say that farmers are not a politically powerful force in Britain. In fact, the National Farmers' Union (NFU) has one of the most effective lobbying machines in British politics, which a number of interest groups representing other (and larger) economic sectors have sought to emulate. However, the relative lack of political power on the part of farm workers is in marked contrast to the political efficacy of the 'corporatist' involvement of the NFU with the British state, through its influence on policy-making and close ties with the Ministry of Agriculture, Fisheries and Food. Farm workers in Britain are one of the least unionized sections of the workforce and, apart from the delights of working in the countryside, enjoy low pay, long working hours, dangerous working conditions and numerous other 'benefits'. Strike action by farm workers is almost unheard of, a result of atomization of the farm labour force: it is rare for farms to employ more than a handful of workers, so connected strike action is very difficult.

Agriculture in Britain has become, in the last century, an economic activity carried out increasingly by landowners – in Britain's case, by farmers who own the land they farm – using their own or their family's labour to run their production of food. Average farm size has grown considerably at the same time as the farming sector has shed labour, as mechanization has replaced men with machines in many farm tasks.

The net result of such trends is that farming has become an increasingly *family*-based form of production, unlike most other sectors of capitalist economies where the logic of capital concentration has meant larger units employing considerable numbers of workers. Industrial development of the type experienced by Britain and the other 'advanced' capitalist societies would have been impossible, if the unit of production had become *more*, rather than *less*, dependent on the family group. But this is precisely what has occurred in agriculture. Even where agribusiness interests have generated a close (even contractual) link between farms and food-processing companies, the tendency to industrialize food production has generally not meant the creation of large capitalist farm units, with professional managers and large numbers of wage-workers. Food processors have tended to avoid vertical integration by purchasing farms and staffing them, in favour of the simpler arrangement of extending credit for machinery purchase, and by offering lucrative production contracts, to those farmers willing and able to produce food to demand. Whilst this does lead in many cases to close control by the processor over stages of the crop cycle, the farmer remains an independent producer. Since there is also an incentive to mechanize as highly as possible, contract farming of this type encourages farms to shed labour and to rely as much as possible on the work of the farmer and his family.

It is not unreasonable to argue that agriculture's incorporation within capitalism has led to trends which do not appear to conform to the generally accepted logic of capitalist development. Although the number of agricultural producers in many (but not all) capitalist economies has been reduced quite dramatically in the last fifty years, capital concentration has produced quite different consequences in farming than those produced in other industrial sectors. In Britain a century ago, 90 per cent of farmland was tenanted by farmers who, in a large proportion of cases, employed agricultural labourers to work the land. In the 1980s, almost 80 per cent of farmland is worked by owner–occupiers, who outnumber their hired workers by almost two to one.

In order to comprehend this apparently inverted process of capitalist development, it will be necessary to return to the formulations of Karl Marx, around which an important and long-standing debate about agricultural development has emerged. This came to be known as a debate about 'the incorporation of agriculture within capitalism'. In general terms, this debate has its roots in the very emergence of industrial capitalist societies themselves during the nineteenth century, and thus in the historical processes which led to the transformation of agricultural work itself as a concomitant of capitalist industrialization. The French Physiocratic economist, Quesnay, writing as early as the end of the eighteenth century, indicates that the probable effects of this transformation were already well known: 'land employed for the cultivation of grain crops should be put together as much as possible in large farms managed by wealthy farmers, because there is less expenditure in the maintennance and repair of buildings, and proportionately much lower costs and much greater net product, in big farms than in small farms' (my translation).

Marx, responsible for much of the form in which this debate has been conducted, was perhaps as brilliantly one-sided in his insights about how this rural transformation would take place as he was with those devoted to transformations of the urban sector of industrial production. Yet it remains true that his inability to look beyond the case that best fitted his favourite thesis has been responsible for a certain degree of theoretical confusion about the social development of agricultural production within capitalist societies. For Marx built a theory about the forms which capitalism would take in agriculture with excessive regard to what was happening during his own lifetime in Britain. It is not surprising that Britain appeared to Marx to be the leading country in the rise of industrial capitalism, and perhaps no less surprising that industry's counterpart – agriculture – should be seen as similarly indicating the path for all other capitalist societies to follow.

This would not have mattered so much if Marx's ideas about capitalist development in agriculture had simply been confined to projecting trends in British farming. But instead they were directed to predictions about the demise of peasant farming, which ignored the historical particularity of the British case. Furthermore, such ideas were translated into practice in a number of societies where the peasantry was thought to be a bar to agricultural progress, and led directly to the creation of state and collective farms whose results have been generally less impressive than either the peasant farms they replaced or capitalist farms.

In the realm of rural development in the so-called 'Third World' Marx's ideas have received an even more severe test, as they have been adapted to the situation of peasant societies marked by colonial exploitation as well as to indigenous social and cultural conditions quite different to those in the countries of nineteenth-century Western Europe with which Marx was familiar. Hence the development of agricultural capitalism in such societies has taken forms at considerable variance with Marx's predictions, and has led many Marxist development theorists to make quite major modifications to the theses of classical Marxist theory. Indeed, it has even been argued that to take Marx's predictions about the capitalist development of agriculture at face value is to deny that rural development in 'underdeveloped' societies can be differentiated in any significant way from rural development in 'advanced' capitalist societies – the former being simply at a 'lower' level of the process than the latter, and thus at a predominantly 'feudal', rather than 'capitalist', stage in the development of the forces and relations of production.

This is not to say that Marx's ideas about agrarian capitalism have either been useless or simply wrong; indeed the opposite would be nearer to the truth, for the disputes and debates around the classical Marxian concepts and theories have been valuable in clarifying problems concerned with the major changes in rural social structures which have occurred in capitalist and socialist societies since the nineteenth century. In addition, it is worth emphasizing, although this is not strictly relevant to the concerns of the present chapter, that such disputes and debates have also been important to scholars concerned with earlier historical periods.

Thus, despite the problems inherent in his formulations, Marx's prediction of an increasing concentration of the control of farmland in the hands of capitalist entrepreneurs, employing the dispossessed former owners of small peasant farms as agricultural labourers – whilst the landowner is stripped of his role as organizer and master of the production process, becoming no more than a 'receiver of rent' – has for over a hundred years been the focus of debate over the failure of agriculture to follow the same course as manufacturing industry. This debate has called into question the nature of peasant economy and society, of pre-capitalist modes of production, of the transition from feudalism to capitalism, and of the demonstrable survival, persistence – and even expansion – of farming based on familial ownership and labour in countries such as Britain and the USA, where conditions seemed the most propitious for the creation of large capitalist farms.

Karl Marx and Agrarian Capitalism

It was suggested earlier that one major consequence of Marx's model of the development of capitalist relations in agriculture was a tendency for certain recent Marxist writers to see all societies as following the same general path of transition to agrarian capitalism. Thus, for some Marxist writers, the problems faced by peasant farmers in the so-called 'Third World' can be defined as the simple consequence of their societies being *en route* towards industrialization and the development of capitalist productive forces. Such problems result from the fact that these societies are at a preliminary stage, or stages, of a development process which the 'developed' capitalist societies have already traversed. Thus certain key features of the peasantry mirror those exhibited by, say, the French peasantry in the mid-nineteenth century or the Balkan peasantry in the 1920–40 period. In other words, they constitute a type of *transitional* social formation of small proprietors or 'petty commodity producers', whose future role is to become a dispossessed agricultural and urban proletariat (Warren, 1973). This formulation follows Marx's own, which may be seen as a radical rejection of the 'development problematic' *tout court*. Certain readings of Marx's writings (especially from Volumes 1 and 3 of *Capital*) indicate that he viewed the capitalist development of agriculture as an indispensable element of capitalist industrial development. It is perhaps unfortunate that Marx concentrated his attention on the historical experience of Britain in devising an analysis of capitalist agriculture. His theory of industrial capitalism, in taking Britain as a model which other societies would inevitably follow, led to the rather atypical de-peasantized agriculture of Victorian England being constituted as the prototypical form of agrarian capitalism.

For Marx, capitalist society was inevitably committed by the laws of capital formation to the concentration of the social structure into three distinct classes: rentiers, capitalists and proletariat. The two former classes would eventually merge together, as they represented the interests of property and capital. In Victorian England, this type of class structure was already in evidence, especially in the industrial towns. But it was also clearly evident in the countryside, where the advantageous conditions for arable farming in the third quarter of the nineteenth century had encouraged the formation of a tripartite class structure of landowners, tenant farmers and landless agricultural labourers. It is thus not surprising that Marx should have been struck by the apparent symmetry of industrial and agrarian capitalism, and tempted into seeing contemporary rural England as the prototype of the capitalist penetration of agriculture which would eventually be generalized throughout Europe. However, far from being the model for a universal process, English agrarian capitalism in its tripartite form has proved to be unique, in essence because it was only in England (and lowland England at that) that the indigenous peasantry was abolished *before* industrialization (Newby, 1983). As Newby has pointed out:

> Britain and its white-settler colonies (Canada, Australia, New Zealand and – for these purposes – the United States) are distinguished by their very absence of a peasantry, whereas in virtually every other country in the world the peasantry has survived the onslaught of *subsequent* industrialization. The value of the 'English model' of agrarian development is therefore limited in the extreme. *It is the*

persistence, not the disappearance, of the peasantry which has turned out to be the most distinctive feature of agricultural capitalism. (Newby, 1983, p.000, my italics)

If Marx was led up a theoretical blind alley by the historical particularity of the British version of agrarian capitalism, it is not perhaps surprising that he committed a similar error with his treatment of the peasantry. Marx's analysis of the peasantry relies on a small range of historical sources: principally the wine-growers of the Moselle and Rhine in his native Germany, and the French peasantry of the 1840s and 1850s. As a young journalist, he wrote at length on the hardships experienced by the former, and his commentary on the political role of the latter in 'The Eighteenth Brumaire of Louis Bonaparte' was written only a few years later in 1851. In characterizing the French peasantry as 'a vast mass [whose] members live in similar conditions but without entering into manifold relations with one another', Marx was led into a way of conceptualizing peasant social structures as merely anomalous social formations whose rationale had disappeared with the demise of the feudal mode of production. His treatment of the peasantry is rather one-dimensional and gives the impression that he almost shared the prevailing bourgeois view of peasants as a backward, ignorant, superstitious and savage race – indeed, a race apart from the townspeople:

> Their field of production, the small holding, admits of no division of labour in its cultivation, no application of science and therefore no diversity of development, no variety of talent, no wealth of social relationships. Each individual peasant family is almost self-sufficient; it itself directly produces the major part of its consumption and thus acquires its means of life more through exchange with nature than in intercourse with society. A small holding, a peasant and his family; alongside then another small holding, another peasant and another family.
>
> A few score of these make up a village, and a few score of villages make up a Department. In this way the great mass of the French nation is formed by simple addition of homologous magnitudes, much as potatoes in a sack form a sack of potatoes. Insofar as millions of families live under economic conditions of existence that separate their mode of life, their interests and their culture form those of the other classes, and put them in hostile opposition to the latter, they form a class. They are consequently incapable of enforcing their class interests in their own name, whether through a parliament or through a convention. They cannot represent themselves, they must be represented. (Marx, 1962, vol. 1, p. 334).

It is important to recognize that Marx's conceptualization of the peasantry constituted the other side of the coin to his model of agrarian capitalism. For Marx, movement towards the tripartite system is only possible through the concentration of land in the hands of a smaller and smaller number of landowners, and the consequent dispossession and proletarianization of peasant farmers. His writings clearly recognize a contradiction:

> between the dynamic growth of industrial capitalism and the persistence of a system of landownership that was pre-capitalist in form. Marx's own position was that capitalist society had replaced one form of exaction with another; the peasant family was now subjected to taxes and increased rents in place of feudal dues. (Goodman and Redclift, 1981, p. 5)

In effect, the new forms of surplus appropriation created by capitalism meant that peasant producers had no obvious place within it. In this sense, the peasant production unit shared the same eventual fate as all other small-scale enterprises, since it would be wiped out by competition from large enterprises in which the concentration of capital and labour enabled production be carried out at much lower cost than would be possible in the peasant farm. The only feature could be that of 'dissolution of private property based on the labour of its owner', for the 'production of capital and wage workers is ... the major product of the process by which capital turns itself into value'.

Marx could not see why the French peasantry, and thus all others opened up to the full force of capitalism, should not be subject to the same panoply of technical changes that had dealt such a fatal blow to the English peasantry. He saw enclosure and the 'agricultural revolution' as technological improvements little different to those accomplished in industrial production; by increasing agricultural productivity, they wiped out the small peasant farmer in the same way that factory production had wiped out the hand-loom weaver. As Marx expressed it in a letter to Vera Zassoulitch: 'all the countries of Western Europe will follow the same path as England'.

Engels put Marx's pessimism about the future of the peasantry even more strongly, in a way which interestingly foreshadows modern work. In his study of the 'Peasant Question in France and Germany', we find him pointing to the fact that the peasant is 'a survival of a past mode of production' who is doomed to become a proletarian. In part, this is because of the peasant's incorporation in an economy: he becomes increasingly dependent upon capital goods produced industrially, whilst as the same time unable to satisfy his own subsistence needs. Such a situation produced increasing indebtedness, which comprised the apparent independence conferred upon him by his possession of the means of production. Only paupererization could result from such a situation of increasing indebtedness and improvements in agricultural technology.

It must be evident that in countries like France, Germany and Italy Marx's predictions of a declining peasantry have been proved to be at least *partially* correct – that increasing indebtedness, technological change and relative pauperization *have* taken their toll of the peasant population. But it must be equally clear that, rather than being pushed *out* of agriculture, the pull from expanding urban/industrial sectors has been more important in draining the erstwhile rural populations of their agricultural workforces.

Similarly, many less developed countries have experienced either stability or an expansion in their peasant populations. In Mexico, for example, whilst the proportion of peasants in the total population had undoubtedly declined over the period 1910–70, the actual number of peasants has remained fairly constant during that time. In Brazil, there has ever been an absolute increase in the numbers and proportion of the peasantry within the total population (Lopez, 1976). Such processes as these are occurring in capitalist societies, even if they are ones which are relatively less well advanced along the road of capitalist development than the Western European states referred to above. None the less, the formation of a class of capitalist farmers in opposition to a class of dispossessed agricultural workers has not occurred in such societies where the conditions of capital accumulation could be taken to be at least roughly similar to those obtaining in Marx's nineteenth-century Europe. Marx's model posits a *progressive* replacement of pre-capitalist structures (peasant farms) by agrarian capitalism, rather than what seems historically to have occurred in a number of societies. Even in the USA and Britain, the tendency over the last ten years has been for rapid and continuing contraction of the number of farms and farmers to go hand in hand with a decline in the proportion of strictly *capitalist* farms – in the sense of farms using only hired labour. The most obvious trend has been for the 'typical' farm unit to become based more upon family ownership of the means of agricultural production, and the consequent 'exploitation' of *family* labour, rather than hired workers' labour. Whether it would be correct to call these farms run by family labour 'peasant' farms or not, has been a much-debated question. But the fact that, even in advanced capitalist societies, a return to relations of production associated in the progressive model with an *earlier* stage of development may be observed raises a number of questions about its adequacy.

Kautsky and Differentiation

Clearly, if the peasantry has not been extinguished by the development of capitalism in a number of different types of capitalist societies, then its future appears to be more at issue than might have been predicted if the 'progressist' type of classical Marxian theory just outlined were to be taken at face value. An agrarian transition along 'progressive' lines cannot be assumed and even a 'differentiation of agricultural capitalism' model à la Kautsky raises severe problems. Kautsky's *La Question Agraire* (1900) constitutes a paradigm for portraying the obstacles to progressive argrarian transition to the classic two-class situation. Although his work is rooted in specific political debates concerning the German peasantry's persistence in the late nineteenth century, contrary to Marx's prediction of its disappearance, it constitutes a model of agrarian transition which is of more general relevance.

Kautsky's position was that Marx's progressive model is correct in its isolation of the general tendencies involved in the capitalist mode of production, but that it is unable to identify those special factors which would prevent its conforming to the model in particular socio-historical contexts. Agriculture – and especially peasant or family-labour farms – represents one of these special factors (Hussein and Tribe, 1981). Because agriculture has these special characteristics (one of the most important being its dependence on a form of capital – *land* – that is non-reproducible), it exhibits a set of special laws of capitalist development, which may be clearly differentiated from those of industry.

Although capitalism develops along distinct lines in agriculture, it does, however, share certain general features of the development of industrial capitalism. These include the continuing extension of capitalist production, a certain degree of proletarianization of the agricultural labour force, and the concentration of property in the means of production. However, these similarities in the effects of capitalist development should not obscure the fact that their *structure* is quite different. The extension of capitalism does not so much involve an increase in the *area* farmed by capitalist farms, as it does in an extension of the organizational system under which capital is appropriated – or, in other words, the vertical and horizontal integration of capitalist farms into food processing and agribusiness. Even in 1899, he gave as an example of such a process the development of Nestlé!

Proletarianization also has a special meaning for Kautsky, for it implies the pauperization and loss of liberty of small peasants, their subjection to the interests of the agribusinesses rather than an actual change in the relations of production. Such a process also involved the *differentiation* of the peasant household, as peasants find it necessary to supplement their inadequate land resources by selling labour rather than agricultural commodities in order to provide a monetary income – to ensure family survival. The proletarianization process therefore creates worker-peasants or 'part-time farmers', rather than leading to the disappearance of the non-capitalist petty commodity producer. Indeed, Kautsky argues that the persistence of the small peasant farm is not a consequence of any superior productivity on its part, but a result of its ceasing to be in competition with the large capitalist farm, and its usefulness as a source of manpower for the latter

(Kautsky, 1900, p. 423). In fact, the complementarity of capitalist and peasant farms, which extends even to a specialization by the latter in certain labour-intensive crops which are not a viable proposition for the capitalist enterprise, is a result of the absence of the direct market competition which Marx's model identifies as the main cause of the disappearance of peasant farms.

This point about the potential complementarity of peasant farms and large capitalist farms is of considerable import in societies such as those in Latin America and the Caribbean, where *latifundia* and plantations have been implanted by colonial exploitation. The very fact of the coexistence of peasant farms alongside capitalist plantations in these societies, each type of farm supplying different agricultural commodities, indicates the relevance of Kautsky's model of agrarian transition for such a situation. Furthermore, Kautsky's analysis of the process of concentration in capitalist agriculture emphasizes that this does not necessarily mean, the creation of very large farm units in place of small peasant farms. The latter are undoubtedly affected by a concentration of landownership, due to their own increasing indebtedness. But this means that they are more and more reliant upon loans and mortgages, so that *de facto* control of their land passes into the hands of finance capital, rather than creating a widespread consolidation of small farms into larger farms. In addition, Kautsky was sceptical of the apparent technical superiority of large farms: Marx had assumed (like the Physiocrats) that large capitalist farms were automatically more efficient, in the same way that large factories were more efficient than small factories. But as Kautsky points out, the economies of scale apparent in industrial production are not simply transferable to agricultural production.[2] As he said, 'the expansion of a given enterprise... amounts to a mere extension of the area under cultivation, and thus entails a greater loss of material, a greater deployment of effort, resources, time' (Kautsky, 1900, p. 155).[3] Thus the main effect of Kautsky's model of agrarian transition is to stress the delayed and complex process by which capitalism penetrates agriculture, rather than to posit an alternative to Marx's paradigm itself. Kautsky believed in the ultimate correctness of the Marxian analysis, but he recognized that a complex *differentiation* of the rural social structure would occur before the logic of capitalism reached its conclusions. Within this complex differentiation, the peasantry would find itself with a variety of niches which allowed them to retain non-capitalist production units within a predominantly capitalist society. It is tempting to see the peasantry of many Third World societies as caught within this long-term transitional phase, their farms persisting because of their relative complementarity with plantations and *latifundia* and because of the pluri-activity of a considerable proportion of their labour force.

But it is not just in the Third World that a differentiated rural social structure of the type posited by Kautsky can be seen to persist. In 'advanced' capitalist societies such as France, Italy, Spain, and even West Germany or the Netherlands, agricultural work is quite clearly divided into two main forms: that carried out on a relatively small number of large capitalist farms, which tend to be devoted to the production of commodities where scale economies are significant, or more expensive capital equipment is required; and that carried out on a large number of small and medium-sized family-labour or 'peasant' farms involving a small number of family workers with the occasional hired worker, or, more frequently today, where the head of household has an urban, industrial occupation as well as his farming activity and a large responsibility for farm work therefore devolves on to his wife and children. These latter 'peasant' or family farms may specialize in certain commodities such as fruit, vegetables, free-range livestock and in many cases milk production, which they can produce at lower cost (and higher quality) than capitalist farms. The typical products of the peasant *'basse cour'* in France, for example, such as *foie gras*, rabbits, chicken and ducks, together with a wide range of salads and vegetables, find a ready local market and will frequently find their way to the kitchens of the best regional restaurants. The propensity of peasant farmers to exploit their own and their family's labour for small returns (the other side of the coin to the peasant mentality of penny-pinching and greed so often portrayed in folk-tales) enables their economic niche to be relatively secure, despite competition from capitalist farms. Indeed, the 'rural exodus' that has depopulated continental Europe of a large proportion of its peasants since 1950 or thereabouts was not primarily the result of the economic superiority of the capitalist farm over the peasant farm, but the result of a massive expansion of work opportunities for peasants in the towns, and the decline of a need for security expressed by the ownership or control of small plots of land, on which a family would eke out a meagre living. These are, to be sure, other aspects of the development of capitalism: but they are not evidence of the superiority of capitalist farms, nor a vindication of Marx's progressive model.

Chayanov and the Peasant Mode of Production

Kautsky's recognition that Marx's *progressive* model of the incorporation of capitalism within agriculture faced certain problems when it was divorced from its original *locale* – Victorian Britain – was paralleled by the emergence of a Russian school of rural economists concerned with the differentiation of the peasantry from the capitalist farming sector from the 1900s to the late 1920s. Their most important figure was A.V. Chayanov, who used a vast mass of data on the Russian peasantry to argue for a theory of the *peasant economy* – a mode of production which should be added to those distinguished by Marx: slavery, feudalism, capitalism, socialism and the 'Asiatic' mode of production.

Chayanov's main contributions were 'to provide a theory of peasant behaviour at the level of the individual family farm and...to show that at national level peasant economy ought to be treated as an economy in its own right, and not, as the Marxists claimed, as a form of incipient capitalism, represented by petty commodity production' (Kerblay, 1971, p. 151).

Chayanov insisted that the peasant, rather than being merely an erstwhile capitalist, has at best a set of different motivations: he is concerned above all with securing the needs of his family, rather than with making a profit. Indeed, Chayanov allots a major place in his theory to the idea of some sort of balance between subsistence needs and a 'subjective distaste for manual labour', because it is this which determines how hard the peasant will work and thus how intensely his farm is cultivated and ultimately its net product. Thus peasants do not follow the same rationale as capitalist entrepreneurs: 'the decreasing returns of the value of marginal labour do not hinder the peasant's activity so long as the needs of his family are not satisfied'. In other words, the peasant goes on attempting to increase what his farm produces after a 'rational' capitalist would have reasoned that the extra output would not justify the increased output of work:

> All the principles of our theory, rent, capital, price and other categories have been formed in the framework of an economy based on wage labour and seeking to maximize profits. ... But we must by no means extend its application to all phenomena in our economic life. We know that most peasant farms in Russia, China, India and most non-European and even many European states are unacquainted with the categories of wage-labour and wages. The economic theory

of modern capitalist society is a complicated system of economic categories inseparably connected with one another: price, capital, wages, interest, rent, which determine one another and are functionally interdependent. If one brick drops out of this system the whole building collapses.

In a natural economy human economic activity is dominated by the require-ment of satisfying the needs of a single production unit, which is, at the same time a consumer unit; therefore budgeting here is to a high degree *qualitative*...quantity here can be calculated only by considering the extent of each single need. ... Therefore, the question of comparative profitability of various expenditures cannot arise – for example, whether growing hemp or grass would be more profitable or advantageous for these plant products are not interchangeable and cannot be substituted for each other.

On the family farm, the family equipped with means of production uses its labour power to cultivate the soil and receives, as the result of a year's work, a certain amount of goods. A single glance at the inner structure of the labour unit is enough to realize that it is impossible, without the category of wages, to impose on its structure net profit, rent and interest on capital as real economic categories in the capitalist meaning of the word. ... Thus it is impossible to apply the capitalist profit calculation. (Chayanov, – quoted in Kerblay, 1971, p. 152).

Chayanov's theory is extremely well worked out: he calculated very carefully how the balance between subsistence needs and labour input depends on the size and demographic composition of the peasant family, and how such data could in turn be used to predict the area likely to be cultivated by the peasant farm, and the likely range of land improvements undertaken:

In the capitalist economy land and labour are the variable factors which the entrepreneur tries to combine to obtain the maximum remuneration from his capital, considered as a fixed factor. In a typical peasant economy labour, proportionate to the size of the family, it is the stable element which determines the change in the volume of capital and land. (Chayanov, quoted in Kerblay, 1971, p. 154)

Chayanov argued forcefully against concentration of agricultural production in the form of state or collective farms: such *horizontal integration*, as it is called, appeared to him to offer few advantages (despite the assumption that it reproduced the advantages of *industrial* concentration), although *vertical* inegration of peasant farms with co-operatives and processing plants seemed to him to offer considerable advantages, such was the competitive strength of the peasant farm *vis-à-vis* both capitalist and collective farm.

There is no doubt that Chayanov's theory works best for the socio-historical conditions in which it was designed – the fairly thinly populated rural regions of pre- and post-revolutionary Russia. But it also suggests that certain underlying characteristics of the peasant or family-labour farm may be used to explain its persistence, where assumptions that capitalism necessarily requires the sweeping away of such units through a process of concentration can be seen to be inaccurate.

One possibility raised by the persistence of peasant farms in both 'advanced' and 'dependent' capitalist societies is that they represent a deformed or transitional form of 'peripheral' social organization, thrown up by the somewhat lopsided way in which the capitalist mode of production develops. In such formulations – strongly influenced by studies of *peripheral* (i.e. 'developing') societies such as those in Central and Latin America, and of the historical emergence of capitalism – the main concern is to deal with the question of whether the persistence of peasants is evidence of a problematic transition from feudalism to capitalism. Peasants may be a 'peripheral' social formation in relation to the rest of their society, much as, in the same way, largely agrarian societies are 'peripheral' in the context of the world capitalist economy. Although agrarian transition in the sense of the Marxian progressive thesis – subsumption of labour by capital and the formation of a rural capitalist class and a rural proletariat of wage labourers completely separated from the means of production – remains a theoretical possibility, our attention is drawn to those factors which prevent its completion.

Dependency Theory and the Modes of Production Controversy

The fact that agrarian transition remains incomplete and partial in the Third World as much as it does in Europe (because of the persistence of family-labour farms and petty commodity production) has to be explained in terms of the controversial estimation of the actual subsumption of labour by capital. Such an estimation is controversial because it lies at the heart of the dispute about the nature of the divergent paths taken by the penetration and expansion of capitalism in agriculture, in a wide range of societies.

Mention of this dispute returns us to the issue of centre-periphery relations in the Marxian debate about underdevelopment. As was outlined above, one mode of argument follows Marx more or less directly in predicting that capitalist penetration of peripheral societies will destroy, or is already in the process of destroying, pre-capitalist modes of production. We have outlined this view above in relation to its implications for agrarian transition and the future of the peasantry. Against this, a wide range of scholarship from a Marxist perspective (or, more exactly, a *variety* of Marxist perspectives) has quite recently been concerned with the observable failure in many less developed countries of the penetration of capitalism to eradicate pre- or non-capitalist structures. The most important of these structures is, arguably, the peasantry which may, as we have pointed out, in fact be in the process of expansion in certain areas, rather than on the road to complete disappearance. It is interesting to note in this respect that the historical experience of developed states such as the USA has itself included long periods when non-capitalist forms of production such as family-labour farms were able to compete on advantageous terms with capitalist enterprises: as Friedmann (1978) has argued, in the first three decades of the twentieth century family farm production (even in arable areas) expanded at the expense of capitalist farm production.

The new Marxist development theories are concerned with indicating how underdevelopment may constitute, variously, a 'blocked' transition to normal developed capitalism. Examples of this are the formulation where it is said that 'capital created underdevelopment not because it exploited the underdeveloped world but because it did not exploit it enough' (Kay, 1975); or where Amin (1974) argues for a special *form* of capitalism – 'peripheral' capitalism; or finally that the 'world-system' of capitalism requires a complementary underdeveloped–developed relation of *metropolis* and *satellite*, as is contained in Frank's (1969) and Wallerstein's (1974) theories. Such approaches constitute an attempt in their various ways to move beyond both the classic Marxist model and, more importantly, the conceptions of *dependency* that were associated with the Latin American resurgence of Marxist development studies in the 1960s – a current to which A.G. Frank himself was initially attached.

Within the Marxist wing of dependency theory that is of most relevance to this discussion, the basic hypothesis of the dependency paradigm is that development and underdevelopment are 'partial', interdependent, structures of one global system'. In Dos Santos's formulation:

> Dependence is a conditioning situation in which the economies of one group of countries are conditioned by the development and expansion of others. A relationship of interdependence between two or more economies or between such economies and the world trading system becomes a dependent relationship when some countries can expand through self-impulsion while others, being in a dependent position, can only expand as a reflection of the expansion of the dominant countries, which may have positive or negative effects on their immediate development. (Dos Santos, 1973)

Naturally enough, a variety of possible positions exists within the Marxist wing of dependency theory. Whilst it may not be the most typical of such approaches, that adopted by A.G. Frank has been by far the most influential. Frank is concerned with the dependent development of Latin America as a 'satellite' region of the capitalist 'metropolis'. The situation of Latin American peasants is thus to be seen within the organizing metaphor of 'metropolis–satellite' relations, as we shall see.

It would not be appropriate here to provide an exposition of Frank's theory. However, it is important to remind ourselves that Frank treats the question of agrarian transition quite perfunctorily: in effect, the 'transition' is 'simply and rapidly accomplished by the integration of [such a] peripheral formation in the capitalist world economy' (Frank, 1969). Because Latin America was incorporated into the capitalist world economy so rapidly after the conquest of the sixteenth century, capitalism and prototypically 'capitalist' social relations of production were quickly generalized as commodity production and exchange relations rapidly penetrated all sectors of the peripheral or *satellite* social formation. Thus integration within the capitalist world system is, on Frank's view, incompatible with the persistence of pre-capitalist modes of production. Plantations, *latifundia* and *microfundia* (regions of small peasant farms) hence all appear not as feudal forms of production, but merely as 'degenerate' or obsolescent *capitalist* forms of production. In discussing the *latifundium*, he is quite explicit on this point:

> the growth of the *latifundium* and its feudal-seeming conditions of servitude in Latin America has always been and still is the commercial response to increased demand and...it does not represent the transfer or survival of alien institutions that have remained beyond the reach of capitalist development. (Frank, 1969, p. 15)

For Frank, then, a feudal or pre-capitalist peasantry does not exist in Latin America. The peripheral nature of peasants in relation to capitalist commercial agriculture thus merely reproduces the 'metropolis–satellite' relations of dependency which extend in a chain-link fashion from the Latin American peasant up to the president of the largest multinational corporation. No one escapes the logic of capitalist relations of expropriation/appropriation, and there cannot be any sector so backward as to remove itself even partially into a non-capitalist mode of production. Even subsistence agriculture is sucked into the capitalist chain of 'surplus appropriation'. Discussing the 'myth of Feudalism in Brazilian agriculture', Frank states that:

> While subsistence agriculture and much of small-scale agriculture might seem by definition not 'commercial', they *are* commercially determined because they are residual to commercial agriculture. *They are residual in every way imaginable – residual land, residual finance, residual labour, residual distribution, residual income, residual everything.* Residual agriculture and commercial agriculture are like the two parts of an hour glass. The connection between them may appear small, but the resources do flow from one to the other with each turn of the hour-glass economy. What determines this flow of resources? Evidently not the changing fortunes of the

subsistence sector, at least in Brazil. (The agricultural reform of Bolivia did in a sense turn the subsistence sector at least partially into the primary sector.) The determining forces come either from the commercial sector and its shifting fortunes and/or from the national and international economy as a whole. (Frank, 1969, p. 286, my italics)

As a number of Marxist critiques have emphasized, Frank is more concerned with employing the concept of surplus *appropriation* derived from Paul Baran (1957) than with engaging with the classic Marxist conceptualization of the expropriation of surplus value which underpins Marx's own definitions of classes and of capitalism. As a result, Frank's formulations are imprecise as to the class structure of dependent economies, and confuse organizations, spatial entities and social classes. In the precise context of, for example, the relationships between peasant farmers and plantation systems in one of the Caribbean societies, Frank's paradigm would not be able to theorize the social relations of production under which the latter exploits the surplus labour of the former. Indeed, it is of considerable importance that the dependency model employed by Frank refuses to assign to wage labour the fundamental characterizing feature of capitalism. Frank's paradigm was a very necessary polemic against, and corrective of, the bland functionalist development or 'modernization' studies which saw peasants as an 'irrational' and 'traditional' stratum who would develop an effective agriculture only when their culture and values could be 'modernized' or made more 'rational'. But to place an excessive explanatory burden on what is essentially a theory of inter-nation transfers of economic surplus leads directly to the point where agrarian social structures slip elusively away from concrete analysis. Although it is undoubtedly true that the peasantries of Caribbean societies suffer from the unequal exchange relationships which characterize metropolis-satellite links, this is not a sufficient explanation of the socio-cultural features of rural class structures.

An extension of Frank's paradigm is to be found in the work of Immanuel Wallerstein, who employs a core–periphery model (in some ways similar to Frank's metropolis–satellite metaphor) to develop a 'world-system' paradigm. His work concentrates on the historical emergence, in about the sixteenth century, of the *capitalist* world-system (Wallerstein, 1974). Wallerstein has been concerned with the historical development of the 'modern' world-system, which is based on the 'world-economy' of capitalism. Capitalism has never constituted a world-empire, because it has always contained 'within its bounds not one but a multiplicity of political systems'. Most importantly for our purposes, however, a world-system is one in which:

> There is extensive division of labour. This division is not merely functional – that is, occupational – but geographical. That is to say, the range of economic tasks is not evenly distributed throughout the world-system. In part this is the consequence of ecological considerations, to be sure. But for the most part, it is a function of the social organization of work, one which magnifies and legitimizes the ability of some groups within the system to exploit the labour of others, that is, to receive a larger share of the surplus. (ibid, p. 400)

For Wallerstein, peripheral societies are those where there is specialization in agricultural products: core societies, on the other hand, are those which are characterized by a high proportion of accumulated capital enterprises. Because the latter are also typically more powerful, they are able to enforce an unequal exchange between periphery and core: capitalism involves 'an appropriation of surplus of the whole world-economy by core areas' because 'tasks requiring higher levels of skill and greater capitalization are reserved for higher ranking areas... [the] capitalist world-economy essentially rewards accumulated capital, including human capital, at a higher rate than "raw" labour power' (Wallerstein, 1974, p. 401).

Like Frank, Wallerstein refuses to identify capitalism with wage-labour: he is only concerned with exchange relations which are its primary defining characteristics – 'production for sale in a market in which the object is to realize the maximum profit' (1974, p. 348). Hence, Wallerstein too is unwilling to grant the persistence of feudal elements such as 'peasants' in his capitalist world-economy:

> The ideological descriptions that systems convey about themselves are never true. It is always easy to find presumed instances of 'non-capitalist' behaviour in a capitalist world – all over Europe in 1650 and 1750 but also in 1850 and 1950. The mixture of such 'non-capitalist' behaviour, firms and states with 'capitalist' behaviour, 'capitalist' firms, or (the least happy usage of all) 'capitalist' states within a capitalist world-economy is neither an anomaly nor transitional. The mixture is the essence of the capitalist system as a mode of production, and it accounts for how the capitalist world-economy has historically affected the civilizations with which it has coexisted in social space. (Wallerstein, 1974, p. 402)

As a result of this orientation in his work, Wallerstien sees non-wage-labour forms of work as equally typical of capitalism. Since such forms – i.e. slavery, forced cash-crop production, share-cropping and tenancy – are all *alternative* modes of the way labour is recruited and organized in Wallerstein's model of capitalist agriculture, we are presented with a highly differentiated paradigm of agrarian capitalism in peripheral societies. Thus, the precise form of surplus appropriation found in any particular agrarian structure can be 'read off' from the patterns of trade and international comparative advantage within which it is situated. The observed differences, then, between the peasantries of the societies we are concerned with would be explicable for Wallerstein in terms of market-determined factors. Class structures, or what Wallerstein calls *labour control systems*, thus simply transmit world-market pressures to their constituent personnel. It would seem, then, that we are not far from the original Frankian analysis in which relations of exploitation appear in a dualistic form, both as class relations and as power relations in which surplus is appropriated from weak peripheries by dominant cores. We are not, perhaps, too far from Lenin's definition of imperialism as well: but in any event it is as difficult with Wallerstein's approach as it is with Frank's to isolate explanatory variables which would account for the particular and diverse social structural forms encountered in the rural societies of capitalist economies.

The problems faced by dependency theory in accounting for rural class structures that can only be incorporated within a Marxist framework by jettisoning its central tenets, relating to the specificity of wage-labour as the prime mode of surplus appropriation, have led to a debate about the nature of agrarian transition which takes full account of the paradoxical association of apparently pre-capitalist and capitalist units of production. This debate has centred on a return to classical Marxian concepts of *mode of production*, a formulation quite absent from the Frank–Wallerstein work, the emphasis of which is placed on *exchange relations*.

Laclau's now-famous contribution to the debate about the Frankian paradigm concentrated on the observable dualism evident in Latin American societies once the conceptual focus shifts away from relations of *exchange* to relations of *production* (Leclau, 1971). Norman Long, for example, discussing his work on Peruvian peasants, indicates that:

> both capitalist and non-capitalist modes of production frequently co-exist within the same empirical situation, involving the same or neighbouring peasants in qualitatively different types of production relations. (1975, p. 261)

Laclau's critique emphasizes that, although Frank is correct to insist upon the view that the period of colonial exploitation in Latin America was not one of a 'closed economy', his departure from the use of *relations of production* confuses the question of whether Latin American societies contain or contained either capitalist or feudal modes of appropriation. Significantly, the drive of Laclau's argument is to show that Frank's claim to provide a *Marxist* analysis of capitalist development cannot be sustained.

Despite the fact that we are thus brought back to the dreary world of Marxism internecine conceptual strife, a number of Laclau's points are of relevance. Laclau insists upon the fact that, for Marx, capitalism is a determinate mode of production with quite specific relations of production which determine, in their turn, how surplus labour is appropriated in the form of surplus value. Central to this is the fact that the direct producer is separated from ownership of the means of production and that there is a free labour market in which labour is bought and sold as a commodity. In consequence, a social division of labour exists based on the antagonistic relations of production which oppose the class of wage labourers to the class of capitalists. Because Frank departs from this conceptualization of capitalism, treating it purely in terms of market relations, he is unable to deal with the cases where two distinct modes of production coexisted in parallel. Indeed, Laclau's general argument is that, although expansion of external markets undoubtedly took place during the mercantilist epoch, this did not promote a greater penetration of capitalism, but rather 'accentuated and consolidated' feudalism. Akin to the situation of 'second serfdom' in Eastern Europe from the sixteenth to nineteenth centuries, that in Latin America (where slavery and forced labour were common) led to a relative strengthening of what he calls 'servile relations' as it was progressively and unevenly incorporated into the world economy. Laclau, then, maintains a model of *incomplete* transition to capitalism in Latin America and the Caribbean. In consequence, his position suggests that initially elaborated by Louis Althusser of the 'co-existence' of several modes of production, for he would appear to favour an 'articulation' between the feudal and capitalist modes of production:

> No doubt from the end of the 19th century these conditions were gradually modified in Latin America with the progressive growth of a rural proletariat. It is difficult to say how far peasant proletarianization has reached in different areas today, since we lack sufficient studies of it, but there is no doubt that the process is very far from being concluded, and semi-feudal conditions are still widely characteristic of the Latin American countryside. (Laclau, 1971, p. 31)

Laclau gives a clear example of the coexistence of the two different modes of production: whilst the peripheral export economies of Latin America were clearly capitalist in terms of the social division of labour during the nineteenth century, he identifies the 'feudal regime of the *haciendas*' as an example of the way in which feudal relations of production (evidenced by the increase and intensification of servile obligations – *inquilinaje*) adapted to expanding commercial opportunities. As Goodman and Redclift point out:

> For Laclau, incorporation in capitalist exchange relations has less significance than the existence of specific forms of labour exploitation and surplus appropriation. For Frank, on the other hand, these forms are merely instruments of the overall dynamic of the capitalist world economy. (1981, p. 40)

It should be pointed out that it is not Laclau's intention to assert the existence of a fully dualistic system, where agrarian enterprises constitute a separate feudal economy distinct from the capitalist economy in which the export enterprises solely participate. He is, rather, concerned to posit a structured and differentiated 'economic system' – or even *social formation* – which is in fact capitalistic. The substantial *elements* of feudalism which make up certain parts of this differentiated structure are not exogenous to it, but constitutes intrinsic and vital (even necessary) components of a wider system. The external market, far from dissolving feudalistic elements, has concentrated or even created them and other pre-capitalistic modes of production.

In developing this model of an *articulated* form of capitalism, writers such as Laclau have been able to cope with the development of peripheral economies, a development so apparently contradictory to the progressive or evolutionary model of Eurocentric Marxist theory, while remaining close to Marx's original concepts.

The so-called 'new economic anthropology' practised by French social scientists such as Dupré (1978), Godelier (1977), Meillassoux (1975), Terray (1972) and, most influentially, Rey (1973) has been a primary site for the elaboration of the 'articulation of modes of production' stream in recent Marxist writing. It bases itself on Althusser's usage of the term *articulation* to suggest how, within a particular social formation, specific 'instances' or levels are linked together and expressed. As Althusser puts it: a 'mode of production' is a 'complex structure, doubly articulated by the productive forces connexion and the relations of production connexion' (Althusser and Balibar, 1970, pp. 311, 317). It is in the work of P.P. Rey that the most relevant connection with the problem raised in this chapter appears. Rey's *Les alliances de classes* (1973, pp. 82–7) is concerned to identify both the European transition to capitalism and Europe's articulation with other (i.e. the peripheral) economies. This involves a periodization of the process of articulation:

(i)   an initial link in the sphere of exchange, where ineteraction with capitalism *reinforces* the pre-capitalist mode;

(ii)   capitalism 'takes root', subordinating the pre-capitalist mode but still making use of it;

(iii) (not yet reached in the Third World) the total disappearance of the pre-capitalist mode, even in agriculture. (Foster-Carter 1978, p. 50)

Thus we are returned to the position that progress to agrarian transition, to the full incorporation of agriculture by capitalism, is possible, even if it is blocked. The peasant farmers of Western Europe are on the road to becoming either fully-fledged capitalist farmers, or a rural proletariat – assuming that they remain in agriculture at all.

However, a major departure from the Rye-inspired articulation approach must be referred to here, before concluding this discussion. It should be clear that what is at issue in the articulation debate is the *blockage* of the process of transition from feudalism to capitalism observed in underdeveloped countries, particularly in the case of Latin America and the Caribbean. Certain writers, however, have opposed the notion that articulation can occur in the sense of the coexistence of two modes of production. As Banaji (1972) and Amin and Vergopoulos (1977) variously argue, although capitalism may well permit the coexistence of several relations of *exploitation* (such as wage-labour or slavery), these must be distinguished from relations of production which are determined by modes of production. 'Pre-capitalist' enterprises, although appearing formally distinct, are in fact capitalist where they exist within capitalist systems, since they are subordinated to the laws of motion of capitalist development.

In Vergopoulos's formulation of Amin's concept of *peripheral capitalism*, then, the persistence or even expansion of the peasant sector is evidence of no more than a 'deformed capitalism'. Discussing the prevalence of family farming in Greece and other countries of Southern and Eastern Europe, he argues that such a form of agriculture:

Although based on the family, is nevertheless capitalist, it is within the *family form of production that, in the domain of agriculture, the contemporary movement of capitalism manifests itself.* It is indeed this inequality, this non-correspondence between urban and rural social forms (which are nevertheless integral parts of the same social body and of the same unitary movement of capital) which I have called '*deformed capitalism.* (Vergopoulos, 1978, p. 447, my italics)

Indeed, far from being a curious pre-capitalist survival destined to disappear, peasant family farming in fact constitutes a 'necessary mechanism' for the accumulation of *urban* capital and the development of capitalism (a position not far from that of Kautsky, it should be noted). The deformity of capitalism involved in this process thus results from the fact that peasants typically over-exploit their own labour in order to receive an income from their sale of agricultural products at about the same level as wage workers. Normally they are not able to realize either a ground rent from their land nor an entrepreneur's profit. As a result, the profit and rent foregone represent 'positive gains' for the urban economy – effectively a *transfer of resources.* It is in this light that Amin and Vergopoulos make the case that 'family farming is the most successful form of production for putting the maximum volume of surplus peasant labour at the disposal of urban capitalism. It also constitutes the most efficient way of restraining the prices of agricultural products' (1977, p. 447).

Conclusions

The arguments of Vergopoulos and Amin thus return us from the peripheral *societies* of the Third World to the peripheral *social* formations which peasants and family-labour farms represent for European societies. The most important feature of the debate about agriculture's incorporation within capitalism is that it indicated the range and scope of the underlying socio-economic changes which agrarian transition involves. As we have seen by following the debate into the Third World, issues about the capitalist penetration of agriculture are questions about the structures of societies themselves – far from being simply the residues of previous economic systems, peasant and family-labour farms would appear to constitute a basic feature of capitalist societies. This is not to suggest that the difficult theoretical issues raised about the persistence of small, family-labour farms in advanced capitalist societies have been resolved, but that their continual raising reflects a basic structural feature of those societies. The highly anomalous case of Britain – which may *never* have had a very significant peasant sector, if we are to believe Alan Macfarlane (1978) – can thus be seen to have muddied the waters of theoretical understanding of processes basic to the development of capitalism itself, by diverting attention to a process of capital concentration in agriculture which was highly specific in historical and social terms. The fact that Britain effectively became a less capitalist agricultural economy after Marx's death, in terms of the classic agrarian transition model outlined previously, does no more than confirm the dangers of relying upon the historical experience of one society – however persuasive a model may thereby be created.

Notes

1. This chapter draws in part from an introductory essay in Peter Hamilton and Ronald G. Parris (eds), *Rural Development in Comparative Perspective*, Paris/CEESTEM and Mexico City, UNESCO, forthcoming.
2. It can be argued that only in certain types of farming can scale economies be exploited, for example intensive livestock production such as poultry and pigs.

3. It should be stressed, however, that Kautsky was writing before the development of a highly mechanized farming, which would permit large areas to be cultivated more efficiently than small.

References

Althusser, L. and Balibar, E. (1970) *Reading Capital*, London, New Left Books.

Amin, Samir (1974) *Accumulation on a World Scale*, 2 vols, New York, Monthly Review Press.

Amin, Samir and Vergopoulos, Kostas (1977) *La question paysanne et le capitalisme*, Paris, Anthropos.

Banaji, J. (1972) 'For a Theory of Colonial Modes of Production', *Economic and Political Weekly*, 23 December, pp. 2498–502.

Baran, P. (1957) *The Political Economy of Growth*, New York, Monthly Review Press.

Dos Santos, T. (1973), 'The Crisis of Development Theory and the problem of dependence in Latin America' in Bernstein, H. (ed.), *Underdevelopment and Development: The Third World Today*, Harmondsworth, Penguin.

Dupré, C. (with P.P. Rey) (1978) 'Reflections on the Relevance of a Theory of the History of Exchange', in D. Seddon, (ed.), *Relations of Production: Marxist Approaches to Anthropology*, London, Frank Cass.

Foster-Carter, A. (1978), 'The modes of production controversy', in *New Left Review* no. 107.

Frank, A.G. (1969) *Capitalism and Underdevelopment in Latin America*, New York, Monthly Review Press.

Freedman, H. (1978) 'World Market, State and Family Farm: Social bases of household production in the era of wage labour', *Comparative Studies in Society and History*, vol. 20, no. 4, pp. 545–86.

Godelier, M. (1977) *Perspectives in Marxist Anthropology*, Cambridge, Cambridge University Press.

Goodman, D. and Redclift, M. (1981) *From Peasant to Proletarian*, Oxford, Basil Blackwell.

Hussein, A. and Tribe, K. (1981) *Marxism and the Agrarian Question*, 2 vols, London, Macmillan.

Kautsky, K. (1900) *La Question Agraire*, Paris, Giard et Brière.

Kay, G. (1975) *Development and Underdevelopment: A Marxist Analysis*, London, New Left Books.

Kerblay, B. (1971) 'Chayanov and the Theory of Peasantry as a Specific Type of Economy', in T. Shamin, (ed.), *Peasants and Peasant Societies*, Harmondsworth, Penguin.

Laclau, E. (1971) 'Feudalism and Capitalism in Latin America', *New Left Review*, no. 67.

Long, N. (1975) 'Structural Dependency, Modes of Production and Economic Brokerage in Rural Peru', in I. Oxaal, (ed.),

Lopez, J.R.B. (1976) *Capitalist Development and Agrarian Structure*, CEBRAP 26.

Macfarlane, A. (1978) *The Origins of English Individualism*, Oxford, Basil Blackwell.

Marx, K. (1962) 'The Eighteenth Brumaire of Louis Bonaparte', in *Selected Works*, vol. 1, Moscow, Foreign Languages Publishing House.

Meillassoux, C. (1975) *Femmes, Greniers et Capitaux*, Paris, Mapero.

Newby, H. (forthcoming) 'European Social Theory and the Agrarian Question: towards a sociology of agriculture', in P. Hamilton, (ed.), *Socio-Economic Change in Rural Society 1945–80: Britain and France*.

Oxaal, I. et al (ed.) (1975) *Beyond the Sociology of Development*, London, Routledge & Kegan Paul.

Rey, P.P. (1973) *Les alliances de classes*, Paris, Maspero.

Terray, E. (1972) *Marxism and 'Primitive' Societies*, New York, Monthly Review Press.

Vergopoulos, Kostas (1978) 'Capitalism and Peasant Productivity', *Journal of Peasant Studies*, vol. 5, no. 4.

Wallerstein, I. (1974) *The Modern World System*, New York, Academic Press.

Warren, B. (1973) 'Imperialism and Capitalist Industrialization', *New Left Review*, vol. 81, September–October.

SECTION III

Work and Society

The debate about the labour process, stimulated by Braverman's work in the early 1970s, arose out of reflections on the rash of disputes in industry, which seemed to represent new worker demands and a widespread dissatisfaction with the conditions of work in industrial society. That was during a time of relatively low unemployment. Since then a prolonged economic slump has brought other issues and problems to the forefront. Employers have sought to reduce labour costs by laying off workers and by getting more work from those they have kept on, which entails reducing the resistance of workers to changes in work practices. Greater competitiveness is believed to follow from the replacement of workers by technology, where possible, and the reduction of job security. Women workers are particularly subject to being laid off or taken on for part-time work, and there is less inclination to take on young apprentices for lengthy training. Consequently the prospects for work among certain sections of society look bleak. In such circumstances, the meaning of work, or ideologies of work, need to be revised. There are also questions to be asked about work outside the formal economy and work that is unpaid.

Pahl (in Chapter 11) examines the implications of a decline in manufacturing jobs and a slowing down in the expansion of service jobs, which had previously taken up the slack. Some commentators view this as a temporary shortfall, which will be put right when the service sector expands again. Others doubt whether there will ever be a sustained expansion. Pahl puts forward the possibility, suggested by his research in association with Jonathan Gershuny, that there will be no compensating expansion of service jobs, because many of the services previously provided by the market or by public authorities are increasingly being provided by the household (for example, cinemas and public transport are replaced by household goods such as television sets and private cars). In this sense, the changes in the division of labour may be even more profound than is commonly believed, as the balance between the formal economy, informal economy and household is possibly shifting, and this could constitute a revolution in patterns of everyday life.

There is another side to the household economy, and that is represented by the sexual division of labour and women's role in the performance of the majority of domestic work. Oakley (in Chapter 12) points out that, in pre-industrial society, there was little 'housework' in the modern sense of cleaning, dusting, tidying and shopping. With industrialization, women's relationship to domestic work changed from production for family use to consumption for family use. Shopping for consumption and home maintenance activities loom large, constituting what has been called the 'crypto-servant' functions of consumption administration. Even that does not fully reveal the chief significance of the housewife's invisible and unpaid work for the maintenance of the economy – she produces and maintains workers for industry in the form of her husband and children. Changes in the social division of labour, and in the household economy, particularly impact on women's work.

Taking up a theme raised elsewhere in this book (by Kumar, Pahl and Oakley), Finch (in Chapter 13) shows that the idea of a division and separation of work in the formal economy from household and leisure activities is misleading. It is not only businessmen who take home their work in more ways than simply in their briefcases. Wives and children find that their lives and relationships are greatly determined by the work preoccupations of husbands and fathers, and similarly when the woman is in paid employment.

A popular diagnosis of the problem of high youth unemployment and of workers' unsuitability or inefficiency, especially among industrialists, is that the schools do not prepare young people for work. Various reports on this subject have put forward the view that many of industry's problems are due to unfavourable attitudes held by workers, and that the best agency for changing these was the schools. Jamieson and Lightfoot of the Schools Council Industry Project report (in Chapter 14) on the effects of schools' attempts to respond to external pressure to teach more about industry. They found that one of the reasons for the relative lack of success of the schools' attempts to produce favourable attitudes towards industry was that pupils share the subculture of industrial workers, which itself contains attitudes that diverge from those that industrialists would like workers to hold. There are clearly limits to what can be achieved by schools in the way of counteracting a culture which is itself a product of experience of workplace relations. One of the findings was that learning about work was not often placed in its political context – the broad social, economic and political forces shaping work. Teaching about work, in schools, tended to be at the level of the individual and his or her reactions to social forces. Where political questions were broached, they usually related to trade unions (which were seen as political), but not to employers, reflecting the dominant ideology in society according to which the position of employers is regarded as 'natural' and 'normal' (a point made by Armstrong *et al.* in Chapter 8).

The question of the meaning of work and its relation to spheres other than that of paid employment in the formal economy is particularly acute for the young unemployed. Roberts *et al.* argue (in Chapter 15), on the basis of their research, that theories about responses to unemployment derived from the experience of earlier generations cannot be reconciled with the behaviour and attitudes of contemporary youth. To make sense of current developments, and in particular to understand the relevance of recreation in an age of rising youth unemployment, the authors insist that we need to reappraise work and leisure, and recognize the qualitative as well as quantitative aspects of the changes in process. A reappraisal of ideologies of work and ideologies of consumption is also called for by Moorhouse (in Chapter 16), who criticizes sociologists for not taking account of the ways in which ideologies of consumption have come to occupy a dominant role in forming people's self-images and commitments. Although he focuses on the classic study of the American automobile workers, published by Chinoy in 1955, and its assumption that they were having to accommodate themselves to failure to attain the American dream of occupational success, Moorhouse's critique applies even more to the sociology of work in our contemporary society.

11 Employment, Work and the Domestic Division of Labour

R.E. PAHL

Employment in the formal economy in advanced industrial societies such as Britain or the United States seems certain to decline, particularly in the manufacturing sector. Earlier assumptions that the service sector of the economy would expand to absorb displaced labour are now being seriously questioned. Economists approaching the problem from sharply different ideological perspectives agree that it seems extremely improbable that full-time employment in the formal economy will expand in the next decade. Evidently there is scope for substantial argument about the causes of the economic change, decline or 'crisis'. I do not want to enter into that debate here, although I recognize that there are some among those contributing to such a debate who would argue that the levels of unemployment, which I appear to be 'accepting', could be avoided by radical economic and political restructuring. That may or may not be so. For present purposes I intend to focus on the consequences of a shift out of 'employment' into 'work', which may be highly productive, although hidden in terms of national accounting. I further want to explore the implications of this and other shifts within local labour markets and how these interact with the household economy.

The decade of the 1970s provoked substantial discussion about 'deindustrialization' (Blackaby, 1979), 'the post-industrial society' (Bell, 1974), 'the recapitalization of capital' (Miller, 1978), 'the self service economy' (Gershuny, 1978), 'the political economy of inflation' (Goldthorpe and Hirsch, 1978), 'corporatism' (Winkler, 1976), 'capitalism in crisis' (Gamble and Walton, 1976) and many other similar themes. Such explorations and analyses were curiously disembodied. We had very little detailed, empirical work which would show the interconnections between 'public issues and private troubles' in the phrase of C. Wright Mills. This was doubtless partly due to the disillusion with the atheoretical and uncumulative 'community' studies of the previous decade, which had been so vigorously, indeed almost scathingly, attacked (Bell and Newby, 1971). It was also due to the lack of any clear methodology which could link macro and micro analysis. Descriptions of modest little protests here and there were puffed up in an arbitrary and cavalier way into grandiose theories of political or societal change. And whilst much was made of the unsavoury impact of an expanding state monopoly capitalism in 'everyday life', there was precious little detailed analysis of this everyday life. People seemingly, had to fit the macro-models and even those committed to more local urban and regional analysis were often more interested in flows of capital at the level of the economy than in the distribution and allocation of work and resources in the household (Castells, 1977; Harloe, 1977; Pickvance, 1976).

Any attempt to develop a social anthropology of inflation or 'post industrial

R.E. Pahl, in *International Journal of Urban and Regional Research*, vol. 4, 1980, pp. 1–19.

society' is fraught with difficulty. One is forced into a conceptual wilderness with few methodological guidelines and the hostility of colleagues ready to attack one with the deadly darts of 'mindless empiricism' or 'travellers' tales'. However, partly in reaction to my own earlier work (Pahl, 1977a; 1977b), I began a two year pilot study in 1977 in an isolated working-class labour market with a high level of unemployment.[1] In this paper I draw on this empirical work in a rather diffuse way in an attempt to illuminate a larger model about the nature of the changes which will, I suggest, become more common in industrial societies in the 1980s. I am preparing a more substantial research project which will develop and explore the ideas which are discussed below.[2]

The Decline of Employment in the Formal Economy

In Britain the continued net fall in employment in manufacturing industry seems inevitable, at least through the 1980s. 'Between 1966 and 1976 the net fall in employment in manufacturing was 1.34 million, an average of 134 000 per annum' (Thatcher, 1979, 33). In 1960 35.8% of the total employment was in manufacturing, but in 1975 the proportion had fallen to 30.9%. Similar proportionate declines were shared by Belgium, Denmark, Germany, Holland, the US and Sweden (Brown and Sheriff, 1979, 239). In an increasingly competitive situation raising output per head seems inevitable and this raises an awkward dilemma. 'Failure to raise productivity in this way could lead to further loss of markets and a fall of employment at some stage in the future. On the other hand, deliberate action to raise output per head, by de-manning or by labour-saving investment, will lead to a fall in employment now' (Thatcher, 1979, 46).[3]

Up until the early 1970s it is likely that the expanding service sector compensated at a societal level for the fall of employment in the manufacturing sector. Thus, there were about 1.5 million more workers classified as professional and scientific in 1976 than in 1961 in Britain, compared with a fall of 1.3 million in manufacturing over the same period. The fastest growing category was professional and scientific services (mainly in health and education) which increased its share of total employment from 9.6% in 1961 to 15.7% in 1976. However, there are strong indications that this period of expansion has come to an end and further expansion in the 1980s is unlikely.

At a general level it may be argued that this slowing down of the expansion of the service sector of tertiary employment is simply part of the general problems afflicting advanced capitalism. Once the economic order 'has been put right', some may argue, jobs will expand once again. This position has been vigorously and most effectively criticized by Gershuny, who has shown how services provided by the market or by public authority are increasingly being provided by the household; thus, for example, cinemas and public transport are replaced by household goods (TV sets and privately owned cars). Indeed when he retabulates census material for the UK to distinguish between 'goods-related' service workers and service workers directly concerned with services proper, he concludes that hardly more than two fifths of those in tertiary occupations are actually involved in the provision of final services (Gershuny, 1977, 111). More and more, it seems, we substitute the purchase of goods for the purchase of final services and it may well be that our satisfaction as consumers increases[4] (Gershuny, 1978).

It is *work* with goods purchased in the formal economy which is the clue to an alternative world of economic activity which has, until recently, been relatively unnoticed and unexplored. In an earlier stage in the process of industrial development the centralization of functions and the more specialized division of labour provided increases in productivity and efficiency. Thus, for example, laundries handled the washing of clothes and linen quickly and efficiently and, for those who could afford it, there was a clear benefit in having the service performed out of the house. Similarly different craftsmen provided services which could not be done by ordinary, untrained workers. Now, however, work is done in the home by using capital equipment such as washing machines and power drills. This shift to the domestic economy, most dramatically evidenced by the Do-It-Yourself movement, had led to a reevaluation of *time*. I am not making a simply contrast between 'employment' in the formal economy (that is the straight sale of labour power in a market) with 'work' in the informal economy. I distinguish between the household economy, the communal economy (exchange of services in the neighbourhood without cash being involved) and the informal economy proper which may be more or less legal and which typically involves cash-based transactions.

In order to clarify this, let us now consider the various options available to someone who wanted a particular job done – repairing a broken window pane for example.

1. He could hire a glazier through the formal economy paying the full cost including any value added or local taxes.
2. He could do the job himself in his own time with his own tools and perhaps with his own satisfaction.
3. He could find someone in the locality who is known to be able to mend windows and pay him or her cash for the job. (He would not necessarily know whether such a person was declaring all his or her income, paying all his or her taxes or working in time already paid for by another employer. Unless the glazier were cross-examined and he or she was prepared to answer truthfully the degree of illegality of this solution could not be known.)
4. He could ask someone to do the work for him in exchange for some other goods or service which could be made available then or at some later time. Thus, if the person with the broken window had some exchangeable skill such as tuning a car or coaching for examinations these could serve as useful currency. Some *specific* reciprocal relationship would be established.
5. He could draw on the skill of a kinsman and he could either pay him cash, exchange in some specific way or, being a kinsman he could draw on *generalized* reciprocity not paying back at a particular time or in a specified way.

There is nothing particularly new about any of these categories: what is new and significant is that their relation to each other may be changing. The informal economy is probably growing faster than the formal economy. Fewer people choose option (1).

It is now time to link together some of the strands in the argument I am developing. In the short term employment in manufacturing industry is likely to decline, partly due to the need to be competitive and to maintain high productivity by increasing output per man, and partly due to the restructuring of capital and the shift of certain kinds of industrial production to the newly industrializing countries. Unemployment in more advanced countries may be a form of hidden aid subsidy to the less industrially advanced. At the same time the cost of providing services is increasing so that we are obliged to serve ourselves in banks, shops and filling stations or provide services for ourselves with our own tools and capital equipment. A new point may be introduced here: it may be more satisfying and rewarding to produce our own service or to engage in reciprocal exchanges with others. Our crafts of cooking, carpentering or coaching are intrinsically rewarding but may be more satisfying if they are rewarded by the actual social approval of significant others. Furthermore, we have more choice and control over what we do and how and when we do it. Those who discuss the process of 'deskilling' in the formal economy may neglect to observe the reskilling in the informal economy (Braverman, 1974).

Unemployment in the 1980s may, therefore, be a different kind of experience from that described for the period half a century ago (Angell, 1936; Garraty, 1978; Jahoda *et al.*, 1971; Pilgrim Trust, 1938). A man with his own tools, his own time and a long-stop income in the form of unemployment pay may not be in such a vulnerable position: his *work* identity can still be maintained even if his employment identity is in abeyance. When the conditions of work are bad in the formal economy and the opportunities for informal work are good, unemployment could, under certain specified conditions, be a positive benefit.

Uneven Access both to Employment and to the Informal Economy

The impact of unemployment will be uneven. Peripheral regions may be hit the hardest and national rates will mask wide variations between groups divided by age, sex or class and between regions. Internal geographical differentiation of the economy is likely to develop rapidly during a recession and some labour markets may virtually collapse. Certain age and skill groups will be more likely to hold their market positions, and more diversified labour markets may hold or attract new employment. This is known and unexceptional, if not necessarily well documented. What is less well known is how accessible and universal the informal economy is.

Paradoxically, the poor have been obliged to develop an informal support system or social economy in the past which may now come to be valued even more.[5] In some specific geographical contexts there may be more scope for its encouragement and expansion. The 'new working class' or the middle mass of uniform public or private housing estates who have not needed such support may be more seriously disadvantaged. The narrower the range of occupations and skills required in the formal economy, the less individuals may have available to be traded informally. Where houses are privately owned and there is land for gardens or allotments, the opportunities for informal home improvements and production are likely to be that much greater if *time* and *skills* are available to utilize these resources. Typically *whom* you know is as important as *what* you know in the informal economy, so that those who have developed locally-based social networks are likely to be in a stronger position than those who are entirely dependent on the market – whether formal or informal.

This enables us to develop a model of the social structure of the informal economy which would not necessarily parallel that based on the capitalist relations of production reflected in the formal economy. A preliminary categorization of the informal social structure in a particular labour market might be as follows:

1. Those with skills and service available for sale or for exchange and who have the local knowledge and contacts to provide access to informal markets.
2. Those with few or no tradeable skills or products but who have access to

      local networks and have the resources to buy such skills and facilities that they need.

3.   Those who have neither skills, knowledge or resources to contribute to the informal economy. In terms of a more traditional system of stratification such a disadvantaged category might fall in the middle of the social hierarchy, being the petty bourgeoisie with some clerical or minor bureaucratic or managerial administrative skill and which has been geographically and possibly also socially mobile. They are isolated from communal resources and do not have enough surplus income to buy their way in.

Evidently these categories are imprecise and need to be modified and amplified. Assuming we are referring to households and not simply to individuals, then it may be that one member of the household provides the tradeable skill and the other markets it through a social network. A wife may publicize her husband's ability to tune cars or a husband might find clients for his wife's skills as a dressmaker. Other less sex-stereotyped examples might be suggested, although it is more often the case that when the husband commutes the wife develops the resources of the local network (Cohen, 1978). Where the husband is unemployed and the wife is in employment, then it is he who builds up gossip networks and perhaps serves as agent for the skills of a larger family group. Single, mobile people may then be at a disadvantage. Similarly those households with links to other areas and other products may be able to strengthen their position in the informal economy by introducing 'cheap' farm produce or raw materials for example.[6] Not only may some labour markets or regions be able to cope with unemployment more readily than others but so may whole social strata or, indeed, societies. Those categories or strata which have resisted most effectively incorporation into the dominant values of industrial capitalism may be able to survive the problems imposed by the decline of formal employment in the years ahead more easily.

    Strength in the labour markets may become a disadvantage if the recession bites very hard. In the past those with marketable knowledge or skills have moved to take advantage of their market position and have built up a life style based on the assumption that any one locality is merely a staging post in the long haul up a career. In the early stages of economic decline such people may use their strength to move to where the jobs are available. These last moves may be advantageous in the short term but in the long term it inevitably disadvantages them in cutting them off from community and probably familial resources.

    Exploring the irregular or informal economy is notoriously difficult. One of the few successful studies is that by Ferman *et al.* (1978). The first place of this study was a period of participant observation by students, which explored the categories and range of activities which were to be the focus of the second, more structured phase, based on a prepared interview schedule. The aims of the study were to discover what goods and services were exchanged; what mechanisms of exchanges brought together the seller and purchaser of services and goods; what norms and values shaped these exchange relationships; what were the processes by which workers seek, acquire and sustain jobs in the irregular economy and what role this work played in an individual's career. One possible hypothesis, which suggested that this kind of work was likely to be more attractive to the unemployed, was not confirmed, but, perhaps surprisingly, it was shown that the irregular economy was widespread throughout all social levels.

    However, a specific list of twenty activities were taken from the ethnographic phase as being representative of the full range of irregular services. Respondents were asked who provided these services and how, if at all, they paid for them. The researchers were then able to distinguish between social sources (that is free services provided either by members of the household or someone else), *irregular* sources (someone outside the household who received cash but was not considered to be a firm or a business) and a *regular* source paid officially in the formal economy. Half the respondents used irregular sources at some time.

An inevitable weakness of the Ferman *et al.* type of study is that it is hard to generalize from one locality to the whole society and, despite a valiant effort to provide quantified results, respondents are plucked out from their social moorings so that social meanings are hard to identify and the researchers are inevitably dependent on the accounts provided by their respondents. Different labour markets have different characteristics and it would probably be a mistake to attempt more than to establish some kind of typology into which specific studies could be slotted. The need for social anthropological studies seems to be self-evident but very few of these have been done (Henry, 1978; Stack, 1974).

I now turn to give a modest example of the style pattern of analysis which could be developed. Much more sociology of production and consumption is needed and the two case studies which follow provide a limited and small-scale beginning. Later work must face the problem of making generalizations based on more finely developed case studies.

Getting by in Everyday Life: Two Case Studies

The Parsons

Mr Parsons was made redundant five and a half years ago when the company for which he worked closed down the plant as part of its rationalization programme. He was lucky to be young and fit enough to be taken on as a postman, a job which he much enjoys. Now that his children are older he can afford to accept a much lower wage, particularly as his wife works full-time in a wallpaper shop. He was trained in the army as an electrician and he can do most jobs round the house himself. As he finishes his work as a postman at 1 pm he has the rest of the day to work for himself and this he does very vigorously: as he says, 'I'm a gardening fanatic'. Mrs Parsons works in an annual cycle using her deep freeze to store the vegetables which come in from the January Brussels sprouts to the October runner beans. 'He used to bring in a terrific amount and it was too much for me to stand there and do. Now he'll bring me perhaps five or six pounds and then I put them into half-pound bags. I'm working for some nights here until 10 o'clock freezing them down.' When I interviewed her she was just finishing the rhubarb and starting on the gooseberries. A slacker period in June is followed by a hectic period from July to September. They both enjoy the pressure of their work and see it as fun. When the last vegetables are frozen they turn, in November, to decorating. Mrs Parsons gets a 40% discount through working in the wallpaper shop and the couple agree on an annual work programme for keeping their house, rented from the Council, immaculate. She has wallpaper put aside for every room in the house. The only way that they can manage their full and energetic life is to have the capital equipment to support them. Machines to help cut and wash the vegetables and a pressure cooker to reduce cooking time are much prized. Since Mrs Parsons works until 5.30 it is her husband who often cooks the meals. She happily complimented him on the fruit cake he had recently made and told me, 'We had spaghetti Bolognese tonight', 'Not out of a tin', Mr Parsons quickly added, 'I can come home to a meal that's already waiting for me when I come home. It's a great help really.' The Parsons household is a mini vegetable factory: 'I think I could supply this whole road', says Mrs Parsons, and Mr Parsons admitted that he sold vegetables, 'It's nothing for me to go and pick twelve cucumbers in one day, well obviously I can't eat twelve cucumbers a day'. Unfortunately pressure on space in the deep-freeze had left Mrs Parsons without potatoes and she was obliged to fall back on the formal economy. 'It's heart-breaking. I've got to go out and buy them now.' Generally Mr Parsons uses his position as postman to buy things like potatoes; he travels and compares prices, but Mrs Parsons never does that,

> For me to go out and buy vegetables, I wouldn't know where to start because I'm so used to going to my freezer and getting it. It's a lot of hard work but I benefit by it in the end. When people are out dashing from shop to shop looking for the best buy, all I've got to do is walk out to the shed and I've got the best buy in the freezer.

The domestic economy ties Mr and Mrs Parsons to their home for most of the year. Even Sunday mornings are fully occupied as Mr Parsons is chairman of the local Allotment Society and sells horticultural supplies at discount rates from a shed. As Mr Parsons said, 'We try to arrange it to have every other Sunday off but it doesn't always work'. Mrs Parsons explained, 'Then he's on his allotment and he's there if they want him. The 'phone has been ringing quite busily lately for chrysanthemum plants which he sells as well. They've just had a spring market and took four hundred pounds.' All the goods and tools for the Allotment Society are delivered to the Parsons' house. He uses his carport as a store. Nothing ever gets stolen, 'Never a thing is touched. Nobody will touch that. We have a neighbour keep an eye on it, or his dad – Oh, Peter's had a delivery. I'll just go over and see what's what'.

Mr and Mrs Parsons live in a familiar world of friends and relations. Mr Parsons' mother was the twenty-second one of her family so he was not short of uncles and aunts and his wife's mother was one of twelve. Neighbours, too, link in to a tightly-knit social world. The woman a couple of doors away works in the same shop as Mrs Parsons and their husbands were at school together, 'You're frightened to speak to people sometimes, in case you might say something that you shouldn't'.

Mr Parsons' work in the formal economy is poorly paid but it provides him with a social position. 'I poke letters in the same letter-boxes every day but I enjoy it. Because I'm out in the air, I've got nobody to govern me. I leave the governor back in the office and you meet a lot of people. I say "good morning" to the same people practically every morning.' The money he gets pays for gas and electricity and rent. His wife's pay helps towards the extras: they go away for a holiday each year and they are both keen on buying machinery to support their domestic economy. Mrs Parsons has decided to switch from an electric cooker to a gas cooker to save fuel but her husband will use it as much as she does. Their daughter, who is just about to leave school, earns money by baby sitting for her married sister or cutting someone's hair (she is hoping to be a hairdresser). The local coalman keeps horses and she helps him and gets more money delivering dung in a barrow to the allotment. But sometimes the dung is paid for in vegetables.

The Simpsons

Mrs Simpson's husband is unemployed: aged 33 he is unlikely to get a job again. He is an unskilled worker and finds it difficult to get more money than he presently receives through various forms of social security payments. His wife works informally in the hidden economy doing various kinds of homeselling and home manufacturing, putting together electrical components in an outwork system. She makes her children help her and the whole family has to sit round for hours on end. As she correctly remarked, 'It's slave labour'. Mrs Simpson organizes her work force. 'The little girl (five next month) sticks the labels on the boxes and the two boys (9 and 10) have to do two hundred each each lot that we do'. Their speed 'depends on whether they want to get out to play quick'. As she explains, 'There's a lot of people do it, we're not the only ones that are out of work and do it. I can tell you what it's paying for – washing machine, it pays my gas, my electric, it helps to buy things for the kids.' She also sells Avon cosmetics. 'I sometimes manage to buy Christmas presents out of it and my own talcs and what have you. That's what I mainly started doing it for.'

While Mrs Simpson is doing work for money (she also runs a small newspaper and sweet shop once a week) her husband is doing other unpaid work. His uncle has a large garden from which he produces the family's vegetables. He also decorates various relatives' homes for which he sometimes receives money. 'Actually he's been over helping an uncle today, painting. I'm waiting for my bathroom to be done but he won't do that. He can't do everybody else's...'

> Q. 'Perhaps you could get your brother-in-law to do that for you?'
> 'Yes I said perhaps if I get a neighbour or something to do it for me, it'll be alright.'
> Q. 'Does a lot of that go on, all doing turns for each other like that?'
> 'I think so.'
> Q. 'But mainly in the family?'
> 'Well, the ones that he's been doing for today, they're good, they lend him money. Like they've given a lovely piece of meat today.'
> Q. 'Straight meat?'
> 'Oh straight meat yes. He bought a bullock. I think it was a bullock. He went over there this afternoon and he was chopping it all up. Bones for the dogs.'
> Q. 'Where did he get it?'
> 'He bought it.'
> Q. 'From the market?'
> 'No. He knows a farmer. It was killed on the farm yesterday. We can keep that till Sunday.'
> Q 'A nice bit of meat?'
> 'It is. It's a lovely piece. He does favours for them and they do favours back.'

Mr Simpson sometimes gets money, which he likes to spend on beer, for the odd jobs he does. Sometimes he goes out fishing with his friends and brings the fish home. 'I never know what they're called. I just eat them and enjoy them.' At other times he goes out to get meat with his ferret or his gun. As Mrs Simpson remarked laconically, 'Yes, he goes poaching. We get everything illegally'. And she enjoys the fruits of her husband's labours, 'We lived well last winter on ducks'. She really likes duck and is not entirely happy with the reciprocities her husband gets bound up in. 'He'll start giving them here, there and everywhere. You know – he's promised somebody one, but I did alright.'

The trouble with Mrs Simpson's domestic economy is that she has nowhere to store the meat, fish and vegetables that come into the house.

I haven't got round to getting myself a freezer. I keep saying I'm going to get one. I will, I will get one...very often we could have had things like the fish and the rabbits and the ducks come to that, if we'd had a freezer. It doesn't matter how many you get they can go in the freezer and you didn't have to give them away. Well, I don't think he does give them away. I think he flogs them. Well, it covers the shots and buys him a pint. I think that's what he does in some ways, although I don't see what he does.

The children's clothes present a problem but Mrs Simpson prefers to get the money herself for these or exchange clothes within the family rather than making special claims on the social security system. She feels very strongly it is *her* responsibility to find the resources to 'keep them well rigged out' and feels confident that she need not be dependent on either the state or her husband for this. Indeed he takes money from her for beer, cigarettes or gunshot. 'He probably has more money for himself than I have. I mean I never have money for me. I never class money as mine personally.'

> Q. 'Whose is it? The family?'
> 'Yes.'

She borrows money from her mother to whom she is probably permanently in debt. She thinks hard about her Christmas presents and attempts to give her something substantial. She and her sister have just given her a spaniel. 'It's just my way of showing her how much I do think of her...without her I think I can honestly say I don't know how I'd manage. She'll lend me money for the gas bill; as long as she's got it she'll lend it to me.'

Discussion of the Case Studies

I do not think that these two families are particularly exceptional and indeed I have substantial further material on which I could draw. Furthermore a graduate student living in the community for nine months has accumulated a body of field notes which document in detail the informal style of economic activity in the place.

In the case of the Parsons it is clear that the hours Mr Parsons works as a postman free him to lead a full and active work life outside employment. It is this informal, but perfectly legal, activity which impinges on the domestic division of labour. This couple shared the production and preparation of food and they work as a team both in the busy summer months of food production and in the winter months of house maintenance. Since Mr Parsons is busy with his seeds in his greenhouse in his back garden early in the new year there is very little 'spare time' in the yearly cycle. He is, however, proud of his collection of records which he showed me. It was characteristic that this couple were interviewed together, seeing themselves as a combined unit. There are a number of jobs in the formal economy which allow men to become more involved in the domestic economy and the care of children. Cooking the evening meal is a common example, but young manual workers also clean the house and handle the dirtiest aspects of infant care if their wife is in employment. How far unemployed male workers will take on the complete burden of housework is unclear, although there are certainly signs that in this traditional working-class community distinctions between 'men's work' and 'women's work' in the home are breaking down. When I questioned couples very closely on this matter the answers among the younger, newly married respondents were generally pragmatic. If the employment conditions allowed the man to have more time during the day to collect children from school or to cook meals then it was obviously good sense that he should do so. A certain amount of money was needed from the formal economy: the couple assess their relative positions in the labour market and their various constraints and obligations to children and parents. They then work out the best strategy. This will often involve the wife's mother or 'nan' who may provide accommodation for the couple early in their married life or care for the young children when her daughter is in employment. Alternatively the mother may take employment for herself, either to accompany her daughter or to get money to 'lend' to her daughter to cover large bills. This balance of help and support is a delicate one and I sometimes heard men complain that they did not get enough time with their infant children who were being cared for too much by the grandmother.

It is possible that the overall participation rates of women in the formal economy will increase in the medium-term future. This may be due partly to women's willingness to choose or to accept the obligation of working part time. Employment protection legislation may encourage firms to shift to part-time workers as other, full-time workers retire. Thus, in Britain from 1971–76 male industrial workers declined (– 443,000 full time and – 116,000 part time). Full-time female industrial workers also declined by 10,000. However, part-time female industrial workers increased by 854,000 over the same period (Thatcher, 1979, 31). These, and more recent figures, need to be analysed with care, but there may well be something in the argument that the employment of part-time workers helps to reduce labour costs and avoids certain kinds of redundancy payments. Certainly it is true that the nimble fingers of women are more use in the assembly of small and intricate components than the more clumsy strength of men. Be that as it may, my field studies certainly show that a stronger position of women in the formal economy leads to a shift in the sexual division of labour in the household.

The Simpsons raise different issues: here, Mr Simpson has reverted to a pre-industrial pattern of hunter and gatherer and he is also using whatever opportunities he can to gain resources in the informal economy, which he keeps for himself. The only hope of resources from the formal economy is through Mrs Simpson, who longs to work full time as soon as her children are old enough to enable her to do so. Already she is in some kind of hidden or dual labour market in the formal economy, being exploited in the conventional way. She is formally and legally paid but as she is in receipt of social security payments there is a limit on how much she may legitimately earn each week. With three employers, each quite possibly giving her less than the legal maximum, her 'crime' is more a matter of cumulation than of individual illegal acts. She is gaining considerable experience in entreprenurial skills and is being socialized into being a more productive worker in the formal economy than her husband will ever be. She is also, presumably, saving the state from dispensing further discretionary payments. As her independence and market power increases, the role of Mr Simpson in the household becomes more and more marginal. Since he beats her when he's drunk and that is not infrequently, it is possible that the couple will split up and Mr Simpson will stay in all-male company which, in many ways, he finds more comfortable. There is a well-established informal, male culture in the community, supported by the underground economy and focused on the pubs, which provides an attractive alternative for those men who are not yet ready to play a more subordinate and supportive role within the household.

Anyone who has followed the argument thus far may be forgiven some irritation for knowing so little about the characteristics of this labour market which may, to some readers, appear a curious mixture of 'urban' and 'rural'. I find these terms sociologically unhelpful in themselves (Pahl, 1966) but I do see that labour markets differ markedly in the access they offer to alternative sources of food or income. Many industrial cities in Britain are within easy reach of fields, moor or coast. It is, after all, a collection of islands and the gathering of cockles, mussels and whelks is a time honoured working-class activity. So also is fishing and the gathering of the fruits of the land. These relate to ancient common rights which 'are specifically those by which one or more persons have the right to take or use some portion of the profit that another's soil produces' (Ditton, 1977, 40). Hence there was the Common of Pasture, the Common of Shack (the right of cattle to glean hay after the harvest), Rights of Pangane and Mast, the Common of Estover to take wood for either the Plough, Hedge or House Bote (i.e. for essential repairs in the household economy) and so on. The Acts of Enclosure led to the annexation of these common rights but they were not forgotten. In some parts of the country, where the power of the squire was less strong, this informal pattern may have lingered on, despite official attempts to stamp out poaching. In the locality where I am doing my field work the main landowners withdrew in the late seventeenth century and only smaller farmers actually lived on the land. Many of the workers in factory or steel mill come from farming backgrounds and preindustrial attitudes may linger on. Mr Simpson has been convicted for poaching. His is an unusual and admittedly uncommon life-style response to contemporary circumstances.

Concluding Discussion – Towards a Revolution in Everyday Life?

In the third volume of *Das Kapital* Marx seemed to accept the idea that alienation could never be completely overcome. In any future society, however advanced the level of technology, the division of labour in the process of production would continue to exist. Collective and rational control of the process of production would allow more humane and liberated social relations to emerge and the most wearisome toil would be ameliorated or abolished. But the 'realm of necessity', which I take to be Marx's rather quaint way of referring to the formal economy, would always, inevitably, remain. Only outside the formal economy in, as Marx put it 'the realm of freedom' could there be the true development of human potentialities for their own sake. That realm of freedom could only flourish if it had the realm of necessity as its base. Marx, therefore, logically concluded that 'the shortening of the working day is its fundamental prerequisite'.

It was Marx's assumption that capitalism has to transform itself through the dynamic of its own internal contradictions and the force of its proletarian revolution into socialism and then, ultimately, communism. Yet paradoxically the very drive of capitalism to expand and to continue to accumulate means that it is forced to shed labour on such a scale that an increasing proportion of the potentially economically active are obliged to leave 'the realm of necessity'. And, in the interests of social control and social cohesion, it might save the dominant class a lot of trouble if it didn't enquire too closely into what people do in the 'realm of freedom'. Fishing, hunting and discussing politics in the pub after dinner is a pretty harmless way for potential revolutionaries to spend their time. Indeed this fits the vision of the earlier, more romantic Marx, who seemed to wish to abolish the societal division of labour and who extolled the virtues of rustic craftsmen.

Mr Simpson who is not involved with the formal economy, and Mr Parsons, who leaves it at 1 pm each day, have their own tools, their own skills and the time to employ these in the creation of use values. However, it is true that Mrs Simpson and Mrs Parsons are not quite so liberated. They both work longer hours in the formal economy than their husbands and also spend long hours in the informal and domestic economies. They both prize the tools produced by advanced capitalism such as freezers and pressure cookers which they perceive as means of enlarging their own freedom. They both get satisfaction from maintaining their tools in good order and in consuming the meat and vegetables which their husbands as hunters and tillers produce. Their incursions into the formal economy initially, perhaps, just to provide holidays or better clothes for the children gives them an independence and autonomy that they value. This clearly affects their power position in the household. Mrs Simpson is severely handicapped by being tied by her children but, with the help of her mother and as they get older, she will be more free to allocate her time and resources in whatever way she chooses.

In this particular labour market the two employers who pay the highest wages (almost entirely for men) do not want workers when they are too young or too old. The work is hard and tiring. And the men adopt an equally instrumental view towards their employment. When they are young and strong and they need to have money to buy a home, capital equipment and services they will do a deal with the formal economy. The pay in these two industries is very good and the work is either boring or tiring, but it is money that they want and so they do it. 'I wouldn't want to do that all my life' is a frequent remark.

The factories which employ women have a different culture: there the expressive aspects of work are emphasized. Women work together, help each other to cope with difficult tasks, support those with personal problems and generally infiltrate the norms of the informal and domestic economies into the formal one. Many of these women need their position in the formal economy in order to be in a position to renegotiate their previously subordinate position in the domestic economy. Socializing their husbands into their role as partners in the reproduction of labour power is easier when at a pinch, they could manage without their husbands altogether.

I am arguing that my field studies suggest that in this labour market there are a number of patterns of 'getting by' which involve more or less interleaving of work in the formal, informal and domestic economies by different members of the household. Despite the high level of unemployment there are many ways of getting money. In terms of national statistics and general surveys of poverty, the Parsons and the Simpsons are at the bottom of the pile. A postman's wage of £48 is low and there are no formal means of augmentation. The Supplementary Benefits payments to a couple with three small children is about a third less than that. But these wages and benefits must be seen in context. The degree of control over and access to resources is a function of the local labour market and the opportunities in the informal economy.

The criticism that I am basing my argument on a handful of cases in one labour market is inevitably correct, although I am confident that my interpretation is not distorting the general culture of that labour market nor am I picking out strikingly unusual cases. It may indeed be the case that there are peculiar conditions and circumstances which favour unconventional ways of getting by. Perhaps I have been looking at a curious anomaly – a section of the working class which has not been fully socialized into industrial capitalism and which still has something of the preindustrial English individualism in its culture. I would like to hold such a romantic view of those inhabiting what most middle-class visitors see as an ugly and polluted industrial wasteland. However, I think it would be nearer the truth to see the emerging economic and social relations which I am attempting to describe as a pragmatic response to conditions of life where certain tools and opportunities are available, so that money and resources can be obtained without the sale of labour power to an employer.

Some see these tendencies as revolutionizing capitalism from within. Thus Scott Burns in his much neglected but important book argues that 'the emergence of something that might be called "household capitalism" ... must, inevitably, result in the reordering of society' (1977, 48). He foresees the market economy accounting for no more than 50% and perhaps as little as 25% of the economic activity of the United States in twenty years' time. The combination of the analyses of Burns, Ferman *et al.* (1978) and Feige (1979) provides a convincing argument for the widespread incidence and inevitable expansion of the informal and domestic economies in the United States. The manner in which the three economic spheres coexist and interpenetrate offer a substantial challenge for empirical research. A brilliantly imaginative and witty attempt to portray these matters in a new and stimulating way has been recently published in France (Mendras, 1979). Different kinds of arguments, which have a direct bearing on my theme, have been advanced by economists such as Hirsch (1977), Schumacher (1974) or Scitovsky (1976).

Others may not be so ready to welcome either the developments or the kinds of analyses that go with them. Partly this may be due to the unexpected nature of these changes, which do not derive from conventional class bases. Many Marxist scholars are understandably uneasy about their difficulty in finding appropriate concepts with which to handle these changes. Feminists, too, may be uneasy about the implications of a growing emphasis on the domestic economy when they have struggled to avoid women being confined solely to that sphere. Some conceptual rejigging will be necessary to consider potentially new forms of oppression as men may seem to push women into the market place, while men stay at home doing the garden. Classical economists and all those who believe it is still within their capacities 'to get the economy right' – that is high growth and low levels of unemployment – may find that there will soon be nothing left for them but economic history.

It is unlikely that my theme consititutes a paradigmatic shift of such dimensions, despite the confident assertions of some of the authorities I cite. My claim is much more modest and is simply this: the way work gets done and the way people get by and use their time, tools and other resources in everyday life is changing. These changes may be linked to macrochanges in the political economy of capitalism. The formal economy appears to have shrinking manpower requirements both as its productivity increases and as the informal economy flourishes, growing, as it does, at a faster rate than the formal economy. Release from the realm of necessity by capitalism's inevitable desire to continue accumulation and to maintain rates of profit, and protected in the realm of freedom by the need of the state to maintain social control, it seems as though some workers are slipping out of their chains and walking out of the system's front door.

Expressing the issue as glibly as that forces difficult and, at present, unanswerable questions upon me. What is the range of variation between labour markets which prevent, permit or encourage informal domestic and communal work to be done? What are the constraints of milieu, of labour market, of town or country, which Marx recognized would be the hardest and most intractable divisions to overcome? What are the links which the formal economy must maintain with other economic and social spheres in order for nasty and necessary work to get done? Can two different systems of motivation and values exist side by side? In the same way that multinationalism and localism may come to threaten the nation state in Europe, so the tensions between the formal, the informal and the domestic economies put a strain on the conventional economic system and its supporting system of educational socialization. I find these and other similar questions difficult and challenging (Gershuny and Pahl, 1979). I hope that this article will encourage others to join me. It is just possible that the remaining two decades of the twentieth century will be a period of revolution in everyday life. It would be a pity if social scientists were too busy with their theories to notice it.

Notes

*Editor's note: This influential article is reprinted in its original form, but it should be noted that a fuller and more up-to-date report of Ray Pahl's important research is being published in book form in his *Divisions of Labour* (Blackwell, 1984). In this most recent work, Ray Pahl is much more sceptical than is perhaps implied here about envisaging the informal economy (or economies) as a separate and self-standing sector and revises his earlier assumption that the 'hidden' or 'black' economy is still growing (on the contrary, he holds that it may now have passed its peak in Britain). In addition, the two case-studies here are set in perspective by his fuller analysis. The basic argument and challenge of this article remain valid, however, and it is reprinted here as a classic paper which has given rise to much debate and thought in the sociology of work.*

1. This pilot project was financed by a grant from the Nuffield Foundation and I am glad to acknowledge its support.

   At this stage in my work I do not wish to divulge the geographical location of my area of study. For present purposes it is perhaps enough to say that the overall level of unemployment fluctuates between 10% and 14%, rising to between 25% and 40% for school leavers or the 16-18 year olds. The main employment is semi-skilled work in factories or mills. There is very little white collar or skilled manual work. Some clothing factories provide employment for young girls who are probably in a marginally better labour market situation than their male peers.

2. Published in Pahl, 1984. [Ed.]

3. The microelectronic revolution is likely to exacerbate this problem.

4. A trvial example may clarify this point. I have recently bought a small coffee-making machine for my university office. I have been prompted to do this by the increasing cost of an inferior product which is provided collectively. Much of the increase in cost is due to the wages of those who make the coffee but there is also a non-monetary cost in the time I have to give up in leaving my office, queuing or waiting for the coffee, which may not be at its best when I want it, and being absent from my office at times when I am likely to be called on the 'phone. My new machine enables me to have fresh coffee when I want it, and, after some time when the cost of the machine has been discounted, at a cheaper price.

5. For the informal support systems of the poor recent work in oral history and working-class autobiographies are valuable sources. See Meacham (1977) and Thompson (1975, for example, pp. 55, 67 and 177–9). See also Lowenthal (1975); Stack (1974) and many other ethnographies of the poor.

6. An interesting anecdote to illustrate this point comes to mind. I was in a provincial Romanian town on the Sunday evening before Christmas Day on the following Tuesday. A visiting group of Opera Singers was helping the local talent to put on a performance of *Die Fledermaus*. Normally the local theatre would be packed, but on this occasion it was embarrassingly deserted, the cast outnumbering the audience by about 10 to 1. The explanation was that the whole town had gone in search of chickens, butter, wine and almost anything that a friend or relation could provide of better quality than the admittedly totally inadequate provision in the shops of the formal economy.

References

Angell, R.C. (1936) *The family encounters the depression*, New York.

Bell, C. and Newby, H. (1971) *Community Studies*, London, George Allen and Unwin.

Bell, D. (1974) *The Coming of Post-Industrial Society*, London, Heinemann.

Blackaby, F. (ed.) (1979) *De-industrialization*, London; Heinemann for the National Institute of Economic and Social Research.

Braverman, H. (1974) *Labor and Monopoly Capital*, New York and London, Monthly Review Press.

Brown, C.J.F. and Sheriff, T.D. (1979) 'De-industrialisation: a background paper', in Blackaby, F. *De-industrialisation*, London, Heinemann for the National Institute of Economic and Social Research, ch. 10.

Burns, S. (1977) *The Household Economy*, Boston, Beacon Press.

Castells, M. (1977) *The Urban Question*, London, Edward Arnold.

Cohen, G. (1978) 'Women's solidarity and the preservation of privilege', in Caplan, P. and Bujra, J.M. (eds) *Women United, Women Divided*, London, Tavistock.

Ditton, J. (1977) 'Perks, pilferage and the fiddle; the historical structure of invisible wages', *Theory and Society*, vol. 4, pp. 1–38.

Feige, E. (1979) 'How big is the irregular economy?' *Challenge Magazine* (November) pp. 5–13.

Ferman, L.A. *et al.* (1978) *Analysis of the Irregular Economy: Cash Flow in the Informal Sector*, Report to the Bureau of Employment and Training, Michigan Department of Labour; Institute of Labor and Industrial Relations, University of Michigan – Wayne State University.

Gamble, A. and Walton, P. (1976) *Capitalism in Crisis*, London, Macmillan.

Garraty, J.A. (1978) *Unemployment in History*, New York and London, Harper and Row.

Gershuny, J. I. (1977) 'Post-industrial society: the myth of the service economy', *Futures* vol. 10, no. 2, pp. 103–14.

(1978) *After Industrial Society*, London, Macmillan.

Gershuny, J.I. and Pahl, R.E. (1979) 'Work outside employment: some preliminary speculations', *New Universitites Quarterly*, vol. 34, no. 1.

Goldthorpe, J.H. and Hirsch, F. (eds.) (1978) *The Political Economy of Inflation*, London Martin Robertson.

Harloe, M. (ed.) (1977) *Captive Cities*, London and New York, Wiley.

Henry, S. (1978) *The Hidden Economy*, London, Martin Robertson.

Hirsch, F. (1977) *The Social Limits to Growth*, London, Routledge and Kegan Paul.

Jahoda, M., Lazarsfeld, P.F. and Zeisel, H. (1971) *Marienthal: the Sociography of an unemployed community*, Chicago.

Lowenthal, M.D. (1975) 'The Social economy in urban working class communities', in Gappert, G. and Rose, H.M. (eds) *The Social Economy of Cities*, Beverly Hills, Sage.

Meacham, S. (1977) *A Life Apart: the English working class 1890–1914*, London, Thames and Hudson.

Mendras, H. (1979) *Voyage au pays de l'utopie rustique*, Mas Martin BP2 13125 Le Paradon, Editions Actes/Sud.

Miller, S.M. (1978) 'The recapitalization of capital', *International Journal of Urban and Regional Research*, vol. 2, pp. 202–12.

Pahl, R.E. (1966) The rural – urban continuum, *Sociologia Ruralis*, vol. 4, pp. 299–329.

(1977a) 'Collective consumption and the state in capitalist and state socialist societies', in Scase, R. (ed.) *Industrial Society: Aspects of Class Cleavage and Control*, London, George Allen and Unwin.

(1977b) 'Stratification, the relation between states and urban and regional development', *International Journal of Urban and Regional Research*, vol. 1, pp. 6–18.

(1984) *Divisions of Labour*, Oxford, Blackwell.

Pickvance, C.G. (ed.) (1976) *Urban Sociology: Critical Essays*, London, Tavistock.

Pilgrim Trust (1938) *Men without Work*, Cambridge, Cambridge University Press.

Schumacher, E.F. (1974) *Small is beautiful: a study of economics as if people mattered*, London, Sphere Books.

Scitovsky, T. (1976) *The Joyless Economy*, Oxford, Oxford University Press.

Stack, C.B. (1974) *All Our Kin: strategies for survival in a black community*, New York and London, Harper and Row.

Thatcher, A.R. (1979) 'Labour supply and employment trends', in Blackaby, F. (ed.), *De-industrialization*, London, Heinemann for National Institute of Economic and Social Research, ch. 2.

Thompson, P. (1975) *The Edwardians*, London, Weidenfeld and Nicolson.

Winkler, J.T. (1976) 'Corporatism', *European Journal of Sociology*, vol. 17, pp. 100–36.

12   Domestic Work

ANNE OAKLEY

> You didn't know that domestic work was Britain's largest industry? Well, it is, and it is also the largest consumer of time. We hear a good deal about manhours at present: more are spent on domestic work than anything else ... It is time that you and I, the women of Britain, took up this matter. Domestic work is our problem. (Burton, 1944, p. 3)

Calculations of the importance of housework in relation to other industries set the figure at more than a third of the GNP – 39 per cent in Britain, 35 per cent in the USA (Wickham and Young, 1973). These figures are based on time-budget studies of housework and calculate the total market value of the housewife's services in her various capacities as cleaner, cook, laundress, nursemaid, etc. However, the exercise of adding up the hourly rates for these jobs to see what housework is 'worth' is an academic one only. For the first characteristic of women's work as housewives is that it is not paid. All over the world in the late 1960s and early 1970s, feminists rediscovered what earlier feminists knew: that the question of women's equality with men cannot be restricted to the world of paid employment and public power, but resides firstly in their domestic relationships.

What is Housework?

An all-consuming function of production
According to J.K. Galbraith, housework exists to service the consumption function of the economy. The rising standards of consumption made possible by advanced capitalism are only attractive economic goals if they do not mean the loss of labour power. A gourmet meal is enjoyable when not preceded by long hours in the kitchen; a well-furnished house soothes the eye as long as its maintenance has not already worn one out. It is the conversion of women into a 'crypto-servant class' that renders consumption pleasurable to the dominant economic group. 'True' servants are available to only a minority of the population, but:

> the servant–wife is available, democratically, to almost the entire present male population ... If it were not for this service [of women as housewives] all forms of household consumption would be limited by the time required to manage such consumption – to select, transport, prepare, repair, maintain, clean, service, store, protect and otherwise perform the tasks that are associated with the consumption of goods. The servant role of women is critical to the expansion of consumption in the modern economy. (Galbraith, 1974, p. 33).

Before the establishment of industrial capitalism, housework had the character of manufacture rather than service. In the southern colonies of America in the seventeenth century, for example, the housewife's duties included the gathering, drying and distilling of herbs for curing the sick, the making of conserves, syrups, jellies, pickles and wines, and the construction of 'Oyles, Oyntments and Powders

---

Anne Oakley, *Subject Woman*, London, Fontana, 1982; pp. 163–86

to Adorn and add Loveliness to the Face and Body' (Spruill, 1972, p. 210). The eighteenth-century Purefoy family of Shalstone Manor in Buckinghamshire in England recorded their domestic organization in a series of letters (Purefoy, 1931; quoted in Davis, 1966). Mrs Purefoy and her adult son Henry produced the basic food consumed by themselves and their six servants at home. They had several cows, sheep, asses, goats, pigs, poultry, a dovecote and three well-stocked fishponds. They brewed their own ale and made their own bread. Clothes and household extras – tea, fancy spices and herbs, sugar, coffee-berries – had to be purchased, either in London or in the local shops, usually by letter. More of these commodities were bought than a generation before as rising living standards allowed them to be redefined as necessities instead of luxuries.

The majority of British and American homes before and during industrialization were not places where much housework, in the modern sense of cleaning, dusting, tidying and polishing, could be done. Rooms did not have individual uses and were plainly and sparsely furnished as places of work – in the undifferentiated sense of production for use and for exchange:

> The labor needs of the household defined the work roles of men, women and children. Their work in turn, fed the family. The interdependence of work and residence of household labor needs, subsistence requirements, and family relationships constituted the 'family economy'. (Tilly and Scott, 1978, p. 12)

The architecture and furnishing of homes reflected this: beds and spinning wheels or other tools of the family's trade shared rooms; cooking, eating, 'working' and relaxing were activities all housed in the same space. The idea of the kitchen as a special room where women prepared food started to emerge among the upper class in the late sixteenth century but was not a general feature of working-class homes until the early twentieth century (Chapman, 1955; Henderson, 1964). Margaret Plant describes the typical eighteenth-century rural home in Scotland as follows:

> There was normally one main living-room where the family had their meals, slept, did their work and chatted with the neighbours who dropped in for the evening. Its social centre was the common fireplace, which ... was large and open and surrounded, beneath the great wide chimney, with seats for family and guests ... toughly hewn boughs formed a not unattractive ceiling, and the space between them and the roof proper was floored with brushwood covered with dried moss or grass. The resulting attic made a useful storeroom; or, if the main living-room would hold no more beds, an extra bedroom, the entrance to it being by way of a ladder and a trap-door.
>
> Behind the living room was the 'spence' or parlour, where the housewife put the best furniture and kept the Sunday clothes, and, on great occasions, received company. A passage known as the 'through-gang' joined the living-room to the cow-house and stable (a rather doubtful advantage). (Plant, 1952, pp. 24–5)

'Carpet' meant a tablecloth and what went on the floor was turf. People tended to eat out of the same wooden dish and share a single glass, and those attending meals elsewhere were well-advised to take their own knife and fork; it was the custom for the diner to wipe and re-use utensils between courses.

Housekeeping is also a simple activity in pre-literate societies where women's (and men's) energies are concentrated on the production of food. The African Nyakyusa, considered among the most well-to-do of all 'primitive' cultures, live in permanent well-built houses, but these are still one-room dwellings made of traditional wattle and daub (Hammond and Jablow, 1976). There is little in the way of household furniture in such cultures, few pots and pans, no complicated recipes to absorb a cook's time.

As the level of material possessions rises and definitions of women and work change, a radical transformation is brought about in women's relationship to their work. Production for family use is converted into consumption for family use. Commodities become available on the market that require little of the housewife even in the way of preparation. At the same time, more energy and hours are needed in home-maintenance activities – dusting, polishing, carpet-shampooing, curtain-washing and so forth. These may be, in Galbraith's terminology, 'the crypto-servant functions of consumption administration', but such language hides the chief significance of the housewife's invisible and unpaid work from the viewpoint of the maintenance of the economy. The housewife's work remains productive, for what she produces is workers for industry: her husband with his clean clothes, well-filled stomach and mind freed from the need to provide daily care for his children; the children fed, clothed, loved and chastised ready for their own adult gender-specific role as workers or worker-producers.

To say that the modern housewife is still a productive worker, despite the changes that have stripped the housework role of its manufacturing aspect, is an important restatement of the position of women. In the early years of the women's liberation movement when feminists began to grapple with the theoretical problem of how women's subordination might be explained, it was the situation of women as unpaid workers in the home that came to be seen as the central enigma. Margaret Benston, in one of the first analyses, stated that housework:

> is pre-capitalist in a very real sense. This assignment of household work as the function of a special category 'women' means that this group *does* stand in a very different relation to production than the group 'men'. . . The material basis for the inferior status of women is to be found in just this definition of women. In a society in which money determines value, women are a group who work outside the money economy. Their work is not worth money, is therefore valueless, is therefore not even real work. And women themselves, who do this valueless work, can hardly be expected to be worth as much as men, who work for money. In structural terms, the closest thing to the condition of women is the condition of others who are or were also outside of commodity production, i.e. serfs and peasants. (Benston, 1969, pp. 15–16)

Housework is pre-capitalist according to Benston because it produces only 'use values' – products and services consumed directly by the family. The disadvantage of this argument is that it allows housework to be seen as some kind of incongruous historical relic; its advantage is that it shifts women's labour from a marginal to a central economic position: it thus 'completely changed the terms on which a discussion of women's work had to be carried on' (Malos, 1977, p. 7).

Since Benston wrote, a great deal of discussion both in and outside the women's movement has been devoted to the thorny question of the exact meaning of the term 'productive labour' as applied to the housewife's work. Did Marx himself define housework as productive? Apparently not:

> In volume one of *Capital* be said that the reproduction of labour power was *productive consumption*, but he did not say it was productive *labour*. (Malos, 1977, p. 15)

> Domestic labour is unproductive (in the economic sense) and conforms with Marx's description of an unproductive labour 'exchanged not with capital but with revenue , that is wages or profits'. (Secombe, 1974, p. 11)

'Production' in capitalism, according to Marxist theory, means the creation of surplus value – the part of labour that enables capitalist profits to be made. (Workers sell their labour power to capitalists who extract profits from their use of this labour power by paying workers less than the amount for which they sell the products of labour on the market.) Housewives create goods through their labour as producers and consumers in the home, but these goods do not enter the commodity market. Wally Secombe maintains that, while housework is productive in the sense of actually transferring and creating value, it is not productive 'in the specific context of capitalist production' because it is not 'conducted in direct relation with capital' and it does not produce surplus value. (Just to complicate matters, others have countered that it does, on the other hand, produce a surplus-value-creating commodity: labour power – Dalla Costa and James, 1972.)

The central point in the Marxist domestic labour debate is 'that the housewife works for the maintenance of capitalism rather than simply being a worker for her family' (Glazer-Malbin, 1976, p. 919). Industrial capitalism as an economic system requires *somebody* to buy the food, cook the meals, wash the clothes, clean the home and bear and bring up the children. Without this back-up of domestic labour the economy could not function – or, at least, enormous and profit-handicapping resources would have to be devoted to catering for these personal and reproductive needs. Women as housewives who meet these needs are thus the backbone of the economy, and their contribution, whether viewed as the psychological welfare of children, the stability of marriage or the employer's pocket, is certainly 'productive'; only Marxist purists need concern themselves with any epistemological uncertainty on this point.

The promotion and prevention of housework

Leonore Davidoff (1976) has observed that the Marxist model of domestic labour can interpret the housewife's oppression (by privatized, unpaid and socially trivialized work) but cannot show why this oppression takes the form it does. Early industrial capitalism in England bred a factory system based on female and child labour that was only transformed into one based on male labour through the propagation of a domestic ideology of women.

The relationship between material conditions and gender ideology was (and still is) a complex one, and nowhere better illustrated than in the fate of women's household labour in socialist economies. Following Marx and Engels, the 1917 Revolution in the USSR promised women a new era of equality based on their emancipation from the privatized oppression of household labour. Sixty years later, there have certainly been achievements in the public role of women (not only women's 51 per cent share in employment, but their 40 per cent uptake of engineering posts, 59 per cent of technical jobs and 50 per cent use of places in higher education), but the amount of time demanded by household chores is the same now as it was in the 1930s (Lapidus, 1978, p. 128) and most of this work continues to be done by women. In fact, looking at time-budget studies from the 1920s to the 1960s in the USSR, Michael Sachs has shown that the female–male ratio in domestic work has remained unchanged: 'Males continue to have as much free time as females have housework' (Sachs, 1977, p. 798). Moreover, while 13 per cent of male housework time in the 1920s was spent on gardening and the care of animals, this figure was 30 per cent in the 1960s.

Soviet women's double burden has been justified since the 1930s by an official conception of femininity that has yoked a glorification of wifely and maternal responsibilities to the national duty of economic productivity:

> Our feminine hearts are overflowing with emotions [proselytized a fictional heroine in 1937] and of these love is paramount. Yet a wife should also be a happy mother and create a serene home atmosphere, without, however, abandoning

work ... She should know how to combine all these things while also matching her husband's performance on the job. (Quoted in Lapidus, 1978, p. 131)

The story of a young Moscow technical worker published in the Russian magazine *Novy Mir* attracted a flood of sympathetic letters for the familar strains it documented. Olya, the story's central character, is also the mother of two young children. She is asked to fill in a questionnaire at work aimed at discovering the reasons for the falling birth rate:

> how many hours do I spend on '(a) housework, (b) occupation with the children, (c) cultural leisure pursuits'. 'Leisure' is explained: radio and television broadcasts, visits to the cinema, theatre, etc., reading, sport, tourism, etc.
> Ah, leisure, leisure ... The word sounds clumsy, somehow – lei-sure'. 'Women fight for cultural leisure!' What rubbish ... Lei-sure. Myself, I'm addicted to sport: running. I'm always running: to work, from work, shopping – a shopping basket in each hand ... upstairs, downstairs, trolley bus – bus, into the underground – out of the underground. There aren't any shops near our new housing estate yet, we have been living there now for more than a year, but they still haven't been built.

She is also asked to provide the total number of workdays lost last year through her own or her children's illness. This she works out later, while doing the ironing – 78. Her husband responds:

> 'What do you think, Olya darling, maybe it would be better if you didn't go out to work? Just think nearly half the year you're sitting at home anyway.'
> 'So you want to lock me up for the whole year? Do you think we can live on your salary?'
> 'If I am freed from these jobs' – Dima glares round the kitchen – 'then I could earn more. I could probably get two hundred to two hundred and twenty. In fact, if you work out the unpaid days, you only earn about 60 roubles a month. It just doesn't pay!'
> 'Great', I say, 'Just great. You mean all these boring jobs' – I also glance round the kitchen – 'will be for me alone, and you'll have all the interesting work. Just fancy, "doesn't pay" – capitalist!'
> 'Capitalist indeed', Dima gives a short laugh, 'the money isn't the only point. The children would benefit from it. The nursery school isn't so bad, but the creche...Gulka hardly ever goes for a walk in winter. And these endless colds!'
> 'Dima, do you really think that I wouldn't like to do what's best for the children? Of course I would. But what you suggest is just ... it would destroy me. And my five years studying? My diploma? My working record? My job? It's easy for you to chuck all that overboard! And what'll I be like, sitting at home? As cross as hell: I'll nag at all of you, the whole time. But what are we talking about? We can't survive on your salary, and you haven't been offered anything else ...'
> 'Don't be hurt, darling, you're probably right. I shouldn't have started it. I just had a glimpse of some sort of ... sensibly organized life. And also that, if I didn't have to rush after the children, I could work differently, not restrict myself ... maybe that's selfishness, I don't know. Let's stop this though, OK?'
> He goes out of the kitchen. I follow him with my eyes, and suddenly I want to call him and say: 'Forgive me, Dima.' But I don't. (*Spare Rib*, December 1976; June 1977)

This situation can be traced directly to the lack of prominence given to household work in Marxist theory. While some Soviet economists in the 1920s propounded the view that all social forms of labour that promote national welfare are productive, the theoretical position that came to predominate in the 1930s was the more orthodox Marxist one, according to which only labour that directly creates national income is productive. The limited economic resources of the Soviet Union were hence directed into the most 'productive' sphere of the economy – heavy industry – and away from public services. Despite a subsequent investment in state childcare (Olya's two children attended a state-run creche and nursery school) and in some communal dining, the inadequate development of the service sector combined with the limited production of consumer durables and general shortage of consumption goods and retail outlets inflated women's domestic burden to a point exceeding that of many women in the West. One ironic consequence is that advanced capitalism has done more *potentially* to lighten the burden of domestic labour than state socialism. There are more semi-processed foods, rationalized shopping facilities, specialized laundry services and mechanized household appliances in the West than the East; for example, in 1970 the USSR boasted 4,400 laundries and dry-cleaners for a population of 244 million, while the UK had 5,593 for a population of 55 million (Heitlinger, 1979).

It is part of the conventional wisdom of family life that, just as 'the' family has historically lost its functions (of production to industry, of reproduction to the hospital, of child socialization to the educational system), so women within families have lost their function to household technology – it is the washing machine, not the vote, that is the true liberator of women. However, it is nearer the truth to see mechanical household aids as rather like the Marxist model of women's emancipation: theoretically, both ought to free women from housework, but in practice neither does so. One factor is that housewives have not benefited to the same extent as other segments of the population from technological advance; it is obvious to anybody who does housework that existing household equipment is not designed with maximum efficiency in mind.

Second, the machines-liberate-housewives view ignored, as Cowan (1974) has pointed out, the possibility that the component activities of housework are merely profoundly transformed when they undergo mechanization. Technological innovation always occurs in a social context, and Leonore Davidoff has described how the hierarchical structure of the household (master versus mistress, mistress versus servant) acted against the 'rational' application of science and technology to household work from the very beginning:

> For example, it must have been known by experience that soaking very dirty pans in water overnight made it both much easier and much quicker to clean them, but it was the rule that every single pan had to be scoured and polished and put away before the servants were allowed to go to bed, no matter how late the hour, and young scullery maids could be hauled out of bed to scrub the pans if they had neglected this duty. (Davidoff, 1976, p. 144)

(It is still a mark of bad housewifery to leave dirty unscrubbed pans in the sink overnight.) What is 'rational' in household management is what is dictated by prevailing ideas of the kind of activity housework is (and the kind of people houseworkers are).

Thirdly, to assume that domestic technology liberates housewives is to ignore all that is known about the social impact of technology on work. Increasing division of labour and increasing routinization are the almost inevitable products of general technological 'improvements' in the work process, and what *these* lead to for the worker is an intensified sense of powerlessness, not a feeling of freedom from the bondage of work. As Betty Friedan so aptly pointed out in *The Feminine Mystique* (1963), technology cannot in itself mitigate the psychological law that 'housewifery expands to fill the time available'. Touring American suburbs in the 1950s, she confronted the same question again and again: given the same house and the same housewife, the same work could take one or six hours.

The answer to the paradox identified by Friedan was the 'glorification' of women's domestic role. Occurring at the same time as 'barriers to her full participation in society were lowered', this evidenced 'society's reluctance to treat women as complete human beings; for the less real function that [women's] role has, the more it is decorated with meaningless details to conceal its emptiness' (Friedan, 1963, p. 239). Against the 'need' to change and wash the sheets once a week is set the 'need' to change them two or three times a week and to get them 'whiter than white'. For this reason, housework hours have actually risen with the invention of new household appliances (Vanek, 1974). In my own interviews with British housewives (Oakley 1974), there was a strong association between the standards housewives set for themselves and their weekly hours of housework, as shown in Table 12.1. The average working week in this sample of housewives was 77 hours. Other time-budget studies show an increase in housework in urban as opposed to rural conditions, and a definite increase of the last fifty years in the time spent on housework despite the raised level of household mechanization and the rise in housewives' employment outside the home. (In fact, some studies actually suggest that outside employment raises housework hours.) Other studies point to the fact that the employment of wives and the addition of more children to the family only in extreme cases raises the amount of housework done by men (Meissner, n.d.; Szalai, 1972).

Table 12.1 Housework hours and specification of standards and routines[1]

Standards and routines	Weekly housework hours		
	40–69 No. (%)	70 or more No. (%)	Total No. (%)
High	2 (10)	19 (91)	21 100)
Medium	4 (29)	10 (71)	14 (100)
Low	4 (80)	1 (20)	5 (100)
Total	10 (25)	30 (75)	40 (100)

Source: Oakley (1974) p. 111.

[1]'Specification' here refers to the detailed rules about the way housework should be done evident in housewives' accounts of their work. These may derive from many sources (feminine socialization, media stereotypes, etc.), but the point is that they are felt as psychologically binding.

One mechanism for the decoration of housewifery is the advertising industry, which sells to housewives through the sexist messages of the media not only X brand of carpet shampoo and Y brand of washing powder, but an immensely powerful imagery of virtuous womanhood. The image is constructed and propagated through the use of stereotypes: 'A particular reality is presented as if it were the only reality. A particular idea of what life is like is presented as if it were the only, or at least the best, way of life' (Millum, 1975, pp. 51–2). Housewives in Millum's analysis of women's magazine advertisements are typically, of course, shown in the home, but the most invidious message is that the hardworking housewife is at one and the same time the calm, satisfied, attractive woman; housework is a labour of love performed with scarcely a hair out of place and a permanently unruffled, cosmetically enriched grin. (It is instructive to compare this with the attitude of the drug companies promoting tranquilizers and anti-depressants as the housewife's necessary aids – (pp. 79–80.) The message 'this product takes the hard work out of housework' appeals to the very notion of femininity that got women into their present predicament: the idea that real femininity is incompatible with real work. At the same time, it most sympathetically acknowledges that housework *is* work, hoping to win the hearts of its female customers by taking their side in the sexual politics of marital domesticity.

> I always say housework's harder work, but my husband doesn't say that at all. I think he's wrong, because I'm going all the time – when his job is finished, it's finished ... Sunday he can lie in bed till twelve, get up, get dressed and go for a drink, but my job never changes. (Oakley, 1974, p. 45)

The prison-house of home

The *unendingness* of housework, together with its repetitious character, were the most frequently named 'worst' aspects of being a housewife in my own study of housework carried out in London in 1971. Most (70 per cent) of the housewives in this study were dissatisfied with housework as work – a finding that was not confined to the middle-class women, but applied equally to working-class house-wives. While housewives valued the autonomy of their role ('You're your own boss'), the effects of this were described as an intensification of responsibility: since no one else tells the housewife how and when to do her work, she has to be her own supervisor and arbitrate her own standards. Rules – a 'job definition' – are even more necessary because housework is not paid. Apart from the appreciative remarks of husband, children and others, the housewife gets no feedback on her job performance; the only remaining course open to her is to reward herself by laying down standards and routines for housework and then achieving self-satisfaction by meeting them.

Yet the pat on the back is a constant struggle – against the pervasive cultural devaluation of housewifery ('only' or 'just' a housewife) and against those aspects of housework that render it a displeasing activity). The more a housework task (and the tasks that make up housework *are* different) resembles assembly-line factory work, the more it is disliked. Ironing comes top of the 'dislike' list; cooking, a potentially creative act, is the best-liked chore. Overall, three-quarters of the women found housework monotonous; 90 per cent complained about its fragmentation – its character as a series of unconnected tasks, none of which requires the worker's full attention. 'The routine is never quite routine, so the vacuum in one's mind is never vacuous enough to be filled. "Housework is a worm eating away at one's ideas" ' (Peckham Rye Women's Liberation Group, 1970, p. 5). Table 12.2 compares the experiences of monotony, fragmentation and excessive pace (having too much to do) among housewives and factory workers. The parallel between housewives' and assembly-line workers' attitudes is striking.

Table 12.2 The experience of monotony, fragmentation and speed in work: housewives and factory workers compared

Workers	Percentage experience		
	Monotony	Fragmentation	Speed
Housewives	75	90	50
Factory workers*	41	70	31
Assembly-line workers*	67	86	36

* These figures are taken from Goldthorpe *et al.* (1968) p. 18.
Source: Oakley (1974) p. 87

But perhaps most disturbing of all is the isolation of the housewife and her work. As Margery Spring Rice said in a unique record of working-class women's domestic labour in the 1930s:

> She eats, sleeps, 'rests' on the scene of her labour and her labour is entirely solitary... Whatever the emotional consequences, whatever her devotion, her family creates her labour, and tightens the bonds that tie her to the lonely and narrow sphere of 'home'. (Spring Rice, 1939, pp. 105–6)

Over half the women in my own study felt they did not see enough people during the day, and this feeling was more likely, not surprisingly, in those who were dissatisfied with housework. Aside from the question of how many people housewives actually see and talk to during the day, there is also the general sense of captivity noted in countless research reports and personal testimonies:

> Twenty five per cent of the working class wives had no friends at all... Many middle class wives felt that they were becoming rather isolated. (Gavron, 1966, p. 142)

> The lack of contact with other people coupled with the almost non-existence of a social life or leisure activities participated in by women outside the home, presents a depressing picture of the lives of many women. (Hobson, 1978, p. 87)

One woman in Hobson's study looked out of the window of her ninth-floor flat and counted the cars going by on the road 'just for something to do'; another talked to her cat until her first baby arrived to give her 'a bit of company'.

But children, for many women the *reason* for being at home, necessitate work of a different kind from housework. 'I could never consider the possibility of staying at home as a housewife, even part-time', said one housewife 'if I had no child to humanize the work for me'. Yet:

> My feelings of satisfaction or happiness are never connected with the housework, and are often in strict opposition to it, because Carl's vivacity and lawlessness oppose the reign of order and hygiene... It is a waste socially, psychologically and even economically, to put me in a position where my only means of expressing loyalty to Carl is by shopping, dishwashing and sweeping floors. (Gail, 1968, pp. 147–8)

Of course, not *every* woman perceives contradiction and ambivalence in this situation; not *every* housewife is dissatisfied. But the fact that some are should not be taken as indicating personal disorder. Because housework is private and feminine, attitudes to it are easily and erroneously laced with the moral invective of individualized discontent. Any description of the structure of the housewife's oppression 'assumes querulous and complaining tones, the tones of a private neurosis to express a social fact' (Peckham Rye Women's Liberation Group, 1970, p. 6). The private neurosis of housewives is depression, a psychiatric label that most adequately hides the social fact of the housewife's loneliness, low self-esteem and work dissatisfaction.

Who Does Housework?

Obviously women do, and that is why a chapter on domestic work is of such importance in a book of this kind. Definitionally speaking, a housewife is 'the person wholly or mainly responsible for running the household' (Hunt, 1968, p. 25) – 85 per cent of women aged 16–64 in this survey were classed as housewives. Through upbringing and social pressures of various kinds, it is women's fate to have the description 'housewife' as an inseparable part of their self-images, at least as these can be tapped by social science researchers. Asking women to describe themselves is liable to yield the following kinds of self-portrait:

I am a housewife	I am a good housewife
I am a mother	I am good to my children
I am ordinary	I am good at housework
I am a wife	I am good to my husband
I am happy	I am good at washing
I am reasonably attractive	I am fed up at times
I am a sister	I am bad tempered at times
I am a neighbour	I am very happy with my work
I am a friend	I am happy with my children
I am sociable	I am seldom unhappy (Oakley, 1974, pp.122, 124)

Of 40 women asked to describe themselves by completing the sentence 'I am...' ten times, 25 wrote 'I am a housewife' somewhere in their lists of self-descriptions and 20 of these put it in first or second place; 41 per cent of all the statements concerned housework or domestic roles generally ('I am a cleaner', 'I am a slave', 'I am a good houseworker').

This intense personal involvement in housework poses a considerable problem for women who wish to share it with men or with other women. To do so implies the obligation to examine one's own standards; where did they come from, and how 'rational' are they? Requiring other people to adhere to uncritically reviewed personal standards is hardly liberation – for others or for oneself. From a slightly different but related perspective, anthropologist Mary Douglas, in her analysis of concepts of pollution, acknowledges a debt of inspiration to her husband. 'In matters of cleanliness his threshold of tolerance is so much lower than my own that he more than anyone else has forced me into taking a stand on the relativity of dirt' (Douglas, 1970, p. viii). Dirt is not absolute. Every culture has its own notions of dirt and defilement; these stand in opposition to its notions of the positive structure that must be preserved. For, as Mary Douglas argues, the elimination of dirt is not a negative movement; rather, it is a positive attempt to organize one's environment to conform with some prior notion of order. So it is these cherished classifications we must understand.

Current European and American preconceptions about housework originated in the domestic hygiene movement that developed in the late nineteenth century. In America, Ellen Swallow Richards, a 'firm-jawed, heavy-browed, confident' ex-chemist, was an early popularizer of the message of domestic science. This was a direct result of discrimination against women in her chosen profession: at the Massachussets Institute of Technology she had been forced to study apart from the male students and was commandeered by her professors to sort their papers and mend their suspenders. But not even suspender-mending could qualify her for a graduate degree or for a job in the male world of chemistry. What she did instead was to teach people 'the science of right living', a mixture of chemistry, biology and engineering geared to the practical tasks of housekeeping. The idea was, as a colleague of Richards put it, that

> Nature has assigned to her [woman] special duties which man has deemed safe to be trusted to her instincts, yet in reality need for their performance the highest scientific knowledge. (Cotten, 1897, p. 280)

Biochemistry could reform cooking and economics would revolutionize shopping. But behind it all was the magnificent Germ Theory of Disease, whose foundations were laid when Pasteur discovered micro-organisms in 1857. Pasteur's discovery had the advantage that disease could be reclassified as in principle under man's control – or, more specifically, as controllable by means of the cleanliness and common sense of women. It had the disadvantage that germs, being invisible to the human eye, might be anywhere. By the 1890s an epidemic of public anxiety about contagion was in full swing. When the typhoid epidemic of the 1870s nearly killed the Prince of Wales, wealthy householders began to confront the problems of indoor sanitation. In America, the case of 'Typhoid Mary', an Irish-American cook who communicated typhoid to 52 people in the homes of her employers, was seen to raise in an especially urgent form the question: who is responsible for the public health?

For various cogent reasons the answer seemed obvious – women. In the first place, women were already defined by their domestic function – if not as housewives in the modern sense, then at least as the moral guardians of the home and as domestic servants. In the second place, the domestic science and sanitary reform movements were seen as relevant to an issue that was of direct biological concern to women: the question of infant mortality. Germs played a large part in the diarrhoeal diseases of infants responsible for a quarter of all infant deaths (1 in 6 babies died in their first year in 1899). Diarrhoea was diagnosed as a 'filth disease' to be prevented only by 'scrupulous domestic cleanliness':

> Infant mortality, it became clear, was a matter not so much of environmental hygiene, but of personal hygiene. It was more a social problem . . . The mother was evidently the factor of paramount importance. (McCleary, 1933, p. 35)

Mothers were taught not only how to feed babies artificially without giving them gastro-enteritis, but also how to eliminate germs from their homes. The penalty of a dead baby for careless maternal housework provided an immensely powerful moral justification for the zealous housewife: bad housecleaning equals child abuse.

While the intrusion of 'science' into housekeeping was argued as a strategy for *reducing* housework, its overall effect was undoubtedly to *increase* it. Instead of mindless routine, housework became a quest for new knowledge, became white-collar work (analysing, planning and consulting with the experts). The education of consumers eventually became their manipulation into the belief that good housewives had to employ a wide range of expensive products to achieve a clean home and a satisfied family. And the moral imputation that proper womanhood is a state of grace only gained when everyone's health and domestic comfort has been cared for, was, of course, presented in such a way as to be quite irresistible.

Yet a third reason why women were seen as guardians of the public health has to be dredged out of the buried subsoil of cultural attitudes. Pollution and purity rituals such as housework are attempts to impose cultural patterns on the natural world, and, in particular, to maintain boundaries between people, activities and places that are felt to be antithetical: the kitchen versus the dining room, poor people versus rich people, urination versus conversation. Because women can more easily be construed as natural creatures than men (only they have the body products of menstrual blood, babies and milk), their social position is more readily defined as marginal than that of men. As Douglas (1970) has shown, it is people at the margins of society – not only women, but little children, ethnic minorities, and lower castes and classes – who are felt to be most potentially dangerous and polluting. The paradoxical consequence of this is that they are required to act as the agents of other people's purity, in order to guarantee their own. Ideas of physical cleanliness as communicated by the nineteenth-century domestic economy movements in Britain and America are mixed with ideas about social and moral purity. A belief in the threatening contamination of femaleness struggled with an intransigent vision of women's inherent goodness to produce a situation in which women can never be just ordinary but must be either angels or devils.

It is not of course the case that only women do housework. In many pre-literate societies, what we call housework is turned over to small children or old people of both sexes who are not able to do other kinds of work. In colonial societies, as Davidoff (1976) points out, native men in preference to native women have provided most of the domestic labour for the foreign dominant group. Table 12.3 shows the division of domestic and childrearing tasks among the Tanulong and Fedizilan people of the Philippines. Of the 29 tasks in this Table, 12 are shared equally, 15 are shared, but less equally, and only cloth-weaving (feminine) and pig-killing (masculine) are one-sex activities.

In some cultures men regularly do the cooking (Firth, 1965), or they may participate only on ritual occasions (Little, 1954). In others, who cooks what is determined by the division of labour in procuring food. Among the Tiwi of Northern Australia, foods are divided into men's and women's, with men hunting

Table 12.3 Tasks and their performers in Tanulong and Fedilizan

Task	Performer
Domestic household chores	
Cooking	B
Washing dishes	B
Feeding animals	B
Skinning sweet potatoes	FM
Pounding rice	B
Keeping floors clean	FM
Gathering sweet potato leaves for pigs	FM
Waking up to cook in the morning	B
Splitting wood	MF
Cutting wood from the forest	MF
Preparing pig's food for cooking	B
Preparing cotton thread for weaving	FM
Weaving cloth	F
Washing clothes	FM
Sewing/mending clothes	FM
Washing dishes and pans	FM
Dressing and sacrificing chickens	B
Killing pigs	M
Distributing meat	MF
Cutting up meat for meals	MF
Fetching water	B
Babysitting	B
Keeping the child clean	FM
Feeding the child	B
Washing the child	FM
Cutting the child's hair	MF
Seeing the medium when child is sick	B
Taking care of sick child	FM
Counselling children	B

Note: B = tasks performed equally by females or males; F = tasks performed by females only; M = tasks performed by males only; FM = tasks performed usually by women; MF = tasks usually performed by men.
Souce: Adapted from *Bacdayan (1977)*, p. 282.

the products of the sea and air and women those of the land (Goodale, 1971); for the Ilongots of the Philippines, the division is between rice, which is cultivated, cooked and distributed by women, and meat, which is provided, cooked and allocated by men (Rosaldo, 1974). Malinowski, discussing *The Family Among the Australian Aborigines* (1963) noted that Kurnai men's work was confined to hunting oppossums and making rugs and weapons, a strange combination from a Western point of view. Among the Tungus of Siberia, men who are too old to hunt share with women their work of caring for reindeer herds, dressing and preparing skins for clothing and managing tents and their belongings (Forde, 1957). Men of the Mbum Kpau tribe in Africa fetch water and sweep the courtyards of houses, weave mats and baskets and dress skins; but they will not pound grain, make beer or oil or render salt (O'Laughlin, 1974).

The Servant Problem

Mrs Wrigley, a plate-layer's wife, was born in a Welsh village in 1858. At the age of 9, she became a servant:

> the doctor's wife came to our house and said a lady and gentleman wanted a little nurse for their child, to go back with them to Hazel Grove, near Stockport. My little bundle of clothes was packed up and I went in full glee with them. Instead of being a nurse I had to be a servant-of-all-work, having to get up at six in the morning, turn a room out and get it ready for breakfast. My biggest trouble was that I could not light the fire, and my master was very cross and would tell me to stand away, and give me a good box on my ears. That was my first experience of service life. I fretted very much for my home. Not able to read or write, I could not let my parents know, until a kind old lady in the village wrote to my parents to fetch me home from the hardships I endured. I had no wages at this place, only a few clothes.

Her last job in domestic service before her marriage to Mr Wrigley, was a happier experience:

> Here there was four servants, and I was engaged for the cook. It was a real gentleman's house. They kept coachmen, farmer and gardener, the very best place I had in all my life. We had plenty of freedom, going out in our turn. We were not treated as servants but as all one family, and the children was taught to treat us kindly and with respect. The servants was thought so much of, and when we had a ball the kitchen staff was allowed to have one dance with the guests ... I was there five years, and I married from there ... I was sorry to give up such a good home. (Davies, 1977, pp. 58, 60)

Personal accounts such as Mrs Wrigley's are rare, for, as Theresa McBride notes, the most completely ignored social group in European history has been the servant class:

> Historians have been content to take servants for granted in the same way that their employers expected them to be always unobtrusively present. (McBride, 1976, p. 9)

Servants are the counterparts in the market economy of housewives – ubiquitous and essential, but working in the coerced silence of a double oppression as women and as secret agents maintaining the all-important cultural boundary between personal and public life. It is not coincidental that servants, like women, were defined as the dependants of men (property-owners) and were the last social group to receive enfranchisement as citizens.

The experience of leaving home for domestic service was a fairly typical one in the nineteenth century; in 1871, 12 per cent of female servants were aged less than 15 (McBride, 1976, p. 45). At the end of the nineteenth century in Britain, around 20 per cent of households employed servants, and around one-sixth of all English women were domestic servants. The number of 'indoor' female domestic servants exceeded by some 300,000 all the women employed in textiles, nursing, teaching, shop work and the civil service put together (Davidoff and Hawthorn, 1976, p. 73). Even the families of skilled working men often had a young living-in servant girl to do the scrubbing and dirty work and babyminding. Roughly two-thirds of all female servants were 'general' domestics of this kind (McBride, 1976, p. 14). Conditions of work were poor. In the early 1800s, for instance, servants slept in the kitchen or in cupboards under the stairs. Later, when allocated the attics, employers often forbad their servants to display pictures or any personal objects, and considered it their right to look through servants' belongings. Servants were not allowed to sing or laugh at work, were expected to do their work noiselessly, never to speak unless spoken to, to stand in the presence of their employer and to walk out of the room backwards (Davidoff and Hawthorn, 1976).

Until about 1840, domestic service continued to be the major occupier of women throughout Western Europe and in the United States, but a decline set in in the late nineteenth century as more women took jobs as clerks, shop assistants and factory workers in preference to domestic service. There was also a trend away from living-in servants and towards daily 'charring' as the ideology of family privacy intensified to exclude strangers – even those who would lighten the rapidly mounting burden of married women's domestic work. Magazines for women such as *Housewife* (1886), *The Mother's Companion* (1887), *The Ladies' Home Journal* (1890), *Woman at Home* (1893), *Home Notes* (1894), *Home Chat* (1895) and *Home Companion* (1897) arrived to bemoan 'the servant problem' and provide manuals of advice on 'the conduct and management of the home'.

Because research into domestic work is almost non-existent, the current position of paid domestic workers in industrial societies is not well-documented. One survey of the home help service in England and Wales carried out in 1967 found that the women who worked for it tended to be older and have more domestic responsibilities themselves than the average employed woman.(Home helps are paid by local authorities to do housework and generally look after people either temporarily or permanently unable to look after themselves.) Half had children under 16; one in six had to look after at least one elderly or infirm person in their family. Pay was between 23p and 28p an hour; only one in four were paid travelling expenses, and one in six were not paid for their travelling time between jobs. Many received no sick pay. One in five were issued with no protective clothing, and only one in ten were provided with equipment. Many of the women worked in homes where equipment and amenities were poor: a quarter had no hot water supply, half did not possess a vacuum cleaner; a third of the home helps used their own equipment or bought items with their own money for use in the homes they worked in. Not surprisingly, 85 per cent wanted improvements in their working conditions (Hunt, 1970).

Nightcleaning is another form of paid domestic work:

Q: Why do you actually do night work?
A: Because of my children, you see, I cannot manage to work in a hospital fulltime, I had to see about one [daytime job] this morning: 7.30 to 1.00 for £10, which is a good salary for me, but 7.30 to 1.00 I can't manage because of my youngest child. The others are alright, they can look after themselves to go to school, but she, I cannot leave her here on her own ...

Q: What else do you have to do during the day besides get the children off to school?

A: Well, I have to take them to school. I have to come home and prepare something for them to eat because I cannot afford a full dinner money for four of them at school. I have to take them back to school and go and collect them in the afternoon, do my housework, cook and wash.

Q: How much sleep do you get?

A: Well, two hours, when my husband is in, he's working in the afternoon, he helps me do a bit of cooking when he's in, but when he's not in, I'm not getting no rest.

Q: Can you get along like that or does it make you feel irritable and nervous?

A: If I don't get any rest I always feel nervous, because my doctor has stopped me from my night job once, he told me I'm not getting enough rest with all the children, [*Shrew*, December 1971, p. 5]

Nightcleaning is 'contract' labour: large offices contract their cleaning to cleaning companies who contract to provide a certain number of women to clean so many feet of office space. Since no one checks how the work is actually done (those who might do so are asleep in bed), there is a golden opportunity to make huge profits out of employing fewer women to do more work than the contract states. Nightcleaners are women who are too old, too untrained or too burdened with childcare to get other work. They often put in a full working week, but they do so at a time, in a place and for the kind of rates that lead their jobs to be dismissed as 'casual' part-time work.

All in a Day's Work

Factories at night mimic the invisibility of the home:

> Jean works in her bedroom. She machines pillow ticks while watching the clock. She's pleased because she can make 21 in 1 hour and soon she hopes to be quick enough to make 24. She finds it difficult to build up speed, though, because she is always being interrupted by the demands of her family. Jean has four children of school age. Her husband, John, works in a shoe factory and with 5 hours overtime he brings home £27 a week, not enough to support a family. (Hope *et al.*, 1976, pp. 91–3)

Jean and her family live in two rooms plus a kitchen and they share a lavatory with fifteen people that is cleaned by Jean 'because no-one else will do it'. Jean earns 2p for each pillow tick she makes and she averaged 48p an hour.

Thousands of women in Britain are in paid employment as homeworkers, although it is hard to get national figures because the opinion of those who organize the work of the government statistical service has been for half a century that homework doesn't exist in any significant sense. Jean was one of those interviewed for a small North London survey – one of the few attempts to find out about homeworkers' conditions. It uncovered atrocious conditions (low pay, no allowance for overheads such as heating and lighting, no training and no expenditure by the firms on capital equipment such as sewing machines). Another investigation of homeworkers in the toy industry showed that four-fifths of homeworkers were paid less than the legal minimum for piecework. Two of the 178 surveyed got holiday pay; none got sick pay. All said that the money they earned was not just pin money, but was a large part of the family income (Advisory Conciliation and Arbitration Service, 1978).

However, one approaches the subject of domestic labour, one is thus returned

constantly to the same theme: the benign refusal to call housework proper labour.
I shall end this chapter by mentioning two further consequences of this.

One is that the conditions of family life do more than mark the prosperity or
poverty of families: they are work conditions. According to the *General Household
Survey*, in Britain one in twenty homes still do not have baths, or inside lavatories,
half lack central heating, a third have no washing machine and one in ten no
refrigerator (*General Household Survey*, 1978, Table 2.20, p. 36). Similarly,
occupational hazards of housework as work are not recognized. One – depression
or 'housewife's disease' – has already been mentioned. Another is accidental
injury or death. 'Twenty people die each day from accidents in the home, and the
kitchen is the single most dangerous place' (Politics of Health Group, 1979, p. 26).
Whereas men are more likely to die in violent accidents and from suicide, women
predominate in deaths from accidental falls and in deaths caused by fire (Office of
Population Censuses and Surveys, 1977), many of these occurring at home. More
than a third of all fatal accidents in the UK are domestic. The double-think of
assigning childcare to housewives is exposed by the stark fact that more young
children die accidentally at home than anywhere else; fires, the inhalation of food
and suffocation are the commonest causes (Macfarlane, 1979).

Secondly, housework has prevented women from pursuing many avenues of
self-development open to those who do not do it.

> The house seems to take up so much time [wrote Katherine Mansfield to John
> Middleton Murry], I get frightfully impatient and want to be working [writing].
> So often this week you and Gordon have been talking while I washed dishes. Well,
> someone's got to wash dishes and get food ... And after you have gone I walk
> about with a mind full of ghosts of saucepans and primus stoves (Cited in Olsen,
> 1972, p. 108)

The reason why women do not produce works of art is that they are perpetually
involved in an unrecognized and unremitting labour of love (which must be
considered a work of art of equal value, if of another kind).

The psychological effect of housework combines with women's economic
dependence to mould a certain opportunity structure. Housework remains an
incredibly important limit on what women are able to do and become.

References

Advisory Conciliation and Arbitration Service (1978) *The Toy Manufacturing Wages Council
   Report no. 13*, London ACAS.
Bacdayan, A.S. (1977) 'Mechanistic co-operation and sexual equality among the Western
   Bontoc', in Schlegel, A. (ed.), *Sexual Stratification: A Cross-Cultural View*, New York,
   Colombia University Press.
Barker, D.L. and Allen, S. (1976) *Sexual Divisions and Society*, London, Tavistock.
Benston, M. (1969) 'The political economy of women's liberation', reprinted from the
   September issue of *Monthly Review* by New England Free Press, Boston, Mass.
Burton, E. (1944) *Domestic Work; Britain's Largest Industry*, London, Frederick Muller.
Chapman, D. (1955) *The Home and Social Status*, London, Routledge and Kegan Paul.
Cotten, S.S. (1897) 'A national training school for women', in *The Work and Words of the
   National Congress of Mothers*, New York, D. Appleton.
Cowan, R.S. (1974) 'A case study of technological and social change: the washing machine
   and the working wife', in M. Hartman and L.W. Banner (eds.), *Clio's Consciousness
   Raised: New Perspectives on the History of Women*, New York, Harper Colophon.
Dalla Costa, M. and James, S. (1972) *The Power of Women and the Subversion of the Community*,
   Bristol, Falling Wall Press.
Davidoff, L. (1976) 'The rationalization of housework' in Barker and Allen (eds.) (1976).

Davidoff, L. and Hawthorn, R. (1976) *A Day in the Life of a Victorian Domestic Servant*, London, Allen and Unwin.

Davies, M.L. (ed.) (1977) *Life as We have Known It*, London, Virago. (First published in 1931 by Hogarth Press.)

Davis, D. (1966) *A History of Shopping*, London, Routledge and Kegan Paul.

Douglas, M. (1970) *Purity and Danger: An analysis of Concepts of Pollution and Taboo*, Baltimore Penguin.

Firth, R. (1965) *Primitive Polynesian Economy*, London, Routledge and Kegan Paul.

Forde, C.D. (1957) *Habitat, Economy and Society*, London. Methuen.

Friedan, B. (1963) *The Feminine Mystique*, London, Gollancz.

Gail, S. (1968) 'The housewife' in Fraser, R. (ed.). *Work: Twenty Personal Accounts*, Harmondsworth, Penguin.

Galbraith, J.K. (1974) *Economics and the Public Purpose*, London, André Deutsch,.

Gavron, H. (1966) *The Captive Wife*, Harmondsworth, Penguin.

General Household Survey 1976 (1978) Office of Population Censuses and Surveys, Social Survey Division, London, HMSO.

Glazer-Malbin, N. (1976) 'Housework', *Signs: Journal of Women in Culture and Society*, vol. 1, no. 4 (Summer), pp. 905–22.

Goldthorpe, J.H., Lockwood, D., Bechhofer, F. and Platt, J. (1968) *The Affluent Worker: Industrial Attitudes and Behaviour*, Cambridge, Cambridge University Press.

Goodale, J.C. (1971) *Tiwi Wives*, Washington, University Press.

Hammond, D. and Jablow, A. (1976) *Women in Cultures of the World*, Meno Park, California, Cummings Publishing Co.

Heitlinger, A. (1979) *Women and State Socialism: Sex Inequality in the Soviet Union and Czechoslovakia*, London, Macmillan.

Henderson, A. (1964) *The Family House in England*, Los Angeles, Phoenix House.

Hobson, D. (1978) 'Housewives: isolation as oppression', in Women's Studies Group, Centre for Contemporary Cultural Studies, University of Birmingham, *Women Take Issue: Aspects of Women's Subordination*, London, Hutchinson.

Hope, E., Kennedy, M and de Winter, A. (1976), 'Houseworkers in North London', in D. L. Barker and S. Allen (eds.), *Dependence and Exploitation in Work and Marriage*, London, Longman.

Hunt, A. (1968) *A Survey of Women's Employment*, London, HMSO.

(1970) *The Home Help Service in England and Wales: A Survey Carried Out in 1967*, London, HMSO.

Lapidus, G.W. (1978) 'Sexual equality in Soviet policy: a developmental perspective' in Atkinson, D., Dallin, A., and Lapidus, G.W. (eds.) *Women in Russia*, Sussex, Harvester Press.

Little, K. (1954) 'The Mende in Sierra Leone', in D. Forde (ed.) *African Worlds*, London, Oxford University Press.

McBride, T.M. (1976) *The Domestic Revolution*, London, Croom Helm.

McCleary, G.F. (1933) *The Early History of the Infant Welfare Movement*, London, H.K. Lewis and Co.

MacFarlane, A. (1979) 'Child deaths from accidents: place of accident', *Population Trends*, vol. 15 (Spring).

Malinowski, B. (1963) *The Family Among the Australian Aborigines*, New York, Schocken Books.

Malos, E. (1977) 'Housework and the politics of women's liberation', reprinted from January–February *Socialist Review* by RSM. publications, 11 Waverly Road, Redland, Bristol BS6 6ES.

Meissner, M., Humphreys, E., Meis, S. and Scherr, J. (n.d.) 'No exit for wives: sexual division of labour and the cumulation of household demands', unpublished paper.

Millum, T. (1975) *Images of Women: Advertising in Women's Magazines*, London, Chatto and Windus.

Oakley, A. (1974) *The Sociology of Housework*, London, Martin Robertson.

Office of Population Censuses and Surveys (1977), *Mortality Statistics: Acidents and Violence*, London, HMSO.

O'Laughlin, B. (1974) 'Mediation of contradiction: why Mbum women do not eat chicken' in Rosaldo and Lamphere (eds).

Olsen, T. (1972) 'When writers don't write' in Cornillon, S.K. (ed.), *Images of Women's Fiction: Feminist Perspectives*, Bowling Green, Ohio, Bowling Green University Popular Press.

Peckham Rye Women's Liberation Group (1970) 'A woman's work is never done', paper presented at Women's Liberation Conference, Oxford, March; reprinted by Agitprop, 160 North Gower Street, London, NW1.

Plant, M. (1952) *The Domestic Life of Scotland in the Eighteenth Century*, Edinburgh, Edinburgh University Press.

Politics of Health Culture Group (1979) *Food and Profit*, London, Politics of Health Group.

Purefoy, E. (1931) *Purefoy Letters*, ed. G. Eland, London, Sidgwick and Jackson.

Rosaldo, M.Z. (1974) 'Woman, culture and society: a theoretical overview' in Rosaldo and Lamphere (eds).

Rosaldo, M.Z. and Lamphere, L. (eds) (1974) *Woman, Culture and Society*, Stanford, California, Stanford University Press.

Sachs, M.P. (1977) 'Unchanging times: a comparison of the everday life of Soviet working men and women between 1923 and 1966', *Journal of Marriage and the Family*, November, pp. 793–805.

Secombe, W. (1974) 'The housewife and her labour under capitalism', *New Left Review*, vol. 83, January–February.

Spring Rice, M. (1939) *Working Class Wives*, Harmondsworth, Penguin.

Spruill, J.C. (1972) *Women's Life and Work in the Southern Colonies*, New York, W.W. Norton. (First published 1938.)

Szalai, A. (1972) *The Use of Time*, The Hague, Mouton.

Tilly, L.A. and Scott, J.W. (1978) *Women, Work and Family*, New York, Holton, Rinehart and Winston.

Vanek, J. (1974) 'Time spent in housework', *Scientific American*, November, p. 116.

Wickham, M. and Young, B. (1973) *Home Management and Family Living*, Report of the questionnaire of the Home Economics Sectional Committee, National Council of Women, 36 Lower Sloane Street, London, SW1W 8BP.

13   Married to the Job

JANET FINCH

Time Elements: Patterns, Structures and Competition

The structuring effect of a man's work is most clearly visible in the patterns imposed by his working hours. Of course these patterns will be modified by a number of other elements: a wife's own paid employment, having children at school, taking care of the elderly parent, and so on. Each of these in a sense sets its own timetable, and indeed family life can be seen as a series of overlapping and interacting timetables (Roth, 1963, pp. 112–14), with which wives in particular have to juggle. But the argument here is that a husband's working hours intrude in a special kind of way: in particular, the effects of a husband's working and a wife's working are not symmetrical. In so far as the couple maintain a sexual division of labour, even in a modified form, a wife normally is assigned to 'covering' domestic tasks, especially child care. This leaves her free to pursue other activities, at best only when he is *not* at work, unless she is able to make alternative arrangements for discharging these responsibilities.

The need to 'cover' child care is not the only way in which a man's work imposes patterns on his wife's life. The man himself has to be serviced, and since many wives remain the household *managers*, even where couples share a number of specific domestic tasks, the organisation of household routines is likely to be significantly oriented to the man's working day. The traditional organisation of life in a mining community was such that 'The rhythm of domestic life is the rhythm of the working-day, of the working-week and the weekly wage packet' (Dennis, Henriques and Slaughter, 1969, p. 184). A very similar note is struck in a rather more recent account of village life in the Fens, where women's lives are organised around the needs of their husband: 'their man, and his needs, must take precedence over all else. Many men come home to lunch and expect a hot meal waiting for them' (Chamberlain, 1975, p. 71). These experiences are not confined to rural life. Deem's much much more recent study of women's leisure in Milton Keynes documents the same phenomenon: 'Where men worked unsocial hours, or irregular hours, the routines of their households had to be adjusted to suit these, sometimes precluding [their wife's participation in] regular activities outside the house at particular times each week ... or allowing only irregular attendance and also making advance arrangements to go out very difficult' (Deem, 1981, p. 7). Similarly, Hunt, in her recent study of an industrial village in the Midlands, notes that, especially where wives are not employed outside the home, 'All women in this group make some adjustments to their husband's work. The preparation and serving of meals is planned to correspond with the wage-earner's hours of work, and leisure is also tailored to fit in with his movements' (Hunt, 1980, p. 49).

The most extreme examples of 'patterning' are found where work is also based in the home. In a study of British Rail resident railway crossing workers, one wife of a respondent described how her husband's working routine impinged on her day:

Janet Finch, *Married to the Job*, London, Allen and Unwin, 1983; Chapters 2 and 3.

Mr Johnson is able to get an average of only five hours sleep a night and Mrs Johnson has to wake at the same time each morning to make sure he gets up...throughout the day Mr Johnson is unable to move out of earshot of the block bell which warns of a train coming and is a sign to open the gates. The longest period of time that elapses without a train passing through is fifty minutes between 7.40 p.m. and 8.30 p.m. and it is during this time that Mr Johnson eats his evening meal.

Hardly surprisingly the wife commented, 'we are both working for them [BR]' (Owen, 1980, p. 18).

Patterns and timetables imposed by a man's work obviously vary with men's working hours. Some inevitably run counter to what are otherwise considered to be 'normal' daily routines. This may be one reason why only about half of the couples interviewed in a study of shift working were happy with the husband's working shifts (Marsh, 1979, p. 83).

A particular implication of all this for a wife concerns the prospects for her own employment. In so far as she is left 'covering' in the home, and especially if child care is involved, effectively she can only take employment when he is known to be available to substitute for her: hence, presumably the comparative popularity of twilight shifts (Marsh, 1979, ch. 2).

Women's employment prospects are closely circumscribed by the domestic responsibilities which are assigned to them as a consequence. As Hunt puts it, in relation to wives in her study, 'One reason why women face such a lack of occupational choice is that they take on jobs to fit in with their domestic duties ... sometimes the clash between the domestic and the paid job finds expression in people turning down promotion' (Hunt, 1980, pp. 124, 126). The extent to which a wife is *able* to fit her employment around the patterning imposed by her husband's work and the assigning of the 'covering' domestic responsibilities to her, depends, somewhat upon her husband's actual working hours, especially if she can only work when she can rely on his being at home. The logistics of this must become well nigh impossible for some people: where can you find a job, for example, which fits in with a pattern of your husband's shift working, where the shifts change on a four-weekly cycle (Young and Willmott, 1973, pp. 185–6)?

Competition for the Breadwinner's Time

A 'special case' of the patterning effects of a husband's working hours is provided by jobs where there are no set working hours, or where work can 'spill over' into non-work time. In the literature on these kind of occupations there is often discussion of tensions between work and family, which in some circumstances seem to develop into direct competition over the worker's time.

A sense of this can be found in some of the work on executives, such as the Pahls' study, where they quote one of their manager's wives as saying:

His work is not only his hobby but his life, and he has no spare time...he will never alter...In the past this has caused considerable upheavals. (Pahl and Pahl, 1971, p. 256)

Cain notes that one general dissatisfaction with police work is that it gives 'insufficient time for family life' (Cain, 1973, p. 7), and that police wives often 'felt cheated of the companionship which they as married women were entitled to, and on behalf of their children, who were similarly entitled to a father like the others' (ibid., p. 137). The Rapoports, in discussing the family life of politicians, give an example where the balance of the pressures is in the opposite direction: an individual may be regarded as unsuitable for high office precisely because of his commitments to his wife: 'the public image of professional work tends to assume that family requirements are inherently incompatible with those of work...When the former British cabinet minister, Maudling, was being considered in 1963 as a possible successor to Macmillan, it was said that he was too happily married to make a good Prime Minister' (Rapoport and Rapoport, 1969, p. 390).

The conditions are set for this tension to develop into competition over the male worker's time, when his work begins to encroach significantly upon time which a wife has assumed was going to be 'free time': to be spent with the family, or to free her from total responsibility for domestic commitments. Then wives may begin to look with envy at other wives whose husbands are freer. As one of Cain's respondents put it:

> I've only one quarrel with the police force, the hours he has to work. They're just not considerate. I can't remember when he last had a rest day... I don't mind that so much, except when I see all these other men doing their gardens, and doing their wives windows and leaning over the fence and talking and not knowing what to do with their off duty. They should never have put our house with theirs. It's just not the same job. They do eight hours and then they're finished but my husband's never finished...They should put the C.I.D. houses separately. (Cain unpublished data)

There are all sorts of reasons for a male worker to allow encroachment upon 'free' time to take place: financial gain, personal advancement, the inherent interest of the work and attractions of the workplace. Whyte, in his well-known study of American company executives, argues that a man's living standards are much higher at work than they are home:

> the corporation now provides a man with a higher standard of living at work than in his home – and, it might be added, a higher one than his wife enjoys. From 9 to 5 he may be a minor satrap, guiding the destinies of thousands, waited on by secretaries and subordinates; back in his servantless home, he washes the dishes. Nor is it merely the fact of his satrapy; the corporation virtually rigs it so that he can have more fun away from home. (Whyte, 1971, pp. 84–5)

The possibilities for this competition exist in a number of occupations, but its particular character and its outcome may vary. The character of the work done is probably of especial significance, since work which a wife herself values highly, or is culturally designated as especially important work, is likely to be accorded the priority in every possible case of competition with family demands. This point is made rather graphically in a book by a journalist about American politicians' marriages.

> The wife of a politician can appear not only petty, but downright unpatriotic if she complains about a husband who is under the lofty illusion that he is saving the country. It is more like the dilemma faced by wives of men who immerse themselves in such professions as the ministry, science or medicine; it is tough to ask for equal time with noble endeavours as your competition. (McPherson, 1975, p. 24)

So wives of men who undertake noble endeavours (or perhaps more accurately, men with wives who *believe* that they are engaged in noble endeavours) may find that the potential competition between work and family, far from being expressed in conflict between husband and wife, results in the husband being given *more* space to get on with the great work. A wife who sees work taking over her husband's whole life, and who endorses the legitimacy of its claims upon him, may well respond by taking on *all* responsibility for domestic tasks, leaving him free to concentrate on his work. This certainly seems to be the case for clergy couples.

Although one might imagine that home-based work, with no set working times, would result in a husband's taking on *more* responsibility for domestic work and child care, the opposite seems to be the case. The sentiment expressed by this wife in my study was a very common one:

> My husband would hate it if he had to fend for himself. It's not that he's not practical, he *is*; but he would not be happy having to do it, because he would be feeling all the time that he wanted to do other things. (Spedding, 1975, p. 295)

In this study, it was very clear that the potential competition between work and family became expressed very much in a presumed dichotomy between spending time on church work and spending time on household work or child care. Since a clergyman's work is based on the home, and work can be done at any time of day or even night, the situation is structured so that any performance of domestic tasks appears to be an *alternative* to work; and a clergyman's wife who suggests that her husband might take on some of these tasks feels that she is taking him away from his work. Since most clergymen's wives value their husband's work highly it is hardly surprising that their response is to create the domestic conditions which ensure that he is not distracted (Spedding, 1975, ch. 12). They provide a good illustration of how the combination of flexible working hours and home-based work can creat a *more* rigid sexual division of labour, not less, despite Young and Willmott's utopian belief that these are precisely the conditions which will create great symmetry in family life and especially in the division of labour between husband and wife (Young and Willmott, 1973, p. 272).

A further twist to the potential competition for the male breadwinner's time is provided where his work has the particular characteristic that he is always, or considers himself to be, potentially 'on duty', even when he is officially 'off'. This is an important characteristic of certain occupations, especially where the worker has a particular skill which may be needed at any time, perhaps in emergencies. However, people engaged in other types of work may also regard themselves as potentially always on duty, especially if they hold some position of responsibility where they would always want to be on the spot to take a particular *decision*, even if no specialised skill is involved. An example of this can be found in Young and Willmott's study, where a computer manager, whilst officially on duty at certain times only, clearly considered himself responsible for his computer at all times:

> My hours are supposed to be from nine to five past five. I arrive every day between eight and eight thirty, and I never leave before six thirty, or seven in the evening. I come in here one Saturday morning out of two, and sometimes both. Occasionally I look in on a Sunday to see if everything is going as it should be. Last Saturday I worked from nine thirty until one. Go on – tell me I'm a fool. My wife does (Young and Willmott, 1973, p. 136)

For people with those kinds of responsibilities, the telephone provides what Young and Willmott have called a 'means of trespass' between work and home (ibid., p. 167), since it affords the opportunity to call them into work. A graphic illustration is provided by one of Fowlkes's respondents, an American doctor's wife:

> It's pretty bad when you get in bed and you're making love and you hear the g— d— phone ring. It interrupts arguments, it interrupts meals, but sex is the ultimate of interruptions. (Fowlkes, 1980, p. 84)

The opportunities for trespass by telephone are not limited to men in professional occupations. One of Cain's respondents described how her policeman husband could be called out by his superiors:

One morning I really had a row with them about it. He was off duty but had been called out early from something or other, and do you know, at half past six that phone started ringing and I said, no, I'm not going to answer it, and that went on until half past eight. But I wasn't going to answer it; that was his rest day. Anyway, at half past eight I did answer, and that was the inspector,...And he was really rude to me. "Didn't you hear the phone ringing?" he said, "Yes" I said, "Why didn't you answer it then" he said. Just like that. "I was busy", I said, "with the children". "Where's your husband then", he said, really rude to me you know. "He's out", I said, "anyway, he's on rest day". "Where's he gone?". "If you must know, to help an old lady with moving", I said, I never did tell him where he'd gone. Why should I? He was off duty. (Cain, unpublished data)

The ethos of being always available opens up the opportunity for work to trespass, and this is a characteristic feature of a number of occupations. Haberstein's study of American funeral directors provides a good example here, and no doubt the same would be true in Britain:

Clients, particularly of 'local funeral homes', want the services of a funeral director who they know personally, or who has served their families in the past. Consequently, such a funeral director feels the need to be constantly at hand: there is really no moment of his life safe from the demands of his clientele. (Haberstein, 1962, pp. 241–2)

The clergy are another example of an occupational group where constant availability is considered essential. Their situation provides an illustration of how the competition for the breadwinner's time can become focused around one particular issue: arranging time off. The unreliability of time off was an issue discussed with some enthusiasm by many of the clergy wives in my study. In the sample of wives of non-conformist ministers, twenty-four out of thirty-three wives said that the husband took *no* regular time off, and only three took as much as one day a week. The issue was a major cause for complaint and concern among all clergy wives, both anglican and nonconformist, and it was often blamed upon a husband's lack of personal organisation and discipline. However, for clergy the situation is compounded by adherence to the ethic of the availability of the minister at all times; one respondent put it like this:

Theoretically, Monday is the day he would like to set apart, but more often than not, it's hopeless. I suppose we don't discipline ourselves enough on this and say, right, we're having this day off whatever happens, it can't work like that. Last December we were all set up to go Christmas shopping, and someone unexpectedly died. And of course by the time we had visited the widow, and one or two other people...But what can you do in those circumstances? You can't say, I'm sorry, it's my day off. (Spedding, 1975, p. 302)

The competitive elements set up in situations where the worker has to be constantly available serve as perhaps the most extreme example of a point which has become apparent through this consideration of the patterning effects of a man's working hours: the structures imposed by the time dimension are overlaid both by the character of the particular occupation, and the spatial relationship between home and work.

Work Characteristics: Implications Inside and Outside the Home

An examination of the literature on occupations suggests three common ways in which the characteristics of work can 'spill over' into non-work life. These are: being mentally 'at work' for most of the time; the replication of patterns of working relationships; escaping *from* work and the need to counteract its effects.

The potential effects of bringing home the *consequences* of work, if not the work itself, are widely recognised in our culture, and the ability of some individuals to 'leave their work behind' at the factory gates or the office door is often much admired. Far more people can bring home work in their heads than bring it in their briefcases, and the possibility that a worker can be mentally 'at work' when overtly engaged in non-work activities presumably occurs in almost any occupation, since he or she may be thinking about features of the work itself, or about aspects of the relationships located in the workplace. A woman also may 'bring home' her work in this way, but it will be argued that its effects upon others in the household are unlikely to be the same as the effects of her husband's work, because of the continued significance of his being cherished as the family breadwinner.

Although one might find examples of carrying over the effects of working *relationships* in almost any occupation, examples of being mentally 'at work' are found mainly in literature about occupations seen as inherently stressful, or where the worker carries quite a high degree of individual responsibility. Morris, writing of the experience of prison officers, sees this as partly a two-way traffic of problems, the tensions of which can best be absorbed by wives, not the men themselves:

> Work problems spill over into his leisure time and private problems may be accentuated by his work experience and spill over into working hours, thus placing a great strain on marriages. It is constantly asserted by officers with a long service that *an understanding and tolerant wife is the best asset a man can have in this job.* (Morris, 1963, p. 8) (my italics)

Sometimes, if work is regarded as an intrinsically enjoyable experience, the ability to be 'at work' when apparently doing something else may be welcomed by the worker. Examples of this were given by some of Young and Willmott's managing directors:

> When I'm in the bath or mowing the lawn, I'm often trying to figure out some problem or other.

> If you saw me very happily sitting in the garden with a drink at my side I might be thinking over a problem. If you came along beside me you might be talking to me for ten minutes and I wouldn't hear you, I'd be so concentrated. (Young and Willmott, 1973, p. 166)

Enjoyable and welcome as this facility may be for the worker, it may not be so for others in the household. Another respondent in the same study recognises that the effects may be unpleasant for his wife, but seems to regard this as part of some sort of normal domestic pattern:

> One has problems. You might think about them and drift off into a haze and don't pay any attention to what your wife is telling you. I said I never take work home – that's true, not paperwork. But unfortunately it remains in my head. There are *the usual domestic problems* as a result. (ibid., pp. 166–7) (my italics)

The second way in which characteristics of work carry over into non-work time is through the continuation or replication or particular patterns of relationships. A number of studies provide examples of out-of-work friendships being based on workplace relationships almost exclusively: ranging from the mobile middle-classes in Bell's (1968) study to a stable working-class community, especially if it is based mainly on one industry. Salaman, in his study of architects and railway workers, quotes one railwayman's wife as saying:

> It's railways, railways, railways with him. All railwaymen are like it, they just want to get together and talk railways. As though they didn't have enough. If you want

to find out about railways, ask the wives. We're the ones who've had railways all these years. (Salaman, 1971, p. 398)

This wife clearly felt that not only her husband's leisure time but also her own life was dominated by his work.

Another way in which patterns of relationships are carried over from the workplace is not through *actual* friendships, but when the *style* of relationships is replicated in non-work settings. The Rapoports suggest this in one of their earlier papers: 'Presumably there are soldiers who organise their families like platoons, computer technicians who program their families as they do their machines, and boxers who use physical violence at home' (Rapoport and Rapoport, 1969, p. 392). No doubt there are, but it is fairly difficult to find actual examples of this in the literature, and there is a real possibility of caricature by overstatements here. Banton gives an example in his study of the police, when he quotes a respondent:

I'll tell you another thing that I've noticed myself doing, if there is something wrong in the house you begin to question your wife as if you were questioning a suspect. It's actually true – you ask a police sergeant – you begin to get into a routine. (Banton, 1964, p. 208)

An example of the replication of police relationships in the home is given by one of Cain's respondents:

Policemen make bad fathers. They can't help bringing the job into the home. They're too strict. It's alright with some children, but it's a nightmare with our son, especially when he was about twelve. We had dreadful rows. My husband's unimaginative and my son's just the opposite. My husband's very rigid. I've got a psychiatrist friend who said it was probably the thought of being a policeman going through his head. (Cain, unpublished data)

In a rather less direct way, Fowlkes suggests that the style of professional relationships adopted by doctors results in the development of a style of family life in which they remain emotionally disengaged (Fowlkes, 1980, pp. 162–3).

The case of the clergy of the Church of England provides an example – albeit quite a rare one perhaps – where a worker is formally *expected* to replicate work relationships in the home, since he is specifically required to promise at the time of his ordination that he will try to create his home as a model for the church. In the modernised version of the ordination service, this reads, 'WIll you strive to fashion your own life and that of your household according to the way of Christ?' (Church of England, 1980, Ordination of Priests, p. 358).

The examples so far have been about continuities between work and home and their implications for wives, but plenty of examples of the opposite can be found – the use of non-work time and relationship to *get away from* work. The distinction developed by the Rapoports between isomorphism and heteromorphism is relevant here (Rapoport and Rapoport, 1969, p. 391). Whilst this perhaps has some use as a conceptual tool, it would be misleading to suggest any individual or occupational group is characterized *either* by similarity between home and work *or* by contrast. It seems more likely that some features of work will be replicated and others contrasted, and the more interesting questions centre around the way in which the two are combined, although insufficient detailed empirical data exists for clear patterns to be identified.

The theme that the home is a place where workers can escape from the work and recover from its effects is a common one. The home often makes its appearance in this form in structural functionalist analyses of the family and work and, as Dorothy Smith writes, commenting on Smelser's work, 'Essentially...from this point of view, the home is a place where people are stored when they are not at work, where they are maintained and serviced, fed and cleaned, where they are psychologically repaired and the injuries of daily routine and the tensions generated on the job made good' (Smith, 1973, p. 10). In this account the wife of course is the key figure, since she creates a home as the kind of place where recuperation is possible. Dennis *et al.*'s account of miners' wives stresses that they feel they must create a comfortable home to contrast with the rigours of their husband's working environment (Dennis, Henriques and Slaughter, 1969, p. 179). The same pattern can be repeated in a completely different occupation, as when the wife of an airline pilot described the effects of his work, and her response to them:

> I often say BOAC is his mistress. He gets very tired. The first day home I have learned to keep quiet and not mention any problems. He still has the noise of the jet engines in his ears. His face is white and fatigued. (Young and Willmott, 1973, p. 165)

In so far as wives do respond to these 'needs' created in work by providing what is regarded as an appropriate contrast – a comfortable, undemanding and well-organised home – they can be seen as contributing their labour towards the production of a husband with a greater capacity for work. The other side of it, however, is that, in so far as it is accepted that a legitimate (and even an important) part of being a wife is to create the kind of domestic setting which will provide for the male worker's work-generated 'needs', then a wife's life is further structured and constrained thereby.

Public Figures

Some occupations are characterised by their ability to define the worker as a 'public figure'. Although this undoubtedly is a minority experience, it is worth looking at its consequences since, it will be argued, it is an extreme example of a wife's life being structured by her identification with her husband's work.

Being a public figure essentially means being defined in terms of work for the purposes of almost all social contacts. Such situations seem to be produced by a combination of characteristics of the work itself, and the setting in which it takes place. Doctors, for example, may find it easier to establish a private identity if they work in a large hospital than if they are general practitioners, and probably find it most difficult of all if they work as a GP in a rural community. The rural doctors studied by Horobin and McIntosh certainly found this difficult. What the authors call their 'embeddedness in the community' had both its rewards and its problems, and meant that they could never really be off duty (Horobin and McIntosh, 1977, p. 96).

Banton has called this phenomenon the 'contamination' of the private person by the occupation (Banton, 1964, p. 197). In his own analysis of the police, he suggests that there are two particular characteristics of police work which require that the police be 'set apart' to some extent: they have access to privileged information, and they do a job which requires that everyone be treated on an equal footing (ibid., ch. 7). If he is correct, then a number of other occupations have the same characteristics: doctors, clergy and Members of Parliament, for example, all do jobs in which they have privileged access to information, and are assumed to treat everyone alike. The reason why these occupational features have the effect of 'setting apart' the incumbents would seem to be the presumed dangers of breach of confidentiality and of favouritism. Those dangers are greatly enhanced if the work is conducted in a settled and identifiable community, and it is in those settings especially, therefore, that certain jobs carry with them the 'public figure' status, where the individual is not available for some of the normal processes of community life, like purveying gossip or taking sides in local disputes. As Banton observes, 'The policeman, like the clergyman, is required to be a bit better than everyone else' (ibid., p. 190).

It would be misleading, however, to imply that the processes of contamination apply only to professional work, or only to stable 'community' settings. *All* doctors, for example, will be subject to the expectations of confidentiality and impartiality. But those who work in cities and in hospitals do have more opportunities to develop a lifestyle in which they can foster alternative identities. The use of the police as one of the main examples of contamination should already have underlined that this does not apply solely to professional work. Prison officers are another group to whom it can apply, and again the inability to talk freely about work provides one of the main mechanisms by which they are set apart. 'Even if the prison officer wants to have social relationships with ordinary people outside, the prison officer is under a special kind of constraint. His work has a strong, macabre kind of fascination for the ordinary citizen, yet the officer, bound by the Official Secrets Act, cannot talk freely about his job as can the busman, foreman or office worker' (Morris, 1963, p. 8). One important mechanism for the setting apart of certain non-professional workers is the wearing of a uniform, which enables them to be identified as 'public figures' and distinguished from other members of the working classes, with whom they might otherwise be confused because of their accent and manner. Thus Morris notes that prison officers are identified with the prison even on their journeys to work through the wearing of a uniform (ibid., p. 8). Some professional workers who are set apart also wear a uniform, although they may well not wear it all the time: the clergy, for example. For professional 'public figures' a uniform is less necessary, since their accent and manner (produced through their background and training) should be enough to mark them out.

If 'public figures' are contaminated by their work, it is equally true that their wives experience a kind of vicarious contamination. This means that they experience some of the consequences of being a public figure without having been appointed, elected, or paid to be one. Nevertheless, in certain circumstances a wife will be expected to behave *as if* she had been. Papenek refers to this as situations where 'the wife's participation is almost, but not quite, formally institutionalised – the ambassador's wife, the mayor's wife, the wife of a large foundation representative abroad, the wife of a company president, the First Lady, and so on. All of these women are expected to give acknowledged public performances, as are the wives of political candidates' (Papanek, 1973, p. 862).

What effects does this vicarious contamination have upon a wife? In various situations these seem to include: expectations that she will conduct herself 'appropriately', being held at arm's length by other people, being treated with deference or hostility. In short, she seems to experience in routine social relationships the same patterns which her husband experiences in his particular occupational location. But there is an additional element for his wife, since her vicarious setting apart means she is also on show as a *wife*, and liable to be subject to additional expectations as a consequence.

Studies of police wives provide good illustrations of feeling that one is expected to act in certain ways – to be a bit better than everyone else – because one is married to policemen. 'A higher standard is expected of the policeman and his family in many matters, and they are all very much aware of this...the country policeman is highly vulnerable to criticism from his neighbours' (Whittaker, 1964,

p. 125). In Mitchell's survey, although about a quarter of all wives felt that 'the nature of their husband's job affected the way they were treated by neighbours', Mitchell argues that the extent to which a police wife will be seen as an extension to her husband depends upon the 'visibility of the police family's status' (Mitchell, 1975, p. 84), so that wives of city police are less at risk.

Wives of the clergy also feel very much under scrutiny about their own conduct, and that of their families. They often feel particularly uncomfortable on their children's behalf. As one anglican said,

> They expect you to do what they won't do. They expect clergy kids to be marvellous and do this, that and the other; quite honestly they're just ordinary kids and I think they want an ordinary kind of life. (Spedding, 1975, p. 304)

However, it is not easy to simply dismiss these kind of expectations since they also, by implication, put a wife under scrutiny as a good mother. As one baptist minister's wife admitted,

> I think there are times when ministers and their wives expect more of their children, or tend to want them to conform, simply because of what Mrs So and So will say. And often people do look upon them and criticise them if they are not perfectly behaved and so on. (loc. cit.)

Wives of the clergy actually vary very much in their response to being the wife of a public figure. In my study, they were fairly evenly divided on the suggestion that a clergyman's wife ought to make her home and family a model for the rest of the congregation or parish: the majority rejected this idea, some reacting against it strongly, but two-thirds accepted it as an ideal to which to aspire, with anglicans and baptists especially likely to hold this view (ibid., pp. 304–6).

A particular problem for wives of 'public figure' men is to find a basis upon which social relationships can be conducted, and especially to make friends. The two key elements here seem to be: the feeling that one is being kept at arm's length by other people; secondly, the recognition that it might be regarded as inappropriate to have close friends in the community where one's husband holds a 'public' position.

The clergymen's wives in my study reflected both of these very clearly; for example:

> I think that sometimes people don't talk to you about the ordinary things that you would want to talk about...They just think of the minister and his wife as being something different, not one of us. (ibid., p. 314)

The feeling that one is regarded as not available for normal friendly relations is paralleled by queries about the appropriateness of friendship. Although clergy wives are about equally divided about whether they ought to 'allow' themselves to have local friends, almost all recognised this as extremely problematic. The underlying reasons for this relate to the key features of 'public figure' jobs – confidentiality amd impartiality. The consequent setting apart applies equally to the clergy wife – for her to have friends offers the potential for divulging confidences or showing favouritism, both of which would be as inappropriate for her as for her husband. One respondent, a woman in her twenties with three young children, described vividly the kind of dilemma in which this had placed her:

> We were taught at theological college, by the principal's wife, that it is wrong to have close friends; and for the first eighteen months here I was extremely careful. I found it very, very hard going, and I had a terrific struggle with this problem:

> should I or should I not? There was one girl I was particularly drawn to – we get
> on like a house on fire, we are just the same sort of people. I sort of warded it off
> for ages and ages, but I *needed* friendship locally, and she was a Christian. And in
> the end I just thought, well, this is ridiculous. I analysed my reasons for it, and in
> the end I could find absolutely no reason for not having a close friend. Otherwise
> it makes you somehow different, if you decide you're going to be aloof, it adds to
> the picture of being different. So I gave in in the end, and it worked out really well.
> (ibid., p. 318)

It is clear from this that the woman involved went through considerable personal
agony as a result of the presumed bar on friendship deriving from her husband's
job; and it is interesting that, even when she decided to make a friend, she thought
of this as 'giving in'.

Wives of other 'public figures' also experience similar dilemmas, and the
feeling of being kept at arm's length. One police wife described the feeling of
'restraint when they know that my husband is in the police' (Mitchell, 1975, p. 85),
and one-quarter of Mitchell's sample felt that the nature of their husbands' job
affected the way they were treated by neighbours (ibid.).

A further way in which wives experience the effects of a 'public figure' husband
is by being, as it were, bracketed with him, and treated with the same kind of
mixture of deference, awe, sycophancy, or hostility with which he is treated. This
may be quite pleasant if it is deference, but less so if it is hostility. Despite the
scepticism of the May Committee on this point, prison officers believe that other
people often treat them with hostility because of their job (*Committee of Inquiry into
the United Kingdom Prison Services*, 1979, para. 8.2), although the consequences for
their wives are not spelled out. Police wives talk similarly about reflected hostility.
In the milder examples they are simply given a wide berth, as with this example
of a police wife going into a local shop:

> There'll be the usual huddle in the middle of the floor and conversation going on.
> It dries up when they go in, and everyone moves up to the counter to be served.
> After they have been able to get served, they hear the hubbub break out again after
> they come out. I don't know if it's hostility or sheer suspicion. (Banton, 1964, p.
> 200)

A somewhat more extreme example was given to Mitchell by a city police wife:

> I could not leave my house for them shouting abuse at me and if they were near
> enough they spat on me. When I washed my steps or the close, the children came
> and urinated on them – they also rubbed excreta on my doormat. (Mitchell, 1975,
> p. 86)

Whilst not wishing to suggest that incidents of this sort are necessarily a common
occurrence, the very fact that they *can* happen indicates the extent to which wives
of men in certain occupational settings do become very closely identified with their
husband's work, and experience the consequences of it vicariously.

Finally, what strategies are possible for wives who wish to mitigate, or more easily
to accommodate themselves to, the effects of vicarious contamination? First, one
can try to turn it to one's own advantage. Wives of men who are regarded as
important figures nationally or locally presumably can use their position in a
variety of ways, and some may become quite skilful at it. Wives of somewhat lesser
public figures can also turn it to their advantage: some of Mitchell's police wives
said that their association with the police acted as a good character reference when
they were seeking employment.

> You automatically gain a position of trust and respect by employers. (Mitchell,
> 1975, p. 88)

Secondly, wives develop strategies for handling social relationships, in which they try to minimise the significance of their 'wife of' identity. The two main ways in which this seems to be done are concealment and seeking out the company of others in a similar situation. Concealment is a strategy which seems to be used in situations where it is important to preserve a distance from the work – on holiday, for example, which for some workers may be the only time when they are really 'off'. A police respondent in Banton's earlier study described the consequences of failure to conceal successfully:

> I remember being in a boarding house up in Arbroath and it was nice and sociable until someone asked my wife what I did, and as soon as the police were mentioned you could sense a change in atmosphere...I had to make a conscious effort to overcome what happens to you then. (Banton, 1964, p. 200)

Attempts to conceal are a response to recognising that one's occupational identity, or the vicarious one attributed to a wife, will be regarded as one's 'real' identity, or at least the one which takes precedence over all others (Mitchell, 1975, p. 88). Failed attempts to conceal are experienced as a kind of unmasking, as a relevation of the key piece of information about oneself.

Concealment is hazardous because of the constant danger of unmasking, and once the vicarious occupational identity is revealed, a wife probably will find it very difficult to establish her own identity in any other light. So it is not surprising that wives commonly adopt the alternative strategy and seek company among what Mitchell classes 'safe categories', people among whom they have a personal identity, primarily long-standing friends and family (Mitchell, 1975, p. 88). The company of wives of men in the same occupation is also sought, since they too constitute safe categories. Morris has described how social life for many prison officers and their wives centred on the company of like others.

> One of the striking things about the staff community is that whether it is in a city prison or in an isolated country district, socially it is just as remote from the outside world. The reference groups tend to be the staff and families of other institutions, thus coachloads of officers and their wives travel between the social clubs of Pentonville, Wandsworth, Brixton and Wormwood Scrubs. (Morris, 1963, p. 8)

Much more recently, the May Committee still found prison officers, including governors, to be a 'somewhat inward-looking group' (*Committee of Inquiry into the United Kingdom Prison Services*, 1979, para 8.3), and firmly placed the blame for this upon the officers themselves: 'we think the tendency of members of the service primarily to seek out each others' company is substantially a matter of choice and convenience; it does not necessarily flow from their occupation' (ibid., para 8.2). The committee apparently fails to recognise a crucial point: what appears to be an individual as the most convenient and congenial choice is itself partly a product of the conditions under which the work takes place.

These strategies for forming friendships are very important, because they offer some pointers to the process of bargaining of identities, and the extent to which wives are constrained by features of their husbands' work when they undertake this process. Certainly it seems that being the wife of a public figure means that one's room for manoeuvre is very tightly circumscribed.

References

Banton, M. (1964) *The Policeman in the Community*, London Tavistock.

Bell, C. (1968) *Middle Class Families*, London, Routledge and Kegan Paul.

Cain, M. (1973) *Society and the Policeman's Role*, London, Routledge and Kegan Paul.

Chamberlain, M. (1975) *Fenwomen: A Portrait of Women in an English Village*, London, Virago/Quartet Books.

Church of England (1980) *Alternative Service Book*, London, Hodder and Stoughton.

Committee of Inquiry into the United Kingdom Prision Services (1979) (The May Committee), Cmnd 7673, London, HMSO.

Deem, R. (1981) 'Women, leisure and inequality', paper presented to the Annual Conference of the British Sociological Association.

Dennis, N., Henriques, F. and Slaughter, C. (1969) *Coal is our Life*, 2nd edn., London, Tavistock.

Fowlkes, M.R. (1980) *Behind Every Successful Man: Wives of Medicine and Academe*, New York, Columbia University Press.

Haberstein, R.W. (1962) 'Sociology of occupations: the case of the American funeral director', in A.M. Rose (ed.), *Human Behaviour and Social Process*, London, Routledge and Kegan Paul, pp. 225–46.

Horobin, F. and McIntosh, J. (1977) 'Responsibility in general practice', in M. Stacey, M. Reid, C. Heath and R. Dingwall (eds), Health and the Division of Labour, London, Croom Helm, pp. 88–114.

Hunt, P. (1980) *Gender and Class Consciousness*, London, Macmillan.

Marsh, A. (1979) *Women and Shiftwork*, Office of Population, Censuses and Surveys, Social Survey Division, London, HMSO.

McPherson, M. (1975) *The Power Lovers: An Intimate Look at Politicians and Marriage*, New York, Putnam.

Mitchell, S. (1975) 'The policeman's wife – urban and rural', *The Police Journal*, vol. 48, pp. 79–88.

Morris, P. (1963) 'Staff problems in a maximum security prison', *Prison Service Journal*, vol. II, no. 6, pp. 3–15.

Owen, T. (1980) *The wrong side of the tracks*, Low Pay Unit Pamphlet no. 14, London, Low Pay Unit.

Pahl, J.M. and Pahl., R.E. (1971) *Managers and their Wives*, Harmondsworth, Penguin.

Papaneck, H. (1973) 'Men, women and work: reflections on the two-person career', *American Journal of Sociology*, vol. 78, no. 4, pp. 852–72.

Rapoport, R. and Rapoport, R.N. (1969) 'Work and family in contemporary society', in J.N. Edwards (ed.), *The Family and Change*, New York, Knopf, pp. 385–408.

Roth, J. (1963) *Timetables: Structuring the Passage of Time in Hospital Treatment and Other Careers*, New York, Bobbs-Merrill.

Salaman, G. (1971) 'Two occupational communities: examples of a remarkable convergence of work and non-work', *Sociological Review*, vol. 19, pp. 389–407.

Smith, D. (1973) 'Women, the family and corporate capitalism', in M.L. Stephenson (ed.), *Women in Canada*, Toronto, New Press, p. 5–35.

Spedding, J.V. (1975) 'Wives of the Clergy', unpublished PhD thesis, University of Bradford.

Whittaker, B. (1964) *The Police*, Harmondsworth, Penguin.

Whyte, W.H. (1971) 'The wife problem', in C.F. Epstein and W.J. Goode (eds), *The Other Half: Roads to Women's equality*, Englewood Clifts, NJ, Prentice-Hall, pp. 79–86.

Young, M. and Willmott, P. (1973) *The Symmetrical Family*, London, Routledge and Kegan Paul.

14   Learning about Work

IAN JAMIESON AND MARTIN
LIGHTFOOT

Learning *about* work can be treated as logically distinct from (let us say) learning *for* work. It is, however, extremely difficult to separate the two in practice. It might seem at first sight that learning *about* work would be concerned with work in general, while learning *for* work would be concerned with the specific work which the individual pupil will eventually undertake. But learning *for* work must involve the acquisition of at least some skills and knowledge which are general and not specific to the work which pupils will actually do. Conversely, learning *about* work needs to include at least some learning about specific roles which pupils are likely to adopt, if only as a means of relating the (potentially inert) knowledge about work and the working world to individual pupils' interest and aspirations.

If the two forms of learning are difficult to distinguish in practice, it is also difficult to separate out the various pressures from the outside world to persuade schools to pay more attention to such learning. The Schools Council Industry Project has used a categorization based on three overlapping sets of pressures or expectations: 'industrial society', 'employment' and 'technology'. Each starts from different assumptions and different perceptions of the nature of the problems which schools should be helping to solve. Thus the 'industrial society' group include such concerns as the need to understand the way the nation 'earns its living' and the role of trade unions; the 'technology' group is aimed at diminishing the theoretical bias of the scientific curriculum and the higher status which 'pure' science is said to enjoy; while the 'employment' pressure is aimed at greater stress on preparation for work and for specific jobs (SCIP, 1979; for an alternative categorization, see Castles and Wuestenberg, 1979, pp. 156–162).

But such categorizations do nothing to help separate out learning *about* and learning *for*. It would be possible to take any of these pressure groupings and interpret them alternately as general or vocational in either intention or implementation. For example, the technological pressure might give rise to a desire to improve the image of technology in the eyes of able pupils, or to a move to develop the experience of actually designing and making things, or to a programme designed to illuminate the role of technology in modern society.

To understand how external pressures of these kinds become interpreted by the schools, it is necessary to analyse in depth the character of the measures which schools adopt. It is not possible to assess how schools respond merely by analysing the character and motives of the external pressure groups or by examining the form of schools' responses or their stated intentions, which may differ from classroom practice and may in any case be consciously designed to divert outside pressure from having any significant effect on the main ideals and practice of the school. In the most general terms, we can say that the formal nature of any measure introduced by the school does not inevitably predict the degree to which the emphasis which it embodies in practice is general or vocational. Certain kinds of

Ian Jamieson and Martin Lightfoot, in *Educational Analysis*, vol. 2, 1981, pp. 37–51.

measures may certainly reveal a tendency towards one or the other, but separate analysis is needed to reveal more precisely how schools are actually operating on the learning about/for dimension. We might add that there is a further dimension which merits close attention. This could be called the 'political' dimension: irrespective of whether the school tends towards the learning *about* or learning *for*, there are likely to be considerable differences in the degree to which pupils are encouraged to accept the existing order in the working world.

Such an analysis would be complex and is beyond our present scope. It seems likely that it would need to involve some kind of 'profile' of different elements and emphases, along the lines of that developed by a working party of the Further Education Curriculum Review and Development Unit (1980) for the analysis of social and life skills programmes. It is important to stress, however, that the external pressures on schools are not in practice rigid and inflexible, and they are not simply accepted or rejected by schools. In terms of the actual measures adopted, they can be transmuted by the process of interaction, sometimes to the point of becoming unrecognizable. We will illustrate some of the features of this transmutation process by separating out one strand of the national debate, and examining the form the debate takes at local level and some of the responses to it within schools.

The National Debate

At the national level, the past few years have seen an unprecedented series of reports by various bodies which have been wholly or partially concerned with urging schools to teach more about 'industry' (see Department of Industry, 1977; BAAS, 1977; BIM, 1979; AMA, 1980; CPRS, 1980). The main motive for this has been mounting concern about the declining competitiveness of British Industry. Such a concern is long-standing: it goes back to at least the aftermath of the Great Exhibition of 1851, and a formal organization of industrialists seeking to change school practice existed as early as 1911 (Reader, 1979). The post-war formal organization of this pressure, and its universality, seem to derive mainly from the mid-1970s: it is notable that, for example, the needs of industry scarcely figure at all in the Black Papers of the 1960s and early 1970s.

The recent reports differ in many respects, but they are united on two major points. First, they see the source of many of industry's problems as lying in the unfavourable attitudes held towards it by large sections of the population. Two consequences are said to derive from this: that few of the ablest young people choose a career in industry, and that the workforce itself is apathetic and unco-operative, or even hostile. Second, the reports agree that if education is not the source of these attitudes, then it is certainly the major means by which they can be corrected. (It is fair to add that in the series of reports and conferences that took place between 1976 and 1980, the media ran education a close second as both source and means of correction of these alleged attitudes. Moreover, other means of correcting attitudes were also instituted: initiatives were launched focusing variously on the churches, children's publishing, and Women's Institutes.) The report of a working party set up by the British Institute of Management can stand for many of these documents:

> Everyone – and particularly those actually working in industry or industry-linked jobs, and those guiding the attitudes of the young – should understand at least the reasons for the existence of industry, and the essential contribution it makes to the national wealth and therefore to the quality of life in our society.

> Understanding cannot be established without clear and accurate information.
> (BIM, 1979, p.9)

Much the same basic point is also endorsed, through from a rather different perspective, by the Trades Union Congress:

> The Truth is that most young people leave school politically and economically illiterate. (TUC, 1977)

The principal reason advanced for the schools' malign influence is that teachers themselves are antipathetic to industry. This is commonly supported by reference to the belief that teachers as a group have very little experience of industry, most of them having proceeded from school to college, and then back to school. In a phrase used by Sir Alex Smith (then Chairman of the Schools Council and Director of Manchester Polytechnic), teachers are part of a 'benign circle' in which teachers influence pupils to move into the professions, from which the next generation of teachers emerge to continue the process (for an elaboration of this point, though not the phrase, see Smith, 1976, p. 25).

Three things are notable about these arguments. There is the first confidence – which is flattering but surprising to most teachers – that schools and teachers are so influential in forming the attitudes of pupils. Most teachers, and not just in momentary professional pessimism, would rate their influence as dispiritingly slight in comparison with the media, parents and peer groups. Secondly, there seems to be a clear feeling that teachers are a remarkably homogeneous group, more so than (say) 'managers' or even 'engineers'. Finally, there is a consistent assumption that attitudes towards industry derive from a lack of understanding about it, which in turn derives from a lack of information. The recurrence of these assertions and implications is so constant that they might also be called the key elements in a kind of 'lay orthodoxy' about education.

The Debate at Local Level

It is not part of our purpose to examine these assumptions, though we believe that many of the points made by the series of national reports deserve much closer analysis than they have yet received. For our present purpose we need to say how these pressures from the outside become filtered and interpreted at the level of the school. It is here that we can begin to detect differences between the emphases placed at the national and local level.

By and large, the pressure exerted by local employers on local schools has been comparatively short-term in its motives and largely vocational in character. That is, local employers, who for obvious reasons, tend to be mostly concerned with those young people who are coming on to the labour market within the near future, and they tend to concentrate their criticisms on features of the available young people which they regard as impediments to effective operation in the work-place. The commonest criticisms of this kind relate to basic skills, and to attitudes towards what are regarded as the necessary disciplines of the work-place. There are exceptions to this generalization – for example, many of the large multinational firms do take a longer–term view of the role of schools. But while local employers certainly subscribe to the attitudes/understanding/information paradigm which has been a feature of the national debate, they do not on the whole regard teaching *about* work as particularly important. Local employers engage with education largely to solve employment problems which they are experiencing directly themselves.

The differences between the emphases placed at the national and local levels begin to create ambiguities which teachers have to negotiate. Teachers frequently find themselves entering into dialogues in the expectation of taking up a national debate, only to find that local agendas are rather different. At this point a fundamental conflict of interest seems to occur. Many of the problems which employers confront are the direct consequence of changes in the employment structure of the community, or of changes in the educational structure: in particular, more youngsters staying on in the educational system, thus changing the nature of the group from which employers recruit. Schools are concerned with the whole ability range; local employers are largely concerned with lesser-achieving pupils who leave early. Schools see themselves as educating for a lifetime, and not only for the period between 16 and 20; local employers have a narrow focus of interest.

Such differences are exacerbated by the national concern about youth unemployment, which contributes to a feeling in schools that it would be unwise to tie the curriculum too closely for employment prospects. While most teachers are pragmatic about the need for young people to acquire jobs which they like and which are suited to their abilities and aptitudes, they are also acutely aware that the role of the school is, in large part, to diminish the predictive effects of social class, parental attitudes, and the immediate environment on pupils' aspirations and expectations. Hence teachers' resistance to the notion that a significant part of their function is to prepare pupils for specific jobs. This resistance can even be detected where the realities of certain pupils entering certain kinds of jobs is virtually inescapable.

There is, too, a fundamental ambiguity in the employers' role as agents of curriculum change. On the one hand, employers are suspicious of educational innovation, and many incline to the view that ill-considered changes are the main source of the problems which they are encountering with young people in the work-place. As a consequence, their instinctive response is to press schools to revert to traditional curriculum patterns. On the other hand, since employers are widely concerned about young people's attitudes – towards the disciplines of the work-place if not towards industry in general – they are aware that changes in the character of the curriculum may be necessary.

We have only sketched these ambiguities in a general way: they are complex, and local circumstances can modify them considerably. In general, however, the role of teachers in these exchanges is to *generalize*, while that of employers is to *particularize*. That is, teachers are concerned to convey messages to pupils which are transferable and not specific to particular jobs, while employers are much more concerned to convey what actual jobs are like and what they require of the people who do them. For this reason, the national pressure to teach *about* work is more likely to be supported by teachers than by local employers, though their reasons for supporting this emphasis are different from those advanced nationally. The resulting tension can lead to somewhat tenuous local agreement on programmes which are supported for perceptibly different reasons by local employers and teachers. This is especially true in many of the schools in the Schools Council Industry Project, because the project encourages schools to secure the participation of local employers and trade unionists in curriculum planning and implementation. For example, a work-experience scheme may be introduced: while employers see this as an excellent way of improving career choice and inducting pupils into 'appropriate' attitudes, teachers may be using the scheme as part of an 'understanding industrial society' course with a 'research' element for pupils to undertake while they are in the firm. Or again, mock interviews may be laid on, with real personnel managers from industry: while the employers may see this as a natural piece of training for a situation which the pupils will soon meet, teachers may be more interested in the value of the exercise in improving social skills and developing a self-view.

We have used the words 'ambiguity' and 'tension' to describe the situation we have observed, and this may be unjustified. We might, for example, have called it a 'compromise', which would give the impression of a more balanced attempt to meet the needs of the outside world while respecting the ideals of the schools. Such judgements cannot be made in general terms: the profiles of individual schemes need to be assessed individually. But however the process is described, it seems clear that in practice the schools tend to transmute the national pressure to teach *about* work into a means of modifying local pressure and delaying or blurring vocational influences on pupils. Hence a common feature of schools as they go through this process is not the introduction of 'industry' or 'work' into the curriculum as a distinct academic offering, in the way that economics or French is offered, but the use of techniques which have usually been associated with vocational choice and preparation to serve a much wider purpose. Such techniques include work experience, interviews, the use of adults other than teachers in the classroom, simulation and role-play. At the same time, it is this local 'compromise' that makes analysis so difficult. If activities are instituted and labelled as part of a kind of *entente* between conflicting local interests, how can we distinguish the label from the reality?

Curriculum Strategies

Despite these difficulties, we believe that it is worthwhile attempting to analyse in some detail how schools cope with the task of learning about work. We must realize that not only do schools very often 'convert' these national and local pressures into a variety of different schemes to secure a wide range of educational objectives, but that teachers have to accommodate all this into the structure and process of a school. At this level any 'solution' to the problem of learning about work has to deal with organizational constraints like the timetable 'cover' arrangements, and the examination system. A simple but useful way of looking at the way schools handle learning about work is to pose the question: how does it get on to the timetable? There are three main solutions adopted by schools: the general course; the examination course; and the across-the-curriculum approach.

In the Schools Council Industry Project, from which we are drawing a lot of the data for this article, the most common way of including teaching about work was by incorporating the topic into a general course that already existed in the school for the fourth and/or fifth years. The majority of these courses are based round the theme of 'living in a modern industrial society'. Such courses are very often designed, or at least used, by schools to accommodate a variety of 'demands' made by those outside the school (for example, parents, industry, or the LEA) for the inclusion of subject matter which is thought to be necessary for a child's education, but which does not easily fit into the existing curriculum slot. Examples of these topics include health education, moral education, political education, economic education, occasionally careers education, and 'the world of work'. One can immediately see the potential difficulties of such courses. The treatment of each issue area is likely to be relatively superficial because of the large amount of ground to be covered. The course is likely to lack conceptual coherence, particularly if it is taught by teachers from a variety of subject backgrounds, which is commonly the case. The most usual organizing framework in Industry Project schools was one that started from the standpoint of the individual and considered a range of questions and problems which were likely to face him or her in living in a modern society: coping with the world of work was clearly an important one.

Many of these 'general courses' have one important advantage for schools which believe that learning about work is something that every pupil should be exposed to – they are often taken by *all* children. If there are omissions, then it is usually the top ability band which does not take the course, being left to concentrate on its examination courses. It is of course possible for learning about work to be itself dealt with via an examination course. This was, however, the least common mode of approach adopted by schools in the Industry Project. There are several reasons for this which are worth noting. In the first place, making such a course culminate in a public examination invariably means that it becomes an option, so that many pupils will not take it. Furthermore, such courses discriminate against the less-able pupils who, on one view of learning about work, have the most to gain from this area of the curriculum. Again, an examination course very often means that the school has to clear a space in the timetable for the new option, and this is always difficult. It also upsets the existing balance of the various subject interest groups, and either requires a remarkable degree of consensus amongst the teachers on the importance of the new subject, or a good deal of political adroitness on the part of the management team: the 'liberal education' caucus is likely to be sufficiently strong in many schools to articulate considerable opposition to what can often be construed as vocational education. And even supposing that there is consensus in the school on the importance of learning about work for a child's education, it is not likely that this will be translated into an *examination* subject, or indeed even into a subject at all. There are no examinations in 'careers' as a subject, and it is difficult to think of the consequences of 'failing' to learn about work.

Another problem with the examination course in this area of the curriculum is that there is a tendency for examinations to foster the acquisition of facts and content at the expense of attitudes and skills. We have already suggested that teaching about work tends to rely more heavily on exposing pupils to a wide range of experience and processes than do many other areas of the curriculum, and although it is by no means impossible to accommodate activities like work experience, factory visits, role-plays and simulations in examination courses, it is generally accepted that it is more difficult. The main source of the difficulty can be well illustrated by the case of pupil work experience, where the control of the experience which is to be examined passes out of the hands of the teacher. It is difficult to examine what pupils have learned about work from work-experience placements which have all been markedly different from one another. Such problems can only be partly ameliorated by the use of a suitably designed Mode 3 CSE, where course-work makes an important contribution to the final results.

Many existing examination syllabuses cover, in one way or another, learning about work. Those that seem to make it an important issue include: economic and social history; social studies (including sociology); industrial studies: civics (including political studies and government); economics; history; business studies and commerce; and a miscellaneous category, which would include community studies and religious studies. It is difficult to draw out generalizations from these courses, particularly as so much depends on the way the teacher handles them, but we would offer two observations. First, unlike many of the general courses that we have already referred to, the emphasis tends not to be at the level of the individual, but rather on the institutions of work (and those impinging on it): this shift of emphasis partly accounts for the greater stress on content than on processes in these courses. Second, we would note the rather limited attention to the study of the trade unions, much of it concentrating on historical aspects of unionism.

One of the main objections that could be brought against having an examination course on work or industry is that it compartmentalizes an issue which is of relevance right across the curriculum. This can lead to a situation where individual subject specialists believe that they have been relieved of the responsibility of relating their subject to the world of work. One solution to this problem is to try to get teachers of every subject in the school timetable to think about the implications of their subject for learning about work, just as subject departments in many schools have been encouraged to think about language use, or the multi-ethnic implications of what they teach. The main advantages of this across-the-curriculum approach are easy to list: learning about work occurs naturally in the general learning process; there is minimal disruption to time-tabling; every pupil is exposed to learning about work. The disadvantages are also clear: in particular, unless there is a 'lead subject' like careers or social studies or social economics, or unless there is a degree of across-the-curriculum planning which is unusual in schools, there is no guarantee that the pupil will learn anything fundamental about the world of work. Furthermore, the fate of other 'across-the-curriculum' approaches like language across the curriculum and multi-racial education shows the extreme difficulties in getting a wide range of subjects to take on issues which, in principle, most teachers would accept as affecting most subjects.

Methods

Schools have been encouraged from a variety of sources not only to reflect the world of work in what they teach, but also to bring pupils closer to the realities of the working world. We can recognize three main ways in which they try to do this: through pupils going on work visits or work-observation schemes to industry; through pupils going on work experience; and through industrialists coming into schools to help in the process of learning about work. The use of these process-based teaching strategies reflects certain changes in the teacher's role, whereby he sees himself no longer as the sole or even main source of information for his pupil – the expert teaching the ignorant – but rather as the manager of learning situations and resources. There are a number of reasons for the greater stress on process-based teaching in this area. One is that many of the courses are interested in transmitting not so much a body of knowledge, as certain skills and attitudes. Again, insofar as work is placed alongside such topics as health education or moral education, they too stress the acquisition of attitudes rather than knowledge, and tend to be heavily process-based. Moreover, with industry so powerfully represented in the hinterland of many schools, often in the role of critical consumer, some teachers regard it as sensible and prudent to involve them in the process of learning about work.

The three processes of learning about work that we have enumerated above are all different, but they raise some general problems for teachers. First, managing these learning experiences is quite different from straight didactic teaching. The major difference is that, as we have already suggested, the teacher has much less control over the learning situation, particularly in the case of work experience. This difficulty is compounded by the fact that these experiences are much more *public* than most teaching that goes on in schools, and mishaps are therefore potentially much more damaging to the teacher and the school. The second general problem relates to whether the teacher is likely to receive support for this form of learning from colleagues in the schools and the wider community. Schools still tend to be relatively isolated institutions, and their organizational arrangements reflect this. Pupils going out of the school on an industrial visit or to a work-experience placement disrupt an organization that is likely to be relatively inflexibly timetabled in order to cope with the complex business of teaching a lot of different subjects to a large number of children of various ages. Neither are many secondary schools well equipped to receive outsiders, particularly if the outsider does not wish to participate in units dictated by the school organization (for example, thirty pupils for forty minutes). Moreover, the teacher cannot be sure that such process-based learning will gain whole-hearted approval from parents. 'Remoteness from industry' does not seem to figure high on the list of parental (or teacher) concerns: a *Sunday Times* survey of parents which examined the matters that parents said worried them most showed it second to bottom of a list of 14 items, only religious education causing less concern (Wilby, 1978). Again, research evidence seems to suggest that many parents, particularly those in the lower socio-economic groupings, favour the control-and-content' style of teaching over the more 'discovery-oriented' style (Musgrove and Taylor, 1967). On the other hand, there is plenty of evidence to suggest that parents *are* concerned about the future job prospects of their children.

Work visits and work observation

Work visits should really be separated from work observation: in the former case typically a group of pupils tour a work-place in a relatively short space of time, certainly within the confines of a day: in the latter, individual pupils, or *very* small groups, observe a particular job or a limited range of jobs for a period of time, often extending over a number of days. What is learned about work on a visit depends on two main factors: the nature of the briefing given to the pupils (this acts like a pair of spectacles through which jobs can be seen); and what is shown to the pupils. The most common curriculum framework for visits is science and technology, and here the concentration is likely to be on the physical process of work operations rather than on the work itself. The curriculum framework of many such visits is also relatively weak, partly because teachers have to arrange the visits to suit the firms rather than to suit the appropriate place in the curriculum, and partly because many firms tend to offer schools a standardized package, a 'Cook's tour', which is the same for all pupils.

Even on work observation it is relatively rare for pupils to gain much of an insight into the feelings and satisfactions of ordinary workers. The pupil often has to contend with public-relations messages from the representatives of management. It is difficult to appreciate from the outside the demands and satisfactions of many manual jobs. Pupils (and many of their teachers) witnessing mass production for the first time frequently comment that the only conceivable attractions from such jobs must be purely instrumental – the money. They rarely get to meet and talk to ordinary workers on such visits and observations, and almost never meet trade-union representatives.

Work experience

In many ways it might be thought that pupil work experience would get round some of these difficulties. Certainly the incidence of such schemes is growing: probably one-third of all schools in England and Wales now have a scheme. It is tempting to argue that one of the best ways of learning about work is by doing a job within an educational setting (it is the educational framework which primarily distinguishes such work experience from vacation or 'Saturday jobs'). It is difficult to judge how satisfactory work experience is in bringing about learning, partly because of the enormous variety of such schemes with different aims, durations and pupil selection policies (for an extensive review of such schemes, see Watts, 1980). On the basis of the experience of the Industry Project, however, it would seem that large numbers of schools operating work experience do not place such schemes in an adequate curriculum context to maximize the potential learning gains. Pupils are rarely given assistance in focusing their observations whilst at work: rather it is generally assumed that the experience will 'rub off' on the participants with beneficial effects. A DES survey found that half of the schools which offered work experience failed to find 'adequate' time for preparatory and follow-up work (DES, 1979). Schools often find themselves completely dominated by administrative considerations (for example, finding enough placements) rather than curricular ones. This lack of a curricular framework is exacerbated in those schemes which are run centrally by the LEA, where individual schools find it difficult to relate to the scheme.

Schools have a tendency to locate the work-experience scheme within one department and to compartmentalize it there. There is a particular problem if this department is careers: the other staff are then inclined to take the view that the experience is narrowly connected to some vocational aim, and thus of no concern of theirs. This can have the effect of reinforcing the 'career choice' framework that many children naturally bring to such an experience, and of dissuading non-careers staff from drawing on the experience to widen the pupil's conception of the world of work.

How work experience is organized has a bearing on what a pupil is likely to learn about work. The evidence from our own pupil survey – based on a sample of 684 fifth-year pupils who had been on work-experience schemes in five different LEA regions – strongly suggests that sex and ability stereotyping occurs in selecting pupils for placements. We found no evidence to suggest that the social-class origins of pupils made any difference to the placement decision, but girls and high-ability pupils, although no less likely to go on work experience, were steered away from manual jobs, and from jobs in the manufacturing sector of the economy (all these differences were statistically significant). Such results, we believe, are consistent with a vocational conception of work experience, rather than one whose primary objective is concerned with learning about work. We were also disappointed to note the widespread use of non-union firms in work experience, and the general failure to involve the pupils with trade-union representatives in the firms.

It is difficult enough to assess what pupils learn from traditional subject teaching, and even more difficult to judge what is learned from a period of work experience. Our own evidence was gleaned from asking pupils an open-ended question on what they thought of their work-experience placement(s). The results are detailed in Table 14.1, and provide some support for the view that pupils did learn something about work.

Industrialists in the classroom

If pupils going out of school to learn about industry is an increasingly important part of schools–industry liaison, this can be matched in many schools by the more frequent use of industrialists inside the schools. We have observed three types of involvement. The first type, where the industrialist is involved in making a 'technical' contribution to a school subject, most often in science and technology, has little relevance to learning about work, although it is one of the most common types of school–industry activities.

Table 14.1 Pupils' reaction to work experience

Helped in career choice (pos. or neg.)		Insight into working/work skills		Social/life skills		Cheap labour exploitation		Miscellaneous	
N	%	N	%	N	%	N	%	N	%
109	(23.1)	212	(44.9)	47	(10.0)	17	(3.6)	87	(18.4)

The second type is very much more relevant, and involves the employer trying to convey the ethos of work: what it is like to work, the rhythm and discipline of industrial life, attitudes and social skills required, etc. Teachers outside the careers area often find it difficult to fit such a contribution in, but we have noted its use in broad social-education-type courses, and in subjects in the humanities area of the curriculum. It rarely works well in formal teaching situations, but lends itself more to group discussions, role-play exercises, etc. This is partly because there are potential conflicts of perspective in this area. Certainly, as we have already suggested, there is considerable evidence to suggest that employers regard pupils' attitudes towards work, and their ability to adapt to the discipline of industrial life, as fundamental. But some pupils are only too well aware of the attitudes and qualities required by much of the world of work, *and reject them*. We would reiterate here our earlier point that knowledge does not automatically change attitudes. Moreover, as writers like Epperson (1964) and more recently Willis (1978) have shown, there is in fact a marked continuity between the values, attitudes and behaviour of large sections of the low-achieving school population and much of the sub-culture of industrial manual workers. When management comes to school it tells the pupils about a set of values, attitudes and behaviour it would *like* to see, although this is often passed off as that which prevails. However, pupils have access to the experience of their parents and siblings and, via the mass media, to a much wider population. The spread of industry–education liaison also allows them personal access to the world of work. Our experience shows that they are quick to digest the messages, and that the results are not always to the advantage of employers.

The third type of involvement for employers with schools involves the employer as a purveyor of knowledge about the world of work *per se*: that is, knowledge of the various functions within a business (marketing, production, etc.), the way a firm is run, industrial relations, and so on. In many ways this might seem akin to our first type, in that the employer might be thought of as passing on some purely *technical* knowledge. In fact, there are some differences, and it is because of a failure to appreciate them that this type of involvement often runs into a series of difficulties. Much of what employers have to say about work they treat as 'plain facts', when in reality views on matters concerned with industrial relations, or the economics of the firm, are extremely tendentious. There also may be doubts in the minds of some teachers about whether many of the managers know very much about (say) industrial relations in the UK, even though they may have a distinct view about industrial relations in their own firm or industry. More generally, teachers often find that there are problems in reconciling differences between the 'real world' and textbook theory, particularly in subjects like economics.

When schools invite people from the world of work in to talk with pupils about various aspects of work, it is noticeable that these representatives are nearly always managers or supervisors. Only rarely do they include people representing the ordinary employee or the trade union. This is a pity because the 'ordinary employee' represents by far the largest section of the working population. There are several reasons for it. The contact invariably starts on the managerial level, and there is a natural tendency for it to stick there. There also seems to be a general worry on the part of industrial managers about how employees located further down in the organization might perform in an educational context. Sometimes this seems to be just a worry about competence, but there is also evidence of employers being worried that their employees may not put forward an image of the firm with which they would be altogether happy.

Work and the Trade Unions

The trade-union dimension to the world of work is a wider and more serious problem. The national debate referred to earlier, which provided many schools with an impetus to help their pupils learn about work, made scant reference to the trade unions. Few of the national projects in the school-to-work area include trade-union interests, a notable exception being the Schools Council Industry Project. And even the Industry Project found it more difficult to involve trade unionists in the schools than it did employers. The reasons for this are complex, but include greater scepticism on the part of local trade unionists themselves about the worth of such projects, difficulties in trade unionists getting release from their place of employment, and the teachers' belief that the trade unionists' contribution is less likely to be useful than the employers' (all children eventually need jobs, but few are thought to need unions in quite the same way).

Learning about work is not often placed in its *political* context: that is, in the context of the broad social, economic and political forces shaping it. In many schools, indeed, there seems to be a conscious attempt to keep many of the issues non-political. Part of the explanation lies in the type of courses which generally accommodate such teaching. In the broad 'living in society' courses, or courses organized under the banner of 'social education', the accent is at the level of the individual and his or her *reactions* to larger social forces. Thus, in dealing with unemployment, it is the consequences for the individual that are highlighted rather than the causes of the phenomenon itself. Similarly, rather than dealing with the distribution of rewards at the level of the society, the analysis tends to be at the level of the individual worker's pay packet.

Of course, course content can reflect the abilities and training of the teacher as well as the philosophy of the teaching programme. It is probably true that it is easier to teach about the individual pay packet than about the determination of wages, and it is also easier to relate the former to the experiences of the pupil. We are further inclined to the view that the teachers' subject background is important: the majority of teachers in this area of the curriculum are drawn from careers (itself often consisting of teachers drawn from a very wide spectrum of subject specialisms), commerce and business studies, none of which are subjects that are used to dealing with political questions. This subject bias probably also accounts for our observation that many topics which are potentially full of political questions (for example, how does a firm work) are in the classroom reduced to a series of technical questions, purged of any wider analytical framework.

It is interesting to note that most of our strictures about the avoidance of political questions in dealing with the world of work apply mainly to the employer's world. Teachers appeared to be much more aware of the broader issues surrounding trade unionism: when trade unions were discussed, questions about the closed shop, the right to strike, and the necessity of trade unions, were nearly always considered. We presume that this reflects the culture of our society, where the existence of employers is regarded as 'normal' and 'natural', an accepted part of the fabric of society, whilst the trade unions do not occupy such a legitimate place. There was also some evidence from the Industry Project of teachers being concerned about the possible reaction of employers to what was taught, particularly when there were a lot of liaison activities between the school and employers. In this sense a certain amount of what Bachrach and Baratz (1962) call 'non-decision making' went on in respect to a syllabus content: although there was little evidence of employers actively disapproving of material that was critical of the business world, they exercised power over the situation through the way in which – consciously or unconsciously – they created or reinforced barriers to the public airing of conflicts.

Conclusion

The relationship between the content of education and the world of work is one full of paradoxes at the present time. The industry–education debate which was fuelled by the then Prime Minister's Ruskin speech in 1976 has certainly had an effect on LEAs and teachers. Many feel obliged to be seen to be doing something to knit industry and education closer together. And yet at a time when the mood is favourable on the education side for closer contacts, the interest of industry, and its ability to forge contacts with schools, seems to have waned. The economic recession has meant that many firms no longer have much of a recruitment problem, and this would appear to have been the major reason (though not the sole one) for the participation of many companies in schools–industry work. Furthermore, the recession has damaged the capacity of many firms to assist schools. Nowhere can this be better witnessed than in the case of work experience. The demands of the MSC for placements for the unemployed, and the paucity of work for *anybody* in many companies, have made considerable inroads in the availability of work-experience placements for school pupils. Moreover, although we have argued that the climate on the education side is ripe for greater contact with industry, we must also acknowledge that the depression takes its toll amongst even the most willing teachers. The cut-backs in teacher provision and in public spending on education make *any* changes in educational practice more difficult: it is difficult enough even to hold the *status quo*. And the question 'Are you teaching about the world of work?' would be responded to in many staffrooms by a further question: 'What work?'

References

Association of Metropolitan Authorities (1980) *Education and the World of Work*, London, AMA.

Bachrach, P. and Baratz, M. (1962) 'Two faces of power', *American Science Review*, vol. 56.

British Association for the Advancement of Science (1977) *Education, Engineers and Manufacturing Industry*, Birmingham, University of Aston.

British Institute of Management (1979) *Industry, Education and Management*, London, BIM.

Castles, S. and Wuestenberg, W. (1979) *The Education of the Future*, London, Pluto Press.

Central Policy Review Staff (1980) *Education, Training and Industrial Performance*, London, HMSO.

Department of Education and Science (1979) *Aspects of Secondary Education in England*, London, HMSO.

Department of Industry (1977) *Industry, Education and Management: a Discussion Paper*, London, Department of Industry.

Epperson, A. (1864) 'A reassessment of indices of parental influence in "The Adolescent Society", *American Sociological Review*, vol. 29.

Further Education Curriculum Review and Development Unit, (1980) *Developing Soical and Life Skills: Strategies for Tutors*, London, FEU.

Musgrove, F. and Taylor, P.H. (1967) *Society and the Teacher's Role*, London, Routledge and Kegan Paul.

Reader, D. (1979) 'A recurring debate: education and industry' in Bernbaum, G. (ed.), *Schooling in Decline*, London, Macmillan.

Schools Council Industry Project (1979) *Interim Report*, London, SCIP.

Smith, A. (1976) 'Wisdom lost in knowledge', Bolland Memorial Lecture, Bristol Polytechnic (mimeo).

Trades Union Congress (1977) 'Note of comment on the Government's consultative paper "Education in Schools", London, TUC (mimeo).

Watts, A.G. (1980) *Work Experience Programmes – the Views of British Youth*, Paris, OECD (mimeo).

Wilby, P. (1980) 'Schools: What one thousand parents think', *Sunday Times*, 22 October.

Willis, P. (1978) *Learning to Labour*, Farnborough, Saxon House.

15   Youth Unemployment:
An Old Problem or a
New Life-style?

KENNETH ROBERTS, MARIA NOBLE AND JILL DUGGAN

This paper draws on the findings from 551 interviews among 16–20-year-olds from high unemployment areas in Liverpool, London, Manchester and Wolverhampton. It argues that theories about reponses to unemployment, derived from the experience of earlier generations, cannot be reconciled with the behaviour and attitudes of contemporary youth. To make sense of current developments, and in particular to understand the relevance of recreation in an age of rising youth unemployment, the authors insist that we need to reappraise work and leisure, and recognize the qualitative as well as quantitative aspects of the changes in process.

The Return of Youth Unemployment

During the 1970s mass youth unemployment reappeared, not only in Britain but throughout most Western economies. Levels are expected to rise as we move into the 1980s (OECD, 1980). Everywhere it is described as a worrying trend. The overall gloom owes much to the persuasiveness of those social scientists who spent the decades following the 1930s explaining the debilitating consequences of unemployment. Even economists became convinced that jobs mean more to people than just ways of earning a living. Psychologists and sociologists broadcast their message: jobs structure time, provide individuals with identity and self-respect and are therefore vital for their acceptance as legitimate members of the community. Without work, it was argued, individuals' self-concepts collapse, and the shame and stigma of being workless drive the victims to social isolation (Jahoda, 1979). Theories about these tragic effects of unemployment were derived from research conducted during the inter-war years. As the arguments became widely known they helped create a public climate in which politicians of all parties condemned mass unemployment as an intolerable evil. For young people, passing through a critical phase of personal growth, unemployment was judged potentially disastrous, and since the Second World War this conventional wisdom has remained unchallenged.

We shall not be proposing unemployment and leisure as interchangeable concepts, nor arguing that the young unemployed are a new leisure class whose members are enjoying the time of their lives, or would be if only they were given

Kenneth Roberts, Maria Noble and Jill Duggan, in *Leisure Studies*, vol. 1, No. 2, 1982, pp. 171–82.

ample recreational opportunities. However, we intend to query whether the unemployment theories of the 1930s have the full measure of the current situation. Writers on unemployment have never enjoyed exclusive commentary-rights on the decline of work. Leisure scholars have an equal stake, and have never treated the lifetime being released from work as a calamity. Trimming the working day, week, year and life has been regarded as a legitimate and desirable fruit of industrialism. The perspectives of unemployment and leisure experts have rarely meshed, but this paper argues that cross-fertilization is essential if we are to understand and devise solutions to the predicaments of jobless youth.

Confronting the alleged injuries inflicted by unemployment with the liberating claims made for the growth of leisure obliges us to question the conditions under which time released from work becomes a valuable resource rather than a malady, and to explore whether there might be elements of leisure behind the unemployment statistics. In turn, as we shall see, this forces us to reassess what we mean by leisure and work.

Our evidence is drawn from survey investigations conducted between 1979–81 in six high-unemployment inner-city areas: Brixton, Harlesden, Shepherds Bush, Liverpool, Manchester and Wolverhampton.[1] In each area, between 80 and 100 young people aged 16–20 were identified through systematic household canvassing, and information sought about their experiences since leaving school. The Brixton and Shepherds Bush respondents had spent 17% of their 'working lives' unemployed, those in Wolverhampton 23%, in Harlesden 25%, in Manchester 29% and in Liverpool a massive 45%. In the absence of governmental special measures, all these figures would have been even higher. The aim of the research was to discover what a 25% or 40% level of unemployment means in terms of the career trajectories awaiting school-leavers, and to learn how the individuals directly affected respond. The arguments developed in the following passages are inspired by our informants' stories, which lead us to query whether their predicaments are best understood, and their problems addressed, by making unemployment the central concept.

The Young Unemployed

Many specialist youth and careers workers recently appointed to minister to the young unemployed, who ventured forth expecting to find morale sagging and self-concepts in tatters, have found it impossible to enact their anticipated roles. Some have found themselves needing to convince their clients that unemployment is a problem. Today's young unemployed often fail to react as the classic theories say they should. To understand this obstinacy, the first point to grasp is the extent to which unemployment is normal and accepted in the communities where the jobless young are clustered.

Official measures which record the percentages of those who are out of work at specific points in time underestimate the numbers unemployed at some time or another. In all the areas surveyed *the majority* of our 16–20-year-olds had tasted unemployment. In the different surveys, 44–81% became unemployed immediately on leaving school. No more than 36% of the sample in any area had escaped joblessness competely. With unemployment (conventionally measured) as 'low' as 17%, it appears that approximately two-thirds of school-leavers in a locality can expect some first-hand experience of it. Within our subjects' neighbourhoods, joblessness was neither socially isolating nor stigmatizing (see, also, Rathkey, 1978; Phillips, 1973). Unemployment is probably harder to bear in areas where it is exceptional. Our respondents were not a representative sample of Britain's school-leavers. But Britain's young unemployed are not scattered evenly across the country: they are concentrated in territories resembling our survey areas, where joblessness is common, sometimes almost as commonplace as working.

The next point to underline is that the overwhelming majority spent the greater part of their post-school lives in work. Most left school at 16 either completely unqualified, or with modest qualifications: many more lower-grade CSEs than O-levels. Nearly all found employment within six months of leaving school, though in jobs which tended to be unskilled and short-lived. Job-changing became common throughout our subjects' early years in the workforce, and approximately two-thirds of all departures were voluntary.

As careers officers will often explain, a great deal of youth unemployment is in some senses self-imposed. Over a half of the unemployment episodes recorded in our surveys (other than those immediately on leaving school) were precipitated by voluntary job departures. The young unemployed are not all strenuous job-hunters. Only a minority of our subjects had made weekly or more frequent visits to local careers offices or Jobcentres during their spells out of work. Furthermore, to the frequent annoyance of employment service staff, they sometimes refused the jobs they were offered. This behaviour might outrage taxpaying workers, but it is entirely rational, viewed from the adolescent dole queue. Job-hunting can be soul-destroying. Repeated rejections can hurt more than joblessness itself, which is why so many individuals will wait for reliable tips from friends or relatives, or until careers offices or Jobcentres recommend vacancies for which they believe they will be seriously considered. And even the unemployed maintain some standards. They certainly hesitate before accepting jobs where the wages less travelling and other costs hardly exceed social security entitlement.

Few of the young people we interviewed, with working lives composed of short-lived unskilled jobs, interspersed with spells of unemployment, considered this predicament ideal. Most would have preferred skilled, secure and well-paid occupations. None actually enjoyed being out of work. The main irritations were boredom and lack of money (see, also, Daniel and Stilgoe, 1977). Social isolation and loss of self-respect were not so much the problem as the daily dilemma of what to do and where to go. But these problems often persisted when the young people were working. Many jobs are boring and low paid, and 'desultory' is a recurrent adjective in studies of young people at leisure (Willis, 1979).

If individuals are not officially employed in the formal economy, it does not always follow that they are not working. In the different areas, up to 38% of our respondents admitted to having worked casually, being paid cash in hand for sessions in shops, pubs, cafés and betting offices, for cleaning offices and windows and so on. Few had discovered viable long-term alternatives to regular employment. In areas of high unemployment there is considerable competition for casual work, and as in the formal labour market, young people tend to lose out. But a minority succeeded in supplementing their 'regular' incomes, and however modest its economic contribution, casual work is of cultural significance. In some teenage peer groups, 'hustling' is a status role (Pryce, 1979). Rather than tolerating regular hours for low pay, there can be more status in proving one's ability to get by without surrendering to the system.

Young people not only move rapidly between jobs; they also have a habit of drifting in and out of the labour market with unusual frequency. Young female workers retire into (temporary) domesticity. Some school-leavers look for work unsuccessfully before returning to full-time education. Other young workers leave their jobs to return to college. A few of the registered unemployed are officially part-time, but *de facto* full-time students. In areas of high unemployment, and elsewhere, young people are often marginal members of the workforce in an objective sense, and also, in some cases, on a subjective level. They regard their officially permanent jobs as temporary. Rather than enjoying the conferred identities, many young 'drifters' feel it necessary to distance their real 'selves' from their occupations. There are other statuses to which some can turn.

Describing youth employment as voluntary is usually less than the whole truth. For most of those involved, unemployment is structurally inevitable, since there are fewer jobs on offer than would-be workers. But it remains the case that for some young people intermittent employment becomes part of their preferred life-styles. In districts where jobs are available and firms complain of labour shortages, many young people still prefer to take 'breaks'. To the press and public these individuals are 'work-shy scroungers', but given the types of job locally available, is it fair to assume that their own and society's best interest would be better served if the young people were 'permanently' employed?

The sub-cultural solutions to youth unemployment now being pioneered differ from those that became ingrained during the Great Depression. Society has changed. The welfare state is now taken for granted, many families are able to support the young jobless, and education beyond 16 is more common. The social and economic pressures that produced job-dependence have weakened. Internationally, today's youth are earning renown for 'occupational marginality', preferring independence and novelty to commitment to any single occupation (Gordon, 1979; Gaskell and Lazerson, 1980). A 1978 EEC survey among member nations reports that unemployed 15–24-year-olds display exceptional 'intransigence': they prove less willing than other age groups to lower their expectations, learn fresh skills and move to different towns, and are more likely to regard it as sound advice to refuse unsatisfying work, and to seek jobs in the black economy (EEC, 1979).

Reappraising Work

The now-customary connotations of the term 'unemployment' distort the real situations of many young people without regular jobs. To understand what is happening and to recognize the range of future possibilities, we need theories of employment and unemployment, of work and leisure, attuned to contemporary realities. To begin with, we need to distinguish work from employment. The former is a broader concept. Any action on nature, people or ideas intended to increase their value for future use can be defined as work. The opposite of work, thus defined, is not leisure, but consumption, when we use up value by doing things for their intrinsic satisfaction.

Work need not be remunerated. We can work for ourselves, as when repairing cars and tending gardens, or for our families, as with housework. Some individuals work voluntarily for the wider community, and employment is just one of many possible social relationships within which paid work can be performed. Throughout history men have devised numerous ways of harnessing other people's labour. In feudal times serfs tilled their lords' fields in exchange for the right to work their own plots. Under slavery individuals have been obliged to work in exchange for their lives. Employment, where individuals sell only their 'labour power', for wages, not customary rights, rose to prominence with industrialisation. Flexibility has been its commending feature. Labour can be employed by the week, day or even hour. A lifetime's commitment is unnecessary. Furthermore, employers quickly learnt that financial incentives could be an effective way of motivating employees. Slavery and serfdom fell out of fashion not because people became more humane; they proved less efficient.

Industrialism has been associated with a growth of employment in two senses. Firstly, own-account workers, both artisans and professionals, have declined in prominence. Secondly, various forms of voluntary work have become incorporated in the formal economy, and are now performed by employees. The care of children and other dependent members of the community, and the rise of the leisure industries are prime examples. These trends have made work and employment synonymous in many people's minds, but a great deal of work has always remained outside the formal economy, and since the 1950s we may have been crossing another historic threshold, involving not a 'collapse of work' but a decline in employment. There has been a modest revival of 'own account' working. Even more significant, there appears to have been a transfer of some work into informal economies (Gershuny and Pahl, 1980; Wallace, 1980). The Inland Revenue certainly believes that a black economy has prospered, principally on account of its opportunities for tax evasion. In addition, domestic do-it-yourself and other types of self-service including car maintenance have flourished (Gershuny, 1978). The rising cost of labour has been one contributing factor. Senior managers and professional workers now find that they can save by taking unpaid holidays to renovate houses and decorate lounges, and discover intrinsic satisfaction available from craft-work in one's own time, and at one's own pace. Some of the officially unemployed prefer informal community work to orthodox jobs (Wallace, 1980). Northern Ireland's para-military organizations have been among the beneficiaries.

This 'decline of employment' should not be over-played. Married women have been escaping from full-time domestic labour into the formal economy. Among women, employment is more popular than ever, but this does not obliterate the evidence of non-employment and work-free time becoming decreasingly synonymous. Married women normally return from paid employment to their domestic shifts.

Where does youth unemployment fit in? Firstly, it is misleading to imagine that the lives of the officially unemployed are devoid of work. Some are involved in casual remunerated activities. Others have quasi-occupations based in the domestic economy and part-time education which structure time, confer identity, and earn status in the eyes of peers. Secondly, one alternative to addressing youth unemployment by endeavouring to provide all 16-year old school-leavers with regular jobs would be to recognize and support other types of work.

The Growth of Leisure

To comprehend the reality of today's youth unemployment we need to reappraise work, and understand leisure, a notoriously difficult concept. The standard definitions all say that leisure occurs in non-working time, but no one of repute designates the whole of life minus work as leisure. Its scholars agree that leisure is different from work, but in endeavouring to distinguish their subject-matter from the remainder of non-working life they divide into a panorama of debate within which three main approaches to identifying leisure's character can be discerned.

Some define leisure as a *type of experience*, doing things for their own sake, for the intrinsic satisfaction; what economists call consumption. These definitions do not tie leisure to any particular activities. It is said that everything hinges on the quality of the experience. Gardening, playing football and preparing meals can be work to one person, and intrinsically rewarding to another. A second approach insists that leisure is a *particular type of activity*, or play. We play games, our recreations, whose essential property lies in their separation from ordinary life. Since it is 'only a game' the result does not really matter. Needless to say, many people take their games very seriously. Players normally want to win. This desire is essential to make games enjoyable. But Monopoly is still 'just a game' since the losers do not forfeit all their worldly assets. The consequences of games are contained within the 'field of play', which is why we are able to 'let ourselves go', reveal aspects of our characters that are ordinarily concealed, develop new skills, and try out new personae. The third approach treats leisure as a *type of time*, spare or free time, when we have performed our work and other 'obligations', e.g., sleeping, eating and all the other things we 'have' to do. The residue is labelled 'leisure time', when we can please ourselves.

There is no need to debate the respective merits of time, activity and experience when conceptualizing leisure. Once these 'elements' have been disentangled, the need for any single definition evaporates: we realize that modern leisure is no one 'thing', but has been created by the manner in which industrialism fuses free time, play and opportunities to do things for the intrinsic satisfaction. Modern leisure's elements are not historically novel, but prior to industrialism they were dispersed, alongside work, throughout most people's family, community and religious lives. Industrialism separates production and consumption. It compartmentalizes work, which becomes employment in specialized work organizations for specified times during which the employee is subject to whatever rationality his employer dictates. A consequence is that opportunities to engage in intrinsically satisfying pursuits are concentrated in free time, where they become associated with play. We work at certain times producing certain things in order to consume other things at other times. Leisure thereby becomes the deferred reward for working. Under industrialism, work and leisure form an inseparable couplet, materially and ideologically. Industrialism creates a powerful tendency, though it has never been more than a tendency, towards fusing the elements of leisure, and such a concept becomes necessary to describe the product of their combination.

No one would deny the growth of leisure since the early phases of industrialism. The trends have been towards a diminishing proportion of lifetime in employment, rising levels of consumption and recreational activity. Where arguments arise is on whether this growth has amounted to more than a quantitative progression. Some writers claim that we are now on the verge of a 'society of leisure' in which our self-identities and values that supply meaning to behaviour in other spheres will be derived from leisure interests (Dumazedier, 1974; Kaplan, 1975). Everyone realizes that there will remain more to life than leisure. The 'society of leisure' is offered as a conceptual equivalent to industrial society, suggesting that leisure will become the central process structuring time, shaping our life-styles and self-concepts, acting as the sub-structure for the wider social order by assuming the non-economic functions hitherto associated with employment.

We sympathize with this view that the growth of leisure has involved more than simple quantitative expansion, more people spending more time playing more games for their own sake. At the same time, we suspect that orthodox 'society of leisure' scenarios mistake the nature of the qualitative changes in process. In our view these are best understood as unlocking the time/activity/ experience package that was forged with industrialism. People have gained time free from employment and cash for discretionary spending, but neither has been devoted wholly to play. Individuals have preferred to spend a great deal of their extra time and income on their homes and families, often developing new kinds of 'work' to enhance their overall quality of life. Despite the quantity of time it accounts for, more than any other single leisure activity, television is rarely named as a particularly enjoyable pastime (Young and Willmott, 1973). The activities from which people derive the greatest intrinsic satisfaction are not always the games they play, but sometimes educational, domestic and community work (Andrews and Withey, 1976), and a consequence of the containment of employment, alongside the growth of real incomes, but has to enable people to develop and combine these activities in diverse and novel ways, nurturing life-styles that reflect their varied interests. Writers are acknowledging these trends when they reject 'residual' concepts and advocate treating present-day leisure as a ubiquitous process, or as a quality of life in general, rather than linking it to any specific times, activities or experiences (Murphy, 1974; Nuelinger, 1979).

Its prophets recommend 'flexibility' in order to nourish this quality of life, tolerating diversity in style of marriage, family careers and uses of education, and allowing individuals to arrange the demands of employment to fit their preferred life-styles. There is little evidence of work being humanized by leisure values, but there is a trend towards flexitime, giving individuals scope to arrange their weekly hours of work, and towards flexible work scheduling throughout the life-span. In the near future it is likely that the still orthodox sequence of education, then work, then retirement, will be recognized as just one among many options (Best, 1978) which is where the young unemployed re-enter our discussion.

Youth in a Society with Leisure

Many young people deliberately opt for flexible work schedules. They prefer to work part-time, not every week throughout the year, but by taking full-time jobs for several weeks or months, followed by holidays. They manipulate work so as to gain maximum flexibility. Vacations are taken whenever *they* choose. They have no qualms about taking odd days off. Dismissal for bad time-keeping does not shatter their career plans. If these young people were offered progressive careers and satisfying jobs, perhaps many would change their priorities. But whilst we insist on preserving a market economy that breeds hundreds of marginal occupations and firms that are unable to offer the pay, working conditions or prospects to attract the quality of labour the employers would wish to engage permanently, why should we expect the individuals who are confined to this sector of the work-force to display the commitment of those with 'status jobs'? *Hassle* is one of the most frequently used terms in the young unemployed's vocabularies: 'hassle' by police who want to keep the streets tidy, by Jobcentre staffs and careers officers who believe that all the able-bodied young ought to be working, by parents and teachers who believe that everyone should settle in a permanent occupation on leaving full-time education, and from social workers who assume that the young unemployed must be sad or mad. Why not recognize the sub-employed life-style as a legitimate option that a society with leisure can support?

This suggestion has little relevance to the predicaments of some unemployed young people. The classic theories of unemployment retain some contemporary relevance. School-leavers from 'respectable' families still feel stigmatized when denied employment and protect themselves by withdrawing from social intercourse. Some subemployed young people, particularly those seeking training and career opportunities are anything but reconciled to their circumstances. Then there are the 'unemployables': individuals who prove unable to hold any job for more than a few months or weeks, or even days. During the 1950s and 60s these individuals were seen as chronic job-changers, at odds, and drifting aimlessly. They appeared incapable of settling in any structured situation. In the tighter labour markets of the 1970s and 80s, these same characters have re-emerged as the chronically unemployed. Their volatile career histories quickly diminish their attractiveness to employers, while careers officers and Jobcentre staffs become unwilling to jeopardize their agencies' reputations by recommending such individuals.

The young unemployed are a heterogeneous bunch, and we are not seeking to encapsulate all-comers within a new stereotype. Quite the reverse: we are urging recognition of one aspect of the reigning heterogeneity that has major policy implications. It appears unlikely that additional jobs will be created during the 1980s at a pace matching the current growth of the labour force, thus how to handle school-leavers seems destined to remain a live issue. Some will argue for expanding the Youth Opportunities Programme and subsidizing teenage employees. Others will urge retaining 16-, 17- and maybe 18-year-olds in education. We are warning that some of the intended beneficiaries will resent the hassle. Why not accord young people the legitimate option of not working permanently? Many are able to use the time as productively as the over-60s. If education is to be prolonged, why should it not be through teachers making their courses more attractive? Widening young people's options could have a thoroughly beneficial effect on the quality of the employment they are offered. A working life of 50 years in low-paid, uninteresting jobs is not an attractive prospect. That some young people prefer to delay its onset should surprise no one. Employers realize that marriage and parenthood induce 'responsibility'; hence their prejudice against teenage employees. Why not adopt an equally tolerant response to the young people who wish to defer settling into work habits that employers deem responsible?

Our present-day leisure industries have grown from foundations laid in the 19th century, during the creation of industrial society, when most of our sports and games were rescripted as spare-time activities, consistent with the rhythm of industrial life. If the meaning of leisure is once again changing, we could be on the threshold of another period where our forms of recreation will be revised. Rather than games to be pursued at the end of the working day or week, jobless youth need quasi-occupations, compatible with intermittent paid employment, but which can structure time throughout days and weeks, sometimes years, and supply credible statuses in the community. Will our recreation professions prove capable of tuning to the coping strategies and life-styles that the young unemployed are evolving? Can they teach the youth of Bristol, Brixton, Toxteth and Moss Side anything about imparting meaning and excitement to work-free time?

Note

1. This research was supported by a grant from the Department of Employment, but the views expressed are solely the authors'.

References

Andrews, F.M. and Withey, S.B. (1976) *Social Indicators of Well-being*, New York, Plenum Press.
Best, F. (1978) 'The time of our lives', *Society and Leisure*, vol. 1, 95–114.

Daniel, W.W. and Stilgoe, E. (1977) *Where Are They Now?* London, Political and Economic Planning.

Dumazedier, J. (1974) *Sociology of Leisure*, Amsterdam, Elsevier.

European Economic Commission (1979) *Chomage et Recherche d'un Emploi*, Brussels, EEC.

Gaskell, J. and Lazerson, M. (1980) *Between School and Work*, Vancouver,, University of British Columbia, Faculty of Education.

Gershuny, J. (1978) *After Industrial Society?* London, Macmillan.

Gershuny, J.I. and Pahl, R.E. (1980) 'Britain in the decade of the three economies', *New Society*, 3 January.

Gordon, M.S. (1979) *Youth Education and Unemployment Problems*, Berkeley, Carnegie Council.

Jahoda, M. (1979) 'The psychological meanings of unemployment', *New Society*, September.

Kaplan, M. (1975) *Leisure: Theory and Policy*, New York, John Wiley.

Murphy, J.F. (1974) *Concepts of Leisure*, New Jersey, Prentice-Hall.

Neulinger, J. (1979) 'A report of and comments on the symposium 'Reasons for Leisure: research of factors which influence leisure behaviour', *Leisure Newsletter* 7 pp. 6–7.

Organization for Economic Co-operation and Development (1980) *Youth Unemployment: Causes and Consequences*, Paris. OECD.

Phillips, D. (1973) 'Young and unemployed in a northern city', in D. Weir (ed.), *Men and Work in Modern Britain*, London, Fontana.

Pryce, K. (1979) *Endless Pressure*, Harmondsworth, Penguin.

Rathkey, P. (1978) 'Youth Unemployment on Teesside', unpublished manuscript.

Wallace, C. (1980) 'Adapting to unemployment', *Youth in Society*, vol. 40, pp. 6-8.

Willis, M. (1979) *Youth Unemployment and Leisure Opportunities*, London, Department of Education and Science.

Young, M. and Willmott, P. (1973) *The Symmetrical Family*, London, Routledge and Kegan Paul.

16 American Automobiles and Workers' Dreams

H.F. MOORHOUSE

Introduction

In his classic study of automobile workers Chinoy tried to uncover the ways in which they reconciled the pressures of American culture with the opportunities objectively available to them.[1] He presented the problem as one of the existence of a gap between the grand imperatives of the American Dream and the prosaic possibilities of advancement at a time when long-range occupational mobility or success as an entrepreneur were, virtually, impossible for such men. According to Chinoy this gap was bridged in a variety of ways: some men admitted they were not smart enough or had taken decisions in early life which torpedoed their chances; some were quite cynical about the prescribed means; some contrived to inject 'meaning', 'skill', 'mastery', 'identification' and 'moral worth' into the most mundane, machine-paced and standardized tasks and products; others maintained that they still would, 'one day', start their own business. However, it is two other responses to the disparity between sanctioned goals and real changes which Chinoy emphasizes in his analysis. First, some men reoriented their aspirations away from paid labour and into leisure. Such workers sought to be 'happy' rather than 'successful', or pinned their hopes to their children's lives, or, most significantly, stressed consumption goals and regarded their jobs as just a means to the ends. Second, these workers explained the opportunities that were available to them – in consumption, but especially movement into more secure, regular and less physically onerous jobs in the accents of the cultural imperatives. The nub of Chinoy's argument was that the vocabulary of the 'tradition of opportunity' was now applied to the acquisition of consumer goods, and to the striving for small-scale advance in the work-place. This translation was socially useful for the male individual in proclaiming that he had not reneged on the claims of the culture *but*, so Chinoy believed, it did not actually assuage self-doubt and guilt, and these, insisting on the personal failure and not the structural constraint, were extremely functional for the maintenance of the status quo of American society.

It is rather disquieting to read Chinoy's brief book and to realize how little it has been surpassed as a schematic analysis of reactions to impoverished labour in advanced societies. For all the rediscovery of the significance of the labour process by Marxist writers,[2] and for all that mainstream sociology has kept beavering away, I believe that an analysis of the failings of Chinoy's study can stand as a much more general critique of the conceptual and theoretical approaches of a great deal more work that has been produced, and is constantly being reproduced, in the quarter of a century since he wrote. I make this claim because the assumptions that underlie Chinoy's monograph are shared by most sociology – especially in the

H.F. Moorhouse, in *Sociological Review*, n.s., August 1983, pp. 403–26.

sub-disciplines of social stratification and industrial sociology – and virtually all Marxism. So Chinoy:

1. emphasizes paid labour as the crucial sphere of being, at least for a male life – his dream centres on occupation and production – all the rest of life is determined, is residual and is less worthy of sustained study;
2. utilizes a mainly implicit, qualified, but still vital notion that the dominant values of capitalist society do stress paid labour as the significant arena of male life, the sphere in which men *should* find identity, meaning, personal growth and so on;
3. tends to concentrate on the *formal* structures of time in paid labour – on labour as detailed in procedure manuals and union rules, rather than on the real rhythms of paid labour – how it is actually lived and experienced.

So, and characteristic of a lot of other studies, Chinoy approaches his men as automobile workers – that is what defines them and groups them. He is characteristic too in holding them up for contrast not, I will admit, in the now fashionable glow of some mythical age when every worker was a craftsman, but with some equally idealized group of entrepreneurs, farmers and professionals who, so it is asserted, do identify self with occupation. And again, he insists his workers must suffer from the labour they do. No real evidence or argument is offered as to why the various bridges which he outlines do not actually serve to remove these workers from some experience of 'alienation'. Chinoy describes a number of significant mechanisms which would seem to be able to cope with the apparently disturbing features of factory work in the American milieu only, at the last, to *assert* that these must be unsuccessful. Such labour cannot give a 'rich and full sense of self[3] which Chinoy believes is the cultural demand. The mental ploys he alludes to are dismissed by him as 'makeshift substitutes for full-bodied emotional satisfaction on the job'.[4] They are 'attenuated meanings' which cannot give 'real satisfaction'. While this kind of assertion about the inescapable costs and psychological travail of factory work has echoed in a thousand and one studies since, it does, in fact, cut somewhat oddly across the grain of much that has gone before in Chinoy's analysis, and much that has been uncovered since by perceptive analysts of shop floor life.[5]

Moreover, Chinoy's resort to some axiom that men *must* obtain some vital quality of experience in paid labour, is made all the easier because the cultural benchmark with which he operates – the American Dream – is never really detailed theoretically or empirically but is merely invoked as the creator or at least a buttress of the deleterious effects of factory labour. It is clear that Chinoy believes that the dominant culture of American society somehow foregrounds paid labour as a crucial area of individual endeavour and individual experience for men, but he never states convincingly what social mechanisms are involved here nor argues why his workers should interpret the dream in this way. Thus he alludes to moving up, economic success, personal progress, getting ahead, wealth, occupational advancement, unremitting effort, personal development, meaning in work, independence, and more besides as parts of the Dream and the 'tradition of opportunity', but does not describe when these elements ever hung together or consider whether, in post-war America at any rate, they may have become differentiated and, in certain cases, antithetical. He does not examine whether the very vagueness of the terms he uses may make any Dream susceptible of different interpretations by different groups,[6] nor does he really investigate whether any American Dream may be made up of contradictory messages presented by different social sources. In short, Chinoy fails to detail the dominant values of American society. Had he done so, had be been more rigorous in his specification of the content and forms of the cultural imperatives and of their diverse social sources, he could not have believed that expectations of paid labour and actual experience of it were in the unaligned state his argument assumes. In fact, it is quite easy to argue that the individualism, personal development and meaningful activity which the Dream as work ethic was supposed to encourage was and is actually discovered and displayed well outside the factory walls.[7]

Now, it is true, that in some passages of Chinoy's text there is some recognition of what is at issue here. When he is considering evidence that some of his workers redefined their aspirations away from occupational achievement and wealth towards being 'happy' Chinoy noted:[8]

> Such assertions do not represent a radical rejection of American values. The importance of moral integrity, the happiness to be found in humble surroundings, the spuriousness of the single-minded search for fortune when human values are neglected are all familiar, though usually minor themes in American culture.

However, because of his overall perspective, and the strong desire to pin these workers to an alienation induced by paid labour Chinoy is at pains to argue that such a shuffling of the pack of values governing behaviour does not deny the emotional desirability of economic success (defined as occupational advance), so much as re-weight it in the system of goals. In effect, though, this half recognition of alternative readings of any Dream poses considerable difficulties for the study's overall thrust. For it becomes quite possible that some of the subjective bridges workers used to 'escape' psychological travail are, in fact, part and parcel of the Dream itself, reflections of a profound socialization to the dominant values of US society. For example, Chinoy insists that the urge to purchase consumer goods represents some behavioural shift by workers away from the substance of the Dream towards its symbols. He does note mass media messages urging consumption but sees these as of secondary cultural weight. Chinoy categorizes his workers' stress on consumption goals as 'rationalizations' of their 'real' failure, as attempts to sidestep self-deprecation, doomed to failure because of the insistence of the true American Dream. What seems much more plausible is that different social sources in American society promoted rather different packages of the Dream, and that some of these imperatives were actually quite consonant with, and probably actually helped to produce, the subjective responses to labour of the men of Autotown. It seems quite likely that the themes of the Dream had altered in ways Chinoy did not get to grips with, that the dominant ideas of American society in the middle of the twentieth century had become a good deal more complex and variegated than he allowed and that what he chose to categorize as 'defensive rationalizations' may have stood square in the mainstream of the flow of the Dream for a lot of workers.[9] Indeed, it is quite arguable that the kind of product his men were engaged in making clearly exemplified some of these changes. To put it bleakly, these men and their children may have heard about Abe Lincoln at school but in post-war America their dreams were much more likely to involve a Lincoln in the garage.[10]

As much is suggested in another sociological classic, co-written by Chinoy's mentor, Robert Lynd. Writing about rather similar men in a rather similar town in 1935 the Lynds spoke of 'their great symbol of advancement – an automobile. Car ownership stands to them for a large share of the American Dream, they cling to it as they cling to self respect.'[11] The Lynds' treatment of leisure in *Middletown in Transition* severely undercuts the objectivism of statements by Chinoy that his men faced problems of self-justification because they 'live in a world in which they have manifestly gained no substantial advancement.'[12] Once the role of consumption, consumer goods and a rising standard of living are seen *not* as somehow peripheral to, or challenging, or substituting for some 'real' American Dream, but at some point in time becoming the evidence about, and tools for the experiencing of, personal success, it should no longer be possible for analysts to operate with a notion of an alienation based on paid labour pervading all contemporary life, nor should it be possible to privilege the factory, office, shop or mine as *the* crucial sites of human experience and self understanding, though this is continually done in a lot of sociological and most Marxist theorizing.

Some indication of what is at issue here is contained in another classic of the same vintage as Chinoy's work which provides rather more complicated suggestions about the nature of the dominant values of American society, workers' responses to them and the implications for the basis of individual esteem and significant social relationships in American society. Mills's main focus was on non-manual workers but his analysis had relevance for the lives of all workers – whatever the hue of their collar.[13] Mills was attracted to, but could not accept, the metaphysical notion that the person's self is crucially formed and expressed in the activity of paid labour. The origin of this view, Mills argued, represented some attraction to an idealized craft version of work which, in so far as it had ever represented reality, certainly did not fit the situation of post-war America. Most people had no experience of craft work in practice, nor had they grasped it as an ideal meaning of paid labour. Mills suggested that there are all manner of satisfactions which are obtainable from work which are by no means restricted to the nature and quality of the task itself, but of the greatest significance was the 'big split' of modern life; the sharp division of work and leisure, with the cultural devaluation of paid labour as a significant area of the individual's life – its main, and only crucial importance being the income it generated. Most workers, Mills averred, 'try to build their real life outside their work. Work becomes a sacrifice of time, necessary to building a life outside it.'[14]

In the America of the 1940s and 1950s the gospel of work had been replaced by the ethos of leisure. Leisure, free time, had become *the* crucial existential sphere. The individual, Mills proposed, held two different images of self: the everyday one based on work, and a weekend or holiday one based on leisure and consumption. Associated with this was an alteration, though perhaps it would be more proper to say a diversification, of the messages which explained what 'success' was. Mills noted Lowenthal's work of a decade or more earlier showing a shift to a presentation of heroes of consumption in biographies in popular magazines, with the course of their lives explained in terms of inherent personalities and 'breaks' of the lucky or bad variety. Mills argued that the display by the mass media of a group of celebrities, particularly the Hollywood elite, gave ordinary people a series of models with which they could fantasize, identify and emulate on a lower but parallel level. He also discerned a new literature of inspiration in America in which those who were successful in the Chinoy sense of the American Dream were shown as spiritual failures, as internally unfulfilled and unsatisfied, with no peace of mind. The more positive aspect of this 'Readers Digest philosophy'[15] was that 'the new literature of inspiration holds out internal virtues, in line with a relaxed consumer's life rather than a tense producer's.'[16] Yet this was no simplistic appeal to the power of the mass media – though later studies do seem to reveal significant alterations in media messages in the war and post-war period.[17] Mills was ready to point to a change in the nature of the social ties that bound people. Concomitant with changes in the presentation of values were institutional and structural changes which had affected the nature of status hierarchies and the individual's response to inequality. In the cities of the USA the individual was removed from localized small-scale groupings within which prestige was claimed and acknowledged. Rather the person moved through diverse and separate communities in each of which the individual could advance claims unrelated, or only broadly limited, by his or her position in others. For such claims often depended on consumption and expenditure, and so were limited by income, but anyone could fake or localize in time or space such expenditure so as to 'pass' as a higher status individual for a while. Such efforts, Mills suggested,'[18]

> provide a temporary satisfaction of the person's prized image of self, thus permitting him to cling to a false consciousness of his status position. They are among the forces that rationalize and make life more bearable, compensate for economic inferiority by allowing temporary satisfaction of the ambition to consume.

Mills's analysis is certainly a good deal more compelling than that contained in *Automobile Workers and American Dream* and its like. Mills does pose pertinent problems about the relation of time and 'experience', and of the relative salience of paid labour and free time to the ideas and emotions people have about their own identity and their relations with significant others; problems all too easily ignored in that cyclopoean perspective which, searching for the person, sees only the labourer.

However, Mills' analysis is flawed too, While he empirically rejects the notion that paid labour is somehow *the* crucial existential sphere he is clearly drawn to it as a moral ideal. This uneasy position tends to attenuate and impoverish his analysis of unpaid time. Indeed many of those who, like Mills, have appreciated some of the ideological and behavioural shifts in contemporary capitalism still tend to drift back into an overall approach – hallowed in the sacred nineteenth-century texts of sociology and Marxism – that emphasizes time in paid labour as, literally, the vital part of life. Mills's oftquoted lines, 'Each day men sell little pieces of themselves in order to try to buy them back each night and weekend with the coin of "fun",'[19] deceive in their neatness and are quite incongruous in context as Mills has previously argued that it is just in the buying that people create and feel 'themselves'. Here rhetoric swamps reason, so that, rather like Lowenthal, the stress is all on the triviality of leisure, its passive quality, its formation as a reaction to the forced seriousness and restrictions of degraded paid labour: a viewpoint still paramount with radicals in the 1980s. There is no real appreciation in Mills that there is not just one elite of celebrities in advanced societies but a plurality of elites and that it is just this plurality which promotes some of the cardinal themes of the contemporary Dream – those of individual choice and individual happiness. Nor does Mills appreciate that it is simply not true that the media stories and publicized personalities of all these elites serve to encourage a passive consumption. Often to pursue parallels, to emulate, to identify, involves considerable activity and skill: a creative consumption of commodities, backed up, often with a literature which is quite as urgently inspirational as the prescriptions of any Dream as work ethic. There has been no simple transition in the history of capitalist societies from active and engaging work to a passive and alienated leisure. Moreover, while Mills recognizes that people can locate themselves in structures of status differently at separated times and places, he does not draw out the point that modern society can be conceptualized as consisting of a host of separate status structures, each with its own elite, and one's standing in one of these structures is relatively indirectly linked to one's standing in another. There is, indeed, a relative autonomy of leisure from paid labour *and* it is arguable that it is just in this autonomy that social meaning is found and identity fashioned.

There is, in short, in most sociology and virtually all Marxism a failure to think very seriously about consumption and its place and weight in modern life and autobiography. This intellectual failure is, ironically, clearly demonstrated by the automobile. Both modes of analysis have concentrated on it as *the* production object of the twentieth century[20] but have more or less ignored it as an item in consumption. Yet it is an instrument of mobility and pleasure for most of the population, it is a key commodity in free time and an important icon of the twentieth century, of American 'advance', of 'freedom' and 'affluence'. In the next sections of this paper I want to consider two aspects of the automobile in the sphere of consumption at a period roughly contemporaneous with Chinoy's study to try to uncover what these might suggest about the relation of the automobile and workers' dreams.

The Automobile as Hot Rod

Just as Chinoy was interviewing his workers the 'hot rod' became significant in the lives of a large number of young Americans. A culture was created around the term with definite values, interests, a special vocabulary and a variety of informal institutions: used car lots, races, clubs, events, shops, magazines, local and national associations. The term was used for abuse and admiration in the news media of the time, while the cinema drew on the culture for background and for symbolism: refining and spreading its messages.[21]

The main theme of the culture was the modification of 'Detroit iron', the 'lead barges' which were the American production car. There was both a technical and an aesthetic aspect to such modification. The aura which hung around the culture, and its presentation in the media certainly was that of a 'hot' car, a speedy vehicle engaged in racing, often illegally on public highways, but, in fact, engineering and ornamentation, the desire to go faster and the wish to look sharper were combined or separated in all manner of ways to provide a variety of sub-cultures, styles and specialisms. And, of course, like any other activity, there was a continuum of commitment: from simply bolting a few shop bought accessories onto your car, to creating, through one's own labour over many months, a streamlined dry-lake special.[22] The horizontal and vertical dimensions of attachment to the hot rod culture provided many niches for individual placement and certainly did allow the exercise of skilled manual labour and the mental work of design, costing and racing. The ethos of this culture, expressed through the magazines and books of post-war America, is not one of passive consumption but rather the prescriptions are to labour, to strive, to plan, to exercise skill, to compete, to succeed, to risk: themes like those alluded to by Chinoy but located in unpaid time.

What is revealed when we look at the hot rod culture of the 1940s and onwards are directives in the literature and the carrying out in practice of personally chosen projects felt to be personally fulfilling and unconnected to paid labour or connected to it in rather special ways. In this culture, for example, Henry Ford is appreciated in a particular way: not as industrial magnate nor as the destroyer of skill but as the producer of solid cars and, even more tellingly, as the prototype self-taught mechanic and backyard tinkerer. The literature often alludes to his racing and record breaking and draws a close analogy between the hot rodder and the early automobile enthusiasts like Ford with the promise that the rodders' innovations are having their effects in Detroit.

It may be objected that this culture was a model only for middle-class youth in the sunshine suburb of California, irrelevant to the vast majority of American workers. To this I can reply that in the literature little attention is paid to rodders' occupations, and if we look at such occupations as are recorded these by no means suggest a middle-class monopoly, and such objections would also fail to grasp the point that in post-war America California itself became a main theme of the American Dream. Still it is true that the hot rod was for most involved, an affair of youth, and some sociology tends to concede the enthusiasms of the young only to assume that people grow up, out and into a real world of work, politics and so on. But, of course, the passions of youth can live on in the adult.[23] So while 'hot rodder' must have been a master status for very few for a rather brief period in their existence its part-time, historical and fantasy weight in lives must have covered a lot more of the male population, while general car expertise, the routine maintenance and upkeep of a family car, also contain similar directives to skill and study as is found in the hot rod culture. Certainly, while the evidence is scarce because most researchers simply do not bother with such matters or stow them away into that conveniently misleading category labelled the 'reproduction of labour power', it is clear that American workers – and car workers among them – *do* take pride in their expertise about cars. Le Masters's study of a working-class tavern reports workers bragging about their skill in getting good used cars.[24] Moberg's infrequent references to the outplant life of Lordstown workers suggests that tinkering with cars is a major activity.[25] When Lane asked his small sample of the American common man what was the most important event in their lives, 'most say "getting married", a few mention buying a new car.'[26] While Chinoy, puzzling over the difficulties posed by his own presentation of the problem, said, 'The issue here is not laziness, an aversion to work. One could see this in the persistent activity around workers' houses as men tended their gardens, painted their houses, worked on their cars.'[27] The hot rod was but one aspect of a variety of ways in which creative activity surrounds the car not in what is conventionally taken to be production, but what is called consumption. The rod may have been the clearest sign but in many other ways, in fantasy no doubt but in activity too, the post-war male American worker drew a connection, in leisure time, between cutting metal and cutting a dash.

The Automobile as Exhibit

Another role of the automobile in the sphere of leisure, fun and free time was its use as an exhibit to entertain and instruct. The car, indeed cars – several were touring the country at one time – in which the gangsters Bonnie and Clyde were shot, was an attraction whose power waxed, waned, then waxed again from the 1930s to the 1970s.[28] It appeared at state fairs, carnivals and local shows as did the rather tidied-up wreckage of the Porsche in which James Dean died in 1955:[29] both curious icons of the frailty of occupational success.

More novel than this, increasingly in post-war America automobiles came to be exhibited for their intrinsic merits of beauty and workmanship or for the evidence they offered about technological advance and the growth of America rather than, or as well as, their association with famous individuals. The hot rods, more especially their cooler cousins the custom cars, were part of this.

After the war the companies arranged shows at which personalities, performers and products sought and received public and media attention. Along with the model line the companies also displayed the special vehicles made for the media elite and experimental automobiles of all kinds. Some of these were prototypes of short term trends in automobile design displayed to test reaction and to whet the consumer's appetite. Others were bolder design exercises revealing possible sharp changes in automobile styling in the long term. Others – usually designated as 'dream cars' – were wild extravaganzas – usually without engines – in metal shaping, colours, gadgetry and the like.[30]

All of these kinds of shows, I would suggest, had various effects relevant to the issues I am considering. They certainly were new festivals for communities of interest, new markers of time passing, sources too of media content and excitement. More than this they were messages about progress, change and modern life. The cars of the stars (alive or burnt out) related personality and commodity, detailing sophistication, luxury, but tragedy too. The useless metal and dazzling colours of the custom cars and design exercises suggested individual imagination and dream futures, while the more staid design prototypes revealed tomorrow today: progress as a tangible incremental process. Technical data was presented at such shows but reading about them and looking at the photographs it is hard to escape the notion that they were meant to be dramatizations of progress, providing evidence for Bell's contention that in modern capitalism the idea of change overshadows actual change.[31] Of course, underneath the styling the cars would all have been rather similar. Perhaps it is tempting to see the prevalence of 'dream cars' without engines as some neat manifestation of the lack of substance of an older Dream but rather, I suggest, they herald a new stress in capitalism on style, display and beauty.

The automobile as exhibit, in the examples I have sketched out, was meant to speak about change and progress and such themes can also be traced, in environments cleansed of overt commercial concern, if we note that in post-war America automobiles began to be placed in museums. One aspect of this was the display of automobiles in museums of fine art, a development I intend to deal with elsewhere, but more crucial to my theme here was their use in collections or special exhibitions designed to illustrate the history of technology and its relation to American culture.

Now, a perceptive critic of American technological museums has noted that their collections and display tend to be organized around themes of a smooth evolutionary progress and of technological solutions to human problems. Rarely is any criticism of technology offered nor are the social relations which produced it revealed or discussed. The machine is shown as both symbol and source of plenty but the human organization of the outpourings is left obscure. The vacuum in explanation arising out of this isolation of technology from its social base is filled by an ideology of technological progress as a force in its own right.[32] To this I would add that the stress on individual invention and constant evolution add weight, often expressed in the associations of the visual impact of old machines, to a romantic view of science. In short, such museums endorse and constantly portray a very particular kind of history. The progress which is the keystone of presentation, is explained as a matter of quantity, to be understood in terms of increased output whether by machine or society. The reverse of the emphasis on progress is nostalgia – an evocation of quaintness rather than any realistic attempt to display work or life for most in the past. Such museums exude an optimistic account of the develoment of society with a sideways glance at a stylized past which was poorer, perhaps better than now, but quite unrepeatable because of the march of time and the drive of the machine. So as well as rendering what modernism is not, museums tell us directly what modernism is and will be.[33]

As an example we can consider the Smithsonian Institution in America's capital. It had automobiles in its collection for some time but in 1964 it opened a new museum – the National Museum of History and Technology – visited in its first year by five million people and in its first decade by almost fifty-five million.[34] Just one part of this was the automobile and truck collection and the associated catalogue certainly supports the generalizations made above. The pictures are of machines as isolated objects to be contemplated, the text is all about inventors, specifications and performance. There is little information about the companies who produced such vehicles or why they did and such references as do occur are, like similar references to planned obsolescence in fine art catalogues, quite facile, with in this case a marked tendency to reification and overwhelming optimism: 'Assembly line manufacture, which is based on interchangeability of parts, made possible the high production records that the automobile industry has achieved in times of both peace and war.'[35] Racing and competition have 'spurred manufacturers and engineers to develop better and better tyres, alloys, lubricants and other components of the automobile. The result has been that our cars have become more serviceable and last longer.[36]

Similar observations can be made about the Henry Ford Museum at Dearborn, Michigan, opened in 1933 and drawing one and a half million visitors yearly in the 1970s.[37]

Now sociologists and Marxists tend not to investigate the social significance of the visual impact of objects. These disciplines, rooted in the nineteenth century, dwell on words not images, on texts not colours, shapes or sounds.[38] To pose the problem of what people in advanced capitalist societies read out from the look of common artefacts about the society and their place in it is to tread on to a virtually uncharted terrain of social understanding and causation. But one can at least speculate that abstract notions, prevalent in the culture at various levels of sophistication, can be the more easily assimilated when given a physical form – indeed this is a tenet of modern museum display. When the automobile is considered as an exhibit – by no means confined to the examples given above – it is the case that it is amidst a set of explanations and cues which locate its shape, size, style and performance to notions of technical advance and scientific achievement. If, as Habermas argues, there exists an important background ideology in modern capitalist society which legitimates the present structures as the products of humanly unstoppable forces of technical and scientific change, then such exhibitions and, indeed, the automobile itself could be one of the ways this ideology is laid down.[39] In this way the condition of modern labour becomes quite comprehensible and the ideology provides the material for dreams of technological solutions to social and individual problems. The repeated claim that car workers (among others) do not know how their activity 'fits in' to the whole is rendered quite ridiculous by the availability of such explanations in schools, press shows, museums and, probably most important, in the car parks, freeways or showrooms of America. Of course this is not just a streamlined account of an untramelled advance. There are discordant aspects and obvious problems. Indeed people often allude to traffic and transport when referring to the 'pace' of modern life, the loss of community and so on. None the less automobiles do contain easy lessons, personally related lessons, to the advantages of modern technology. In post-war America the automobile was probably most people's most immediate experience of the machine and so its messages about progress had a special basis too. People could feel, use and control its power, know its idiosyncrasies, enjoy its styling. In Lane's study of the ideology of the American common man in the late 1950s, men whose own self-images are purposeful and striving, we are told:[40]

The men of Eastport believe with all their heart and soul in progress; over and over again they take satisfaction in the technical things they have that their parents did not have, and, with less certainty, the things their children have that they did not.

And that for these men movement[41]

> is not at all an ascent up the status ladder, it is more likely to be the purchase of a new machine or the payment of debts for an old one.

Which is to stress just that which is often forgotten in analysis of the modern worker: that they do not just confront technology in paid labour but in all parts of their lives and, outside the factory, both the display and experience of it are likely to convince them of its broadly benign and progressive nature, and to locate the modern world in a commonsense vision of the march of science.

Discussion

The automobile and the social relations it provokes have been scrutinized in the social analysis of advanced societies. But this examination has been blinkered, for attention has been focused almost entirely on the automobile in production and its role in grouping people in paid labour. Neither sociology nor Marxism have noticed the place of the automobile in consumption, the social relations and understandings it inspires there.

Chinoy's interviews were mainly carried out in 1946–7 and his book was published in 1955. In 1947 *Fortune* magazine published an issue 'Dedicated to American Selling' which estimated that while real incomes had risen by 40 per cent in the period 1940–47 the amount available for discretionary spending was up by 160 per cent.[42] This figure, and the rise and shifts in population, caused *Fortune* to speak of 'portentous changes' in the American market, and this was soon to be proved a correct assessment. During the 1950s consumer indebtedness rose three times as fast as personal incomes, while in the decade which ended in 1957 credit for the purchase of automobiles rose by 800 per cent.[43] Between 1947 and 1955 forty-five million new cars were registered in the USA.[44] By 1955 around one third of spending units in the *lowest* quintile of incomes owned a car, and advertisements sought to convince the better-off of the horrors of 'one-car captivity'. Americans began to travel a billion miles a day on tyres, and the eccentricities of the social ritual of the annual model changes became prime news.[45] Car parking space in some New York garages shrank by 15 per cent in four years as cars grew bigger, and, in a real flavour of the times, Moscow, Idaho boasted it had more service stations than Moscow Russia.[46]

In short, the years after the war was that period of 'affluence' when most Americans became comfortable and well-off compared to their parents or to their earlier lives. The automobile was the exact symbol of this change coming to a new peak as a commodity and as a cultural symbol. By the 1970s Middletown was a driver's nightmare, its inner city decaying and choked with traffic, its suburbs flourishing. It was encircled by important venues for the newly popular auto-sports.[47]

Now, it seems unlikely that the kind of changes sketched above, plus, of course, media interpretations of them had no effect on workers' group and individual ideologies, their comprehension of society plus their place within it and, centrally, the weight they placed on paid labour in their own biographies but the analysis of this has been attenuated and disappointing. *The Affluent Worker* and similar American studies convincingly closed off *one* avenue of discussion here – that the working class was becoming middle-class, but many others remain open and largely unexplored. The views of Mills outlined above or the somewhat similar argument of Burns[48] are sometimes quoted but have not led to much research. It is, and only for example, difficult to find an informed study which traces the paths of the Hollywood elite through their careers and lifecycles, both in their fictional and 'factual' existence.[49] In broad terms the consumpion of commodities is an area of social life and social affect largely ignored by the most powerful forms of social analysis. It is a part of life which is labelled and then put to the back of the shelf of concerns.

I have detailed the place of the automobile in two distinct areas of time free of paid labour in post-war America, juxtaposing them, somewhat artificially I will admit, to a classic work of sociology, the better to emphasize the weakness of the habitual perspectives of a good deal of sociology and more Marxism. Both forms of analysis tend to conceptualize people – adults anyway – as labourers and proceed from this to present accounts of living in capitalism which scarcely ring true. Feminist and other gender-based critiques have diagnosed the blinkered scrutiny such a theoretical vision ensures but still, the real force of their objections has not altered the meta-theoretical foundations of the powerful forms of social analysis. Rather, these have tried to incorporate the critique by extending their terminology, by insisting on the determined nature of non-paid time, and so on. But the intellectual problems associated with discovering how people construct an identity, the processes of self-evaluation and the experience of a trajectory through social relationships are *not* to be answered by reducing life to labour and being to occupation as is routinely done in sociology and Marxism. However plausible this may once have been it really will not serve today. For most people, and by no means only those in objectively routinized work, the felt centre, the *real* part of life, is experienced outside pay labour.[50] Chinoy's Dream with its vague allusions to occupational success surely has an attenuated and meagre content compared with the actual dreams and daydreams of human beings which turn more on freedom from control and constraint, and self-realization.

Studies, like Chinoy's, which take it as axiomatic that paid labour *is* the vital existential sphere of life assume away what most needs to be examined. Even within their own meta-theoretical stance they tend to avoid complexities, usually taking labour to mean 'paid work task', ignoring the actual experience of labour time, evading the point that all productive labour is not paid labour, and that not all work on nature is paid labour – even for men. More than this, such analyses avoid confronting the way paid labour is ideologically presented in advanced capitalist societies and, like Chinoy, tend to vaguely assert that work is still, somehow, presented as crucial to being by the main agencies of socialization. To this it is necessary to counter-claim – for claim is all that is involved – that a theoretical concentration on occupation, paid labour, and work task tells us very little about most people's hopes and fears, desires and dreams: little about who people think they really are and how they relate to others. Everyone knows they are more than they seem to be at work. For most people's prized image of self, work as such is an annoying irrelevance. Their dream is usually to be free of its shackles. This reflects significant changes in the material basis of most people's lives, the greater willingness of workers to assert an old distaste for labour of all kinds and a change in dominant values or, rather, a reweighting of the significance of various sources of dominant values. Many of these now stress non-paid time as the real place of being and, as one part of this, a displacement of the craft ideal into free time, if not into a total concern with making the self.

What this kind of argument suggests is that labour and labour time cannot be taken to be so central to self and to consciousness as Chinoy and a myriad other studies assume. 'Lived experience', like the working day, is given order and infused with meaning by its rare high points and special events and we cannot apportion a similar subjective weight to every passing moment. References to the amount of time spent in paid labour or its centrality in the organization of all life are sociologically simplistic. It is not the quantity but the quality of time which provides 'meaning'. The stopwatch can measure the speed of the line but not, in all truth, the tempo of a life passing. That which is mused on by the individual, which is offered as evidence in the constant court room of self-assessment is, in most cases, quite unlikely to be paid labour experiences except in so far as these involve the crucial limitation of the amount of money earned. It may be true that labour time restricts and orders the possibilities of the use of time away from work but, for the individuals, it is just this free time which will resonate with meaning and the general rise in the standard of living, along with concomitant structural changes involving work, community, mass media messages and so on, has allowed many more degrees of freedom, much greater variation in individual decision as to just what kind of person one really is, *once* the tedious necessity of 'earning a living' is done.

Which is all to say that as production has changed so has consumption: in its forms, in its relations, *and* in its weight in personal biography and yet, except in very simplistic arguments concerning the role of goods as status symbols in some, presumed, relatively consensual hierarchy of taste and knowledge the study of social stratification or industrial sociology has scarcely been touched by such notions. The crucial effect of 'affluence' in post-war capitalism has surely been to justify the ideology and allow the practice of individualism and to link the acquisition and use of consumer goods to values which emphasize the importance of the search for personal identity and authenticity, yet this has scarcely begun to be investigated by those disciplines which purport to describe and explain contemporary capitalism. There is no sophisticated sociology of consumption, while Marxists, virtually forced to regard this part of life as determined, make do with specious references to commodity fetishization on the one hand or generalized references to the role of advertising on the other. I hope I have said enough about automobiles and their location in consumption activities to suggest that, if social analysts wish to understand the dreams of modern workers, we need to construct a sociology of consumption and to refine some of the basic assumptions of the core texts of sociology and Marxism.

Notes

1. E. Chinoy, *Automobile Workers and the American Dream*, (Beacon, Boston, 1955).
2. Two recent theses which survey the American automobile industry and workers from a Marxist perspective are D. Moberg, 'Rattling the Golden Chains: Conflict and Consciousness of Auto Workers', PhD thesis, University of Chicago (1978); and W.D. Gartman, 'Autoslavery: the Development of the Labor Process in the Automobile Industry of America 1897–1950', PhD thesis, University of California, San Diego (1980). Both concentrate almost exclusively on the paid labour experiences of car workers.
3. Chinoy, *Automobile Workers and the American Dream*, p. 86.
4. Ibid., p. 131.
5. The insights of Donald Roy are quite unsurpassed here and have not been confronted in most of the literature about the experience of work or the creation of the labour process. See for example D. Roy, 'Banana time: job satisfaction and informal interaction', *Human Organisation*, vol. 18 (1959–60) and 'Sex in the factory: informal heterosexual relations between supervisors and work groups', in C. Bryant (ed.), Deviant Behaviour (Rand McNally, Chicago, 1974).
6. Thus Chinoy does not consider his Dream as divided into gender, racial or ethnic varieties, let alone considering class variants or the reworking of dominant values into sub-cultural specificities. At the time Chinoy wrote around 9.5 per cent of all automobile

factory workers were women and 9 per cent were black. *Census of the Population*, vol. IV, Special Reports Part I, chapter on 'Industrial Characteristics'.

7. Similar points, of course, were made by J.H. Goldthorpe *et al.* in the *Affluent Work* study some time ago. See, especially, J.H. Goldthorpe, 'Attitudes and Behaviour of Car Assembly Workers: a deviant case and a theoretical critique', *British Journal of Sociology*, vol. 17 (1966), pp. 227–44. It is noticeable that despite all the criticism and research this study provoked certain of its concepts and findings, for example that of a 'normative convergence' between social groups or 'privatization', remain almost uninvestigated.

8. Chinoy, *Automobile Workers and the American Dream*, p. 127.

9. Some indications of this are contained in David Reisman's introduction to Chinoy's book which, while highly complimentary in tone, does raise issues in a way which jars with the main text's arguments. See Chinoy, *Automobile Workers and the American Dream*, pp. xix–xx.

10. The Lincoln was, and is, the luxury car for the top of the market produced by the Ford Company. The 1955 Lincoln Continental is a particularly famous model. For details see B.R. Kimes, *The Golden Anniversary of the Lincoln Motorcar*; T. E. Bonsall, *The Lincoln Motorcar: sixty years of excellence*, (Bookman Dan, 1981).

11. R.S. Lynd and H.M. Lynd, *Middletown in Transition* (Constable, London, 1937).

12. Chinoy, *Automobile Workers and the American Dream*, p. 123.

13. C.W. Mills, *White Collar*, (Oxford University Press, New York, 1951, esp. ch: 10 and 11).

14. Ibid., p. 228.

15. It is tempting to note that when Berger interviewed a hundred automobile workers living in a Californian suburb in the 1950s he found an extraordinarily high readership of the *Reader's Digest*. This sample was not a random one. B. Berger, *Working Class Suburb* (University of California, Berkeley, 1960), p. 76.

16. Mills, *White Collar*, p. 283.

17. See J. Kasen, Portraits from the Dream: the Myth of Success in the Comic Strip, PhD thesis, Rutgers University (1978); E. Long, 'Themes of Success in American Best Selling Novels 1945–1975, PhD thesis, Brandeis University (1978). These reveal patterns of change in presentation of 'success' rather like those Mills predicted. T.P. Greene, *America's Heroes:the changing models of success in American magazines* (Oxford University Press, New York, 1970) suggests that the ideal of 'self-improvement' has a rich and varied history in the USA with the work-centred, competitive striving individualistic ideal being only one aspect.

18. Mills, *White Collar*, p. 258.

19. Ibid., p. 237.

20. So there are a number of studies of working for Ford, General Motors, Citroen, etc. but hardly any of the social meanings of *driving* a Ford, etc. An almost unique attempt is: G. Maull, 'Driving as Social Action,'manuscript submitted for a PhD to the Department of Sociology, University of Essex (1980).

21. Apart from the items listed below, a short introduction to the hot rod culture is contained in J. Storer, 'Coachbuilding to customizing', in S. Murray (ed.), *Petersens Creative Customizing* (Petersen, Los Angeles 1978), pp. 4–13. W. Parks, *Drag Racing: Yesterday and today* (Trident, New York, 1966) also has details of the early period. The presentation of the hot rod in the mass media of the time include H.G. Felsen's novel, *Hot Rod* (Dutton, New York, 1950) (and into its twentieth printing by 1967); films like *Hot Rod* (1950), *High School Confidential* (1952) and *Rebel Without a Cause* (1955); and various records like the Beach Boys *Little Deuce Coupe*.

22. See the typology set out by Gene Balsley, 'The hot rod culture', *American Quarterly*, vol. II, no. 1 (Spring 1950). This is the only contemporary academic piece – Balsley was a student of Reisman's – that I have been able to find.

23. And in this regard it should be remembered that 41 per cent of Kinsey's respondents noted the automobile as a common place for pre-marital sex relations. Quoted in E.A. Smith, *American Youth Culture* (Free Press, London, 1962), pp. 170–1.

24. E.E. Le Masters, *Blue Collar Aristocrats* (University of Wisconsin, 1975), p. 32.

25. Moberg, 'Rattling the Golden Chains', p. 48.

26. R. Lane, *Political Ideology* (Free Press, New York, 1962), pp. 284–5.

27. Chinoy, *Automobile Workers and the American Dream*, p. 70.

28. C.Y. Rich, 'Clyde Barrow's last Ford', *Journal of Popular Culture*, vol. VI, no. 4 (1974), pp. 631–40.

29. G. Barris and J. Scagnetti, *Cars of the Stars* (Jonathan David, New York, 1974), pp. 20–3.
30. For details see M. Frostick, *Dream Cars: design studies and prototypes* (Dalton Watson, London, 1980); and J-R Piccard, *Dream Cars* (Orbis, London, 1981).
31. D. Bell, *The Cultural Contradictions of Capitalism* (Heinemann, London, 1976), p. 34.
32. G. Basalla, 'Museums and technological utopianism', in I.M. Quimby and P.A. Earl (eds), *Technological Innovation and the Decorative Arts* (University of Virginia, Charlottesville, 1974).
33. So in his excellent book trying to analyse modern sensibility and experience, MacCannell only gets at some of the functions of the museum. D. MacCannell, *The Tourist* (Macmillan, London, 1976), pp. 78–85.
34. Smithsonian Year 1965, p. 12 and 1974, p. 170.
35. S.H. Oliver and D.H. Berkebile, *The Smithsonian Collection of Automobiles and Motorcycles* (Smithsonian, Washington DC, 1969), p. 21.
36. Ibid., p. 22.
37. See L.R. Henry, *America's Foremost Automobile Collection*, pamphlet available from the Henry Ford Museum, Dearborn. No pagination.
38. So most of the sociology of popular music concentrates on lyrics for 'meaning', while mass media studies tend to avoid the visual impact of television or press presentation.
39. J. Habermas, 'Technology and science as ideology', in *Toward a Rational Society* (Heinemann, London, 1971).
40. Lane, *Political Ideology*, p. 290.
41. Ibid., p. 386.
42. *Fortune*, vol. 36, no. 5, (November, 1947).
43. M. Dubofsky, *et al.*, *The United States in the Twentieth Century* ((Prentice-Hall, London, 1978), p. 427.
44. R.P. Smith, *Consumer Demand for Cars in the USA* (Cambridge University, London 1975), appendix A, table 1.
45. J. Jerome, *The Death of the Automobile* (Norton, New York, 1972), gives the flavour; see also Smith, *Consumer Demand for Cars in the USA*, appendix A, table 3.
46. V. Packard, *The Waste Makers* (Longman, London, 1961), p. 37; K. Schneider, *Autokind v Mankind* (Norton, New York, 1971), p. 108.
47. L. Mandel, *Driven* (Stein & Day, New York, 1977),ch. 2.
48. T. Burns, 'The Study of Consumer Behaviour, A Sociological View', *Archives Européennes de Sociologie*, vol. 7 (1966).
49. L. May, *Screening out the Past* (Oxford University Press, 1980) is an interesting attempt to examine the new Hollywood stars of the early part of the century as providing national models of leisure experts.
50. Here is what commercial artist and designer Walter Lundquist said: 'I was a kid in 1942 when I got out of art school. I wanted to make a lot of money and become famous. In five years I'll own the world. I'll be in New York driving a Cadillac and owning my own plane. I want gold cufflinks and babes and the big house in the country. The whole bit. The American Dream', in S. Terkel, *Working* (Wildwood House, London, 1975), p. 425.

17 Work: Past, Present and Future

RICHARD BROWN

Sociological research and writing reflect the time and place in which they are produced. The sociology of work is no exception to this truism. Indeed there are numerous examples within this area of enquiry of the ways in which an interest in particular topics can be seen, at least in a general sense, to be the product of specific historical circumstances in a specific society or societies. Unemployment, for example, has understandably attracted far more attention when it has been, and has been seen as, a major problem – during the present century: before the First World War, in the 1920s and 1930s, and since the late 1960s. The two periods when most attention had been given to women in paid work – before the First World War and during the last twenty years – coincide respectively with the growth and activities of the suffragette movement and of the women's liberation movement, and with concurrent changes in women's social position.[1]

Even better documented is the issue of industrial participation and industrial democracy. As Ramsay (1977), Brannen (1983, pp. 33–48) and Brannen *et. al.* (1976, pp. 9–28) for example, have shown, in Britain over the past century or so there have been recurrent periods of interest in worker participation corresponding to periods when management authority is felt to be facing challenge. At such times, possibilities of increased participation have been explored as a way of restoring managerial legitimacy and control over labour, giving rise to 'cycles of control'. Interest in participation has declined when labour is less threatening, as for instance during periods of increased unemployment. During the last few decades there have been flurries of sociological research and writing on industrial democracy, coinciding with and indeed forming part of these cycles.

One can go further, however, to suggest that in our area of interest the definition and understanding of the object of enquiry, 'work' itself, have varied over time in significant ways. Not all attempts to develop or contribute to a sociological understanding of work have been directed at understanding the same phenomenon. What counts as 'work' and what aspects of work are seen as problematic and worthy of study have varied over the years. We have a situation therefore in which any discussion of the past, present and future of work must consider a number of rather different, though related issues. What do we understand by 'work' and how has this understanding changed and developed? What has been the social organization and allocation of work, as variously understood, in the past; what is it now; and how is it likely to change? How does the organization and allocation of work differ as between societies and cultures? What aspects of work have been seen as problematic and which ones are likely to become problematic in the future? How have changes in the definition and understanding of work, and in its social organization and allocation, and more

The Open University, 1984 (Specially written for this volume)

general developments within sociology, combined to give rise to emphases on the study and investigation of particular issues within particular sorts of theoretical framework? No final or definitive answers will be offered to these questions, but they form an agenda for the discussion which follows.

Definition of Work

As will be apparent from the discussion in other contributions to this volume, there is no universal agreement among social scientists as to the definition of 'work'. Clearly it canot be defined solely in terms of the activities to which it refers, but must also include reference to the purposes for which and the context within which such activities are performed. Thus, for example, for some people to 'work' is to play games to entertain spectators, games such as football, tennis, golf or snooker, which many others play for pleasure or relaxation; reading a book for interest is a different activity from reading it to prepare a lecture or write a review; the significance of digging the garden, driving a car, or even walking, all vary depending on the purpose for which they are done, for their own sake or in order to produce goods or provide a service. Work activities are instrumental activities; this does not mean that they cannot be enjoyable, but whatever intrinsic rewards they offer to those who perform them, they are carried out in order to achieve some extrinsic purpose and not just for their own sake. Within that limitation, however, almost any activity can be 'work'. This wide scope of work activities is perhaps adequately contained if they are defined as any physical or mental activities which transform materials into a more useful form, provide or distribute goods or services to oneself or others, and/or increase or improve human knowledge and understanding of the world.

Many work activities, and certainly the ones we most commonly think of as 'work' are performed in order to provide something – goods or services – either for which others are willing to pay, or for which others would have to be paid if one did not provide them oneself. In the first case, we are talking about work within the context of employment, or self-employment, leading to the sale of the product of one's labour directly, or indirectly in return for a wage, salary or fee. In the second case, we are referring to work within the household and for consumption by the household – domestic work, do-it-yourself, care of the elderly and sick, and so on. Thus work can be and is performed both when conventionally 'at work' (during one's employment, typically located away from the home) and during one's own time (typically spent at home) (see Parker *et al.*, 1972; Parker, 1983, ch. 1; Brown, 1984). Even this broad definition does not exhaust the contexts within which work occurs; some work (e.g. voluntary work, help to neighbours) may be communal, in that its products are not sold or bartered, nor do the producers themselves consume the results of their labours; the benefits go to third parties or to society in general (Gershuny and Pahl, 1980).

The adequacy of the conception and definition of work suggested here should be judged against the discussion which follows, and the discussions of the nature of work in this volume and elsewhere. As we shall see, it has at least the merit of being considerably more broadly and more inclusively – and therefore, in my view, more satisfactorily – than the taken-for-granted conceptions of work which have characterized most popular and social scientific discussions in the past.

The Changing Shape of Work

One of the sources of complexity in any attempt to discuss the past, present and future of work is that over time there have been three distinct, but related sets of changes: first, in the definition of what was to be seen as work; second, in the relative importance of the various types and contexts of work activities (importance in terms of numbers involved, economic contribution, time spent at such work, and so on); and third, in what aspects of 'work', so defined, were seen as problematic and requiring discussion and investigation. To jump ahead of the discussion a little, perceptions in the past as to what counted as work were unduly narrow, although even within such narrowly defined limits there were important changes taking place in the social organization of work; and yet it was an even more limited range of problems and issues that attracted, or were brought to, the attention of social scientists. In the last ten years or so, there have been important changes both in the social organization of work, in the social division of labour, and in the definition of 'work' and what is problematic about it.

Britain is unique in being the first country to industrialize and having, therefore, the longest experience as an industrial society. Indeed, the development of a capitalist agriculture even earlier than a capitalist industry (and as an important precondition for it) has meant that the predominant type of work for most of the world's population for most of recorded history – work on the land, mostly at or near subsistence level – became of minor importance in Britain very early. Work, for the majority, came to mean the production of goods through mining or manufacture, or the provision of services. What dominated and has for the most part continued to dominate observers' perceptions of the 'industrial revolution', however, is not just this shift in the balance of productive economic activity from the primary sector to the secondary and tertiary sectors, but the dramatic change in the social organization of work represented by the growth of relatively large-scale extractive, manufacturing and service enterprises – mines, mills and factories, docks and railway companies. Work came to mean work as an employee, and the stereotype employee was the manual worker, especially in large enterprises in manufacturing industry, the millhand or the factory worker, workers whose productivity was enormously increased by the use and continued development of machinery. Britain was the 'workshop of the world', and manufacturing industry was the dominant element in this image.

In fact, of course, although this transformation of work was dramatic and had enormous and far-reaching consequences for society, social perceptions of work in the past and more recently exaggerated and have continued to exaggerate the extent to which men and women were working as employees in relatively large-scale mines, mills and factories. As a result, not only were household and communal work largely lost to view, but so too was the continuing existence throughout the nineteenth century and more recently of many much more traditional and less 'industrial' forms of work. Samuel (1977), for example, has described in great detail the extent to which hand technology continued throughout the nineteenth century, much of it involving work in small workshops or the workers' own homes, rather than in factories; and employment in 'domestic offices and personal service', which may have included as many as 18 per cent of the occupied population in Britain in 1841, still included over 14 per cent in 1911, nearly half a million men and over 2 million women (Department of Employment, 1971, p. 195). Marsh has usefully summarized the occupational/industrial distribution of the economically active population at the end of the nineteenth century as follows:

> Out of every 100 males and females with specified occupations about 12 in 1881 and 9 in 1901 were engaged in agriculture or fishing; about 5 in 1881 and 6 in 1901 were in mining or quarrying; about 36 in 1881 and 1901 were concerned with making things in factories, workshops or on building sites; about 7 in 1881 and 9 in 1901 conveyed persons, goods or messages or provided gas, water and sanitary services;

about 6 in 1881 and 8 in 1901 were engaged in selling things or in banking or insurance; about 14 in 1881 and 13 in 1901 gave personal service as domestic and other servants; about 2 in 1881 and 3 in 1901 were in occupations connected with Government or defence; about 6 in 1881 and 7 in 1901 were either making or selling food, drink and tobacco, or providing lodging; about 8 in 1881 and 5 in 1901 were general dealers, labourers or in undefined occupations. (Marsh, 1958, pp. 129–30)

Thus even that work which was included within the confines of recognized occupational categories as used in the census was much more varied than was commonly acknowledged.

It is now widely accepted that the relative decline of Britain as an industrial and manufacturing power must be dated back to these years, the last decades of the nineteenth century, when the United States and Germany in particular grew economically much more rapidly and adopted new technology and new forms of work organization more quickly and effectively. However, these changes in Britain's position in the world economy were slow to have effect on the industrial and occupational structure, and perhaps even slower to affect social consciousness. There had never been a majority employed in manufacturing industry and the proportion so employed (a little below 40 per cent), though it fluctuated, appeared to show no long-run tendency to decline during the first half of the twentieth century. Similarly, though coal-mining had clearly declined in importance by the mid-century, there were still over 700,000 men employed in the industry in the early 1950s. New manufacturing industries developed (e.g. motor vehicles, electrical engineering, chemicals), but if anything the dominant image of work as manual work in large-scale manufacturing industry seemed even more justified as firms and plants grew in size and some of the more traditional forms of work disappeared. The main contrary trend was the growth of white-collar work, of the number and proportion of the occupied population working as managers and administrators, in professional occupations and, most numerous of all, in clerical work. Between 1911 and 1951, the number of employees in white-collar work doubled, to comprise 31 per cent of the occupied population, over 40 per cent of them women – itself an important development – whereas the number in manual work rose by only 6 per cent, a proportionate fall from nearly three-quarters to less than two-thirds of the occupied population (Price and Bain, 1976, p. 346).

Past Patterns of Research on Work

It can be suggested that before the Second World War most of the enquiries into work which can now be seen as pre- or proto-sociological were carried out in the course of the formation or administration of social policy and with an emphasis on the social problems of or connected with work. Though there were clearly exceptions to such a generalization, such as notable studies of trade unionism by the Webbs (1894 and 1920) and others, and economists' investigations into wages, many of these enquiries were concerned with groups or situations marginal to what has been taken for granted as the central core of work; they were concerned with the low paid and poor, children, women, unemployment, the sweated trades and so on.

Empirical sociological research on work in Britain can probably effectively be dated from the late 1940s and, in contrast to the earlier investigations of acknowledged social problems, the predominant emphasis in such research for twenty years or so was on the study of male manual workers in the traditional industries – engineering and vehicles, shipbuilding, iron and steel, printing, and

– outside manufacturing – mining and transport. Research which focused on the study of organizations similarly tended to focus on large enterprises in manufacturing industry. Not only were these the most clearly visible areas and types of work, but what was seen as problematic about work in any case directed attention towards these workers and these industries. That was where one could find the large companies and plants, the elaborate management hierarchies, the high levels of trade union membership and well-developed workplace union organization, and the formal mechanisms for consultation and negotiation, which were of interest to students of industrial organizations and industrial conflict. They were the locations associated with problems of management organization, or with strikes and other forms of collective action, which attracted the attention of policy-makers as well as researchers. In a period when Britain's export performance and balance of payments were central issues of economic policy, what was seen as problematic about work were low levels of productivity, low morale, resistance to technical change, and management–worker conflict, and these were all problems to be found most clearly and obviously in these traditional industries.[2] Women, non-manual workers and the service industries other than transport were not entirely neglected; women's employment, especially married women's employment, tended to be studied as a social problem within the rubric of 'women's two roles' (see the discussion in Brown, 1976 and also Beechey, 1978), and both clerical workers and professional employees attracted attention within the general framework of the study of class structure (for example, Lockwood, 1958; Prandy, 1965); but non-male workers and/or non-'traditional industrial' work were seen as far less important and less problematic, and attracted far less attention than their quantitative, or theoretical, significance warranted.

Not only were there these biases and limitations in the substantive coverage of research on work in the post-war period, the theoretical frameworks used have also been subject to considerable, mostly justified, criticism (among many others, see, for example, Rose, 1975; Nichols, 1980; Thompson, 1983, ch. 1). Two elements in this criticism should perhaps be emphasized, though not all research and writing could be so characterised. On the one hand, there was the assumption of an underlying harmony of interests between management and workers, and on the other, a tendency to confine analysis to the workplace, the employing organization itself, or, even if the wider 'environment' was considered, to consider it in a limited and *ad hoc* manner.

The 'human relations' movement, for example, which strongly influenced the study of work in the USA and in Britain in the 1940s and 1950s, certainly had these failings, as did a good deal of work carried out in the structural-functionalist tradition which dominated sociological theory during the same period. Even when, within these traditions, a much more thorough and elaborate conceptualization was developed of the relations between the economy (and industrial organizations) and other societal subsystems, it remained very abstract (See Parsons and Smelser, 1956). In addition, the stress on the (largely harmonious) contribution of the parts to the maintenance of the whole social system meant that structural functionalism was inadequate as a framework for the analysis of the changes and conflicts which characterized the world of work.

Other researchers, particularly in Britain and in the 1960s, accepted that conflict was inherent in the relations between employer and employee. Even when their analysis did not 'stop at the factory gates', however, the significance of the social context within which paid work was carried out was inadequately grasped. Environmental factors were drawn on rather arbitrarily, to explain differences within and between situations which could not be accounted for in terms of factors internal to those situations.[3] In one very influential example, *The Affluent Worker* study (Goldthorpe, *et al.*, 1968), the authors introduced the notion of 'orientations to work', seen as shaped by workers' experiences outside the workplace, to explain two sets of findings; why assembly-line workers in one plant they studied accepted conditions of work of a type which previous investigations has reported as causing considerable dissatisfaction; and why workers in different occupations in three contrasting factories with dissimilar conditions all expressed similar attitudes to work. In both cases, an 'instrumental' orientation to work was satisfied by relatively high pay; conditions of work were seen as relatively unimportant.

Although there is certainly much research and writing in the sociology of work at the present time which largely remains within these perspectives – and much of value which can be gained from the earlier work – the past fifteen years or so have seen the emergence of approaches to the study of work which clearly reflect both different understandings of the phenomena to be investigated and different theoretical frameworks through which to analyse them. First, however, we must consider the ways in which the pattern of work has changed.

Recent Changes in the Social Organization of Work

The roots of recent changes in the social organization of work in Britain can undoubtedly be traced back a long way. It is predominantly during the past twenty years or so, however, that the impact of these changes has become clearly apparent so that laymen and academics alike have been forced to reconsider their understanding of 'work', a fairly painful process which is still going on (see, for example, Chapter 1 of this volume). Without attempting any sort of comprehensive account of causes or consequences, it is possible to indicate something of the nature and scale of the changes which have occurred.

As Littler and Salaman argue (in Chapter 2 above), the changes which have occurred in Britain reflect developments in the world economy specific to a particular stage in the development of capitalism. Britain in particular, despite the benefits of North Sea oil, and Western industrial nations more generally are relatively less powerful; manufacturing industry in both traditional (e.g. shipbuilding, textiles and clothing) and modern (e.g. vehicles, electronics) sectors has increasingly been relocated in 'Third World' countries, for example, in South-East Asia or Latin America, where labour is plentiful and cheap. This new 'international division of labour' has been possible partly due to the fragmentation of work processes, making them 'suitable' for unskilled labour, and to the development of means of communication and transport. It reflects also the activities of multinational corporations which operate on a world-wide basis without allegiance to any one national economy or nation-state (though states may be expected to intervene in national economies to provide, through education and social welfare provision and through measures of economic management, conditions within which modern capitalist corporations can flourish). In Britain's case, the impact on employment of these trends, and of others such as increasing productivity in manufacturing and some service industries and the introduction of microelectronic technology, has been intensified by government economic and fiscal policies.

The most striking effect on employment has been the decline in the number employed in manufacturing industry. Between 1961 and 1981, the numbers employed in that sector (an increasing proportion of whom were in non-manual jobs) fell by $2\frac{1}{2}$ million, from just over 38 per cent of the occupied population to just over 28 per cent; and the numbers have fallen further by more than half a million since 1981. The decline was perhaps especially notable in those industries which had been of greatest importance during the earlier years of industrialization – textiles and clothing, metal manufacture, and engineering and allied activities. During the same period, employment in the service sector grew, especially in insurance, banking and finance, in education and health services, and in miscellaneous services such as catering and personal services. In the past three years, however, this growth has been halted and has been reversed as a result of the recession and cuts in public-sector employment (*Social Trends*, 1982; Department of Employment, 1983, p. 58; for a powerful commentary on these changes, see Beynon, 1983).

Secondly, associated particularly with the expansion of the service sector, there has been an absolute and relative increase in the number of women who are 'economically active'. Whereas the male labour force (employed, self-employed and registered unemployed men) in the United Kingdom fell from 16.3 million in 1961 to somewhat less than 15.7 million in 1981, the female labour force increased in the same period from $8\frac{1}{2}$ million to 10 million, most of this increase occurring after 1971. As a result, women represented nearly 40 per cent of the civilian labour force at the start of the present decade, as compared with less than 35 per cent twenty years earlier. Much of this increase reflected two trends: the increased participation of married women in the labour force (nearly two-thirds of all economically active women in Great Britain in 1981 were married, and nearly six out of every ten married women were economically active outside the home); and the growth of part-time work especially for women (nearly 42 per cent of economically active women worked part-time in 1981, when less than 6 per cent of men did) (*Labour Force Survey 1981*, quoted in Equal Opportunities Commission, 1983).

Thirdly, the decline in the relative importance of manual work has continued, although it has had less effect on men's work than on women's. The numbers and proportions in all the main categories of white-collar work have grown – managers and administrators, professionals, salespersons, and (especially) clerical workers. According to Price and Bain (1983, p. 51) the proportion of employees in non-manual work was just over 30 per cent in 1948: in the next twenty years it grew to just over 41 per cent; and in the following decade to nearly half (49.2 per cent in 1979). Because of their heavy concentration in clerical work, selling and lower professional and technical occupations, however, and their under-representation in skilled manual work, women were much more likely to be in non-manual work than men. In 1981, for example, whereas some 45 per cent of all those economically active were in one of the main categories of white-collar work (Socio-Economic Groups 1–6), the proportion of women so categorized as well over half (59 per cent) and the proportion of men only just over a third (36.5 per cent) (*Census 1981*, 1983, p. 25). Thus, though manual work remains the typical lot of the male worker, male manual workers now represent a minority of the labour force as a whole.

Fourthly, in one form or another the state has become increasingly important as an employer. Employment in national and local government, the armed forces, nationalized industries, and so on totalled 26.5 per cent of all employees in 1979, over 700,000 more than in 1968, despite declining employment in many of the nationalized industries during the same period (Price and Bain, 1983, p. 52).

Fifthly, in recent years, and especially since the end of the 1970s, there has been a massive increase in unemployment. The numbers recorded as unemployed in the United Kingdom reached a million in the post-war period in 1975, $1\frac{1}{2}$ million in 1980, 2 million early in 1981 and 3 million in 1983, when it represented more than

12 per cent of the labour force. The impact of unemployment has been very uneven; recorded unemployment (much women's unemployment may go unrecorded) is particularly severe for the young and those over 55 years old, for men, for manual workers generally and for unskilled manual workers especially (Department of Employment, 1983; Sinfield, 1981). It is significant that neither politicians nor academic forecasters expect the level of unemployment to change in the near future, and some suggest that it may well get a lot worse. One of the consequences of increasing unemployment has been that even greater emphasis has been placed on education and on qualifications as prerequisites for employment, in many cases in jobs where the credentials demanded bear little or no relationship to the tasks to be performed.

Finally, the size of industrial organizations has continued to increase so that private-sector economic activity is dominated by a relatively small number of large corporations, many of them multinationals, and a considerable proportion of them based outside the United Kingdom. The ultimate control of work has become increasingly further removed from the shop or office floor.

Clearly all these changes represent major shifts in the nature of work in our society. Paid work is more likely to involve manipulating symbols or processing people than dealing with things; it is much more likely to be providing a service than making a product; it is increasingly likely to be done by a woman rather than by a man (though there is still clear segregation between most men's and women's work) (Hakim, 1979); and whereas paid work was readily available for nearly thirty years to all who wanted it, except a small residual minority, it has now become scarce. The changing shape of paid work during the last decade has necessitated fairly radical changes in sociological approaches to the study of work. What were the predominant characteristics of employment in the early 1960s, and what was problematic about work then, are no longer an adequate agenda for research work in the 1980s.

Changing Emphases in Research

The relationship between changes in society and changes in what social scientists are encouraged, allowed or want to investigate is far from straightforward, but two related developments in the focus of research during the past fifteen years clearly appear to reflect the ways in which employment patterns are changing. Research on the labour market, that is on the processes whereby people are allocated to jobs, and jobs to people, grew in importance and attracted the attention of social scientists other than economists. This reflected not only a concern with rising levels of unemployment, but also with the persistence of low pay and with institutionalized discrimination in employment on the basis of gender, ethnic origin and/or age, despite repeated official commitment to eliminating poverty and to providing equal opportunities. As the contributions in this volume by Kumar and by Roberts, Noble and Duggan (Chapters 1 and 15, respectively) illustrate, however, the spread of unemployment also clearly called into question conventional definitions of work as equivalent to employment and emphasized that the nature of and relationship between paid work, unpaid work and leisure required much more study.

Secondly, the growth of women's employment in the formal economy stimulated questions about the division of labour between the sexes, an issue which was of central importance to the growing women's movement. As Oakley showed in *The Sociology of Housework* (1974) (see also her contribution to this volume), domestic work was 'work' and could be investigated and analysed in much the same way as paid work. From a wider perspective on work, it was also clear that unpaid work in the household was not peripheral or residual, but was essential, if paid work was to be carried out in the formal economy; and in some occupations, as Finch's chapter in this volume shows, the domestic contributions to the performance of a 'job' are especially great.

In a context in which the perceptions of what was problematic about work were being widened in these ways, an especially significant contribution was made by the publication in 1974 of Henry Braverman's *Labor and Monopoly Capital*. What this book did was to advocate an approach to the study of work in societies like our own which was centred on the analysis of the capitalist labour process and within a Marxist theoretical framework. Littler has provided a concise assessment of Braverman's impact:

> Traditionally the academic study of work and work relations has been distributed among managerial studies and organisation theory, industrial relations, the sociology of occupations, and something called industrial sociology. However, industrial sociology never amounted to an integrated subject. ... Braverman's major contribution was to smash through the academic barriers and offer the potential for the birth of a new, *integrated* approach to the study and history of work. (Littler, 1982, pp. 25–6)

Braverman's argument and some of the criticisms to which it has been subjected are discussed elsewere in this book (especially in Chapter 5, by Thompson), and, of course, the 'potential' has not always been realized in the studies which have followed Braverman. What was important about his approach in the context of the present discussion, however, is that within a coherent theoretical framework it directed attention to a variety of issues and topics which had previously been seen as largely unrelated. Central to any Marxist account of the processes of production, for example, are the processes of production and reproduction of labour itself; in other words, there is a need to ask the following questions. Where does the labour force come from? How is it recruited, and attracted or compelled to enter employment? How are workers socialized, in the family, the educational system and elsewhere, into appropriate orientations to work? How is labour reproduced on a daily, and on a generational basis? Processes of control are also seen as central to an understanding of the labour process under capitalism. Analysing such processes directs attention both to the detailed organization of work and to the social organization of the labour force – the use of divisions between workers on the basis of skill, gender and/or ethnic origin, for example, to prevent collective organization and action contrary to the employers' interests, and the use of the 'reserve army of labour' (the unemployed, women, immigrants) to weaken the power of workers and to reduce labour costs. Thus the relations between work and the family, and work and education, the role of the state, the domestic labour of women (and men), the operation of the labour market and the structure of unemployment all become crucial elements in any study of work, rather than being seen as peripheral or largely unrelated matters.

The products of these new directions in the study of work are now available in books and journal articles (including this volume and the Open University course for which it was originally designed). Initially, the advocacy of the labour process as the focus for analysis often accompanied a fairly critical dismissal of the products of research carried out within other frameworks. More recently, however, criticism of some features of Braverman's argument has led to an awareness of the ways in which the earlier research could supplement and complement it. Before briefly discussing this further, it is necessary to consider the future of work itself.

Work: the Future

Comments on the future of work are inevitably speculative. At least in the short to medium term, however, it seems likely that many of the trends outlined in the previous section will continue. As previously mentioned, high and possibly even increasing levels of unemployment are widely forecast, so that we may soon come to see the 1940s–1960s as the 'exception', a time when a fortunate conjecture of circumstances permitted successful full-time employment politics, rather than regarding three million unemployed as a temporary phenomenon which will soon go away. It is unlikely that the balance of employment in Britain will swing back towards manufacturing industry or manual work, even less likely towards male manual work in large-scale manufacturing plants. Employment in the public sector may decline as a result of privatization and policies to cut public expenditure, but state involvement in regulating work and workers directly and indirectly shows no sign of diminishing. Temporary work, part-time work, work under short-term contracts (perhaps interspersed with periods of unemployment), work (for pay) outside the 'formal economy', home-based work (as home-workers and on a 'self-employed' basis), job sharing and households with multiple 'breadwinners' all seem likely to increase. Patterns of employment have never been as neat and uniform as the dominant images of work assumed, but they are likely to become messier, more varied and more complex. This will have implications for trade union membership and organization; by and large unions have thrived where large workforces with relatively stable employment faced bureaucratic employers (Price and Bain, 1976). It seems likely that most women will spend nearly (or even equally) as large a proportion of their lifetimes 'gainfully occupied' as men do.

All these possibilities are overshadowed and may be significantly affected by the development and application of microelectronic technology.[4] What the silicon 'chip' (and parallel technical developments, e.g. fibre optics) make possible is the very rapid processing of large quantities of information, its storage, retrieval and transmission, all using electronic devices which are increasingly compact, increasingly versatile, and reducing in cost all the time. Attached to electro-mechanical devices (as in robots), physical tasks such as handling goods or using tools can be carried out automatically. Attached to visual display units, printers, graph plotters, and so on, words, numbers and pictures can be displayed and reproduced. The storage facilities of computers make it unnecessary to keep 'hard' copies (papers, files, books, etc.) and electronic storage of such materials has the advantage that it can be available virtually simultaneously to a large number of people, in different locations and at a distance. It can also be amended, updated, sorted, rearranged and deleted without any handling of physical copy. Current developments include attempts to give robots, effectively, the senses of sight, touch and/or hearing so that they are able to cope without operator intervention with irregular and unexpected situations; and to make computers increasingly 'user-friendly', accessible to the untrained and the inexpert, including making them responsive to speech, rather than instructions or questions typed in at a keyboard.

Clearly, if the full potential of these developments were to be realized immediately, it would have enormous repercussions for the nature and organization of work. It seems unlikely that the alarmists' worst fears (or the technological utopians' best dreams) will be realized. All our earlier experiences of technical changes would suggest that the adoption of technological innovations, which are 'available', is uneven and takes place over a considerable period of time. Indeed, technologies of clearly different 'generations' may well coexist in the same situation (for example, the situation described in Nichols and Beynon, 1977). The reasons for this are partly economic: even if the cost of the microelectronic hardware – computers, etc. – is falling, there are still considerable costs involved in its adoption and installation, in devising appropriate programmes, retraining staff and so on; and the costs of abandoning investments in previous generations of equipment, and of compensating employees made redundant. They are also partly social and psychological, such as the resistance to innovation which derives from considerable collective and individual investment in existing systems.[5]

Nevertheless, national and international competitive pressures alone are likely to mean that much of the potential of the 'new technology' will be realized in time, and as a result much existing paid work will become unnecessary. This is, of course, already happening. Robots weld car bodies at Longbridge and elsewhere; computers are programmed to set up type so that the skills of the compositor are no longer needed; cash points dispense banknotes without the intervention of a bank cashier; and computers and word processors now do much of the work previously done by large numbers of clerical and secretarial workers.

On an issue which clearly arouses extreme hopes and fears – the employment implications of microelectronic technology – there could be said to be two polar positions (with a range of others in between). Some argue that, as in the case of technological innovations in the past, there may be temporary dislocation, structural unemployment and hardship, but in the longer term the productivity and wealth creation made possible by the new technology will generate demands for goods and services at the moment unknown and possibly unknowable, and this demand will lead to the creation of new jobs which will absorb those who have been displaced. We can then go on much as before, though with a higher standard of living.

Others hope or fear that the changes are qualitatively different from any in the past, there is no possibility of new demands which will generate enough jobs to replace those lost due to adoption of the new technology. This could be due to a number of reasons: such demand will itself be met using microelectronics and therefore with minimal new jobs; finite world resources – and increasing competition for them – will set limits to what can be consumed in any one society like our own; human consumption of goods and services is inherently limited; and so on. The new technology will, however, allow existing levels of demand to be met with very much lower levels of employment, and of human effort, so that the existing gross national product and therefore existing standards of living could easily be maintained, or increased. Here, the proponents of the view that the new technology will permanently reduce the need and opportunities for paid work divide into optimists and pessimists. For the optimists, the future holds the possibility of everyone spending a much smaller proportion of their day, their week, and/or lifetime in paid work, and consequently all having greatly increased leisure *and* the means to enjoy it. The pessimists fear that the necessary changes in the social organization of work, the (re)distribution of incomes, and so on, will not take place for such an idyllic solution to be realizable. Instead, developments will lead to a situation where a proportion have well-paid jobs requiring skills and education, another proportion may have low-paid unskilled jobs which have not been or cannot be automated, and the remainder, possibly even the majority, are permanently unemployed and without the resources, both material and cultural, to utilize their 'leisure'. In such a society, the prospects of social conflict and disorder are clearly considerable, with the danger that authoritarian solutions will be adopted to meet them.

Whichever of these or other possible scenarios is more likely to be realized, what does seem likely is that the combination of the trends already discussed with the developments made possible by the new technology will alter the meaning and significance of work, and especially of employment, very considerably. Already, as Kumar's contribution to this volume indicates, there is advocacy of a reduction in emphasis on the Protestant work ethic, and of a search for and recognition of other sources of social status, of structure and purpose in life, and of other social contacts outside the home than are provided by an occupation. As the contributions to this volume by Pahl and by Roberts, Noble and Duggan show, there are some signs of 'alternative' life–styles, in which employment plays a much smaller part. Clearly, there will be no shortage of questions and problems for researchers interested in the sociology of work – broadly defined – even if they are unlikely to be the same ones as have so far attracted most attention.

Whether or not current theoretical perspectives will prove appropriate for the study and analysis of the new situations must also be uncertain. It is, however, already clear that the focus on the capitalist labour process, which has done so much to give a fresh impetus to the sociology of work, has limitations. These arise, especially with regard to Braverman's formulation, from the assertions within it as to the inherent tendencies of the labour process to deskill work leading to an increasingly unskilled, powerless and alienated workforce dominated by capital. This view has justifiably been criticized as inadequate on both theoretical and empirical grounds: it attributes an omniscience and omnipotence to capitalists or to a management which is in any case far from monolithic, as Chapter 7 above shows; and it denies the possibility of any effective opposition by workers, thus reinforcing a highly deterministic view of the course of social development. Empirical, especially historical, studies have shown that there were considerable variations in the nature of the labour process in the past, that the developments have been equally varied, and that the outcome in the case of any particular industry or enterprise has been the result, at least in part, of the actions and interactions of specific managements and sets of workers, constrained by particular historical circumstances (see the contributions to Wood, 1982 and also Chapter 9 above). Once such a more varied set of possibilities is recognized, then some of the approaches and research which predated the focus on the labour process, and may have appeared to be superseded by it, become of relevance to help account for such variation – for example, the concerns with orientations to work, with the influence of technology on organizations, with social relations within management, and between workers, and with payment systems. The end result should be a sociology of work which is more coherent and more adequate. Such a sociology of work must also be open to the possibility that in the future work within an employment relationship may be less important as a form of work, and indeed less central to an understanding of society in general, than it has rightly been seen to be for the past 150 years. In any case, the social relations and social processes which make such work possible, and work outside the 'formal' economy and outside employment of any sort, must continue to be regarded as worthy of the sort of attention which they have only received comparatively recently.

Concluding Comments

In this chapter, I have tried to combine discussion of the changing shape of work with discussion of changes in sociological approaches to the study of work, so as to show how both must be located in specific historical contexts. What is to be seen as 'work' and what is 'problematic' about work have varied over time, as have the social organization and allocation of work. There is, however, a further and more fundamental sense in which that which is historically specific enters into sociological discussions, of work or of anything else. On the one hand, the discipline strives to develop general understanding of social relations and social processes, to elaborate concepts and to identify and clarify general tendencies which will provide some understanding of the pattern of social life. On the other hand, the actions and events which go to make up those patterns are unique, and historically and culturally specific; only in a rather general and diffuse sense does history repeat itself and are there any possibilities for the replication of sociological investigation. Thus there is a continuing tension between the attempt to say something of universal significance about the social world and the need to recognize the historical uniqueness of all examples of that world. This tension is probably ultimately irresolvable, and may indeed be highly fruitful. It is equally unsatisfactory to concentrate on either pole to the exclusion of the other. Without concepts and explanatory models – notions such as 'bureaucracy' or 'the labour process', for example – it is not possible to make sense of the bewildering mass of evidence from the real world; but as recent criticisms of some formulations of 'the labour process' have shown, to build a logically coherent framework of concepts and relations partly or entirely divorced from empirical data is ultimately arid and useless. Progress in understanding society and societies depends on both historically specific enquiries and the development and refinement of concepts, models and 'theories', carried out in productive relationship with each other. The sociogical study of work clearly provides examples of such a process and, I hope, of such progress.

Notes

1. These impressionistic judgements receive some support from an analysis of the entries in Bain and Woolven's *Bibliography* (1979). The compilers interpreted the coverage of 'industrial relations' in an admirably broad-minded way and consequently included much of the literature on (paid) work for the period they cover, 1880–1970. A rough count of the entries categorized, respectively, on unemployment (organizations of unemployed; level and structure of unemployment; unemployment – conditions and relief; unemployment benefit) and on women's employment (employee organization – women; female employment; women's wages and equal pay; conditions of employment – women; safety, health and welfare – women workers) produced the following distribution of items by year of publication:

Years	Unemployment (percentage)	Women (percentage)
1880–99	10	17
1900–9	18	15
1910–19	8	20
1920–9	18	7
1930–9	26	5
1940–9	5	12
1950–9	4	5
1960–70	11	18
N =	873	425

    Unfortunately the equivalent bibliography for the 1970s is not yet available.

2. This further impressionistic judgement also receives some support from an analysis of Bain and Woolven's *Bibliography* (1979). Under the general headings of employee organisations; collective bargaining; industrial conflict; level and structure of employment; wages; and conditions of employment, just under 1,800 items published

between 1945 and 1970 were categorized as referring to specific industries or occupations. Rather more than a third of them referred to professional associations and professional work. Of the remainder, 30 per cent were classified as concerned with manufacturing industry (11 per cent, engineering and shipbuilding), 10 per cent with mining, and 18 per cent with transport; (only just over a quarter of the items were concerned with the remaining 'service' industries, nearly three-fifths of these were under the heading public administration.

3. For example, the emphasis on technology in the work of Joan Woodward (1958 and 1965); the influence attributed to changing technology and product markets in Burns and Stalker (1961); and a variety of 'external factors' in Lupton (1963).
4. See Forester (1980). For a provocative discussion of the employment implications of the new technology (and other changes), see Jenkins and Sherman (1979 and 1981), and Gershuny (1978 and 1983).
5. For a discussion of such 'investment' in existing technology, and in an existing sexual division of labour, see Cockburn (1983).

References

Bain, G.S. and Woolven, G.B. (1979) *A Bibliography of British Industrial Relations*, Cambridge, Cambridge University Press.

Beechey, V. (1978) 'Women and Production: a critical analysis of some sociological theories of women's work', in A.Kuhn and A.M. Wolpe (eds), *Feminism and Materialism*, London, Routledge and Kegan Paul, pp. 155–97.

Beynon, H. (1983) 'False Hopes and Real Dilemmas: the politics of the collapse of British manufacturing', *Critique*, vol. 14.

Brannen, P. (1983) *Authority and Participation in Industry*, London, Batsford.

Brannen, P. *et al.* (1976) *The Worker Directors: A Sociology of Participation*, London, Hutchinson.

Braverman, H. (1974) *Labor and Monopoly Capital*, New York, Monthly Review Press.

Brown, R.K. (1976) 'Women as Employees: some comments on research in industrial sociology', in D.L. Barker and S. Allen (eds), *Dependence and Exploitation in Work and Marriage*, London, Longman, pp. 21–46.

  (1984) 'Work', in P. Abrams and R.K. Brown (eds), *UK Society: Work, Urbanism and Inequality*, London, Weidenfeld.

Burns, T. and Stalker, G.M. (1961) *The Management of Innovation*, London, Tavistock.

Census 1981. National Report, Great Britain Part 2 (1983), London, HMSO.

Cockburn, C. (1983) *Brothers: Male Dominance and Technological Change*, London, Pluto Press.

Department of Employment (1971) *British Labour Statistics: Historical Abstract 1886–1968*, London, HMSO.

  (1983) *Employment Gazette*, vol. 91, no. 9, September.

Equal Opportunities Commission (1983) *The Fact about Women is...*, London, HMSO.

Forester, T. (ed.) (1980) *The Microelectronics Revolution*, Oxford, Basil Blackwell.

Gershuny, J.I. (1978) *After Industrial Society*, London, Macmillan.

  (1983) *Social Innovation and the Division of Labour*, Oxford, Oxford University Press.

Gershuny, J.I. and Pahl, R.E. (1980) 'Britain in the Decade of the Three Economies', *New Society*, 3 January 1980, pp. 7–9.

Goldthorpe, J.H., Lockwood, D., Bechhofer, F. and Platt, J. (1968) *The Affluent Worker: Industrial Attitudes and Behaviour*, Cambridge, Cambridge University Press.

Hakim, C. (1979) *Occupational Segregation*, Research Paper No. 9, London, Department of Employment.

Jenmins, C. and Sherman, B. (1979) *The Collapse of Work*, London, Eyre Methuen.

  (1981) *The Leisure Shock*, London, Eyre Methuen.

Littler, C.R. (1982) *The Development of the Labour Process in Capitalist Societies*, London, Heinemann Educational Books.

Lockwood, D. (1958) *The Blackcoated Worker*, London, Allen and Unwin.

Lupton, T. (1963) *On the Shop Floor*, Oxford, Pergamon.

Marsh, D.C. (1958) *The Changing Social Structure of England and Wales*, London, Routledge and Kegan Paul.

Nichols, T. (ed.) (1980) *Capital and Labour*, London, Fontana.

Nichols, T. and Beynon, H. (1977) *Living with Capitalism*, London, Routledge and Kegan Paul.

Oakley, A. (1974) *The Sociology of Housework*, Oxford, Martin Robertson.

Parker, S.R. (1983) *Leisure and Work*, London, Allen and Unwin.

Parker, S.R. *et al.* (1972) *The Sociology of Industry*, 2nd edn, London, Allen and Unwin.

Parsons, T. and Smelser, N.J. (1956) *Economy and Society*, London, Routledge and Kegan Paul.

Prandy K. (1965) *Professional Employees*, London, Faber.

Price, R. and Bain, G.S. (1976) 'Union Growth Revisited: 1948–1974 in perspective', *British Journal of Industrial Relations*, vol. 14, no. 3.

(1983) 'Union Growth in Britain: retrospect and prospect', *British Journal of Industrial Relations*, vol. 21, no. 1, March.

Ramsay, H. (1977) 'Cycles of Control: Worker participation in sociological and historical perspective', *Sociology*, vol. 11, no. 3, pp. 481–506.

Rose, M. (1975) *Industrial Behaviour: Theoretical Development since Taylor*, London, Allen Lane.

Samuel, R. (1977) 'Workshop of the World: Steam power and hand technology in mid-Victorian Britain', *History Workshop*, vol. 3, pp. 6–72.

Sinfield, A. (1981) *What Unemployment Means*, Oxford, Martin Robertson.

Social Trends No. 13 1982 (1982), London, HMSO.

Thompson, P. (1983) *The Nature of Work*, London, Macmillan.

Webb, S. and Webb, B. (1894) *The History of Trade Unionism*, London, Longman.

(1920) *Industrial Democracy*, London, Longman.

Wood, S. (ed.) (1982) *The Degradation of Work?* London, Hutchinson.

Woodward, J. (1958) *Management and Technology*, London, HMSO.

(1965) *Industrial Organisation: Theory and Practice*, Oxford, Oxford University Press.

Index